ANNUAL EDITIONS

Early Childhood Education *07/08*

Twenty-eighth Edition

EDITOR

Karen Menke Paciorek
Eastern Michigan University

Karen Menke Paciorek is a professor of early childhood education at Eastern Michigan University in Ypsilanti. Her degrees in early childhood education include a B.A. from the University of Pittsburgh, an M.A. from George Washington University, and a Ph.D. from Peabody College of Vanderbilt University. She co-edits, with Joyce Huth Munro, *Sources: Notable Selections in Early Childhood Education* and is the editor of *Taking Sides: Clashing Views on Controversial Issues in Early Childhood Education*. She has served as president of the Michigan Association for the Education of Young Children, the Michigan Early Childhood Education Consortium and the Northville School Board. She presents at local, state, and national conferences on curriculum planning, guiding behavior, preparing the learning environment, and working with families. She also serves as a member of the Board of Directors for Wolverine Human Services and The Karla Fund supporting reading to young children.

Contemporary Learning Series

2460 Kerper Blvd., Dubuque, IA 52001

Visit us on the Internet
http://www.mhcls.com

Credits

1. **How the World Treats Young Children**
   Unit photo—Digital Vision/PunchStock
2. **Young Children and Their Families**
   Unit photo—Photodisc Collection/Getty Images
3. **Supporting Young Children's Development**
   Unit photo—SW Productions/Brand X Pictures/Getty Images
4. **Educational Practices**
   Unit photo—Digital Vision
5. **Guiding and Supporting Young Children**
   Unit photo—Creatas/Jupiter Images
6. **Curricular Issues**
   Unit photo—SW Productions/Brand X Pictures/Getty Images

Copyright

Cataloging in Publication Data
Main entry under title: Annual Editions: Early Childhood Education. 2007/2008.
1. Early Childhood Education—Periodicals. I. Menke Paciorek, Karen, *comp.* II. Title: Early Childhood Education.
ISBN-13: 978–0–07–351630–1   MHID-10: 0–07–351630–9   658'.05   ISSN 0272–4456

Twenty-eighth Edition

Cover image Getty Images and Comstock/PunchStock
Compositor: Laserwords Private Limited

Printed in the United States of America   1234567890QPDQPD987   Printed on Recycled Paper

Editors/Advisory Board

Members of the Advisory Board are instrumental in the final selection of articles for each edition of ANNUAL EDITIONS. Their review of articles for content, level, currentness, and appropriateness provides critical direction to the editor and staff. We think that you will find their careful consideration well reflected in this volume.

Preface

In publishing ANNUAL EDITIONS we recognize the enormous role played by the magazines, newspapers, and journals of the public press in providing current, first-rate educational information in a broad spectrum of interest areas. Many of these articles are appropriate for students, researchers, and professionals seeking accurate, current material to help bridge the gap between principles and theories and the real world. These articles, however, become more useful for study when those of lasting value are carefully collected, organized, indexed, and reproduced in a low-cost format, which provides easy and permanent access when the material is needed. That is the role played by ANNUAL EDITIONS.

*A*nnual Editions: Early Childhood Education has evolved over the 28 years it has been in existence to become one of the most used texts for students in early childhood education. This annual reader is used today at over 550 colleges and universities. In addition it may be found in public libraries, pediatricians' offices, and teacher reference sections of school libraries. I have worked diligently to bring you the best and most significant articles in the field. I realize it is a tremendous responsibility to provide a thorough review of the current literature—a responsibility I take seriously. I am always on the lookout for possible articles to be included in the next *Annual Editions*. My goal is to provide the reader with a snapshot of the critical issues facing professionals in early childhood education.

Early childhood education is an interdisciplinary field that includes child development, family issues, educational practices, behavior guidance, and curriculum. *Annual Editions: Early Childhood Education 07/08* brings you the latest information in the field from a wide variety of recent journals, newspapers, and magazines. In selecting articles for this edition, I was careful to provide the reader with a well-balanced look at the issues and concerns facing teachers, families, society, and children. There are four themes found in readings chosen for this twenty-eighth edition of *Annual Editions: Early Childhood Education*. They are: (1) the recent interest in the education of boys and how to best serve the male half of our population in schools dominated by female educators, (2) the continued focus on early literacy experiences being critical for young children prior to public school entry age (3) the importance of a curriculum developed around emergent, local issues relevant to young children and (4) the immense pressure to achieve placed on young children at ever-decreasing ages.

It is especially gratifying to see issues affecting children and families covered in magazines other than professional association journals. The general public needs to be aware of the impact of positive early learning and family experiences on the growth and development of children.

Continuing in this edition of *Annual Editions: Early Childhood Education* are selected Internet References that can be used to further explore topics addressed in the articles. I have chosen to include only a few high-quality sites. The reader is encouraged to explore these sites on their own, or in collaboration with others for extended learning opportunities.

Given the wide range of topics included, *Annual Editions: Early Childhood Education 07/08* may be used by several groups— undergraduate or graduate students, professionals, parents, or administrators—who want to develop an understanding of the critical issues in the field.

The selection of readings for this edition has been a cooperative effort between the editor and the advisory board members. I appreciate the time the advisory board members have taken to provide suggestions for improvement and possible articles for consideration. The editorial and production staff of McGraw-Hill ably coordinate and support my efforts.

I also want to thank Mr. Robert L. Johnston Jr. who this year rekindled the excitement and interest in early childhood education at Eastern Michigan University. His very generous donation made possible the Gail E. Johnston Early Childhood Classroom and Resource Library in memory of his wife. The ECE classroom sends a powerful message to others about the importance of early childhood education. There aren't many university faculty or administrators who can say their most technologically up-to-date and student friendly classroom on campus is dedicated specifically for students in early childhood education. I never had the opportunity to meet Gail but from talking to her friends and family I learned she was a very gifted and special teacher of young children. It is with outstanding educators like Gail E. Johnston in mind that other teacher educators and I work to prepare the very best future generations of early childhood teachers. These teachers will provide the appropriate learning experiences for young children for years to come. Thank you Bob for keeping Gail's passion for teaching alive.

To the instructor or reader interested in the history of early childhood care and education programs throughout the years, I invite you to view my other books, also published by McGraw-Hill. *Sources: Notable Selections in Early Childhood Education, 2nd edition* (1999) is a collection of 46 writings of enduring historical value by influential people in the field. All of the selections are primary sources which allow you to experience first-hand the thoughts and views of these important educators. *Taking Sides: Clashing Views on Controversial Issues in Early Childhood Education* (2002) contains 18 critical issues facing early childhood professionals or parents. This book can be used in a seminar or issues course. The second edition of *Taking Sides: ECE* is in press and will be published by the end of 2007.

I appreciate readers who have corresponded with me about the selection and organization of previous editions. Comments and articles sent for consideration are welcomed and will serve to modify future volumes. Take time to fill out and return the postage-paid article rating form on the last page. You may also contact me at: kpaciorek@emich.edu

I look forward to hearing from you.

Karen Menke Paciorek

Karen Menke Paciorek
Editor

Contents

UNIT 1
How the World Treats Young Children

The concepts in bold italics are developed in the article. For further expansion, please refer to the Topic Guide and the Index.

UNIT 2
Young Children and Their Families

Unit Overview   36

The concepts in bold italics are developed in the article. For further expansion, please refer to the Topic Guide and the Index.

UNIT 3
Supporting Young Children's Development

UNIT 4
Educational Practices

The concepts in bold italics are developed in the article. For further expansion, please refer to the Topic Guide and the Index.

The concepts in bold italics are developed in the article. For further expansion, please refer to the Topic Guide and the Index.

UNIT 5
Guiding and Supporting Young Children

UNIT 6
Curricular Issues

The concepts in bold italics are developed in the article. For further expansion, please refer to the Topic Guide and the Index.

The concepts in bold italics are developed in the article. For further expansion, please refer to the Topic Guide and the Index.

The concepts in bold italics are developed in the article. For further expansion, please refer to the Topic Guide and the Index.

Topic Guide

This topic guide suggests how the selections in this book relate to the subjects covered in your course. You may want to use the topics listed on these pages to search the Web more easily.

On the following pages a number of Web sites have been gathered specifically for this book. They are arranged to reflect the units of this *Annual Edition*. You can link to these sites by going to the student online support site at *http://www.mhcls.com/online/*.

ALL THE ARTICLES THAT RELATE TO EACH TOPIC ARE LISTED BELOW THE BOLD-FACED TERM.

Academics
7. The New First Grade: Too Much Too Soon?
29. Building Positive Teacher-Child Relationships

Accountability
16. What Does It Mean to Educate the Whole Child?

Achievement
5. The Preschool Promise
6. Kindergarten Learning Gap
15. The Trouble With Boys
16. What Does It Mean to Educate the Whole Child?
37. The Overdominance of Computers

Advocacy
8. Taking a Stand: Strategies for Activism

Assessment
16. What Does It Mean to Educate the Whole Child?
24. Second Time Around

At-risk Children
2. Preschool Pays

Behavior
15. The Trouble With Boys
27. From Policing to Participation: Overturning the Rules and Creating Amiable Classrooms
29. Building Positive Teacher-Child Relationships

Boys
15. The Trouble With Boys

Brain Development
14. Reading Your Baby's Mind

Child Care
13. The Uniqueness of Infancy Demands a Responsive Approach to Care

Cognitive Development
16. What Does It Mean to Educate the Whole Child?
20. Uniquely Preschool
21. Rethinking Early Childhood Practices

Computers
37. The Overdominance of Computers

Cost, Educational
3. The High/Scope Perry Preschool Study and the Man Who Began It

Creativity
41. Promoting Creativity for Life Using Open-Ended Materials

Cultures
9. Creative Play: Building Connections with Children Who Are Learning English

Curriculum
21. Rethinking Early Childhood Practices
31. The Plan: Building on Children's Interests
38. Meeting the Challenge of Math & Science

Development
6. Kindergarten Learning Gap
10. Children of Teen Parents: Challenges and Hope
13. The Uniqueness of Infancy Demands a Responsive Approach to Care
18. Back to Basics
23. Successful Transition to Kindergarten: The Role of Teachers & Parents
26. Essential Contributions from Playgrounds
41. Promoting Creativity for Life Using Open-Ended Materials

Developmentally Appropriate Practice
7. The New First Grade: Too Much Too Soon?
8. Taking a Stand: Strategies for Activism
18. Back to Basics
27. From Policing to Participation: Overturning the Rules and Creating Amiable Classrooms
29. Building Positive Teacher-Child Relationships

Discipline
11. Supporting Grandparents Who Raise Grandchildren
30. Unprotected in the Classroom

Documentation
32. One Teacher, 20 Preschoolers, and a Goldfish

Emergent Curriculum
31. The Plan: Building on Children's Interests
32. One Teacher, 20 Preschoolers, and a Goldfish

Emotional Competence
16. What Does It Mean to Educate the Whole Child?

English Language Learners
9. Creative Play: Building Connections with Children Who Are Learning English

Environment
20. Uniquely Preschool

Internet References

The following Internet sites have been carefully researched and selected to support the articles found in this reader. The easiest way to access these selected sites is to go to our student online support site at *http://www.mhcls.com/online/*.

Annual Editions: Early Childhood Education 07/08

The following sites were available at the time of publication. Visit our Web site—we update our student online support site regularly to reflect any changes.

General Sources

Children's Defense Fund (CDF)
http://www.childrensdefense.org

At this site of the CDF, an organization that seeks to ensure that every child is treated fairly, there are reports and resources regarding current issues facing today's youth, along with national statistics on various subjects.

Connect for Kids
http://www.connectforkids.org

This nonprofit site provides news and information on issues affecting children and families, with over 1,500 helpful links to national and local resources.

National Association for the Education of Young Children
http://www.naeyc.org

The NAEYC Web site is a valuable tool for anyone working with young children. Also see the National Education Association site: http://www.nea.org.

U.S. Department of Education
http://www.ed.gov/pubs/TeachersGuide/

Government goals, projects, grants, and other educational programs are listed here as well as many links to teacher services and resources.

Unit 1: How the World Treats Young Children

Child Care Directory: Careguide
http://www.careguide.net

Find licensed/registered child care by state, city, region, or age of child at this site. Site contains providers' pages, parents' pages, and many links.

Complementary Learning Approach to the Achievement Gap
http://www.gse.harvard.edu/hfrp/projects/complementary-learning.html

Complementary learning provides a variety of support services for all children to be successful. These supports reach beyond the school and work toward consistent learning and developmental outcomes for children.

Early Childhood Care and Development
http://www.ecdgroup.com

This site concerns international resources in support of children to age 8 and their families. It includes research and evaluation, policy matters, programming matters, and related Web sites.

Global SchoolNet Foundation
http://www.gsn.org

Access this site for multicultural education information. The site includes news for teachers, students, and parents as well as chat rooms, links to educational resources, programs, and contests and competitions.

Goals 2000: A Progress Report
http://www.ed.gov/pubs/goals/progrpt/index.html

Open this site to survey a progress report by the U.S. Department of Education on the Goals 2000 reform initiative. It provides a sense of educators' future goals.

Mid-Continent Research for Education and Learning
http://www.mcrel.org/standards-benchmarks

This site provides a listing of standards and benchmarks that include content descriptions from 112 significant subject areas and documents from across 14 content areas.

The National Association of State Boards of Education
http://www.nasbe.org/

Included on this site is an extensive overview of the No Child Left Behind Act. There are links to specific state's plans.

Unit 2: Young Children and Their Families

Administration for Children and Families
http://www.dhhs.gov

This site provides information on federally funded programs that promote the economic and social well-being of families, children, and communities.

The AARP Grandparent Information Center
http://www.aarp.org/grandparents

The center offers tips for raising grandchildren, activities, health and safety, visitations, and other resources to assist grandparents.

All About Asthma
http://pbskids.org/arthur/grownups/teacherguides/health/asthma_tips.html

This is a fact sheet/activity book used to educate children about asthma. It gives tips on how to decrease asthma triggers within your house or school. It has both English and Spanish versions of some of the materials.

Changing the Scene on Nutrition
http://www.fns.usda.gov/tn/Healthy/changing.html

This is a free toolkit for parents, school administrators, and teachers to help change the attitudes toward health and nutrition in their schools.

Children, Youth and Families Education and Research Network
www.cyfernet.org

This excellent site contains useful links to research from key universities and institutions. The categories include early childhood, school age, teens, parents and family and community.

I Am Your Child
http://www.iamyourchild.org

Rob Reiner's I Am Your Child Foundation features excellent information on child development.

www.mhcls.com/online/

Internet Resources for Education
http://web.hamline.edu/personal/kfmeyer/cla_education.html#hamline

This site, which aims for "educational collaboration," takes you to Internet links that examine virtual classrooms, trends, policy, and infrastructure development. It leads to information about school reform, multiculturalism, technology in education, and much more.

The National Academy for Child Development
http://www.nacd.org

The NACD, an international organization, is dedicated to helping children and adults reach their full potential. Its home page presents links to various programs, research, and resources into such topics as learning disabilities, ADD/ADHD, brain injuries, autism, accelerated and gifted, and other similar topic areas.

National Network for Child Care
www.nncc.org

This network brings together the expertise of many land grant universities through their cooperative extension programs. These are the programs taped back in early 1965 to train the 41,000 teachers needed for the first Head Start programs that summer. The site contains information on over 1,000 publications and resources related to child care.

National Safe Kids Campaign
http://www.babycenter.com

This site includes an easy-to-follow milestone chart and advice on when to call the doctor.

Zero to Three
http://www.zerotothree.org

Find here developmental information on the first 3 years of life—an excellent site for both parents and professionals.

Unit 3: Supporting Young Children's Development

American Academy of Pediatrics
www.aap.org

Pediatricians provided trusted advice for parents and teachers. The AAP official site includes position statements on a variety of related to the health and safety of young children.

Canada's Schoolnet Staff Room
http://www.schoolnet.ca/home/e/

Here is a resource and link site for anyone involved in education, including special-needs educators, teachers, parents, volunteers, and administrators.

Classroom Connect
http://www.classroom.com/login/home.jhtml

A major Web site for K–12 teachers and students, this site provides links to schools, teachers, and resources online. It includes discussion of the use of technology in the classroom.

The Council for Exceptional Children
http://www.cec.sped.org/index.html

Information on identifying and teaching gifted children, attention deficit disorders, and other topics in disabilities and gifted education may be accessed at this site.

Early Learning Standards: Full report
http://www.naeyc.org/resources/position_statements/ positions_2003.asp

This site provides the full joint position statement by the National Association for the Education of Young Children (NAEYC) and

The National Association of Early Childhood Specialists in the State Department of Education (NAECS/SDE) on early learning standards.

Early Learning Standards: Executive Summary
http://www.naeyc.org/resources/position_statements/ creating_conditions.asp

This site provides the executive summary for the joint position statement by the National Association for the Education of Young Children (NAEYC) and The National Association of Early Childhood Specialists in the State Department of Education (NAECS/SDE) on early learning standards.

Make Your Own Web page
http://www.teacherweb.com

Easy step by step directions for teachers at all levels to construct their own web page. Parents can log on and check out what is going on in their child's classroom.

National Resource Center for Health and Safety in Child Care
http://nrc.uchsc.edu

Search through this site's extensive links to find information on health and safety in child care. Health and safety tips are provided, as are other child-care information resources.

Online Innovation Institute
http://oii.org

A collaborative project among Internet-using educators, proponents of systemic reform, content-area experts, and teachers who desire professional growth, this site provides a learning environment for integrating the Internet into educators' individual teaching styles.

Unit 4: Educational Practices

Child Welfare League of America (CWLA)
http://www.cwla.org

The CWLA is the United States' oldest and largest organization devoted entirely to the well-being of vulnerable children and their families. Its Web site provides links to information about issues related to morality and values in education.

Unit 5: Guiding and Supporting Young Children

Future of Children
http://www.futureofchildren.org

Produced by the David and Lucille Packard Foundation, the primary purpose of this page is to disseminate timely information on major issues related to children's well-being.

Busy Teacher's Cafe
http://www.busyteacherscafe.com

This is a website for early childhood educators with resource pages for everything from worksheets to classroom management.

Tips for Teachers
http://www.counselorandteachertips.com

This site includes links for various topics of interest to teachers such as behavior management, peer mediation, and new teacher resources.

www.mhcls.com/online/

You Can Handle Them All
http://www.disciplinehelp.com

This site describes different types of behavioral problems and offers suggestions for managing these problems.

Unit 6: Curricular Issues

Action for Healthy Kids
www.actionforhealthykids.org

This organization works to assist the ever increasing numbers of students who are overweight, undernourished and sedentary. They feature a campaign for school wellness.

Association for Childhood Education International (ACEI)
http://www.acei.org/

This site, established by the oldest professional early childhood education organization, describes the association, its programs, and the services it offers to both teachers and families.

Awesome Library for Teachers
http://www.neat-schoolhouse.org/teacher.html

Open this page for links and access to teacher information on everything from educational assessment to general child development topics.

Early Childhood Education Online
http://www.umaine.edu/eceol/

This site gives information on developmental guidelines and issues in the field, presents tips for observation and assessment, and gives information on advocacy.

The Educators' Network
http://www.theeducatorsnetwork.com

A very useful site for teachers at every level in every subject area. Includes lesson plans, theme units, teacher tools, rubrics, books, educational news, and much more.

The Family Involvement Storybook Corner
http://www.gse.harvard.edu/hfrp/projects/fine.html

In partnership with Reading is Fundamental (RIF) the Family Involvement Storybook Corner is a place to find compilations of family involvement, children's storybooks, and related tools and information.

Grade Level Reading Lists
http://www.gradelevelreadinglists.org

Recommended reading lists for grades kindergarten - eight can be downloaded through this site.

International Reading Association
http://www.reading.org

This organization for professionals who are interested in literacy contains information about the reading process and assists teachers in dealing with literacy issues.

PE Central
http://www.pecentral.org

Included in this site are developmentally appropriate physical activities for children, also containing one section dedicated to preschool physical education. It also includes resources and research in physical education.

The Perpetual Preschool
http://www.ecewebguide.com

This site provides teachers with possibilities for learning activities, offers chats with other teachers and resources on a variety of topics. The theme ideas are a list of possibilities and should not be used in whole, but used as a starting point for building areas of investigation that are relevant and offer first hand experiences for young children.

Phi Delta Kappa
http://www.pdkintl.org

This important organization publishes articles about all facets of education. By clicking on the links in this site, for example, you can check out the journal's online archive, which has resources such as articles having to do with assessment.

Prospects: The Congressionally Mandated Study of Educational Growth and Opportunity
http://www.ed.gov/pubs/Prospects/index.html

This report analyzes cross-sectional data on language-minority and LEP students and outlines what actions are needed to improve their educational performance. Family and economic situations are addressed plus information on related reports and sites.

Reggio Emilia
http://www.ericdigests.org/2001-3/reggio.htm

Through ERIC, link to publications related to the Reggio Emilia approach and to resources, videos, and contact information.

Teacher Quick Source
http://www.teacherquicksource.com

Originally designed to help Head Start teachers meet the child outcomes, this site can be useful to all preschool teachers. Domains can be linked to developmentally appropriate activities for classroom use.

Teachers Helping Teachers
http://www.pacificnet.net/~mandel/

Basic teaching tips, new teaching methodologies, and forums for teachers to share experiences are provided on this site. Download software and participate in chats. It features educational resources on the Web, with new ones added each week.

Tech Learning
http://www.techlearning.com

An award-winning K–12 educational technology resource, this site offers thousands of classroom and administrative tools, case studies, curricular resources, and solutions.

Technology Help
http://www.apples4theteacher.com

This site helps teachers incorporate technology into the classroom. Full of interactive activities children can do alone, with a partner, or for full group instruction in all subject areas.

UNIT 1

How the World Treats Young Children

Unit Selections

1. **Children at Risk,** Lawrence Hardy
2. **Preschool Pays,** Robert G. Lynch
3. **The High/Scope Perry Preschool Study and the Man Who Began It,** *High/Scope Resource*
4. **Class and the Classroom,** Richard Rothstein
5. **The Preschool Promise,** Julie Poppe and Steffanie Clothier
6. **Kindergarten Learning Gap,** Lynn Fielding
7. **The New First Grade: Too Much Too Soon?,** Peg Tyre
8. **Taking a Stand: Strategies for Activism,** Richard J. Meyer

Key Points to Consider

- What would a crystal ball show for the future of early childhood education?

- If our nation wants to make high-quality preschool education a priority, what are some challenges we face?

- What drove David Weikart to begin his Perry Preschool Project in 1963?

- How much emphasis should be placed on academics in a preschool program?

- What are some innovative solutions to solving the learning gap that exists between children entering kindergarten?

- How are social disadvantage and poverty related to low achievement of young children?

- How can teachers become more involved in advocacy issues related to the care and education of young children?

- Why is more and more pressure placed on first graders to achieve in all areas? How can we combat the pressure from parents and others?

Student Web Site
www.mhcls.com/online

Internet References
Further information regarding these websites may be found in this book's preface or online.

Child Care Directory: Careguide
http://www.careguide.net

Complementary Learning Approach to the Achievement Gap
http://www.gse.harvard.edu/hfrp/projects/complementary-learning.html

Early Childhood Care and Development
http://www.ecdgroup.com

Global SchoolNet Foundation
http://www.gsn.org

Goals 2000: A Progress Report
http://www.ed.gov/pubs/goals/progrpt/index.html

Mid-Continent Research for Education and Learning
http://www.mcrel.org/standards-benchmarks

The National Association of State Boards of Education
http://www.nasbe.org/

I always feel good when I realize that others—outside of the field of early childhood education—recognize that quality care and education for young children can have tremendous financial benefits as well as educational benefits for society. Of course I would always welcome the interest from more people outside of the profession, but the field is receiving increased attention from others for a number of reasons. One reason is that the nation is learning that high quality programs are beneficial for young children's long-term development. Coupled with the knowledge of the importance of ECE programs is a realization that the quality of these programs should be of utmost importance. Another reason is the compelling evidence from brain research that children are born learning. Yet, despite new information on the importance of early childhood, we still tend to hold onto cultural traditions about who young children are and how to care for them. This dichotomy between information and tradition results in an impasse when it comes to creating national policy related to young children. Professionals in the field are faced with the dilemma of how to convince legislators, community leaders, and business people to make the political and monetary investment needed for new research and more high quality programs. In "ECE Meets Economics: The Changing World of Early Education and Care," Gwen Morgan and Suzanne Helburn look at the trilemma quality, compensation, and affordability of early care and education.

This unit, "How the World Treats Young Children," includes articles that lay out national issues related to early education today. The unit begins with the article, "Children at Risk." We have an increasing number of children who do not come to school after having a good night sleep, breakfast, or a warm send off from a caring family member. More and more children are living lives on the edge filled with uncertainty, poverty, violence, and hunger. Teachers can work hard to plan appropriate learning activities, but the fact remains that when children have more pressing concerns, like where they will sleep that night or when will they eat next, it is hard to concentrate on the learning activity in the class. Partnerships are needed between school personnel, the local community, and funding agencies to ensure that all children have the basic necessities so they can be ready to learn.

The work of Dr. David Weikart from The High/Scope Educational Research Foundation provides the research base for what we do. It is interesting to know that back in the early 1960s, Dr. David Weikart, then Director of Special Services for the Ypsilanti Public Schools in Ypsilanti, Michigan, started a small research project with 123 children that 40 years later still provides data that shape policy for young children throughout the country. Since we know the importance of quality early childhood experiences, it is our job to educate others by being advocates for young children to attend appropriate preschool programs. The second half of the unit presents some critical issues for the field. In "Kindergarten Learning Gap," a unique program in one school district in Washington state is presented. Leaders in the Kennewick school district begin working with parents when their children are born to best prepare the children for kindergarten. The work is paying off in higher test scores and a higher level of students reading at grade level. The article "The New First Grade: Too Much Too Soon?" discusses the pressure placed on young children to achieve. It has been 25 years since the release of David Elkind's *The Hurried Child*, in which he takes parents and teachers to task for their seemingly never-ending quest to push children into adulthood earlier along with all of the responsibilities related to growing up. The pressures to do more at an earlier age can be relentless.

With more and more people outside the field of early childhood education telling teachers and caregivers how to best educate children, it is critical for those of us in the field to take a strong stand for what is best for young children. "Taking a Stand: Strategies for Activism" will help motivate the beginning advocate and bring renewed passion to the seasoned spokesperson for what is just and right for young children. We didn't enter the public relations profession, but when it comes to young children, anyone who works with and cares about young children is an activist.

Children at Risk

Many students come from impoverished homes with no history of financial or familial success. How can schools help "at-risk" kids beat the odds?

LAWRENCE HARDY

On a malnourished 5-year-old, the facial fat is the last to go. Bundled against the Boston winter, he looks like a normal child, his plump little face peeking out from inside a discount store parka. But a doctor can tell he's suffering.

"The children are so small, you underestimate their age," says Deborah Frank, director of the Grow Clinic at Boston Medical Center. "If you don't have a clue, you say, 'What a cute little 3-year-old.'"

Frank is seeing 10 percent more of these children this year—an alarming, but not altogether surprising, statistic. Rental costs have soared in Boston and throughout the country. Housing programs have been cut. Wages remain flat even as the nation enters its fifth year of economic recovery. And, since 2000, another 1.3 million children have slipped into poverty, bringing the total to nearly 13 million.

The 5-year-old described above is an "at-risk" child—at risk of failure in school and in life. Before he ever sets foot in a public school, he is months, perhaps years, behind. Now it's the school district's job—your job—to give him the best possible chance at success. What are you going to do?

Poverty: A Common Thread

Social scientists have identified six primary risk factors, all of which are common in low-income households: poverty itself, welfare dependence, absent parents, one-parent families, unwed mothers, and a parent without a high school diploma.

While it is not necessary to be poor to be at risk—children from single-parent families are found all along the income spectrum—poverty usually is the common thread.

How much can schools do to help the poor? That is a matter of considerable debate. Some argue that by becoming more efficient, focused organizations, schools alone can lift children out of poverty. Others say the problems of poor children are so multifaceted and profound that reforming schools is not enough.

Richard Rothstein is in the second camp. For nearly 50 years, researchers and policymakers have been well aware of the link between social and economic disadvantage and the achievement gap, Rothstein writes in *Class and Schools*. "Most, however,

have avoided the obvious implication of this understanding—raising the achievement of lower-class children requires amelioration of the social and economic conditions of their lives, not just school reform."

Critics say Rothstein's position lets schools off the hook: They can blame societal factors for the failure of disadvantaged students without turning a mirror on themselves. Conversely, others would argue that the reverse is true—that putting the onus on schools relieves states and the federal government of the responsibility to truly address the needs of poor and working class Americans.

"I sort of come down in the middle of this," says Bruno V. Manno, a trustee of the Thomas B. Fordham Foundation and senior program associate at the Annie E. Casey Foundation. "It's naïve to think that resources aren't important, but … I think it's disingenuous to say that the resources that are presently available are being used in as best a way as possible.

"Let's start by saying, 'Let's look at what we're doing with present resources' and acknowledge that we will probably need more."

How much more? It's a difficult and complex question, to be sure. But Robert Balfanz, a research scientist at the Center for Social Organization of Schools at Johns Hopkins University, has tried to answer it, at least at the high school level. To staff the kind of small learning community that CSOC advocates would take an additional $780 to $1,124 per pupil, Balfanz estimated in a report this year. This would pay for the kind of supports—such as extra reading and math teachers, counselors, and community liaisons—that disadvantaged students would need to improve their graduation rates.

"Schools have got to take on this larger role, and they have to be resourced to do it," Balfanz says. "That's the other side of the bargain: If we want schools to do more, we have to provide the resources to do it."

The Economic Imperative

There is an obvious moral argument for addressing the needs of poor children. But equally important is the economic imperative. In an aging society that depends on young people for its continued prosperity, the call to leave no child behind becomes an almost literal necessity. As Phillip Longman, author of *The Empty Cradle*, writes in *Washington Monthly*, the Social Security system "assumes that the number of workers paying into the system will increase by 30 percent over the next 80 years. And it assumes that our children and grandchildren will be enormously more productive than today's workers."

As Longman sees it, we live in a society that devalues child rearing—a society in which the average nursery school teacher's salary ($20,940 in 2001) is less than that of animal trainers ($27,280). Families with modest incomes can easily spend more than $1 million raising a child through age 18, he writes, so child rearing "is fast becoming a suckers' game."

And fewer people are playing. According to a recent report by the National Marriage Project at Rutgers University, less than 50 percent of women ages 25 to 29 had minor children at home in 2000, compared with 73.6 percent in 1970. And the number of single, childless households has surpassed married ones with children.

Relatively affluent parents may not like the fact that society is less child centered or that their contributions may go unnoticed, but, on average, their children will do just fine. The same cannot be said for the poor, and especially those with the youngest children.

"The way to be poor in this country is to be a young child, and to be the family of a young child," says Frank of the Boston Medical Center clinic, noting that the poverty rate for children under six is 20 percent. "The younger the child, the poorer the family."

In Boston, as in other cities, the rising cost of housing is increasing poverty—and with it, malnutrition. David K. Shipler, the Pulitzer Prize-winning author of *The Working Poor: Invisible in America*, explains the dynamics:

"You have to make the car payment—about 94 percent of working poor Americans need a car to get to work in this country," Shipler says. "You have to pay the electric bill and so forth. But the part of the budget that is squeezable is for food. Families that are paying 50 to 70 percent of their income for housing, because they don't have Section 8 vouchers or they're not in public housing, have to squeeze the food part of the budget."

That kind of belt-tightening doesn't come without consequences. According to the Center on Hunger and Poverty at Brandeis University, the number of people who reported experiencing actual hunger rose 43 percent in America between 1999 to 2004, from 3.1 million to 4.5 million, while food insecurity—defined as limited or uncertain access to healthy food—increased from 31 million to 38.2 million, a number that includes 14 million children.

The fact that poor children suffer from obesity at rates at least equal to that of all children does not diminish the seriousness of hunger and food insecurity. Frank says poor families often gorge on cheap, fattening, non-nutritious food—soda and french fries will keep a child feeling full overnight—when food money is available.

Flat wages coupled with rising housing costs mean families are spending a greater percentage of their incomes on mortgages and rent, according to the U.S. Census' 2005 American Community Survey. In Dearborn, Mich., and Detroit, monthly rents are up 36 percent since 2005. In Newark, N.J., 72 percent of mortgage holders are spending more than 30 percent of their income on housing. Likewise, in Chicago, 40 percent of renters were spending more than a third of their income on housing in 2005, compared to 29 percent five years earlier.

Meanwhile, $1.5 billion has been cut from public housing operating funds nationally since 2001. And the tear down of aging public housing in cities like Chicago—coupled with insufficient investment in replacement housing and the rapid gentrification of central cities—has left low-income families with few options, says Rene Heybach, director of the law program at the Chicago Coalition for the Homeless. She says displaced people try to double up with relatives or friends, move to "inner ring" suburbs, or find a shelter with space for families.

At Chicago's McClutchen Elementary School near downtown, homeless liaison Annie Pugh says the number of homeless students—70 out of an enrollment of 320—has increased 10 percent this school year.

"Most of them are living in shelters," Pugh says. "Some people are doubling up. Some of the shelters have their own individual rooms, and some of them don't. Even with the public housing—rents are rising there. There are increasing working poor who are homeless as well."

The At-Risk Environment

Certainly, not all poor Americans suffer so acutely. In fact, the number of chronically poor is far below the 12.6 percent national poverty rate, suggesting that the most dramatic cases of homelessness and poverty are not the norm. On the other hand, there is a much larger group of people who move in and out of poverty, including a stunning 43 percent of Americans in their 30s who experienced at least one year of poverty in the 1990s, according to Monica Lesmerises, a consultant to the Century Foundation. Are their children any less "at risk?"

The chronically poor "are not a very large number," says Isabel V. Sawhill, co-director of the Brookings Institution's Center on Children and Family. "But I don't want us to get too hung up about who is just below or above some arbitrary poverty threshold. What puts children at risk is not being above or below some arbitrary line; it's the entire environment in which they're growing up."

Of course, much of that environment is of their own making. Drug use, gang membership, teen pregnancy—these are all consequences of the poor decisions young people make. No one is forcing young people to embrace the violent culture of the street, to listen to hateful and misogynist gangster rap, or to buy magazines like *Felon*, which, as the *New York Times'* Bob Herbert recently pointed out, featured a "Stop Snitchin' issue that included headlines like "Hundreds of kilos of coke," "Over a dozen murders," and "No one flipped."

A pathology, to be sure—and one for which neglectful parents, and the young people themselves, are largely to blame. But there is the reality we create and the reality that is thrust upon us; in the case of the poor, that latter reality is full of deprivation, uncertainty, and the very real possibility of failure. Who can say, for certain, which has the greater impact on any given child's life?

At the Center for Social Organization of Schools in Baltimore, they're not puzzling over such questions—they're busy trying to create high schools that transform the environment in which poor children are educated.

"Poverty has lots of negative impacts that people have to overcome, but schools are one of the major institutions of social intervention that we have," Balfanz says. "It's the one sort of public institution that's everywhere. And so I think, ultimately, we still have to do it through the schools."

One CSOS-affiliated institution, George Washington Community School in Indianapolis, has made remarkable progress with a student body in which 89 percent of the school's seventh through 12th-graders receive free and reduced-price lunch. "Nobody pays for lunch except the adults," jokes Community School Coordinator Jim Grim. "I pay—three bucks!"

Grim is the point person for 49 school partnerships, which help bring community services and outside expertise into what he calls "a full-service community school." There is a Teen Health Clinic so parents don't have to miss work taking students to the doctor. There are partnerships with the combined Indiana University/Purdue University campus, and with the city park department, which will operate the school swimming pool once renovations are completed.

"No excuses," was a slogan the school used when it opened in 2000, and it applied to both faculty members and students. "If you don't like it here," Grim remembers the former principal telling teachers, "there are 78 other Indianapolis public schools that you can go to."

Standardized test scores have steadily increased over the past five years. But it was the event last May 24 that was the most rewarding to staff members. Eighty seniors matriculated in the first graduating class. Of those, 81 percent planned to go on to post-secondary education—college, community college, or vocational training.

It is an encouraging turnaround for a school that was closed just a few years ago because of its dismal academic record. And, as always with such break-the-mold success stories, the question for educators and policymakers is not just "Can it

be replicated?" but also "Can it be brought to scale? Can we conceive of a nation where all disadvantaged teenagers could have the opportunity to attend such a school?"

The pessimists among us might say "not likely." After all, wasn't it the very uniqueness of the school that attracted its cohort of committed teachers and long list of influential community sponsors? Try to replicate it across 78 other Indianapolis schools, and would you get the same thing?

Others might say while there may be no second or third George Washington Community School, the lessons learned from this school can be applied to other schools as well—if only we have the energy, will, and resources to do it.

Schools as Gateways

The nation's official poverty level has not changed significantly since the 1970s, and many experts say there is nothing on the horizon that suggests it will move significantly in the near future. Barring some unexpected shift of public sentiment, there will be no Marshall Plan to fix poor neighborhoods or rescue poor schools.

But educators are perennial optimists, and the past 30 years have taught them a lot about what works, whether it's quality early childhood education or smaller, more focused and personal high schools that strive to become as they once were, the intellectual and social hubs of their communities.

"I think you have to think of various institutions in society as potential gateways," says Shipler, the author of *The Working Poor.* "And schools are perfect for that because all poor families encounter the schools, and teachers see a lot of these problems without being able to do anything about it. It's an ideal place. It's an absolutely perfect setting, if we're willing to devote the funds to it."

Schools will need help, adds Balfanz. "I'm not saying they can do it alone. But they have to be the fundamental driver for giving kids a chance to come from poverty and go on to success.

"Ultimately, it's got to be the public schools. If not them, who?"

LAWRENCE HARDY (lhardy@nsba.org) is a senior editor of *American School Board Journal.*

Preschool Pays

High-Quality Early Education Would Save Billions

Robert G. Lynch

The youngest children suffer the highest poverty rates of any age group in the United States. Nearly one in five children under age 6 lives in poverty, and the number is rising.

Poor children often have inadequate food, safety, shelter, and healthcare. In school, poor children too often fall far short of achieving their academic potential, making them more likely to enter adulthood lacking the skills to compete in the global labor market. As adults, they are more likely to suffer from poor health and participate in crime and other antisocial behavior; they are also less likely to be gainfully employed and contributing to economic growth and community well-being.

There is a strong consensus among the experts who have studied high-quality early childhood development (ECD) programs that these programs have substantial payoffs. Although the programs vary in whom they serve and in the services they provide, most high-quality ECD programs have the following characteristics in common: well-educated and trained staff; a low child-to-teacher ratio and small classes; a rich curriculum that emphasizes language, pre-literacy, and pre-numeracy activities, as well as motor, emotional, and social development; health and nutritional services; and lots of structured and unstructured play. Good programs also typically include parental involvement and education.

What benefits have such programs produced? We can answer this question thanks largely to carefully conducted, long-term studies that have compared the school and life outcomes of participants in four high-quality ECD programs—the Perry Preschool Project, the Prenatal Early Infancy Project, the Abecedarian Early Childhood Intervention, and the Chicago Child-Parent Center Program—with a control group of children who attended no such program.[1]

These studies have established that participating children are more successful in school and in life than children who were not enrolled in high-quality programs. In particular, children who have participated in high-quality ECD programs tend to have higher scores on math and reading achievement tests, have greater language abilities, are better prepared to enter elementary school, are more likely to pursue secondary education, have less grade retention, have less need for special education and other remedial coursework, have lower dropout rates, have

higher high school graduation rates, higher levels of schooling attainment, improved nutrition, better access to healthcare services, higher rates of immunization, better health, and experience less child abuse and neglect. These children are also less likely to be teenage parents and more likely to have higher employment rates as adults, lower welfare dependency, lower rates of drug use, show less-frequent and less-severe delinquent behavior, engage in fewer criminal acts both as juveniles and as adults, have fewer interactions with the criminal justice system, and lower incarceration rates. The benefits of ECD programs to participating children enable them to enter school "ready to learn," helping them achieve better outcomes in school and throughout their lives (Barnett, 1993; Karoly et al., 1998; Masse and Barnett, 2002; Schweinhart, 1993).

Parents and families of children who participate in high-quality ECD programs also benefit. For example, mothers have fewer additional births, have better nutrition and smoke less during pregnancy, are less likely to abuse or neglect their children, complete more years of schooling, have higher high-school graduation rates, are more likely to be employed, have higher earnings, engage in fewer criminal acts, have lower drug and alcohol abuse, and are less likely to use welfare (Karoly et al., 1998).

Because of these positive results, there is now a consensus among experts of all political persuasions that investments in high-quality ECD programs have huge potential long-term payoffs. Investments in high-quality ECD programs consistently generate benefit-cost ratios exceeding 3-to-1—or more than a $3 return for every $1 invested. While participants and their families get part of the total benefits, the benefits to the rest of the public and government are even larger and, on their own, tend to far outweigh the costs of these programs. Several prominent economists and business leaders (many of whom are skeptical about government programs generally) have recently issued well-documented reviews of the literature that find very high economic payoffs from ECD programs. For example, Nobel Prize winning economist James Heckman of the University of Chicago has concluded:

> Recent studies of early childhood investments have shown remarkable success and indicate that the early years are important for early learning and can be enriched through

external channels. Early childhood investments of high quality have lasting effects. . . . In the long run, significant improvements in the skill levels of American workers, especially workers not attending college, are unlikely without substantial improvements in the arrangements that foster early learning. We cannot afford to postpone investing in children until they become adults, nor can we wait until they reach school age—a time when it may be too late to intervene. Learning is a dynamic process and is most effective when it begins at a young age and continues through adulthood. The role of the family is crucial to the formation of learning skills, and government interventions at an early age that mend the harm done by dysfunctional families have proven to be highly effective.[2]

The director of research and a regional economic analyst at the Federal Reserve Bank of Minneapolis, Arthur Rolnick and Rob Grunewald, have come to similar conclusions:

> . . . recent studies suggest that one critical form of education, early childhood development, or ECD, is grossly under-funded. However, if properly funded and managed, investment in ECD yields an extraordinary return, far exceeding the return on most investments, private or public. . . . In the future, any proposed economic development list should have early childhood development at the top.[3]

This Federal Reserve Bank of Minneapolis study (Rolnick and Grunewald, 2003) further determined that annual real rates of return on public investments in the Perry Preschool project were 12 percent for the non-participating public and government and 4 percent for participants, so that total returns exceeded 16 percent. Thus, again it is advantageous even for non-participating taxpayers to pay for these programs. To comprehend how extraordinarily high these rates of return on ECD investments are, consider that the highly touted real rate of return on the stock market that prevailed between 1871 and 1998 was just 6.3 percent.[4]

Likewise, after reviewing the evidence, The Committee for Economic Development (CED), a nonpartisan research and policy organization of some 250 business leaders and educators, concluded that:

> Society pays in many ways for failing to take full advantage of the learning potential of all of its children, from lost economic productivity and tax revenues to higher crime rates to diminished participation in the civic and cultural life of the nation . . . . Over a decade ago, CED urged the nation to view education as an investment, not an expense, and to develop a comprehensive and coordinated strategy of human investment. Such a strategy should redefine education as a process that begins at birth and encompasses all aspects of children's early development, including their physical, social, emotional, and cognitive growth. In the intervening years, the evidence has grown even stronger that investments in early education can have long-term benefits for both children and society.[5]

What If We Provided High-Quality Early Childhood Development to All Poor Children?

How much would it really cost the government to provide such an experience to all poor children? And how much would it actually save the government in terms of crimes not committed, welfare payments no longer needed, reduced remedial education costs, more taxes collected, and so forth?

In a new study published by the Economic Policy Institute and summarized here, I calculate how much taxpayers would save, how much the economy would grow, and how much crime would be reduced over the next 45 years if high-quality programs were provided for all poor children. To create these estimates, I've extrapolated from research on the Perry Preschool Project.[6] Perry was not chosen because it is an ideal program (or even better than the three other programs named above). It is simply the only program with data suitable for these extrapolations. These estimates assume the launch of an ECD program for all of the nation's three- and four-year-olds who live in poverty in 2005, with full phase-in by 2006. (For practical purposes, such as finding appropriate staff and locations, a large-scale ECD program would have to be phased-in over a longer period.) The costs set forth in these estimates may understate the start-up costs of such an ambitious program, especially the costs of recruiting and training teachers and staff and of establishing appropriate sites. On the other hand, the total benefits of ECD investment are also understated in these estimates. Thus, although the benefit-cost ratio of a national ECD program could be somewhat higher or lower than that which is found in the pilot programs, it is implausible that the ratio would be less than the 1-to-1 ratio necessary to justify launching the program.

In the next two sections we'll look at the results of these extrapolations and specifically the effects of ECD investments on 1) government budgets, and 2) on the economy and crime.

What Is the Effect on Government Budgets?

We can expect, based on long-term research on children who participated in high-quality ECD programs and similar non-participating children, that these ECD investments would benefit taxpayers and generate government budget benefits in at least four ways.[7] First, subsequent public education expenses would be lower because participants spend less time in school (as they fail fewer grades) and require expensive special education less often. Second, criminal justice costs would come down because participants—and their families—would have markedly lower crime and delinquency rates. Third, both participants and their parents would have higher incomes and pay more taxes than non-participants. Fourth, the ECD investment would reduce public welfare expenditures because participants and their families would have lower rates of welfare usage. Against these four types of budget benefits, we must consider two types of budget costs: the expenses of the ECD program itself and the increased expenditure due to greater use of higher education by ECD participants.

The ECD programs do not perform miracles on poor children. Substantial numbers of ECD participants go on to do poorly in school, commit crimes, have poor health outcomes, and receive welfare payments. The key point is that ECD participants as a group have far lower rates of these negative outcomes than do non-participants.

Given all of this, what effect would such ECD investments have on government budgets?[8] In the second year of the program, 2006, when the program would be fully phased-in, government outlays would exceed offsetting budget benefits by $19.4 billion (in 2004 dollars). The annual deficit due to the ECD program would shrink for the next 14 years. By the 17th year of the program, in 2021, the deficit would turn into a surplus that would grow every year thereafter. Within 25 years, by 2030 if a nationwide program were started in 2005, the annual budget benefits would exceed costs by $31 billion (in 2004 dollars). By 2050, the net annual budget savings would total $61 billion (in 2004 dollars). In short, for the first 16 years, additional costs exceed offsetting budget benefits, but by a declining margin. Thereafter, offsetting budget benefits exceed costs by a growing margin each year. This pattern is illustrated in the figure, which shows annual revenue impacts and costs in constant 2004 dollars.

The reason for this fiscal pattern is fairly obvious. The costs of the program will grow fairly steadily for the first decade and a half, in tandem with modest growth in the population of three- and four-year-old participants. Thereafter, costs will grow at a somewhat faster pace for a few years as, in addition to the costs of educating three- and four-year-olds, the first and subsequent cohorts of participant children begin to use public higher education services. After the first two years, when the first cohort of children starts entering the public school system, public education expenditures will begin to diminish due to less grade retention and remedial education. After a decade and a half, the first cohort of children will be entering the workforce, resulting in increased earnings and thus higher tax revenues and lower welfare expenditures. In addition, governments will experience lower judicial system costs.

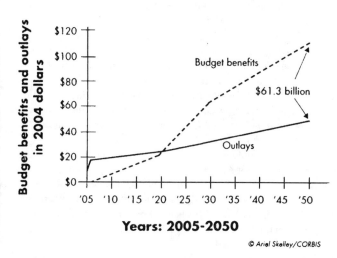

Figure 1 Annual benefits and outlays.

The timing of these fiscal benefits resulting from a nationwide ECD program should appeal to those concerned about the fiscal difficulties posed by the impending surge of retiring baby boomers. The substantial fiscal payoffs from investing in young children would become available to governments just as the wave of new retirements puts the greatest pressure on government resources. For example, the government-wide budget savings in 2030 and in 2050 from ECD investments begun next year would be enough to offset about one-fifth of the deficits in the Social Security trust fund projected for those years. This potential contribution to the solvency of the Social Security system would be achieved without raising social security taxes or cutting benefits.

What Is the Effect of ECD on Crime Reduction, Earnings, and the Economy?

It is important to keep in mind that savings to government is not the only benefit of ECD investments. These other benefits come in many forms. Investments in high-quality ECD programs are likely to substantially reduce crime rates and the extraordinary costs to society of criminality. Some of these reduced costs are savings to government in the form of lower criminal justice system costs. These savings to government would total nearly $28 billion (in 2004 dollars) in 2050, and were included in the earlier discussion of the fiscal effects of ECD investments. But there are other savings to society from reduced crime. These include the value of material losses and the pain and suffering that would otherwise be experienced by the victims of crime. By 2050, these savings to individuals from less crime would amount to $127 billion (in 2004 dollars).

Another major benefit of ECD investments is their impact on the future earnings of participants.[9] The initial increase in earnings occurs in 2020 when the first cohort of participating children turns 18 and enters the labor market. By 2050, the increase in earnings due to ECD investments is estimated to amount to 0.43 percent of GDP, or some $107 billion (in 2004 dollars).

The increased earnings of children who participate in a high-quality ECD program not only allow the U.S. to compete more effectively in a global economy, but also aid both earlier and future generations of children. These increased earnings will benefit earlier generations when they reach retirement age because these earnings will contribute to the solvency of Social Security and other public retirement benefit programs. Future generations will benefit because they will be less likely to grow up in families living in poverty.

A nationwide commitment to high-quality early childhood development would cost a significant amount of money up front, but it would have a substantial payoff in the future. The United States' political system, with its two- and four-year cycles, tends to under-invest in programs with such long lags between when investment costs are incurred and when the benefits are enjoyed. The fact that lower levels of government cannot capture all the benefits of ECD investment may also discourage them from assuming all the costs of ECD programs. Yet, the economic case for ECD investment is compelling.

To recapitulate, I estimate that providing poor three- and four-year-old children—20 percent of all children in this age range—with a high-quality program would initially cost about $19 billion a year. Such a program would ultimately reduce costs for remedial and special education, criminal justice, and welfare benefits, and it would increase income earned and taxes paid. Within about 17 years, the net effect on the budget would turn positive (for all levels of government combined). Within 30 years, the offsetting budget benefits would be more than double the costs of the ECD program (and the cost of the additional youth going to college).

In addition, investing in our poor young children is likely to have an enormous positive effect on the U.S. economy by raising GDP, improving the skills of the workforce, reducing poverty, and strengthening U.S. global competitiveness. Crime rates and the heavy costs of criminality to society are likely to be substantially reduced as well.

Notes

1. All but the Chicago Child-Parent Center Program had random assignment of potentially eligible children into the intervention program or the control group. The Chicago Child-Parent Center Program did not use randomized assignment but the control group did match the intervention group on age, eligibility for intervention, and family socioeconomic status.

2. Heckman (1999), pp. 22 and 41.

3. Rolnick and Grunewald (2003), pp. 3 and 16.

4. Burtless (1999).

5. Committee for Economic Development (2002).

6. The annual average impact for various types of costs and benefits per Perry Preschool Project participant, estimated by Rolnick and Grunewald (2003) of the Federal Reserve Bank of Minneapolis, was used as the baseline for the analysis. (Rolnick and Grunewald used the costs and benefits as described by Schweinhart [1993] and Barnett [1993].) The annual costs and benefits per program participant of the preschool program were adjusted for inflation and/or wage increases every year through 2050 in line with projections made by the Congressional Budget Office (June 2004).

    The numbers of three- and four-year-olds entered in the estimating model were taken from recent population projections made by the U.S. Census Bureau (2004). The total costs and benefits of the preschool program were determined by multiplying the number of participants of a particular age by the average value of the cost or benefit for each year that the cost or benefit was produced by participants of that age as determined by Rolnick and Grunewald (2003). Thus, for example, the reductions in the cost of providing public education per participant were assumed to kick in when that participant entered the public school system at age 5 and were assumed to cease when that participant turned 18 and left the school system.

7. Other savings to taxpayers and boons to government budgets, such as reductions in public healthcare expenditures, are likely to exist. But, we lack the data to quantify all these other potential savings.

8. This analysis considers budget effects on all levels of government—federal, state, and local—as a unified whole. As a practical matter, the source estimates have not made such a distinction, nor should they. All levels of government share in the costs of education, criminal justice, and income support. Responsibilities have shifted in the last half-century and will continue to do so over the nearly half-century timeframe used in this analysis. Although a case can be made that ECD investments should be the responsibility of the federal government to address educational inequalities before children enter the school system, these investments could be made at any or all levels of government. This analysis focuses on capturing national effects of ECD investments.

9. The guardians of participants are also likely to experience increases in earnings since they will have more time for employment as a consequence of the day-care provided to their children by the ECD program. These earnings benefits have not been calculated for our nationwide ECD program.

References

Barnett, W. Steven (1993). "Benefit-Cost Analysis of Preschool Education: Findings From a 25-year Follow-up." *American Journal of Orthopsychiatry, Vol. 63,* No. 4, pp. 500–508.

Burtless, Gary (1999). "Risk and Returns of Stock Market Investments Held in Individual Retirement Accounts." Testimony before the House Budget Committee, Task Force on Social Security Reform, May 11.

Committee for Economic Development (2002). *Preschool for All: Investing in a Productive and Just Society.* New York, N.Y.: CED.

Congressional Budget Office (2004). *The Outlook for Social Security.* Congress of the United States, Washington, D.C., June.

Fuerst, J.S. and Fuerst, D. (1993). "Chicago Experience with an Early Childhood Program: The Special Case of the Child Parent Center Program." *Urban Education,* Vol. 28, pp. 69–96.

Heckman, James (1999). "Policies to Foster Human Development." Working paper 7288. Cambridge, Mass.: National Bureau of Economic Research.

Karoly, L., Greenwood, P., Everingham, S., Hourbe, J., Kilburn, R., Rydell, C.P., Sanders, M., and Chiesa, J. (1998). *Investing in Our Children: What We Know and Don't Know About the Costs and Benefits of Early Childhood Interventions.* Washington, D.C.: Rand Corporation.

Karoly, Lynn (2001). "Investing in the Future: Reducing Poverty Through Human Capital Investments," in *Understanding Poverty,* Danziger, S. and Robert Haveman (eds.), Cambridge, Mass.: Harvard University Press.

Masse, L. and Barnett, W.S. (2002). *A Benefit Cost Analysis of the Abecedarian Early Childhood Intervention.* New Brunswick, N.J.: National Institute for Early Education Research, Rutgers University.

Reynolds, A., Temple, J., Robertson, D., and Mann, E. (2001). "Age 21 Cost-Benefit Analysis of the Title I Chicago Child-Parent Center Program: Executive Summary." Institute for Research on Poverty (http://www.waisman.wisc.edu/cls/cbaexecsum4.html).

Reynolds, A., Temple, J., Robertson, D., and Mann, E. (2002). "Age 21 Cost-Benefit Analysis of the Title I Chicago Child-Parent Centers." Discussion Paper no. 1245-02, Institute for Research on Poverty (http://www.ssc.wisc.edu/irp/pubs/dp124502.pdf).

Reynolds, Arthur (1994). "Effects of a Preschool Plus Follow-on Intervention for Children at Risk." *Developmental Psychology,* Vol. 30, pp. 787–804.

Rolnick, A. and Grunewald, R. (2003). "Early Childhood Development: Economic Development with a High Public Return." *Fedgazette,* Federal Reserve Bank of Minneapolis, March.

Schweinhart, Lawrence (1993). *Significant Benefits: The High/Scope Perry Preschool Study Through Age 27.* Ypsilanti, Mich: High/Scope Press.

Schweinhart, Lawrence (2004). "The High/Scope Perry Preschool Study through Age 40: Summary, Conclusions, and Frequently Asked Questions." Ypsilanti, Mich.: High/Scope Press.

U.S. Census Bureau (2004). *Projected Population of the United States, by Age and Sex: 2000 to 2050.* Washington, D.C.: Population Division, Population Projections Branch, May 18.

ROBERT G. LYNCH is associated professor and chairman of the department of economics at Washington College. His most recent book is *Rethinking Growth Strategies—How State and Local Taxes and Services Affect Economic Development.* This article is adapted with permission from "Exceptional Returns: Economic, Fiscal, and Social Benefits of Investment in Early Childhood Development," published by the Economic Policy Institute, © 2004, www.epinet.org.

The High/Scope Perry Preschool Study and the Man Who Began It

Most researchers don't wake up and say, "Today I'll begin that 40-year study I've been thinking about!" Neither did David Weikart. But although he didn't consciously plan to conduct a long-term study of the effects of a high-quality preschool program on children living in poverty, that is what happened. What began as a small-scale project turned into one of the most influential and well-regarded research studies and educational models in the world of early childhood. With the recent release of the age-40 results of this study and the marking of the first anniversary of Weikart's death, we want to share the story that put Weikart and the High/Scope Curriculum on the map—the story of the High/Scope Perry Preschool study.

Educator, mentor, camp counselor, administrator, researcher, mover, shaker, innovator. David P. Weikart, founder of High/Scope Educational Research Foundation, was all of these and more. This is the story of one of his most influential accomplishments.

The Seeds of the Perry Preschool Study

Throughout his long professional career, David Weikart was interested in changing the practice of education to enable children and youth—especially those who were economically disadvantaged—to attain greater personal, social, and economic success. As school psychologist and director of special services in the Ypsilanti (Michigan) School District in the 1950s, Weikart was frustrated with the lack of options for failing students and the prevailing attitude among school officials that children from impoverished backgrounds were, well, beyond help academically. "I was told that everything possible was already being done; the test scores just represented the way children were," he said. "What could you expect? Their ability was what they were born with."

Weikart was frustrated with the prevailing attitude that children from impoverished backgrounds were beyond help academically.

With his idea for reform of the elementary school curriculum thus dismissed, Weikart and a handful of other reform-minded individuals in the school district came up with a plan for intervention at the preschool level. It seemed a promising way to help children disadvantaged by poverty improve their intellectual and academic capabilities and start their formal schooling on a par with other children. In addition, such a plan posed no threat to existing programs because it required no changes in the schools as a whole, there were funds available for it, and—perhaps most importantly—in this small team of reformers was a principal eager to allow his building to be used for this intervention.

However, experts in the field startled the team by advising that such a program might actually harm the children they were trying to help. "It seemed unethical to just disregard their opinion and continue with our plans," Weikart said. "After several weeks of discussion, we decided that the advisors had asked, but not answered, a legitimate question: Does preschool work?" With this challenging question to be answered, the High/Scope Perry Preschool study was born.

Preschool intervention seemed a promising way to help disadvantaged children start their formal schooling on a par with other children.

The Perry Study Begins

The study officially began in October 1962. From then until the spring of 1967, it was a service project being evaluated. A total of 123 low-income African American children, considered at high risk of school failure, were randomly as signed to either the program group (58 children) or the no-program group (65 children). The children assigned to the program group attended the Perry preschool class three hours a day, five days a week, during the regular school year for two years and had a 90-minute home visit by the same teacher each week. The children in the no-program group remained in the community, at home with their parents, without classes and home visits. From ages 3–11, both groups' progress was assessed each year. Assessment occurred again at ages 14–15, 19, 27, and finally, 40.

The results were beyond what anyone initially expected.

Early Findings

Before the children entered kindergarten, there was an extraordinary increase in program children's performance on intelligence tests. They had an average gain of 15 IQ points, moving them out of the range of mild impairment and into the normal range of intellectual performance. The team was thrilled with these results and felt vindicated in the belief that they could provide an effective intervention in the lives of poor children at risk of school failure. These children could now come to the uncompromising elementary schools better able to engage in traditional education. "We couldn't change the schools, but we could help children be better prepared," Weikart said.

While program children's IQ scores fell back to no-program children's levels in early elementary, their achievement scores were higher.

A worrisome problem emerged, however, as Weikart and his colleagues continued their yearly follow-up assessment. In the early elementary grades the program group's measured level of intellectual performance was not very different from that of the no-program group. This elementary school finding, which had also been found in some studies of Head Start programs, put a damper on the team's enthusiasm. However, by third grade things appeared to change again. While the measured IQ of the program group drifted down to the level of the no-program group, the program group significantly out-performed the no-program group in achievement test scores and some teacher ratings of classroom behavior. While critics pointed to the wash out of IQ gains, the reformers pointed to the achievement gains and lower special education enrollment

figures for program children. "I declared a victory," said Weikart.

But the most dramatic, long-term, real-life program effects were yet to be seen.

Adolescent and Early Adult Years

Not only did the program group continue to out perform the no-program group on achievement tests at age 14, the effect was actually stronger than it had been several years earlier. Throughout the adolescent years, the program group showed stronger commitment to school than the no-program group, and more of the program group graduated from high school—particularly females, a remarkable 84 percent versus 32 percent. In addition, program females were less likely than no-program females to repeat a grade or be assigned to special education classes. The finding of a preschool-program effect on the high school graduation rate is important, because graduation is a gateway to other positive benefits. Jeanne Montie, High/Scope senior research associate and coauthor of the study, would later say, "The preschool program's long-term effects were due to its shorter-term effects on children's educational commitment and success."

By age 27, program participants averaged significantly fewer arrests than no-program group members.

At age 27, more variables were included that offered a glimpse of how participants' life paths were affecting not only themselves but also a new generation. For instance, 40 percent of women in the program group were married at the time of the age-27 interview, compared with only 8 percent of those in the no-program group; and 57 percent of women in the program group were single parents, compared with 83 percent of those in the no-program group.

The effects of the preschool program on participants were extending into the public in general as well. Consider crime rates among the two groups: Program participants at age 27 averaged significantly fewer arrests than no-program group members. By age 27, only 7 percent of adults who had participated in the Perry Preschool program had been arrested five or more times, compared with 35 percent of those in the no-program group. Also, the program group earned more money than the no-program group and were more likely to own their own homes. Through age 27, fewer had received welfare assistance or other social services at some time. Relentless data collection keep overall data loss to only 6 percent—making the results even more impressive.

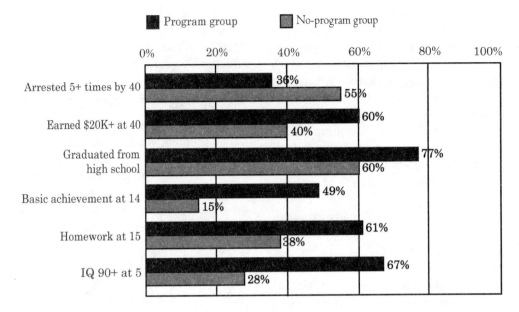

Figure 1 Major Findings: High/Scope Perry Preschool Study at 40.

Age-40 Phase

Would the findings of early adulthood hold through midlife? The age-40 phase was undertaken to answer this. With a continued low attrition rate, the study did in fact find results consistent with those from prior phases. Program participants continued to enjoy more economic success than nonparticipants; in fact, the earnings difference between the two groups was greater at age 40. More of the program group were employed (76 percent vs. 62 percent), and they had a higher median annual income ($20,800 vs. $15,300). Homes, cars, savings accounts—all were owned by more of the program group than the no-program group. Nobel-Prize-winning University of Chicago economist James J. Heckman, a study reviewer, said, "More than 35 years after they received an enriched preschool program, the Perry Preschool participants achieve much greater success in social and economic life than their counterparts" who did not participate in preschool. (See table above.)

At age 40, those in the program group were more likely to be employed and earning more money than no-program participants.

Another trend that continued from earlier phases of the study was a reduction in crime among program participants. The program group had significantly fewer life time arrests than the no-program group, including arrests for violent crimes, property crimes, and drug crimes. In addition, preschool participants were sentenced to fewer months in prison or jail than those who did not attend preschool. Thus, the program group not only had a greater quality of life but also saved taxpayers money. "This study proves that investing in high-quality pre-kindergarten can make every family in America safer from crime and violence," said Sanford Newman, president of Fight Crime: Invest in Kids. "To win the war on crime, we need to be as willing to guarantee our kids space in a pre-kindergarten program as we are to guarantee a criminal a prison cell."

Program participants had fewer arrests and shorter prison or jail sentences than no-program participants.

In addition to issues of economic performance and involvement in crime, researchers asked two major new questions in this phase: What are the participants' health issues? Are personal success and social stability being passed on to a new generation? With regard to health, fewer program males reported abusing drugs, marijuana, or heroin, and fewer members overall of the program group reported health problems for ages 26 to 40 that stopped them from working for at least one week.

Effects on the children of study participants were not as clear. Although more of the program group said they were getting along very well with their family and more program males at age 40 raised their own children (57 percent vs. 30 percent), program males' children did not differ very much from the children of no-program males in education, employment, arrests, or welfare status.

FAQs About the Perry Preschool Study

Because the long-term High/Scope Perry Preschool study is well known and respected and has inspired public investment in early childhood programs, it has attracted many questions that deserve thoughtful answers. Here are some questions commonly asked.

Does the evidence of the effectiveness of the High/Scope educational model come only from programs run decades ago?

No. The Head Start FACES study (Zill et al., 2003) found that 4-year-olds in Head Start classes that used the High/Scope approach improved in letter and word identification skills and cooperative classroom behavior and decreased their behavior problems. In the High/Scope Training for Quality study (Epstein, 1993), High/Scope classrooms were rated significantly better than comparison classrooms in terms of classroom environment, daily routine, adult-child interaction, and overall program implementation. Children in High/Scope programs significantly outperformed children in comparison programs in initiative, social relations, music and movement, and overall child development.

Did the High/Scope Perry Preschool program achieve a level of quality that cannot be duplicated in ordinary preschool programs?

The high level of quality in the Perry program is generally perceived to be due to two factors: well-qualified teachers who were paid public school salaries, and the charismatic leadership of David Weikart. Though it is true that many preschool programs have difficulty attracting higher quality personnel due to low wages, more and more programs are hiring teachers at public school salaries. This trend should lead to more qualified teachers in the field, who are able to provide a high-quality educational experience similar to that of the Perry program. Second, any dedicated preschool program director can exercise similar leadership to Weikart's by insisting on program quality, fidelity to a validated educational model, and providing staff with all the resources and encouragement needed, including adequate salaries.

Was the sample size too small to generate scientific confidence in the findings?

Statistical significance testing takes sample size into account. To achieve statistical significance, group differences must become larger in magnitude as sample sizes become smaller. If the High/Scope Perry Preschool study sample were truly too small, none of its findings would have achieved statistical significance.

Although the program had a strong effect on children's intellectual performance, didn't it fade out over time?

It is true that the Perry program had a statistically significant effect on children's IQs during and up to a year after the program, but not after that. Because the intelligence tests in this study were used to assess preschool program outcomes, they functioned more like achievement tests than intelligence tests. Imagine if achievement tests for grades 4-8 were all combined into one multiage test of achievement—it would not be surprising if a really good grade-4 classroom improved children's achievement test scores on this test at grades 4 and 5 levels but not at grades 6, 7, and 8 levels. This is what happened with the temporary effects of high-quality preschool programs on children's intellectual performance in the Perry study. Children with preschool program experience got more items right on age-specific batteries at their age level but did not get more right on age-specific batteries designed for older children. We might say that their intellectual performance was environmentally sensitive—it went up in intellectually stimulating preschool settings and down in less stimulating elementary school settings. However, all of the subsequent findings of program effects in the Perry study and others—school achievement, high school graduation, adult earnings, crime prevention—demonstrate that high-quality programs for disadvantaged young children do have positive long-term effects.

References

Epstein, A. S. (1993). *Training for quality: Improving early child hood programs through systematic inservice training* (Monographs of the High/Scope Educational Research Foundation, 12). Ypsilanti, MI: High/Scope Press.

Zill, N., Resnick, G., Kim, K., O'Donnell, K., Sorongon, A., McKey, R. H., et al. (May 2003). *Head Start FACES (2000): A whole child perspective on program performance—Fourth progress report.* Prepared for the Administration for Children and Families, U.S. Department of Health and Human Services (DHHS) under contract HHS-105-96-1912, Head Start Quality Research Consortium's Performance Measures Center. Retrieved July 11, 2004, from http://www.acf.hhs.gov/programs/core/ongoing_research/faces/faces00_4thprogress/

"These results are dramatic," said Lawrence Schweinhart, president of High/Scope Foundation and coauthor of the Perry study. "In the areas of crime and earnings, particularly, we found even stronger effects of the preschool program at age 40 than at age 27."

Cost-Benefit Analysis

So the Perry Preschool study demonstrated that a high-quality preschool education helped children better themselves intellectually, socially, and economically. Were there any economic benefits to taxpayers that might convince the public of the value of such education and influence policymakers who had power over preschool funding? There were. At age 27, a cost-benefit analysis showed that for every dollar spent on preschool, the public saved $7.16 in tax dollars.

We need to be as willing to guarantee our kids space in a prekindergarten program as we are to guarantee a criminal a prison cell.

By age 40, the public savings had increased to $12.90 (in year 2000 dollars, discounted at 3 percent). Most of this return came from savings due to program males committing fewer crimes; the rest came from education and welfare savings and increased taxes from higher earnings. Male program participants cost the public 41% less in crime costs per person than they would have otherwise, and they earned 14% more per person than they would have otherwise. Matt Hennessee, president of Quiktrak, Inc., and chair of the High/Scope board of directors, remarked, "The economic return on investment is one of the best ever found for public investment or responsible private investment. Where else can you get [this kind of] return?"

The Future: What Impact Will the Perry Findings Have?

The High/Scope Perry Preschool study is a landmark study that redefines the importance of early childhood education in human lives and economics. It is the first study to find preschool program effects on educational placements, middle school achievement test scores, high school graduation rates, crime, earnings, and employment and the first to establish a large financial return on investment. As of now, it is the only study that has looked at the effects of an early childhood program through age 40.

The latest findings confirm that the benefits of high-quality preschool education extend not only to young adults but also to adults in midlife—these are lifetime effects. High-quality early care and education programs not only raise high school graduation rates and test scores, decades later they lead to higher incomes and lower crime rates. Moreover, the return to the public on its initial investment in such programs is not only substantial but larger than previously estimated.

The Perry project serves as a symbol of what government can achieve. "This study also offers a challenge, a kind of policy gauntlet, for decision makers at local, state, and national levels" said Schweinhart. "We need a good, solid national policy that involves federal and state government in different ways according to what they can do best. It's time we get serious about funding high-quality early care and education for every child in America."

The economic return on investment is one of the best ever found.

Findings from this study and others *have* motivated policymakers to invest more in preschool programs, but these programs have seldom met standards of reasonable similarity to the Perry program. What are some of these standards? According to Schweinhart, they include "teachers who help children plan, do, and review self-chosen educational activities. Teachers who have bachelors' degrees and certification in education. No more than eight children per teaching adult. Teachers who work closely with families, visiting with them at least every month to discuss children's development. Children who are encouraged to solve problems and make their own choices." The Perry findings can be expected of any Head Start, state preschool, or childcare program that has these features. "Given the extraordinary, lifetime effects of such programs, we owe it to all young children living in low-income families to provide access to these programs," Schweinhart said.

As much as these findings support the great value of high-quality preschool programs in breaking the cycle of poverty, however, such programs are only part of the solution. "The report doesn't say you are going to end crime," said Hennessee. "It doesn't say you are going to have zero people on public assistance, but it certainly does say rather clearly that you will have fewer people in the present criminal justice system, fewer people on public assistance." If we truly want to improve the life chances of our neediest children, high-quality preschool education needs to be part of a multifaceted effort to solve our social problems. Affordable housing, ready access to health care, effective job-training programs, reduced institutional racism, and improved educational opportunities at all levels are also essential.

We owe it to all young children living in low-income families to provide access to good preschool programs.

High-quality preschool education needs to be part of a multifaceted effort to solve our social problems.

The landmark High/Scope Perry Preschool study stands as a testament to David Weikart's—and many others'—vision, tenacity, and belief that we can make a difference in the lives of children. The study through age 40 has ended, but it is up to all of us to make sure that its effects will reach far into the future.

The latest results of the Perry Preschool study are chronicled in *Lifetime Effects: The High/Scope Perry Pre school Study Through Age 40,* available from High/Scope Press. See also David Weikart's memoir of High/Scope Foundation, *How High/Scope Grew.* For details on ordering these books, please check our Web site: www.highscope.org/welcome.asp. A downloadable PowerPoint presentation on the Perry study is available at www.highscope.org/PerryProject/perrymain.htm.

Class and the Classroom

Even the best schools can't close the race achievement gap

RICHARD ROTHSTEIN

The achievement gap between poor and middle-class black and white children is widely recognized as our most important educational challenge. But we prevent ourselves from solving it because of a commonplace belief that poverty and race can't "cause" low achievement and that therefore schools must be failing to teach disadvantaged children adequately. After all, we see many highly successful students from lower-class backgrounds. Their success seems to prove that social class cannot be what impedes most disadvantaged students.

Yet the success of some lower-class students proves nothing about the power of schools to close the achievement gap. In every social group, there are low achievers and high achievers alike. On average, the achievement of low-income students is below the average achievement of middle-class students, but there are always some middle-class students who achieve below typical low-income levels. Similarly, some low-income students achieve above typical middle-class levels. Demography is not destiny, but students' family characteristics are a powerful influence on their relative average achievement.

Widely repeated accounts of schools that somehow elicit consistently high achievement from lower-class children almost always turn out, upon examination, to be flawed. In some cases, these "schools that beat the odds" are highly selective, enrolling only the most able or most motivated lower-class children. In other cases, they are not truly lower-class schools—for example, a school enrolling children who qualify for subsidized lunches because their parents are graduate students living on low stipends. In other cases, such schools define high achievement at such a low level that all students can reach it, despite big gaps that remain at more meaningful levels.

It seems plausible that if *some* children can defy the demographic odds, *all* children can, but that belief reflects a reasoning whose naiveté we easily recognize in other policy areas. In human affairs where multiple causation is typical, causes are not disproved by exceptions. Tobacco firms once claimed that smoking does not cause cancer because some people smoke without getting cancer. We now consider such reasoning specious. We do not suggest that alcoholism does not cause child or spousal abuse because not all alcoholics are abusers. We

understand that because no single cause is rigidly deterministic, some people can smoke or drink to excess without harm. But we also understand that, on average, these behaviors are dangerous. Yet despite such understanding, quite sophisticated people often proclaim that the success of some poor children proves that social disadvantage does not cause low achievement.

Partly, our confusion stems from failing to examine the concrete ways that social class actually affects learning. Describing these may help to make their influence more obvious—and may make it more obvious why the achievement gap can be substantially narrowed only when school improvement is combined with social and economic reform.

The Reading Gap

Consider how parents of different social classes tend to raise children. Young children of educated parents are read to more consistently and are encouraged to read more to themselves when they are older. Most children whose parents have college degrees are read to daily before they begin kindergarten, but few children whose parents have only a high school diploma or less benefit from daily reading. And, white children are more likely than black children to be read to in their prekindergarten years.

A 5-year-old who enters school recognizing some words and who has turned the pages of many stories will be easier to teach than one who has rarely held a book. The second child can be taught, but with equally high expectations and effective teaching, the first will be more likely to pass an age-appropriate reading test than the second. So the achievement gap begins.

If a society with such differences wants all children, irrespective of social class, to have the same chance to achieve academic goals, it should find ways to help lower-class children enter school having the same familiarity with books as middle-class children have. This requires rethinking the institutional settings in which we provide early childhood care, beginning in infancy.

Some people acknowledge the impact of such differences but find it hard to accept that good schools should have so difficult a time overcoming them. This would be easier to understand if Americans had a broader international perspective on education.

Class backgrounds influence *relative* achievement everywhere. The inability of schools to overcome the disadvantage of less-literate homes is not a peculiar American failure but a universal reality. The number of books in students' homes, for example, consistently predicts their test scores in almost every country. Turkish immigrant students suffer from an achievement gap in Germany, as do Algerians in France, as do Caribbean, African, Pakistani, and Bangladeshi pupils in Great Britain, and as do Okinawans and low-caste Buraku in Japan.

An international reading survey of 15-year-olds, conducted in 2000, found a strong relationship in almost every nation between parental occupation and student literacy. The gap between the literacy of children of the highest-status workers (such as doctors, professors, and lawyers) and the lowest-status workers (such as waiters and waitresses, taxi drivers, and mechanics) was even greater in Germany and the United Kingdom than it was in the United States.

After reviewing these results, a U.S. Department of Education summary concluded that "most participating countries do not differ significantly from the United States in terms of the strength of the relationship between socioeconomic status and literacy in any subject." Remarkably, the department published this conclusion at the same time that it was guiding a bill through Congress—the No Child Left Behind Act—that demanded every school in the nation abolish social class differences in achievement within 12 years.

Urging less-educated parents to read to children can't fully compensate for differences in school readiness. Children who see parents read to solve their own problems or for entertainment are more likely to want to read themselves. Parents who bring reading material home from work demonstrate by example to children that reading is not a segmented burden but a seamless activity that bridges work and leisure. Parents who read to children but don't read for themselves send a different message.

How parents read to children is as important as whether they do, and an extensive literature confirms that more educated parents read aloud differently. When working-class parents read aloud, they are more likely to tell children to pay attention without interruptions or to sound out words or name letters. When they ask children about a story, the questions are more likely to be factual, asking for names of objects or memory of events.

The achievement gap can be substantially narrowed only when school improvement is combined with social and economic reform.

Parents who are more literate are more likely to ask questions that are creative, interpretive, or connective, such as, "What do you think will happen next?" "Does that remind you of what we did yesterday?" Middle-class parents are more likely to read aloud to have fun, to start conversations, or as an entree to the world outside. Their children learn that reading is enjoyable and are more motivated to read in school.

The Conversation Gap

There are stark class differences not only in how parents read but in how they converse. Explaining events in the broader world to children at the dinner table, for example, may have as much of an influence on test scores as early reading itself. Through such conversations, children develop vocabularies and become familiar with contexts for reading in school. Educated parents are more likely to engage in such talk and to begin it with infants and toddlers, conducting pretend conversations long before infants can understand the language.

Typically, middle-class parents ask infants about their needs, then provide answers for the children. ("Are you ready for a nap now? Yes, you are, aren't you?") Instructions are more likely to be given indirectly: "You don't want to make so much noise, do you?" This kind of instruction is really an invitation for a child to work through the reasoning behind an order and to internalize it. Middle-class parents implicitly begin academic instruction for infants with such indirect guidance.

Yet such instruction is quite different from what policy-makers nowadays consider "academic" for young children: explicit training in letter and number recognition, letter-sound correspondence, and so on. Such drill in basic skills can be helpful but is unlikely to close the social class gap in learning.

Soon after middle-class children become verbal, their parents typically draw them into adult conversations so the children can practice expressing their own opinions. Being included in adult conversations this early develops a sense of entitlement in children; they feel comfortable addressing adults as equals and without deference. Children who ask for reasons, rather than accepting assertions on adult authority, develop intellectual skills upon which later academic success in school will rely. Certainly, some lower-class children have such skills and some middle-class children lack them. But, on average, a sense of entitlement is based on one's social class.

Parents whose professional occupations entail authority and responsibility typically believe more strongly that they can affect their environments and solve problems. At work, they explore alternatives and negotiate compromises. They naturally express these personality traits at home when they design activities in which children figure out solutions for themselves. Even the youngest middle-class children practice traits that make academic success more likely when they negotiate what to wear or to eat. When middle-class parents give orders, the parents are more likely to explain why the rules are reasonable.

But parents whose jobs entail following orders or doing routine tasks show less sense of efficacy. They are less likely to encourage their children to negotiate over clothing or food and more likely to instruct them by giving directions without extended discussion. Following orders, after all, is how they themselves behave at work. Their children are also more likely to be fatalistic about obstacles they face, in and out of school.

Middle-class children's self-assurance is enhanced in after-school activities that sometimes require large fees for enrollment and almost always require parents to have enough free time and resources to provide transportation. Organized sports, music, drama, and dance programs build self-confidence and discipline in middle-class children. Lower-class parents find the fees for such activities more daunting, and transportation may also be more of a problem. Organized athletic and artistic activities may not be available in their neighborhoods, so lower-class children's sports are more informal and less confidence-building, with less opportunity to learn teamwork and self-discipline. For children with greater self-confidence, unfamiliar school challenges can be exciting. These children, who are more likely to be from middle-class homes, are more likely to succeed than those who are less self-confident.

Homework exacerbates academic differences between these two groups of children because middle-class parents are more likely to help with homework. Yet homework would increase the achievement gap even if all parents were able to assist. Parents from different social classes supervise homework differently. Consistent with overall patterns of language use, middle-class parents—especially those whose own occupational habits require problem solving—are more likely to assist by posing questions that break large problems down into smaller ones and that help children figure out correct answers. Lower-class parents are more likely to guide children with direct instructions. Children from both classes may go to school with completed homework, but middle-class children are more likely to gain in intellectual power from the exercise than lower-class children.

Twenty years ago, Betty Hart and Todd Risley, two researchers from the University of Kansas, visited families from different social classes to monitor the conversations between parents and toddlers. Hart and Risley found that, on average, professional parents spoke more than 2,000 words per hour to their children, working-class parents spoke about 1,300, and welfare mothers spoke about 600. So by age 3, the children of professionals had vocabularies that were nearly 50 percent greater than those of working-class children and twice as large as those of welfare children.

Deficits like these cannot be made up by schools alone, no matter how high the teachers' expectations. For all children to achieve the same goals, the less advantaged would have to enter school with verbal fluency that is similar to the fluency of middle-class children.

The Kansas researchers also tracked how often parents verbally encouraged children's behavior and how often they reprimanded their children. Toddlers of professionals got an average of six encouragements per reprimand. Working-class children had two. For welfare children, the ratio was reversed—an average of one encouragement for two reprimands. Children whose initiative was encouraged from a very early age are more likely, on average, to take responsibility for their own learning.

The Role Model Gap

Social class differences in role modeling also make an achievement gap almost inevitable. Not surprisingly, middle-class professional parents tend to associate with, and be friends with, similarly educated professionals. Working-class parents have fewer professional friends. If parents and their friends perform jobs requiring little academic skill, their children's images of their own futures are influenced. On average, these children

must struggle harder to motivate themselves to achieve than children who assume, on the basis of their parents' social circle, that the only roles are doctor, lawyer, teacher, social worker, manager, administrator, or businessperson.

Even disadvantaged children usually say they plan to attend college. College has become such a broad rhetorical goal that black eighth-graders tell surveyors they expect to earn college degrees as often as white eighth-graders do. But despite these intentions, fewer black than white eighth-graders actually graduate from high school four years later; fewer enroll in college the following year; and fewer still persist to get bachelor's degrees.

This discrepancy is not due simply to the cost of college. A bigger reason is that while disadvantaged students say they plan to go to college, they don't feel as much parental, community, or peer pressure to take the courses or to get the grades they need to become more attractive to college admission offices. Lower-class parents say they expect children to get good grades, but they are less likely to enforce these expectations, for example with rewards or punishments. Teachers and counselors can stress doing well in school to lower-class children, but such lessons compete with children's own self-images, formed early in life and reinforced daily at home.

As John Ogbu and others have noted, a culture of underachievement may help explain why even middle-class black children often don't do as well in school as white children from seemingly similar socioeconomic backgrounds. On average, middle-class black students don't study as hard as white middle-class students and blacks are more disruptive in class than whites from similar income strata.

This culture of underachievement is easier to understand than to cure. Throughout American history, many black students who excelled in school were not rewarded for that effort in the labor market. Many black college graduates could find work only as servants or Pullman car porters or, in white-collar fields, as assistants to less-qualified whites. Many Americans believe that these practices have disappeared and that blacks and whites with similar test scores now have similar earnings and occupational status. But labor market discrimination continues to be a significant obstacle—especially for black males with high school educations.

Evidence for this comes from employment discrimination cases, such as the prominent 1996 case in which Texaco settled for a payment of $176 million to black employees after taped conversations of executives revealed pervasive racist attitudes, presumably not restricted to executives of this corporation alone. Other evidence comes from studies that find black workers with darker complexions have less success in the labor market than those with identical education, age, and criminal records but lighter complexions.

Still more evidence comes from studies in which blacks and whites with similar qualifications are sent to apply for job vacancies; the whites are typically more successful than the blacks. In one recent study where young, well-groomed, and articulate black and white college graduates, posing as high school graduates with identical qualifications, submitted applications for entry-level jobs, the applications of whites with criminal records got positive responses more often than the applications of blacks with no criminal records.

So the expectation of black students that their academic efforts will be less rewarded than the efforts of their white peers is rational for the majority of black students who do not expect to complete college. Some will reduce their academic efforts as a result. We can say that they should not do so and, instead, should redouble their efforts in response to the greater obstacles they face. But as long as racial discrimination persists, the average achievement of black students will be lower than the average achievement of whites, simply because many blacks (especially males) who see that academic effort has less of a payoff will respond rationally by reducing their effort.

The Health and Housing Gaps

Despite these big race and social class differences in child rearing, role modeling, labor market experiences, and cultural characteristics, the lower achievement of lower-class students is not caused by these differences alone. Just as important are differences in the actual social and economic conditions of children.

Overall, lower-income children are in poorer health. They have poorer vision, partly because of prenatal conditions and partly because, even as toddlers, they watch too much television, so their eyes are poorly trained. Trying to read, their eyes may wander or have difficulty tracking print or focusing. A good part of the over-identification of learning disabilities for lower-class children may well be attributable to undiagnosed vision problems that could be easily treated by optometrists and for which special education placement then should be unnecessary.

Lower-class children have poorer oral hygiene, more lead poisoning, more asthma, poorer nutrition, less-adequate pediatric care, more exposure to smoke, and a host of other health problems. Because of less-adequate dental care, for example, they are more likely to have toothaches and resulting discomfort that affects concentration.

Because low-income children live in communities where landlords use high-sulfur home heating oil and where diesel trucks frequently pass en route to industrial and commercial sites, they are more likely to suffer from asthma, leading to more absences from school and, when they do attend, drowsiness from lying awake at night, wheezing. Recent surveys in Chicago and in New York City's Harlem community found one of every four children suffering from asthma, a rate six times as great as that for all children.

In addition, there are fewer primary-care physicians in low-income communities, where the physician-to-population ratio is less than a third the rate in middle-class communities. For that reason, disadvantaged children—even those with health insurance—are more likely to miss school for relatively minor problems, such as common ear infections, for which middle-class children are treated promptly.

Each of these well-documented social class differences in health is likely to have a palpable effect on academic achievement; combined, their influence is probably huge.

The growing unaffordability of adequate housing for low-income families also affects achievement. Children whose families have difficulty finding stable housing are more likely to be mobile, and student mobility is an important cause of failing student performance. A 1994 government report found that 30 percent of the poorest children had attended at least three different schools by third grade, while only 10 percent of middle-class children had done so. Black children were more than twice as likely as white children to change schools this often. It is hard to imagine how teachers, no matter how well trained, can be as effective for children who move in and out of their classrooms as they can be for those who attend regularly.

Differences in wealth are also likely to be important determinants of achievement, but these are usually overlooked because most analysts focus only on annual family income to indicate disadvantage. This makes it hard to understand why black students, on average, score lower than whites whose family incomes are the same. It is easier to understand this pattern when we recognize that children can have similar family incomes but be of different economic classes. In any given year, black families with low income are likely to have been poor for longer than white families with similar income in that year.

White families are also likely to own far more assets that support their children's achievement than are black families at the same income level, partly because black middle-class parents are more likely to be the first generation in their families to have middle-class status. Although the median black family income is about two-thirds the median income of white families, the assets of black families are still only 12 percent those of whites. Among other things, this difference means that, among white and black families with the same middle-class incomes, the whites are more likely to have savings for college. This makes white children's college aspirations more practical, and therefore more commonplace.

Narrowing the Gaps

If we properly identify the actual social class characteristics that produce differences in average achievement, we should be able to design policies that narrow the achievement gap. Certainly, improvement of instructional practices is among these, but a focus on school reform alone is bound to be frustrating and ultimately unsuccessful. To work, school improvement must combine with policies that narrow the social and economic differences between children. Where these differences cannot easily be narrowed, school should be redefined to cover more of the early childhood, after-school, and summer times, when the disparate influences of families and communities are now most powerful.

Because the gap is already huge at age 3, the most important new investment should no doubt be in early childhood programs. Prekindergarten classes for 4-year-olds are needed, but they barely begin to address the problem. The quality of early childhood programs is as important as the existence of such programs themselves. Too many low-income children are parked before television sets in low-quality day-care settings. To narrow the gap, care for infants and toddlers should be provided by adults who can create the kind of intellectual environment that is typically experienced by middle-class infants and toddlers. This requires professional caregivers and low child-adult ratios.

After-school and summer experiences for lower-class children, similar to programs middle-class children take for granted, would also be needed to narrow the gap. This does not mean remedial programs where lower-class children get added drill in math and reading. Certainly, remediation should be part of an adequate after-school and summer program, but only a part. The advantage that middle-class children gain after school and in summer comes from the self-confidence they acquire and the awareness of the world outside that they develop through organized athletics, dance, drama, museum visits, recreational reading, and other activities that develop inquisitiveness, creativity, self-discipline, and organizational skills. After-school and summer programs can be expected to narrow the achievement gap only by attempting to duplicate such experiences.

To work, school improvement must combine with policies that narrow the social and economic differences between children.

Provision of health-care services to lower-class children and their families is also required to narrow the achievement gap. Some health services are relatively inexpensive, such as school vision and dental clinics. A full array of health services will cost more, but it cannot be avoided if we truly intend to raise the achievement of lower-class children.

The connection between social and economic disadvantage and an academic achievement gap has long been well known. Most educators, however, have avoided the obvious implication: Improving lower-class children's learning requires ameliorating the social and economic conditions of their lives. School board members—who are often the officials with the closest ties to public opinion—cannot afford to remain silent about the connection between school improvement and social reform. Calling attention to this link is not to make excuses for poor school performance. It is only to be honest about the social support schools require if they are to fulfill the public's expectation that the achievement gap will disappear.

RICHARD ROTHSTEIN is a research associate of the Economic Policy Institute and a visiting professor at Teachers College, Columbia University. He is the author most recently of *Class and Schools: Using Social, Economic, and Educational Reform to Close the Black-White Achievement Gap* (The Economic Policy Institute and Teachers College Press, 2004), on which this article is based. *Class and Schools* includes full bibliographic citations supporting the many claims and generalizations made in this article.

The Preschool Promise

**Going to preschool benefits children their entire lives.
Can states afford to provide it to all kids?**

Julie Poppe and Steffanie Clothier

I f you walk into a good preschool classroom, you might see a teacher reading to a group of kids, children immersed in an art project, little ones playing on a computer or getting ready for a field trip to a nearby museum or public library.

Those children, mounting research shows, will do better in school and are more likely to attend college. As adults they will have better jobs and pay more taxes. They will even be better parents.

The good news is that more and more children go to preschool; in 2002, 66 percent of 4-year-olds attended. Some schools are government supported, others are private. Today, at least 40 states provide state funding for preschool programs, compared to only 10 in 1980.

Parents from all income ranges send their children to preschool, although better educated parents with higher incomes have the highest participation rate.

Preschools are designed to provide education and a safe caring environment. Some states fund programs that incorporate the needs of working parents, sometimes by coordinating their programs with Head Start and child care subsidy programs to ensure full-day services.

Ready for School

One of the striking findings in early education is the size of the achievement gap at the start of kindergarten between children who have gone to preschool and those who have not. That difference hardly ever goes away. It continues in reading and math achievement in the early grades and throughout school and into the job market. Steve Barnett from the National Institute for Early Education Research—an independent, nonpartisan organization that conducts research and follows state early education policy—says that kids living in poverty are 18 months behind the average kid when they start kindergarten. "This is an incredible amount of time for a school to catch up," Barnett says. But the achievement gap isn't just a poverty issue. "The gap continues up the income ladder," he says. Because of these findings and recent brain research showing that almost 90 percent of brain growth occurs in children by age 5, more lawmakers, economists, business leaders and parents are supporting early education.

The Right Programs are Key

What makes a good preschool program? Proper teacher qualifications and training, small class sizes and teacher-to-student ratios, stimulating curriculum and other services that support families. A good program can improve a child's achievement over the short and long term. Recent focus on quality has prompted states to consider enhancements. For example, 23 now require preschool teachers to have a bachelor's degree with additional certification and license.

Most states target their state-funded initiatives to children who are in low-income families or at risk of school failure. Some states are looking to expand their preschool programs in response to state litigation, the need to improve test scores due to No Child Left Behind, and the latest research showing early education improves children's school success. Some states have different goals in mind, such as funding and expanding early education programs to reach more working families.

Paying for Quality Preschool

Arkansas has a state-funded preschool program that started in 1991 for low-income children. In recent years, $40 million in funding has allowed more children to attend. Representative LeRoy Dangeau carried a bill this session that resulted in an additional $20 million over the next two years for the continued expansion of the state's program.

Other preschool funding comes from a beer tax (since 2001) that raises about 18 cents on every six-pack, generating $8 million annually for early education. This April, the Legislature passed a bill to extend the beer tax until June 2007.

Dangeau hopes that by the summer of 2007 there will be a total of $100 million dedicated for voluntary preschool for all 3 and 4-year-olds.

"When I became a legislator four years ago," says Dangeau, "I had no clue about the importance of early childhood. But I saw the research, including the benefits of preschool over time, and how it is the best investment of our money," he says.

In a recent Arkansas Supreme Court case on school funding inequity, the court recognized the importance of preschool (but didn't mandate it) as part of its ruling. "I think that the court

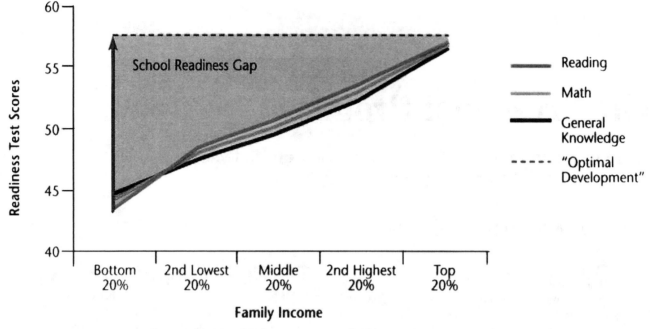

Figure 1 The Achievement Gap at Kindergarten Family income has a great deal to do with how well a child does on readiness tests when entering kindergarten. The school readiness gap is steepest for children from families with the lowest incomes and continues through middle income families, gradually decreasing as income rises.

case had an impact on how the Legislature views preschool," says Dangeau. "We see it as the quickest way to improve test scores. The issue is not whether or not to have preschool. The question is how much money to put into it."

Last year, the National Institute for Early Education Research ranked the quality of Arkansas' preschool program very high.

"I am very proud to say that Arkansas ranked best in terms of quality," says Dangeau. He believes the success is directly tied to legislation passed in 2003 that puts preschool teachers on the same pay scale as K-12 teachers. Any program or school may provide preschool services as long as they meet the state's quality standards, such as one certified teacher per 10 students.

Supporting Working Families

In the mid-'80s, the Illinois legislature established a preschool program for at-risk children. To support working families, the state allows child care centers and Head Start programs that meet standards to provide full-day early education services along with public schools. Local communities determine eligibility; there are an estimated 64,000 3- and 4-year-olds enrolled statewide.

The state has significantly increased funding over the past few years. Since 2003, lawmakers have appropriated $30 million annually for early education and are looking to do the same this legislative session.

The National Institute for Early Education Research gave the state high marks for quality. Teachers participating in the program must hold an early childhood teaching certificate to be on the same pay scale as K-12 teachers.

In 2003, lawmakers created the Illinois Early Learning Council. It builds on the work the state has already done to develop a high-quality early learning system available to all Illinois children up to age 5. Four legislators currently are members of the council, including Representative Elizabeth Coulson.

Coulson, who has a business background, sits on two of the House Appropriation Committee's subcommittees, Human Services and Education, which make funding decisions for early education. She is also a member of the House Human Services

Preschool Popularity

At least 40 states provide state funding for preschool programs.

- The first to expand preschool to all 4-year-olds were Georgia and then Oklahoma. Florida, Maryland, New York and West Virginia are in the process of phasing in their programs.
- Thirty-six states considered early education bills in 2005. At least 28 states considered expanding preschool programs.
- Florida legislators, responding to a state ballot measure, approved legislation for a voluntary preschool program for all 4-year-olds. New Mexico legislators passed a pilot preschool bill with a $5 million initial appropriation.
- Mississippi, Montana, North Dakota and South Dakota have no state-funded preschool programs, but did consider legislation this session.

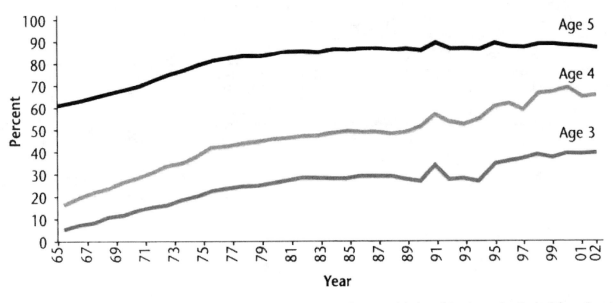

Source: National Institute for Early Education Research.

Figure 2 Kindergarten and Preschool Participation 1965-2002. Over the last several decades, preschool and kindergarten participation has increased steadily for children ages 3 to 5.

Committee. "I'm a link between key committees that focus on early childhood," she says.

She says that Illinois has been concerned for some time about supporting working families and making sure a strong birth-to-age-5 system is in place that nurtures children. In 2003, the legislature increased the percentage of funding for birth-to-age-3 programs from 8 percent to 11 percent of the state's early childhood education block grant. The block grant makes up the state's funding for preschool education, parental training and prevention initiatives. "The formative years have the most impact on education. This is not just a women's issue, but it's also a children's issue and [in terms of economics and business] an important issue for the whole state," she says.

Nearly a third of all Illinois 4-year-olds are in a state-funded preschool program and the number is up from the year before. Coulson says early care is a thriving industry that has an impact on Illinois' economy, and businesses need to be aware of the benefits. Recent research shows that every tax dollar invested in preschool produces $17 for the economy.

"This session, we continue to focus on quality and funding," Coulson says, in the last two years, the state has increased preschool spending by $60 million. "This is a bad budget year for Illinois, but I am optimistic we will find a way to fund another $30 million for early childhood," she says.

Legislative Involvement

During the mid-'80s, Massachusetts set up a state-funded early education program in public schools. Since then, the state has allowed community partnership providers who meet early childhood standards to participate in programs targeting at-risk

3- and 4-year-olds from working families serving almost 16,000 children last year.

During the 2004 session, more than 100 legislators, including leadership in both houses, signed on to a proposal for preschool for all 3-to-5-year-olds to be phased-in over 10 years, at an estimated cost of $1 billion. Two bills that were eventually enacted laid the groundwork for the expansion by reworking state governance of early childhood programs. One law creates a single department to streamline early childhood programs and to expand preschool to all 3- and 4-year-olds. "Hopefully, we will see less duplication of services," says Representative Patricia Haddad.

She co-chairs the legislature's Joint Committee on Education and the state's legislatively created Advisory Committee on Early Education and Care. Nine other legislators participate. They have conducted five public hearings throughout the state. "We had to be a part of the hearings ourselves, because it is nice to read a report, but the passion is different when you are involved," says Haddad. State early childhood advocates also held meetings throughout the state to educate the public on the importance of early childhood education and full-day kindergarten for all.

Last December, the advisory committee completed a report that identified four key components: developing a workforce, defining quality, delivering the system and evaluating progress. Haddad says the next step is providing a good workforce development program for teachers and providers.

The 2004 legislation also created a new board of early education and care, which will start this July. The commissioners from the boards of Higher Education, Education, and Early Education and Care will each sit on each other's boards. "We want the commissioners to be talking to one another, which will lead to better communication between these three entities," says Haddad.

Representative Haddad says people in Massachusetts are starting to realize the importance of preschool and the role that it might possibly play with No Child Left Behind. "If you do not provide the very best for children in the early years, you will continue to see gaps," she says.

JULIE POPPE tracks preschool policy for NCSL. Steffanie Clothier heads NCSL's Child Care and Early Education Project.

From *State Legislatures,* June 2005. Copyright © 2005 by National Conference of State Legislatures. Reprinted by permission.

Kindergarten Learning Gap

Involving parents and caregivers during the powerful early learning years from birth to age 5 gives young children an equal chance at success

Lynn Fielding

Public schools do not create the achievement gap. The five- to six-year gap in reading and math skills between students in the top and bottom quartiles—so painfully evident on the SAT and ACT at 11th grade—is rarely caused by our high schools, our middle schools, or even our elementary schools. Recent data from the Northwest Evaluation Association indicates that virtually the entire gap in language achievement and almost 70 percent of the gap in math achievement are created before the beginning of second grade and most likely between birth and kindergarten.

In Kennewick, Wash., about 20 percent of our students come to kindergarten with language and math skills typical of 2- and 3-year-olds. Another 20 percent come with the skills of 4-year-olds. Do the math. This means 40 percent of our students are already one to three years below grade level when they enter public school. They will continue to lag indefinitely unless we do something about it.

Back in 1996, Kennewick adopted a high but not unreasonable goal: 90 percent of third-graders will leave third grade reading at or above grade level. The board thought our struggling students were just a little bit behind—perhaps by half a year or, in rare cases, as much as a year. We thought we could bring them to grade level by fine-tuning our curriculum, tweaking our teachers' skills, or giving students a little more instructional time.

But when we implemented fall and spring testing in 1999 in first and second grade, and later in kindergarten, we realized our lowest-performing students were much further behind than we expected—and that closing our achievement gap would take a much greater effort than we had thought. When students enter kindergarten with language and pre-literacy skills three years below the average kindergarten student, they have to experience an extraordinary amount of growth each year for two, three, even four years. To bring these students up to grade level by the end of third grade, we had to produce as much as seven years of growth in the four years from kindergarten through third grade.

First, we had to ensure "annual growth"—an average year's worth of growth—in kindergarten and first, second, and third grades. The good news about annual growth is that students who achieve it do not fall further behind. The bad news is that, if they started behind, they don't catch up. They just keep their same place at the back of the line.

To reach our 90 percent goal, we also had to ensure that these students made three years of "catch-up growth." In other words, on top of a year of annual growth, they had to make an additional year of growth in first grade, do it again in second grade, and do it yet again in third grade to read at or above grade level by the end of that year. If they made only annual growth but no catch-up growth in first and second grade, they would have to make as much as three years of catch-up growth (on top of their annual growth) in third grade.

Four years of annual growth and three years of catch-up growth by the end of third grade sound daunting, but the reality is that all elementary principals must now perform this feat under NCLB requirements by 2014.

Reaching Prekindergarten Parents

Our initial strategy—waiting until kindergarten and then ensuring annual growth for all students and accelerated growth for students who are behind—only addressed part of the problem. Four years ago, Kennewick's school board, superintendent, and union leaders realized we would be perpetually reacting to the new wave of entering kindergarten students—40 percent of whom were one to three years behind—unless we got to the root of the problem. We decided to involve parents and childcare providers of children during the powerful early learning years from birth to age 5. The result was a program we call Ready! for Kindergarten.

Some 6,000 adults with children 5 and under have attended 90-minute Ready! sessions in the fall, winter, and spring over the past two and a half years. We train about 900 parents per session. During the sessions, we do five things:

First, we show parents the data on beginning kindergarten students and point out that those who begin behind typically stay behind. We explain that parenting practices from birth to 5 generally determine the academic quartile in which a child starts school. We offer support to families as they prepare their children to enter kindergarten with basic skills at or above grade level. We found parents are very receptive to information on how they can guide their children and enthusiastic about the free training. We also found they enjoy playing with a purpose and reading aloud with their children daily.

Second, we give specific answers to the question, "What should a typical 5-year-old be able to do when he or she begins kindergarten?" Here are our targets, or expectations, for language and literacy: Children enjoy being read to and can retell a story, know 12 to 15 upper- and lower-case letters and their sounds, memorize five to six nursery rhymes, hear ending sounds (rhyme) and beginning sounds (alliteration) in words, speak in complete sentences, and have a vocabulary of 4,000 to 5,000 words.

We also have simple math, social, and bilingual targets, such as counting in order from 1 to 20 and settling into new groups or situations. These targets are focused, narrow in scope, and highly correlated with success in reading and math by third grade. These targets do not include nutrition, safety, physical development, and other important aspects of early childhood that have indirect effects on third-grade academic outcomes.

Third, we share with parents specific age-level activities that can be done in five to 10 minutes a day. We break each of the incoming kindergarten targets into subskills, then sequence each skill at each age level back to birth. For example, to reach the target of knowing letters of the alphabet at age 5, parents do simple eye-movement games with their baby to develop the eye muscles needed for future reading. Parents show 1-year-olds how to feel and match the few simple shapes that form our alphabet with large wooden pieces. This activity wires the young brain for instantaneous recognition of these letter shapes in text. For children ages 2 to 3, parents decorate their home with many five-inch-high copies of the first letter of the child's name, followed by the rest of his name at age 3 and a few more letters at age 4.

We provide free tools, simple activities, and training to make the process manageable and fun for both parent and child. We encourage parents to read with their child 20 minutes a day from birth and spend five to 10 minutes a day with the program's targets, tools, and activities. We teach parents that connecting with their child begins with the interactive eye-contact and smiling "dance" shortly after birth. While the interaction becomes more linguistically complex as time goes on, it is still a dance, with each responding to the other and adding to the stream of interaction. The moment the parent or the child is no longer having fun, we tell them to stop.

We offer different fall, winter, and spring classes at each of the five age levels so the material is fresh while still building on the prior lessons. Parents who start with the newborn lesson will get 15 different sequenced training sessions, with tools and age-appropriate targets, by the time their child starts kindergarten. Ready! provides its instructors, most of whom are community members and kindergarten teachers, with PowerPoint presentations featuring short video clips from outside experts.

Fourth, we assess to determine program effectiveness. We survey parents in the classes each year, and we collect voluntary logs of daily activities with their children. We assess each child on entering kindergarten. These simple assessments let us evaluate the impact of the Ready! program on the children whose parents have attended. The kindergarten assessment allows teachers to see specific initial skill levels in their students.

Our data shows some predictable but powerful trends. Over time, more parents of children birth to age 3 have attended sessions, realizing that they need to be involved early. Fathers have become increasingly involved with their children as they see that simple reading, talking, and reasoning activities are brain building, not merely babysitting activities. And attendance at sessions for Spanish speakers has increased from a few parents to 100.

More low-income parents are attending as well. The free tools and activities (with a retail value of about $65 per session) are a significant encouragement. Although we haven't collected data on this point, we think many negative attitudes toward school, rooted in childhood ("This is frightening. This is embarrassing. This is too hard"), are changing, encouraging parents to seek more learning for themselves.

And best of all, it's paying off. Eighty-five percent of students whose parents attended at least two sessions are meeting the standard on the incoming kindergarten assessment—35 percent more than those whose parents attend no sessions.

Fifth, we are sharing our powerful curriculum and tools with our community partners everywhere. We have adapted the curriculum for child care providers. We modified the lessons for teenage parents, the Headstart and Early Headstart programs, and our own district Early Childhood Education and Assistance Program.

Changing a Culture

We are changing our local culture to value skillful parenting. We did not create the Ready! for Kindergarten program because we are dripping with money. We created it because we are not. We think a dime spent on each child early on will save us a dollar by third grade and maybe 10 dollars by high school. Our initial data after eight sessions seems to bear this out. After two full years, we think we are recouping our investment.

Kennewick has a $112 million general budget. Of that we spend $12 million on special education and $10 million on remedial education, plus we estimate that we reallocated another $10 million inside regular classrooms as teachers spend discretionary time with students who are behind. This totals $32 million—28 percent of Kennewick's total budget, or about $5,400 per year extra for the 40 percent of our students who are behind. Even excluding special education, the cost for remediation would be 20 percent of our budget, or $3,600 per student per year.

We can now say that enough students have already entered kindergarten at or above grade level to pay for the program at our normal remediation rates. But will the program pay off in terms of achievement as well? Will we reach our goal of 90 percent of students reading at grade level by the end of third grade? We have already moved from 57 percent to 88 percent, changing the future of thousands of students. Time will tell, but we're optimistic.

LYNN FIELDING (lynnfielding@hotmail.com), president of the Kennewick (Wash.) School Board, is a business attorney, cofounder of the National Children's Reading Foundation, and coauthor of *The 90% Reading Goal* (1998) and *Delivering on the Promise* (2004). Additional information about Ready! for Kindergarten is available at www.readyforkindergarten.org.

The New First Grade: Too Much Too Soon?

Kids as young as 6 are tested, and tested again, to ensure they're making sufficient progress. Then there's homework, more workbooks and tutoring

PEG TYRE

Brian And Tiffany Aske of Oakland, Calif., desperately want their daughter, Ashlyn, to succeed in first grade. That's why they're moving—to Washington state. When they started Ashlyn in kindergarten last year, they had no reason to worry. A bright child with twinkling eyes, Ashlyn was eager to learn, and the neighborhood school had a great reputation. But by November, Ashlyn, then 5, wasn't measuring up. No matter how many times she was tested, she couldn't read the 130-word list her teacher gave her: words like "our," "house" and "there." She became so exhausted and distraught over homework—including a weekly essay on "my favorite animal" or "my family vacation"—that she would put her head down on the dining-room table and sob. "She would tell me, 'I can't write a story, Mama. I just can't do it'," recalls Tiffany, a stay-at-home mom.

The teacher didn't seem to notice that Ashlyn was crumbling, but Tiffany became so concerned that she began to spend time in her daughter's classroom as a volunteer. There she was both disturbed and comforted to see that other kids were struggling, too. "I saw kids falling asleep at their desks at 11 a.m.," she says. At the end of the year, Tiffany asked the teacher what Ashlyn could expect when she moved on to the first grade. The requirements the teacher described, more words and more math at an even faster pace, "were overwhelming. It was just bizarre."

So Tiffany and Brian, a contractor, looked hard at their family finances to see if they could afford to send Ashlyn to private school. Eventually, they called a real-estate agent in a community where school was not as intense.

In the last decade, the earliest years of schooling have become less like a trip to "Mister Rogers' Neighborhood" and more like SAT prep. Thirty years ago first grade was for learning how to read. Now, reading lessons start in kindergarten and kids who don't crack the code by the middle of the first grade get extra help. Instead of story time, finger painting, tracing letters and snack, first graders are spending hours doing math work sheets and sounding out words in reading groups. In some places, recess, music, art and even social studies are being replaced by writing exercises and spelling quizzes. Kids as young as 6 are tested, and tested again—some every 10 days or so—to ensure they're making sufficient progress. After school, there's homework, and for some, educational videos, more workbooks and tutoring, to help give them an edge.

Not every school, or every district, embraces this new work ethic, and in those that do, many kids are thriving. But some children are getting their first taste of failure before they learn to tie their shoes. Being held back a grade was once relatively rare: it makes kids feel singled out and, in some cases, humiliated. These days, the number of kids repeating a grade, especially in urban school districts, has jumped. In Buffalo, N.Y., the district sent a group of more than 600 low-performing first graders to mandatory summer school; even so, 42 percent of them have to repeat the grade. Among affluent families, the pressure to succeed at younger and younger ages is an inevitable byproduct of an increasingly competitive world. The same parents who played Mozart to their kids in utero are willing to spend big bucks to make sure their 5-year-olds don't stray off course.

> **'I worry that we are creating school environments that are less friendly to kids who just aren't ready . . . Around third grade, sometimes even the most precocious kids begin to burn out.'**
>
> —Holly Hultgren, Principal
> Lafayette Elementary School

Like many of his friends, Robert Cloud, a president of an engineering company in suburban Chicago, had the Ivy League in mind when he enrolled his sons, ages 5 and 8, in a weekly after-school tutoring program. "To get into a good school, you need to have good grades," he says. In Granville, Ohio, a city known for its overachieving high-school and middle-school students, an elementary-school principal has noticed a dramatic shift over the past 10 years. "Kindergarten, which was once very play-based," says William White, "has become the new first grade." This pendulum has been swinging for nearly a century: in some decades, educators have favored a rigid academic curriculum, in others, a more child-friendly classroom style. Lately, some experts have begun to question whether our current emphasis on early learning may be going too far. "There comes a time when prudent people begin to wonder just how high we can raise our expectations for our littlest schoolkids," says Walter Gilliam, a child-development expert at Yale University. Early education, he says, is not just about teaching letters but about turning curious kids into lifelong learners. It's critical that all kids know how to read, but that is only one aspect of a child's education. Are we pushing our children too far, too fast? Could all this pressure be bad for our kids?

Kindergarten and first grade have changed so much because we know so much more about how kids learn. Forty years ago school performance and intelligence were thought to be determined mainly by social conditions—poor kids came from chaotic families and attended badly run schools. If poor children, blacks and Hispanics lagged behind middle-class kids in school, policymakers dismissed the problem as an inevitable byproduct of poverty. Its roots were too deep and complex, and there wasn't the political will to fix it anyway. Since then, scientists have confirmed what some kindergarten teachers had been saying all along—that *all* young children are wired to learn from birth and an enriched environment, one with plenty of books, stories, rhyming and conversation, can help kids from all kinds of backgrounds achieve more. Politicians began taking aim at the achievement gap, pushing schools to reconceive the early years as an opportunity to make sure that all kids got the fundamentals of reading and math. At the same time, politicians began calling for tests that would measure how individual students were doing, and high-stakes testing quickly became the sole metric by which a school was measured.

President George W. Bush's No Child Left Behind Act, which required every principal in the country to make sure the kids in his or her school could read by the third grade, was signed into federal law in 2002. Its aim was both simple and breathtakingly grand: to level the academic playing field by holding schools accountable or risk being shut down.

So if the curriculum at Coronita Elementary School, 60 miles outside Los Angeles, is intense, that's because it has to be. Seventy percent of kids who go there live below the poverty line. Thirty percent don't speak English at home. Even so, No Child Left Behind mandates that Coronita principal Alma Backer and her staff get every student reading proficiently in time for the California state test in the spring of second grade or face stiff penalties: the school could lose its funding and the principal could lose her job. "Our challenges are great," she says. "From day one, our kids are playing catch-up." First grade is like literacy boot camp. Music, dance, art, phys ed—even social studies and science—take a back seat to reading and writing. Kids are tested every eight weeks to see if they are hitting school, district and statewide benchmarks. If they aren't, they get remedial help, one-on-one tutoring and more instruction. The regular school day starts at 7:45 a.m. and ends at 2:05 p.m.;

about a fifth of the students go to an after-school program until 5:30, where they get even more instruction: tutoring, reading group and homework help. Backer says most parents appreciate what the school is trying to do. "Many of them have a high-school diploma or less," says Backer, "but they're still ambitious for their children."

> **'If you push kids too hard, they get frustrated. Those are the kids who act out, and who can look like they have attention-span or behavior problems.'**
>
> —Dominic Gullo, Professor
> Queens College, N.Y.

Parents whose kids attend Clemmons Elementary School near Winston-Salem, N.C., are ambitious for their children, too. But the scale of their expectations is different: the upper-middle-class, college-educated parents in this district don't just want their kids to get a good education, they want them to be academic stars. Principal Ron Montaquila says kids of all ages are affected. Last year, says Montaquila, one dad wanted to know how his son stacked up against his classmates. "I told him we didn't do class ranking in kindergarten," recalls Montaquila. But the father persisted. If they did do rankings, the dad asked, would the boy be in the top 10th? Like almost all elementary schools, kindergarten and first grade at Clemmons have become more academic—but not because of No Child Left Behind. Unlike poor schools, wealthy schools do not depend on federal money. The kids come to school knowing more than they used to. "Many of our kindergartners come in with four years of preschool on their résumé," says Montaquila. Last year nine children started kindergarten at Clemmons reading chapter books—including one who had already tackled "Little House on the Prairie."

In wealthier communities, where parents can afford an extra year of day care or preschool, they are holding their kids out of kindergarten a year—a practice known in sports circles as red-shirting—so their kids can get a jump on the competition. Clemmons parent Mary DeLucia did it. When her son, Austin, was 5, he was mature, capable, social and ready for school. But the word around the local Starbucks was that kindergarten was a killer. "Other parents said, 'Send him. He'll do just fine'," says DeLucia. "But we didn't want him to do fine, we wanted him to do great!" Austin, now in fourth grade, towers over his classmates, but he's hardly the only older kid in his grade. At Clemmons last year, 40 percent of the kindergartners started when they were 6 instead of 5. Other parents say they understand where the DeLucias are coming from but complain that red-shirting can make it hard for other kids to compete. "We're getting to the point," says Bill White, a Clemmons dad whose kids started on time, where "we're going to have boys who are shaving in elementary school."

Parents are acutely aware of the pressure on their kids, but they're also creating it. Most kids learn to read sometime before the end of first grade. But many parents (and even some teachers

Ten Ways to Prepare Your Child for School

For Kindergarten

1. **Read To Them** Pull out the board books, get cozy and channel Mr. Rogers. Kids love repetition and there's no such thing as reading too much to your child.
2. **Talk To Them** Sing songs, recite rhymes and narrate your activities as you go about the day. Ask questions and invite them to name objects and describe whatever they're seeing. At night, recap the day's events together out loud.
3. **Take Them On Trips** No, not Europe. The supermarket, the post office, a museum or the zoo will do. Then, talk about what you see and ask questions.
4. **Write It Down** Kids love to scribble. Give them paper and plenty of pencils, crayons, paints and markers. Finger paints are colorful and feel squishy, too.
5. **Socialize** Whether it's a big birthday party or a one-on-one play date, kids benefit from hearing a range of words in a variety of voices. Story hour at the library or a puppet show can be especially good for encountering new sounds and ideas.
6. **Use Your Fingers** Drawing, cutting and pasting can seem laborious but these activities will help them learn to write more legibly—and result in keepsakes.

For First Grade

7. **Read Some More** Let them "read" to you, too, by flipping the pages—themselves, thank you very much—and retelling a favorite story in their own words.
8. **Teach Recognition** Logos on food packages. Names and addresses on the mail. A stop sign. A "walk" signal. The letter B. Give them opportunities to demonstrate that they know what these things mean and then heap on praise.
9. **Do The Math** Talk about numbers. Count everything out loud. How many grapes do you have on your plate? One more would make how many?
10. **Grow Their Attention Span** Card games, board games, setting the table, picking photos out of a magazine. Set aside time to focus on a single activity or one task before moving on to active play.

Source: Dominic Gullo, Queens College, N.Y.

and school administrators) believe—mistakenly—that the earlier the kids read independently, write legibly and do arithmetic, the more success they'll have all through school. Taking a cue from the success of the Baby Einstein line of videos and CDs, an entire industry has sprung up to help anxious parents give their kids a jump-start. Educate, Inc., the company that markets the learning-to-read workbooks and CDs called "Hooked on Phonics," just launched a new line of what it calls age-appropriate reading and writing workbooks aimed at 4-year-olds. In the last three years, centers that offer school-tutoring services such as Sylvan Learning Centers and Kumon have opened junior divisions. Gertie Tolentino of Darien, Ill., has been bringing her first grader, Kyle, for Kumon tutoring three times a week since he was 3 years old. "It's paying off," she says. "In kindergarten, he was the only one who could read a book at age 5." Two weeks ago Tiffani Chin, executive director of Edboost, a nonprofit tutoring center in Los Angeles, saw her first 3-year-old. His parents wanted to give him a head start, says Chin. "They had heard that kindergarten was brutal" and they wanted to give him a leg up.

All this single-minded focus on achievement leaves principals like Holly Hultgren, who runs Lafayette Elementary School in Boulder County, Colo., in a quandary. In this area of Colorado, parents can shop for schools, and most try to get their kids into the top-performing ones. Two years ago Hultgren moved to Lafayette from a more affluent school, in part to help raise the tests scores, improve the school's profile and raise attendance. Every day Hultgren has to help her staff strike a balance between the requirements of the state, the expectations

of parents—and the very real, highly variable needs of all kinds of 5- and 6-year-olds. She is adamant that her staff won't "teach to the test." Yet, in keeping with her district's requirements, on the day before the first day of kindergarten, students come in for a reading assessment. Sitting one-on-one with her new teacher, a little girl named Jenna wrinkles her nose and in a whispery voice identifies most of the letters in the alphabet and makes their sounds. Naming words that start with each letter is harder for her. Asked to supply a word that starts with B, Jenna scrunches her face and shakes her head.

Hultgren is ambivalent about high-stakes testing. The district reading test, administered three times a year, helps parents see how the school measures up and helps teachers see "exactly what kind of instruction is working and what isn't." But the pressure to improve scores makes it hard for teachers to stay sensitive to the important qualities in children that tests can't measure—diligence, creativity and potential—or to nurture kids who develop more slowly. "I worry," she says, that "we are creating school environments that are less friendly to kids who just aren't ready."

Some scholars and policymakers see clear downsides to all this pressure. Around third grade, Hultgren says, some of the most highly pressured learners sometimes "burn out. They began to resist. They didn't want to go along with the program anymore." In Britain, which adopted high-stakes testing about six years before the United States did, parents and school boards are trying to dial back the pressure. In Wales, standardized testing of young children has been banned. Andrew Hargreaves, an expert on international education reform and professor at

Boston College, says middle-class parents there saw that "too much testing too early was sucking the soul and spirit out of their children's early school experiences."

'When Austin was 5, he was ready for school. Other parents said, "Send him. He'll do just fine." But we didn't want him to do fine, we wanted him to do great!'

—Mary DeLucia, Parent
Clemmons Elementary School

While most American educators agree that No Child Left Behind is helping poor kids, school administrators say a bigger challenge remains: helping those same kids succeed later on. Until he resigned as Florida's school chancellor last year, Jim Warford says he scoured his budget, taking money from middle- and high-school programs in order to beef up academics in the earliest years. But then he began to notice a troubling trend: in Florida, about 70 percent of fourth graders read proficiently. By middle school, the rate of proficient readers began to drop. "We can't afford to focus on our earliest learners," says Warford, "and then ignore what happens to them later on."

Interview: What Would Big Bird Do?

"Sesame Street" began in 1969 with a revolutionary idea: learning could be fun. The cast of furry Muppets and their inimitable songs became so popular among kids of all backgrounds—and not just the disadvantaged kids the show originally intended to help—that "Sesame Street" spawned an entire industry of DVDs, toys and computer games aimed at teaching ever-younger children. The show, meant for 2- to 4-year-olds, is watched today by kids as young as 9 months. NEWSWEEK's Julie Scelfo asked Rosemarie Truglio, "Sesame Street's" VP of education and research, whether she thinks this is a good idea. Excerpts:

SCELFO: Do you Think there's too much Pressure on Young Kids to Learn?

TRUGLIO: People want children to be ready to read in kindergarten, so that pressure is now being passed down to preschool and day-care centers. We're putting a lot of pressure on [teachers] and introducing children to some things that may or may not be age-appropriate. Stress is not conducive to learning. If you're put in a stressful environment, you're not going to learn.

What should Preschoolers be Learning?

The majority of kindergarten teachers want children to be able to function in a group setting. To be able to listen and take direction. Be able to get along. To be able to regulate their emotions. A lot of what I'm talking about is social-emotional development of children. If they can't function in a group setting, it will interfere with learning to read.

So Reading is Important, but it's not the Only Thing?

Every child learns at their own rate. During the preschool years, children's job is to explore and investigate, and adults need to assist learning and facilitate it. I'm not going to say a child can't read by the age of 5. But developmentally, most children in kindergarten are learning the precursors of

reading skills—they have sounds, they do the alphabet, they have rhyming—but they are not reading.

Then why do Parents Feel so Pressured?

One reason may be No Child Left Behind. I don't think the intention was for this kind of hysteria. The idea of accountability is great. But I think it's turned into this testing issue, and there's a lot of pressure about testing and performance which I think might be leading to anxiety.

Is that what is Spurring Sales of all those Videos for Infants?

What's happening now is, everything is getting pushed down to a younger and younger age. There's pressure even on babies to begin achieving, so parents are buying these videos to make their infants "smarter." But there's no research that shows exposure to videos increases learning.

But aren't Kids Watching "Sesame Street" at Younger and Younger Ages?

Yes, and that's not something we can control. "Sesame Street" is a show for 2- to 4-year-olds. If you can get that word out, it would be great. Parents grew up on "Sesame Street" and they know it's a safe, educational viewing experience. They think, Why not have my little ones learn their letters and numbers at an accelerated pace? It makes parents feel proud. There's no harm, but the show's content isn't age-appropriate, so a lot of the learning is going over their heads. Also, they burn out. If you start watching it at 9 months, by the time you're 2 you want something else.

How is this Affecting Children?

Learning should be fun. It shouldn't feel like they're learning, which is what "Sesame Street" is all about. A child's work is through play. I don't think preschoolers should be doing flashcards.

What early-childhood experts know is that for children between the ages of 5 and 7, social and emotional development are every bit as important as learning the ABCs. Testing kids before third grade gives you a snapshot of what they know at that moment but is a poor predictor of how they will perform later on. Not all children learn the same way. Teachers need to vary instruction and give kids opportunities to work in small groups and one on one. Children need hands-on experiences so that they can discover things on their own. "If you push kids too hard, they get frustrated," says Dominic Gullo, a professor of early education at Queens College in New York. "Those are the kids who are likely to act out, and who teachers can perceive as having attention-span or behavior problems."

There are signs that some parents and school boards are looking for a gentler, more kid-friendly way. In Chattanooga, Tenn., more than 100 parents camped out on the sidewalk last spring in hopes of getting their kids into one of the 16 coveted spots at the Chattanooga School for Arts and Sciences (CSAS), a K-12 magnet program that champions a slowed-down approach to education. The school, which admits kids from all socioeconomic backgrounds, offers students plenty of skills and drills but also stresses a "whole-child approach." The emphasis is not on passing tests but on hands-on learning. Two weeks ago newly minted kindergartners were spending the day learning about the color red. They wore red shirts, painted with bright red acrylic paint. During instructional time, they learned to spell RED. Every week each class meets for a seminar that encourages critical thinking. Two weeks ago the first graders had been read a book about a girl who was adopted. Then, the class discussed the pros and cons of adoption. One girl said she thought adoption was bad because "a kid isn't with her real mom and dad." A boy said it was good because the character "has a new mom and dad who love her." The children returned to their desks and drew pictures of different kinds of families. At CSAS, students are rarely held back, and in fourth grade—and in 12th grade—more than 90 percent of students passed the state's proficiency tests in reading last year.

Tiffany Aske says she wishes she could have found a school like CSAS in Oakland. Instead, they're pulling up stakes and moving to a suburban community in Washington where the school system seems more stable and has more outdoor space, and where the kids have more choices during the school day. In some ways, they feel as if they're swimming against the current. Most of their friends are scrambling, paying top dollar for houses in high-performing school districts. The Askes say they're looking for something more important than high test scores. "We want flexibility," says Tiffany. Ashlyn is a bright girl, says her mom, "but she's only a child." And childhood takes time.

With Matthew Philips, Julie Scelfo, Catharine Skipp, Nadine Joseph, Paul Tolme and Hilary Shenfeld.

Taking a Stand: Strategies for Activism

Richard J. Meyer

"I'll close my door and do what I've always done."

Many teachers have said this as a way of dismissing the new curriculum and assessment requirements that conflict with their beliefs as educators. Teachers hope that their classroom doors will insulate them and their students from inappropriate mandates that may limit effective teaching and fail to accurately reflect children's learning. But closing doors does not work.

President Bush, in his inaugural speech, proclaimed the success of the No Child Left Behind Act. Indeed, many families whose children have not met with success in schools view the legislation as hopeful because it appears to finally offer access to education and the American dream. Many educators however, believe that the mandates get in the way of effective teaching and learning. One educator, in fact (Nieto 2004), called the law "mean-spirited," because it ignores the cultural, linguistic, research, and pedagogical realities in an effort to homogenize and simplify what occurs in classrooms.

Many early childhood educators feel they must implement programs that conflict with their understanding of best practice. Some teachers are saddened and some even decide to leave schools in which administrators are not open to dialogue, challenge, and reflection. But there is hope in taking action. This article is about action and activism because it is time for teachers and supporters of public education to respond when imposed curriculum and high-stakes testing (when a test score alone is used to make an important education decision about a child, like being promoted to the next grade) do not reflect what educators know about development, learning, and teaching.

The guiding principle of this Viewpoint is one that could make some early childhood educators uncomfortable because it extends our job descriptions. That principle is this: we may have to act beyond our schools to support authentic learning in our classrooms and to preserve the integrity of our profession.

Ways to Take Action

Action can be simple and private or more bold and public. Some teachers may choose to become more active in an educational organization or association they believe in. Others may become active and vocal in local political issues. A word of caution—if you choose to become involved in a public manner, consider the repercussions of your actions. It is better to act in partnership than alone, unless you are confident that your right to express your views will be respected. My ultimate goals are to support teacher conversations and autonomy, to validate teachers' knowledge, and to advocate for local control so those educational programs can reflect the needs of students.

Talk with Each Other

Teachers may feel isolated or vulnerable when asked to implement curriculum that is based on inappropriate expectations. They can ease these feelings by telling their stories (Ohanian 1999). Teaching colleagues can meet socially to talk about conditions in their school, district, or state. Building a trusting atmosphere might be a gradual process, but once it is built, there will be a safe forum in which the group can begin to understand and plan. One helpful piece of advice is to end a meeting by setting the date for your next meeting.

Knowing that there is a next meeting can serve as a beacon for hope.

We may have to act beyond our schools to support authentic learning in our classrooms and to preserve the integrity of our profession.

Work with Local Advocacy Groups

In some cases, local groups have begun conversations that lead to real action. Ellen Brinkley and her colleagues (1997) describe a group of teachers, other educators, and citizens who formed one such group called Michigan for Public Education (MPE). They advocated for educational equality and excellence and prevented adoption of a curriculum that they thought inappropriate. Their group received support from a number of national organizations. In Florida, groups of individuals talking to each other united to prevent the state from instituting a voucher system (Hallifax 2000). Conversations are forums for thinking and serve to end loneliness and the sense of oppression that some teachers feel, but they can also lead to real change.

Learn Lessons from History

Our advocacy actions become part of the grassroots responses that occur around the country. But we do not necessarily need to invent strategies because many successful approaches already exist. Systematic meetings—open forums in which stories could be told and issues discussed—led to the civil rights movement in the 1960s (Horton, with Kohl & Kohl 1998).

A group of teachers might meet and listen to or read the speeches of Martin Luther King Jr. Many teachers don't know the story of Highlander Center (Horton, with Kohl & Kohl 1998) and would find inspiration in learning how Martin Luther King Jr., Septima Clark, Rosa Parks, and other civil rights workers and union organizers strategized for action under the leadership of Myles Horton.

Studying the past could provide examples for us as we advocate for good teaching practices.

Reading about the women's movement, Mothers Against Drunk Driving (started by Cindy Lightner), Gandhi, and Ralph Nader (consumer advocate) are also ways to learn how others acted to promote social causes. Perhaps we can "recapture some of the experiences of coming together that occurred in the peace movement and the civil rights movement" (Greene 1995, 75). Studying the past could provide examples for us as we advocate for good teaching practices.

Vote

In a metaphorical light, we cast a vote each time we teach. We vote for a book when we engage children with it. We vote for an operational definition of reading when we institutionalize certain practices. We vote for having a voice when we tell our stories to one another in an effort to understand what is happening around us, why it's happening, and consider what we can do about it. We vote for developmentally appropriate teaching strategies when we make pedagogical decisions based upon our students' actions, interests, and performance.

Although the national elections are past, we must ensure that we are informed about local issues and convince pro-education candidates to run for school boards, town councils, and state and national seats that are available every two years. We can encourage teachers and parents who agree with us about appropriate educational practices to vote in elections for candidates that support our work. Activism might involve working with the League of Women Voters (www.lwv.org) to ensure that all eligible people are registered to vote. We can show our presence both by casting a vote and by telling others why we voted as we did.

Partner with Colleagues at Colleges and Universities

Colleges and universities sometimes offer courses that respond in a timely way to the needs of teachers in their surrounding communities. These institutions of higher education may enhance their partnerships *with* teachers and community members to assess curriculum for how well it "accept[s] the children, their culture, their language, and their ways of knowing into the . . . classroom" (Willis & Harris 2000, 81). Early childhood educators might approach faculty at a local university or seek out a distance learning institution to suggest a course or workshop focusing on critical literacy, education and politics, or another area that will address current needs. Perhaps professors would be interested in forming a study group, teaching a course, or engaging in an independent study focusing on local or national issues.

Do Teacher Research

One of the most powerful ways in which teachers can act is to inquire into the effectiveness of our own classroom practices. As teacher researchers, we gather data, systematically analyze it, and present it to audiences of our choosing. Such research helps teachers become more articulate about what happens in the classroom because we are "living the questions" (Hubbard & Power 1999).

NAEYC's online feature Voices of Practitioners (found on the Beyond the Journal page: www.journal.naeyc.org/btj) offers articles and useful resources on teacher research that readers can download to read, share with colleagues and families, and use for staff development and college courses.

Participate in Professional Organizations

Educators can organize and act within professional organizations concerned with issues of teaching, learning, and high-stakes testing. Attending national conventions is always a powerful experience. We might become more active by writing letters to organization officers and joining committees and commissions. Forming a special interest group within an organization is a relatively easy process that typically gives members a meeting time and place—and a public forum—at the national conference. NAEYC, for example, offers members the opportunity to join an existing special interest group or form a new one. Each group has an Online Communities Web page for discussing issues and networking on NAEYC's Web site. (See the members' area at www.naeyc.org for more information.) Write, call, or visit the Web site of educational organizations for information on their groups and activities. Here are a few.

As teacher researchers, we gather data, systematically analyze it, and present it to audiences of our choosing.

The International Reading Association (IRA)—The International Reading Association's lobbyist reports on his activities in Reading Today, one of the IRA's journals. For this and other information on IRA's work, visit www.reading.org.

National Council of Teachers of English (NCTE) and Whole Language Umbrella (WLU)—The NCTE Web site has information about the organization's political actions. NCTE produced a strategy packet for teachers interested in writing to families, various commissions, legislators, editors of newspapers, and more.

In addition, NCTE is affiliated with the Whole Language Umbrella (WLU), which supports professionals interested in developing and implementing whole language approaches in educational institutions. For the past five years, the annual WLU conference (now called the Literacies for All Summer Institute) has offered preconvention workshops on teaching, politics, and activism. WLU invites sessions in which teachers tell stories of their struggles and their actions.

For more information on NCTE and WLU, visit www.ncte.org.

Phi Delta Kappa—This organization has been bold in its use of the Kappan journal as a forum for discussions on controversial issues from many points of view. Phi Delta Kappa has a presence in Washington, D.C., and the News, Notes, and Quotes newsletter that members periodically receive also contains information about what is happening in the legislature and the courts.

Unions—Some teachers feel supported by their unions and others do not. Some unions take stands on curricular, pedagogical, and testing issues. In my opinion, unions should articulate clear agendas that support academic freedom but should not take stands on issues such as teaching materials, methods, and curriculum. Many teachers see unions as negotiating away benefits. Teachers sometimes vote against their union by quitting. If you choose this action, make sure you understand the benefits that you are leaving behind. Some teachers purchase liability insurance from other agencies in order to leave their union.

National Association for the Education of Young Children (NAEYC)—NAEYC has crafted position statements on many important topics in early childhood education. (Educators can view the position statements online at www.naeyc.org/about/positions.asp.) These research-based position statements give guidance to the field and policy makers on critical issues in early childhood education. The Association also engages in public awareness and public policy advocacy to promote a well-financed, high-quality system of early care and education for all children.

Like the organizations mentioned above, NAEYC sponsors national conferences. NAEYC's state and local affiliates offer conferences at a local level. Teachers can attend these conferences as a place to find other colleagues to support them in their activism. Proposing sessions for conferences lets teachers voice what they are experiencing and informs the organization of their interests and needs.

NAEYC offers a number of resources for those who want to advocate for policies that support a system of high-quality early care and education programs.

NAEYC offers a number of resources for those who want to advocate for policies that support a system of high-quality early care and education programs. For links to NAEYC's action center, a toolbox for advocates, and more, visit www.naeyc.org/policy.

Wear a Message

Sometimes we can wear our views and use them to engage in meaningful discussions about educational issues. Harman's (2000) "High Stakes are for Tomatoes"

T-shirts gained much attention at recent national conventions. When I saw her shirts, I had some printed with the words "Raise a child, not a test score" on the front and "High-Stakes Testing" written in a red circle with a line through it on the back. People stopped me in stores to discuss the message and to order a shirt. It's a small action but it felt great to connect with others; the shirt was a magnet for conversations about testing, legislators, and parenting.

I recently learned about a teacher who wore her "Raise a child. . ." shirt to work and was told by her principal not to wear it again in school. The teacher contacted her union and the union lawyer reminded the principal of the teacher's first amendment right to free speech. She wears it every Friday.

Advocate in the Community

I am consistently amazed at the long list of organizations and companies that know little about teaching, learning, and schools, yet tell educators what's wrong with schools and how to fix them (Spring 1997). Teachers, teacher researchers, and college and university faculty could respond to these groups by providing information and making concrete suggestions about ways they could provide help.

In the community where I teach and do research, I attended a meeting of a business group that has been quite vocal about problems with education. The members are convinced that if our city's students achieve high test scores, the economy will improve and more new businesses will want to locate here. They also suggest that higher test scores will result in reductions in poverty. Street (1995) has refuted this idea, noting that just the opposite is more accurate: if there were less poverty, children would perform better in schools.

At a recent meeting of this group, I reported on Street's ideas and suggested what local businesses might do to support literacy efforts in our city. Local businesses could actively work to raise employee incomes in the poorer neighborhoods of the city. These businesses could hire more individuals as full-time employees who receive health and dental benefits. They could also provide quality child care for employees' children. I also told them that the principles of industry should not be applied to schools because children are not products. Of course, the group did not like my suggestions and I'm not invited to these meetings anymore, but the ideas have been aired.

If you choose to confront such a group, there are some guidelines to consider: (1) attend with a colleague; (2) make sure you understand the group's agenda for education; (3) prepare a written statement from which to read; (4) limit your statement to two or three points of action that the group can take to truly be helpful (don't shred their ideas, offer useful ones); (5) distribute copies of your statement to the group and to the press, if the press is present; and (6) prepare a one-sentence response to those who disagree with your statements.

The hope and the challenge

Hope is apparent all over the country as resistance increases to using standardized test scores alone to make critical educational decisions about a child; slowly and cautiously we are finding support. Organizations like the Whole Schooling Consortium, FairTest, and The Rouge Forum are emerging with broad agendas that work to include other organizations. There are always risks when we take any action. There are also risks to inaction, and we may believe that those are not as severe. We won't be fired for *not* speaking out.

Early childhood educators who speak out do risk being reprimanded, suspended, perhaps even fired, depending on the conditions of their employment. The problem is that sometimes inaction means using curriculum and tests that are not good for our students. We need not act radically and risk our jobs; some of the ideas above (talking, doing teacher research) are powerful but low risk. Our goal needs to be to continue our work with children in a way that respects our knowledge base.

There are always risks when we take any action. There are also risks to inaction.

Teaching has changed. Some mandates force us to teach in ways that conflict with our beliefs as educators. Our ability to teach in ways that call upon our expertise as educators is in jeopardy if we remain silent and retreat to our classrooms.

Teaching prescribed programs that seek to raise test scores, complying with narrowly defined standards, using programs that profit others financially or politically, and being forced to apply inaccurate interpretations of research—these chip away at authentic and relevant teaching and learning. Using "one-shot" tests that provide limited and inaccurate snapshots of our students in place of the assessment data from multiple sources that teachers have collected over an entire year diminishes students'

accomplishments. Closing our doors leaves us isolated, lonely, and living with a false sense of safety while our teaching and children's learning are at risk.

It is time to open the doors.

References

Brinkley, E., C. Weaver, P. Campbell, M. Houston, J. Williams, V. Little, M. Freedman Mohaghan, J.B. Bird, & J. Bird. 1997. Believing in what's possible, taking action to make a difference. *Language Arts* 74 (7): 537–44.

Greene, M. 1995. *Releasing the imagination: Essays on education, the arts, and social change.* San Francisco: Jossey-Bass.

Hallifax, J. 2000. Florida judge tosses school voucher law. *Albuquerque Journal,* March 15, p. A9.

Harman, S. 2000. Resist high-stakes testing: High stakes are for tomatoes. *Language Arts* 77 (4): 332.

Horton, M., with J. Kohl & H. Kohl. 1998. *The long haul: An autobiography.* New York: Teachers College Press.

Hubbard, R., & B. Power. 1999. *Living the questions: A guide for teacher-researchers.* York, ME: Stenhouse.

Nieto, S. 2004. "No Child Left Behind and the Community." Panel discussion, Authentic Educational Reform: Teachers and Parents Speak Out! Conference, Queens College, City University of New York, Flushing, New York.

Ohanian, S. 1999. *One size fits few: The folly of educational standards.* Portsmouth: Heinemann.

Spring, J. 1997. *Political agendas for education: From the Christian Coalition to the Green Party.* Mahwah, NJ: Erlbaum.

Street, B. 1995. *Social literacies: Critical approaches to literacy in development, ethnography, and education.* New York: Longman.

Willis, A., & V. Harris. 2000. Political acts: Literacy learning and teaching. *Reading Research Quarterly* 35 (1): 72–88.

RICHARD J. MEYER, PhD, is an associate professor in the Department of Language, Literacy, and Sociocultural Studies at the University of New Mexico, Albuquerque. His areas of research include young children's literacy, the politics of literacy, and beginning teachers' understanding of the reading process and instruction. He taught young children for almost 20 years and continues to do research in classrooms with teachers and children.

UNIT 2

Young Children and Their Families

Unit Selections

Key Points to Consider

- What are some strategies teachers can use to assist English language learners and their families?

- Are teenage parents able to effectively care for their children with support from educators?

- What do grandparents raising grandchildren need to be effective parents for the second time?

- What strategies are the most successful for helping homeless children to be successful in school?

Student Web Site

www.mhcls.com/online

Internet References

Further information regarding these websites may be found in this book's preface or online.

Administration for Children and Families
http://www.dhhs.gov

The AARP Grandparent Information Center
http://www.aarp.org/grandparents

All About Asthma
http://pbskids.org/arthur/grownups/teacherguides/health/asthma_tips.html

Changing the Scene on Nutrition
http://www.fns.usda.gov/tn/Healthy/changing.html

Children, Youth and Families Education and Research Network
www.cyfernet.org

IAm Your Child
http://www.iamyourchild.org

Internet Resources for Education
http://web.hamline.edu/personal/kfmeyer/cla_education.html#hamline

The National Academy for Child Development
http://www.nacd.org

National Network for Child Care
www.nncc.org

National Safe Kids Campaign
http://www.babycenter.com

Zero to Three
http://www.zerotothree.org

I was very fortunate to be included in a group of seventeen educators from southeast Michigan who traveled to China in October, 2006. The purpose of our trip was to begin exploring ways to bring teachers from China to Michigan to teach Chinese and to learn more about the educational system and culture of China. What we learned was China is massive in size, population, and growth, and is making great strides as it moves forward with its lengthy agenda. I especially enjoyed watching young children interact with their parents and grandparents. In much of China the one child only policy is still in effect, reflecting attempts by the government to curb the rapid population growth. Young children in China grow up in a family structure quite different from that which is typical to young children in the United States. They have no siblings; few if any cousins; and usually all four grandparents live nearby. Children in the United States often have siblings however, grandparents and cousins may live another state.

One benefit of working with young children is having the opportunity to interact with family members and get to know what family life is like for the children in our classes. The chance to interact with family diminishes as the student gets older. It is almost nonexistent at the secondary level. In "Creative Play: Building Connections With Children Who Are Learning English," Sara J. Burton and Linda Carol Edwards present ways teachers can help families and children as they work towards learning the English language. In China, every child begins to learn a second language in first grade. English was studied in every school I visited, and children at all levels were eager to practice English with their American visitors. In the United States it is not uncommon to begin to learn world languages in high school; if world languages are taught in the elementary schools, it is often in exploratory courses only. The courses are not of sufficient duration or content to fully learn the language.

The next two articles examine the heads of families at two very different ends of the spectrum. "Children of Teen Parents: Challenges and Hope" and "Supporting Grandparents Who Raise Grandchildren" both present similar advice. In each article the authors stress the importance of individual support and integrated services that meet the needs of that particular family. Younger parents, as well as second-time-around parents, all need support, and they typically welcome the opportunity to have a teacher for their child or grandchild who is understanding of their particular situation.

Almost 20 years after the passage of the Education of Homeless Children and Youth Program of the 1987 Stewart B. McKinney Homeless Assistance Act, that issue remains at the top of the crisis list for educators in predominately low-income districts. Kevin Swick provides strategies for helping homeless children achieve success in school in "The Dynamics of Families Who Are Homeless: Implications for Early Childhood Educators." All families can benefit from parent education, in particular low-income parents who have limited support.

There are more and more examples of teachers adjusting their image of family that go way beyond the traditional "Dad goes off to work and mom stays at home" idea. Only when all educators are accepting of the diversity that exists in family structures will children feel welcomed and comfortable to learn at school. The collaboration of families, the community, and school personnel will enable children to benefit from the partnership these three groups bring to the educational setting. Our hope is that every child will have a strong network of support in their home, community, and school which will enable them to be successful lifelong learners and contributors to society.

Creative Play: Building Connections With Children Who Are Learning English

How can teachers support young children, all of whom are English language learners? Play is a wonderful way to help ALL children gain the confidence and skills they need to succeed in school and life!

Sara J. Burton and Linda Carol Edwards

Six-year-old Ana Belen speaks Spanish. She is in the block center with an English-speaking friend named Malik. Ana Belen tries to get Malik's attention because she needs more blocks to complete her building. She calls out to Malik in Spanish, gesturing with her hands and asking for the block she needs. She looks at him with a confused look when he does not respond to her request. Ana Belen then walks around the block center and points toward the blocks for which she was asking. She then says, to Malik, "Tarugo" (block).

Malik complains to their teacher that he cannot understand Ana Belen and cannot play with her. When the teacher approaches, she explains to Malik, "Ana Belen is asking you to get her the square block—tarugo. Look, she is making a block shape with her hands, too!"

Immediately Malik understands how Ana Belen is communicating. His confused expression changes to a smile. Ana Belen smiles too, as Malik hands her a block. Both children understand that they can communicate, verbally and nonverbally. The teacher observes as the two children continue to play together.

Learning English: Opportunities for Everyone

English language learners (ELL) are learning to listen, speak, read, and write (Silvaggio, 2005). When speakers of other languages begin to acquire English, like all children, they develop at different rates. Teachers may encounter situations such as these with English language learners who already speak Spanish:

- Some children experience a silent period of 6 or more months.

- Other children practice learning by mixing or combining the two languages or use a form of "Spanglish."
- Some children may have the skills (appropriate accent, vocabulary, and vernacular) but they are not truly proficient.
- Other children quickly acquire English-language proficiency (National Association for the Education of Young Children, 1995).

Language acquisition is a very complex developmental process and it may take some students "a minimum of 12 years" to master a new language (Collier, 1989). Even when children seem to express themselves correctly, they may not have mastered the true complexity of the language.

Educators realize that children who are English language learners come to early childhood programs and schools with their own knowledge of the language used in their homes (NAEYC, 1995). Teachers of young children are encouraged to view the inclusion of children who are learning English as an enrichment opportunity for everyone: children who are learning English as a second language, the English-speaking students, and even themselves. Wise teachers embrace classroom diversity and create an atmosphere where all children can thrive and progress.

This article primarily considers children who come from homes where Spanish is spoken, but the premises and suggestions hold true for any of the "nearly 3 million ESL students" in the nation's schools (Shore, 2001). What better way to involve and encourage all children to learn than through play?

What Are the Benefits of Play for English Language Learners?

Play is the primary vehicle through which children learn about themselves and others and about the world in which they live and interact. Through play, children actively explore their world, build new skills, and use their imaginations. Best of all they do it for the simple *joy* of doing it.

Educators are well aware of the lasting benefits of play, but the idea of "playing with language, oral and especially written language, during dramatic play is not nearly as common as it ideally should be" (Korat, Bahar, & Snapir, 2002, p. 393).

Play is extremely beneficial in overcoming communication challenges between English speakers and speakers of other languages (Little, 2004–2005; Reeves, 2004–2005; Oliver & Klugman, 2002). For children who are learning English, self-directed play establishes an informal, non-threatening atmosphere that is one of the most valuable ways of learning.

When children are engaged in the process of play, they usually care very little about an end product. They are free to figure out what they want to do and when they want to do it. They engage in spontaneous activity. In other words, children are in control. Play is a hands-on activity in which children choose their own learning adventures. They learn while doing something they have decided to do. What are children learning through play?

- Children increase the size of their vocabularies and their ability to comprehend language.
- They develop skills in cooperation by sharing and taking turns.
- Play helps children to develop empathy and strengthens their ability to express emotions (Oliver & Klugman, 2002).
- Play enables children to develop patience and tolerance (Dorrell, 2000).
- During play, children feel comfortable enough to take risks. As they gain self-reliance and feel successful (Edwards, 2002) they begin to function more independently and eventually take more risks outside of the play environment.

Play is essential for the sound development of all children, but it is especially important in the growth and development of children who speak English as a second language. How did Ana Belen and Malik benefit from playing? They interacted in the block section, primarily with nonverbal communication, and both learned a new vocabulary word. After resolving their initial lack of knowledge about the Spanish and English words for *block*, they played together in such a way that both students felt comfortable.

Children who are learning a language benefit from play in several ways (Silver, 1999). Play helps establish bonds of friendship among children who do not communicate well in English (p. 67). During play, children who are learning English may exhibit independence and self-assurance that is not otherwise evident.

For example, Silver noted that children who were learning English tended to engage in solitary play when painting or doing cut-and-paste activities. As they got used to the routine, they became involved in play with rules and games. One child was very shy and used mostly telegraphic speech (see sidebar). After engaging in play, he gradually built up his confidence to volunteer to go first when playing a game. Silver concluded that only during periods of play was this child on "equal footing with the others in the class" (1999, p. 67).

Telegraphic speech: Use of only the words necessary to communicate. For example, "I want to be picked up," might be verbalized as "pick up."

How Can Teachers Support English Language Learners?

Teachers have a critical role in organizing their classrooms, structuring activities, and planning the use of materials in order to maximize all children's participation in play. Early childhood educators can celebrate children's strengths and allow them many ways to express their own interests and talents.

Many children born in the United States speak English at school, but speak their native language elsewhere. Speaking Spanish at home and among friends is one way that families cherish their ties to their home country. Silvaggio (2005) notes that children need adult help to negotiate this new world. It is not an easy task for teachers, who often lack resources to work with English language learners. As Shore (2001) explains, there are simple and practical ways that educators can help ESL children succeed. These are a few possibilities.

Assess needs. Find out where students' skill levels are, not only in English but in other areas of development as well. Families' perspectives, previous child care providers' insights, and regular observations are essential resources for understanding children.

Empathize. Imagine how overwhelming it is to walk into a classroom where you only understand part of what you hear. The first author of this article remembers studying in Spain during her college years and being truly scared during the first few months there. Even though she had studied the language for a number of years, she felt helpless, insecure, and disconnected. How much more difficult it must be for a young child!

Foster a sense of belonging. Make sure all children feel welcomed by being patient. Use body language and pictures to communicate while learning welcoming words in their languages. Take care to pronounce children's names correctly. Be aware of children's needs for personal space and privacy, too.

Assign buddies. All children yearn to feel important and included. English-speaking children can be terrific resources to those who speak other language by making sure they can find the way around school, count money at lunchtime, understand directions, and more.

Keep track of language progress. Maintain a portfolio of each child. Save photographs, recordings, artwork, and writing samples. Review records with the child (and family) to see progress over time. This is an important way to acknowledge children's strengths and accomplishments.

Encourage family involvement. Encourage parents of children who are learning English to feel like they are a part of the community and classroom. If needed, arrange for an interpreter at meetings and conferences. Learn more about each family's culture so that interactions with each other are always respectful. Study the language and learn important words and phrases.

Learn key words. Make sure all staff and children quickly learn basic vocabulary words in both languages, such as restroom, clock, teacher, and bus. Picture cards and labels with words are an excellent tool to use with children who are beginning to learn about written language.

Foster an appreciation of cultural diversity. Diverse cultures are an asset for any classroom. Respect each culture's customs, make and taste a variety of foods, learn vocabulary words, create maps, talk with family members, and encourage all children to share their traditions.

Ask and observe to find out how children prefer to be encouraged and supported to succeed—these strategies vary by culture and custom. "Children with high motivation, self-confidence, and low levels of anxiety are more successful second language learners" (Szecsi & Giambo (2004/2005, p. 104)).

Find out how children prefer to be encouraged.

In an ideal environment, children play independently, at their own pace, in their own unique way, and have the necessary materials to facilitate their play. "We need to play in English, not just speak English at school," said one student (Reeves, 2004/2005). Learning centers provide unique opportunities for all children to participate in free play, and this puts children who are learning English on "a level playing field" with their peers (Silver, 1999).

Dramatic Play Enhances Language Development

A dramatic play center is especially useful for children who are English language learners. Pretend play enables them to communicate in an informal setting and gather information that will be helpful to them, even beyond the classroom.

For example, during pretend play, children explore activities and relationships important to them in the real world. They typically investigate the role of family members, community helpers, and health care professionals (Texas Workforce Commission, 2002). Children bring their own knowledge into their play as they cooperate with one another.

In the dramatic play center, children build language and literacy skills. English language learners soon begin to communicate in effective and appropriate ways with both children and adults. They have many opportunities to "practice their language skills with peers" (deAtiles & Allexsaht-Snider, 2002) in a "language-rich environment" (Szecsi & Giambo, 2004/2005).

A language-rich environment is essential in any early childhood classroom. Include props such as telephone books, magazines, and restaurant menus for dramatic play. By labeling items, teachers expose all children to print in both languages. This enables children who are learning English to encounter reading and speaking while they play and gives them a "multisensory approach" (Gasparro & Falletta, 1994) to language acquisition.

For example, Luis Jose and Sophie are pretending to go to the subway station. The props are labeled with text and pictures of a train, ticket, money, a caution sign in both languages, so each child knows each object in his or her language. Even though they speak different languages, they are able to recreate what happens at the subway station.

Unscripted role play is a valuable way for children to interact informally and gain the confidence they need to speak aloud. Similarly, playing restaurant is efficient and helpful for children as they read menus, practice ordering, interact with a waiter, and use table manners. For children, it seems less important that they can engage in English or Spanish conversations. What does appear to matter to them is that they can interact and understand each other.

Teachers can choose relevant, diverse themes for dramatic play and provide props for each theme. Stock the area with tickets, pretend money, many types of groceries, tools, and toy animals. By using mostly familiar items, children find creative ways to play. Playing with real-life materials helps children feel more comfortable.

Teachers can also create a Reader's Theater. Children perform dramatic representations of a story read to them in class or by a friend (Szecsi & Giambo, 2004/2005). The list in the box contains a sample of books that may be helpful in working with Spanish speakers. These books can be integrated into many themes. Some books are also available in English so that children can "read" together.

Teachers who want children to feel at ease in the classroom must "reach past psychological and cultural barriers that lead students to prefer the safety of silence to the danger of speaking" (Reeves, 2004/2005). When children feel comfortable and relaxed, they will speak up and show what they have learned. "Drama places learners in situations that seem real," (Gasparro & Falletta, 1994) so when students use the goal language (English) for a specific purpose, the language is more easily internalized and remembered.

Through a variety of play experiences, children who are learning English become more prepared to engage in everyday interactions with English speakers. They eventually gain the confidence to participate in the community.

What Role Do Families Play?

Parents and extended family members play a large role in helping children learn a new language and successfully adapt to the culture in which they live. Many families who speak another language and value their own culture face a difficult challenge when it comes to maintaining that culture and wanting their children to learn English as quickly as possible (Giambo & Szecsi, 2005).

Celebrate children's strengths.

Keeping children's fluency and literacy (if already acquired) in the native language while developing new language skills is a tremendous benefit because people "who are bilingual have an advantage in our increasingly global economy" (Giambo & Szecsi, 2005). Share these suggestions with families, who can help their children thrive in two cultures and languages.

Many school-related skills that parents teach their children in their native language transfer to their new language and classroom. Translators and resources in other languages are increasingly available in many communities. Families and teachers are urged to work together to facilitate each child's growth in language and in life.

Outlook for the Future

"Young children are just beginning to learn about the world, and because they are still amateurs, they make mistakes, they get confused, and they do not always get things just right. They need a positive reaction from the adults around them, and they need to be recognized for their own individual value" (Edwards, 2005, p. 2).

This challenge is true for teachers and their interactions with all children, including those who are learning another language. Young children construct knowledge by building on familiar experiences. Educators provide young children with an extensive array of meaningful experiences.

When children learn new vocabulary words and practice pronunciation and language conventions, they are gaining skills for life. Taking the time to help children learn English as well as key words in other languages enables them to succeed in their learning environment. They will gain the confidence and abilities to succeed in the diverse culture in which they live.

Hispanics are the largest minority population in the United States, with 39.9 million people as of July 2003 (U.S. Census Bureau, 2005). Hispanic youth also have a high dropout rate: "Nearly one in three students fails to graduate from high school" (Clearinghouse on Urban Education, 2000). Solutions are urgently needed to help children who speak Spanish become fluent in the language and gain skills they need to become productive, healthy adults.

Young children construct knowledge by building on familiar experiences.

Almost every teacher works with one or more English language learners every year. The education challenge is to make every situation a truly beneficial "teachable moment." Partnerships with children (and their families) will benefit children's language and literacy skills and build the confidence they need to succeed. After all, "People who can communicate in at least two languages are a great asset to the communities in which they live and work" (Cutshall, 2004/2005, p. 23).

Summary

As leaders and mentors, teachers can best help culturally and linguistically diverse children and families by respecting the importance of each child's home language and culture. Educators who embrace, respect, and preserve the many ethnic and linguistic backgrounds of students will enable them to increasingly contribute to this diverse culture.

References

Clearinghouse on Urban Education. (2000). *School practices to promote the achievement of Hispanic students.* ERIC Digest Number 153.

Collier, V.P. (1989). How long? A synthesis of research on academic achievement in a second language. *TESOL Quarterly, 23*(3), 509–531.

Cutshall, S. (2004/2005). Why we need "The Year of Languages." *Educational Leadership, 62*(4), 20–23.

deAtiles, J.R., & Allexsaht-Snider, M. (2002). *Effective approaches to teaching young Mexican immigrant children.* ERIC Digest Number 20021201.

How Families Help Children Adjust to a New Language and Culture

- Read aloud in both languages to your children. Many reading skills transfer between languages.
- Get involved in community activities with your children. Go on local history tours, visit nature centers, and attend library story times. Link up with groups with similar interests, such as recreation departments, faith communities, and heritage festivals.
- Play board games. This will enrich skills such as counting, using money, and learning new words.
- Watch a few English-language children's educational television programs together such as *Reading Rainbow* or *Zoom!* The language is easy to understand and the characters are real. Talk about children's ideas afterwards, too.
- Become active in sports. Choose sports suitable for children's ages. These welcoming social interactions enable children to learn new expressions and casual rules of the language. Families are likely to gain new friendships. (adapted from Giambo & Szecsi, 2005)

Put These Ideas Into Practice!

Creative Play: Building Connections With Children Who Are Learning English

by Sara J. Burton and Linda Carol Edwards

What Children Learn Through Play

- Children's vocabularies increase.
- Sharing and taking turns improves cooperation.
- Children develop empathy and express emotions.
- They develop patience and tolerance.
- Children gain self-reliance and feel successful.
- They become more independent.

Ways Teachers Support English Language Learners

- Find out their skill levels in all areas. Ask parents and previous child care providers to share their insights.
- Imagine what it is like to be in a group where you only understand part of what you hear.
- Be patient.
- Make sure children and families feel welcome. Learn a few words of their languages.
- Ask classmates to help each other during classroom routines.
- Regularly observe children and record progress. Keep a portfolio of photos, recordings, art, and (for older children) writing samples.
- Help families feel part of the community and classroom.
- Appreciate diversity.

Enrichment Experiences for Young Children

Focus on the dramatic play area. Add familiar props such as clothing, flowers, restaurant menus, pretend money, foods and tools, toy animals, magazines, and real-life materials. Label items in both languages for older preschoolers and primary children. Encourage informal, language-rich play.

Create a Reader's Theater. Offer age-appropriate and culturally relevant books, puppets, and dress-up clothing. Encourage role play of the stories in both English and children's own languages.

Offer everyday opportunities to use English. Pair an English language learner with an English-speaking student. Ask older English-speakers to read to younger ELL students. Encourage ELL students to read to younger peers.

Enrich learning opportunities. Ask older ELL students to interview a teacher, another student, or a member of the community. Students create their own interview questions, take photos, record the answers, and share the experience with classmates.

Suggestions to Share with Children's Families

- Read aloud in both languages to your children.
- Get involved in community activities with your children. Go on local history tours, visit nature centers, and attend library story times.
- Play board games. This will enrich skills such as counting, using money, and learning new words.
- Watch a few English-language children's educational television programs together. Talk about children's ideas afterwards.
- Become active in sports. Choose sports suitable for children's ages.

Adult Learning Experiences that Build on These Ideas

- Start learning children's languages. Perhaps a child's family member would like to tutor YOU.
- Get to know children's cultures. Shop in ethnic stores their families frequent. Attend community events. Read about diverse families to gain a better understanding of their strengths and challenges.
- Engage staff in a cultural immersion experience. Find a meeting moderator who speaks the chosen language, such as Spanish. Show a clip from a Spanish-language film. Each teacher receives a handout, in Spanish, about the film. After viewing the film, small groups discuss feelings, thoughts, reactions, and realizations as a result of this cultural experience.
- Ask an ELL parent to attend a staff meeting, with a translator, to talk about issues within the school and broader community.
- Identify translators who can attend parent meetings, translate written materials, and otherwise facilitate communication with families.

Note: *Dimensions of Early Childhood* readers are encouraged to copy this material for early childhood students as well as teachers of young children as a professional development tool.

Dorrell, A. (2000, March/April). All they do is play? Play in preschool. Early *Childhood News,* pp. 18–22.

Edwards, L.C. (2002). *The creative arts: A process approach for children and teachers* (3rd Ed.). Columbus, OH: Merrill/ Prentice-Hall.

Gasparro, M., & Falletta, B. (1994). *Creating drama with poetry: Teaching English as a second language through dramatization and improvisation.* ERIC Digest Number 19940401.

Giambo, D., & Szecsi, T. (2005, Spring). Parents can guide children through the world of two languages. *Childhood Education, 81*(3), 164–165.

Korat, O., Bahar, E., & Snapir, M. (2002). Sociodramatic play as an opportunity for literacy development: The teacher's role. *Reading Teacher, 56*(4), 386–394.

Little, C. (2004/2005). A journey toward belonging. *Educational Leadership, 62*(4), 82–83.

Oliver, S.J., & Klugman, E. (2002). Playing the day away. *Child Care Information Exchange,* 66–70.

National Association for the Education of Young Children. (1995). Position Statement. *Responding to linguistic and cultural diversity: Recommendations for effective early childhood education.* Retrieved February 22, 2005, from www.naeyc.org/about/positions/PSDIV98.asp.

Reeves, D.B. (2004/2005). "If I said something wrong, I was afraid." *Educational Leadership, 62*(4), 72–74.

Shore, K. (2001). Success for ESL students. *Instructor, 110*(6), 30–33.

Silvaggio, A.M. ESL demand challenge schools. Retrieved January 11, 2005, from greenvilleonline.com/news/2005/01/11/20050 11156589.htm

Silver, A. (1999). Play: A fundamental equalizer for ESL children. *TESL Canada Journal, 16*(2), 62–69.

Szecsi, T., & Giambo, D. (2004/2005, Winter). ESOL in every minute of the school day. *Childhood Education, 81*(2), 104–106.

Texas Workforce Commission. (2002, Spring). Learning centers: Why and how. *Texas Childcare,* 30–42.

U.S. Census Bureau. *Hispanic Heritage Month 2004.* Retrieved January 24, 2005, from census.gov/Press-Release/www/releases/archives/facts_for_features_special_edition.

SARA J. BURTON, B.A., M.A.T., is a third grade teacher at Goodwin Elementary School in North Charleston, South Carolina. She holds a B.A. degree in Spanish from Wofford College and has traveled extensively to Spanish-speaking countries around the world. She earned her M.A.T. degree from the College of Charleston in Charleston, South Carolina.

LINDA CAROL EDWARDS, ED.D., is Professor, Department of Elementary and Early Childhood Education, College of Charleston, Charleston, South Carolina. Before she began teaching at the college level, she taught kindergarten in the North Carolina public schools. Edwards is the author of two books on early childhood education.

Children of Teen Parents: Challenges and Hope

BARBARA A. WHITE, MIMI GRAHAM, AND SEATON K. BRADFORD
Florida State University Center for Prevention and Early Intervention Policy, Tallahassee

Virtually every publicly funded early childhood program serves teen parents and their children. Some programs serve pregnant and parenting teens, and their infants and toddlers, exclusively. Yet all too often, health services, school-based programs, and home visiting initiatives focus primarily on outcomes for the teen mother (for example, repeat pregnancies) and place very little emphasis on outcomes for the child.

In this issue of *Zero to Three*, we hope to explore as thoroughly as possible the experience of infants and toddlers who have adolescent parents. What is it like, for example, for a baby and her mother to be in foster care together? To have the same pediatrician? How does a toddler feel when he spends the day in a child care classroom in his parent's high school? What happens when a toddler and his parent compete for a home visitor's attention?

The contributors to this issue report from the perspective of the child, but their larger goal is to describe the development of the dyad—the adolescent parent and the child. Taken together, the articles in this issue suggest that in health care settings, center-based services, and home-based programs, practitioners who effectively support the dual development of teen parents and their young children have a number of characteristics in common. They:

- understand the role of multiple risk factors in the lives of the children of teen parents;
- are comprehensive in approach, integrating services from a variety of community partners;
- appreciate the specialized knowledge and skills required to work effectively with teen parents and their children; and
- are committed to providing strength-based, relationship focused services to promote positive outcomes.

Risks Associated with Adolescent Parenthood

Any discussion of young families includes a discussion of risk factors. Teenagers who have had academic difficulty and mental health problems are more likely than their peers to give birth before graduating from high school. These young parents often bring to parenthood a history of poverty, abuse, violence, and unresolved grief and loss. Poverty is a risk factor for adolescent childbearing, which in turn compounds and perpetuates poverty. Children who are born to teen mothers are 8 times as likely to grow up in poverty as are children of older mothers. Babies of teens are less likely than children of older parents to live with both a mother and father. The resulting inadequate financial support translates into poor housing, inferior child care, and limited health care options.

Teens who have been raised in poverty often feel that they have never "had enough." When they become parents, they have difficulty sharing limited resources with a child. Thus programs that serve the children of teen parents should be prepared to provide for babies' needs at two levels. Formula, diapers, and baby clothes ensure basic survival. At a second level, programs must compensate for the "poverty of experience" that is common to young families by offering front-pack carriers, board books, play materials, and, perhaps most important, learning opportunities and life experiences in the community that link to school readiness for the child.

Community-based Strategies to Support Young Families

High-quality services for teen parents and their children are integrated services. Effective program planners identify points of

---

At a Glance

Programs for teen parents and their children promote dual development by:

- Acknowledging the role of multiple risk factors in the lives of the children of teen parents;
- Integrating services from a variety of community partners;
- Employing specialized strategies and specially trained staff; and
- Providing strength-based, relationship-focused, high quality services.

entry, unique to each community, where teen parents are most likely to seek help for themselves and their children. No single service program is likely to be able to address the multiple needs of young families; partnerships among programs and agencies are essential. Community providers also have a responsibility to explore research evidence, recommended practices, and professional development resources that are likely to contribute to positive outcomes for teen parents and their young children.

In the context of well-designed programs for young families, competent practitioners individualize intervention strategies. Drawing on their understanding of adolescent development and early childhood, they find ways to give hope to teen parents and their children. Those professionals who are most successful in their work with young families constantly look for ways to capitalize on the motivation, resilience, and responsiveness of young parents. If skilled support is available, the rapid pace of development in the early years and the baby's powerful drive toward attachment can bring out the best in teen mothers and fathers.

In 2004, the Task Force on Teen Parents and Their Children, convened by the Miami-Dade School Readiness Coalition and the Florida State University's Center for Prevention and Early Intervention Policy, identified 14 components of a comprehensive service system for teen parents and their children. The Task Force recommended that service providers address these components when developing new programs or improving upon existing services for young families (White, Larsen, & Schilling, 2004). These components include:

1. A "medical home" (stable source of health care) for parent and child
2. Good-quality early care and education (child care)
3. Social work services
4. Prenatal and parenting education
5. Family planning counseling and services
6. Comprehensive educational programs/work force development
7. Family violence intervention/protection
8. Mental health/infant mental health services
9. Housing/shelter referrals
10. Legal services
11. Family literacy activities
12. Sexual abuse treatment
13. Substance abuse education and treatment
14. Early intervention

The Task Force further recommended that communities:

- Use co-located programs or carefully crafted interagency agreements to establish a network of service providers;
- Inform teen parents of service options;
- Assure developmental screening for each teen parent and child;
- Educate practitioners, community policy makers, and the general public about the developmental needs of teen parents and their children;

- Provide for the basic needs of young families;
- Identify risk factors for healthy development of young families and build protective factors into community institutions such as schools, the health care system, libraries, recreational programs, and the arts;
- Promote a relationship-based approach in all interventions;
- Use an infant mental health framework to understand the behavior of teen parents and their children;
- Establish multidisciplinary teams to assess the functioning of teen parents and their children, develop intervention plans with parents, and offer comprehensive services;
- Use a continuous improvement model to raise the quality of community services; and
- Integrate reflective practice into all levels of service for young families.

Changing Lives

Although they usually lack the skills, experience, and means to make it happen, most adolescent mothers are determined to make the lives of their children better than their own. Unlike many adult women who seem defeated by years of living in poverty, even the most challenged adolescent mothers have a reservoir of resilience and hope that their new baby will experience success and happiness.

Practitioners who work with young families will attest that most adolescent parents respond positively to caring adults who have an interest in their well-being and that of their baby. Even young parents who have lacked consistent relationships with loving, attentive, responsible, and trustworthy adults during much of their childhood will—eventually—respond to and deeply appreciate kindness that is offered to them.

Well-designed programs with skilled staff work to reduce risk factors and build protective factors—both internal and external—into the lives of teen parents and their children. Committed practitioners know that the children of teens are resilient and that most teen parents want a good life for their child. In the hopeful words of one young mother, "My main dream is to give my baby the life I didn't have . . . a home, a family that I didn't have when I was growing up." Using proven and promising practices, practitioners, programs, and communities can do far more than simply help the children of teen parents survive. As the contributors to this issue of *Zero to Three* demonstrate, systematic efforts to understand young families and thoughtfully designed, skillfully implemented interventions can overcome challenge and justify hope.

References

White, B. Larsen, R, & Schilling, M. (2004). *Interim report of the Task Force on Teen Parents and Their Children.* Tallahassee: Florida State University, Center for Prevention and Early Intervention Policy.

Supporting Grandparents Who Raise Grandchildren

Jennifer Birckmayer, Jan Cohen, Isabelle Doran Jensen, and Denyse Altman Variano

Four-year-old Kyle enters the classroom slowly, clinging to the hand of his grandmother. His friend George runs toward him, shouting "Hey Kyle–wanna play?" Suddenly George stops short and stares. "Who's that?" he asks.

When Kyle's eyes begin to fill with tears, his teacher intervenes. "Hello," she says warmly. "Our director told me Kyle's grandma would be visiting today. George, maybe you and Kyle would like to show his grandma the seeds we are growing on the windowsill."

"OK," George says doubtfully, "but where's your mommy, Kyle?"

In the past 10 years the United States has seen a dramatic increase in the number of children who live without their parents in a household headed by a relative. More than 2.5 million grandparents now raise grandchildren without a biological parent present in the home (Simmons & Dye 2003).

Many other grandparents provide full- or part-time child care for working parents, often as a supplement to early childhood education programs such as Head Start or family child care. Because grandparents are often the ones who see teachers or caregivers at drop-off or pickup times or may be the only adults available, many become the logical family contact for a program.

Grandparents who assume responsibility for their grandchildren are unsung heroes and heroines of the twenty-first century. Without them, many children whose parents are unwilling or unable to care for them would be in the foster care system.

Circumstances and Challenges Differ

A popular image of grandparents portrays them as individuals who provide loving relationships and enriching experiences for grandchildren or give practical help with child care for working parents. But the circumstances under which many grandparents become the *primary* adults in the lives of grandchildren are often unfortunate, even tragic. The reasons include parental drug and/or alcohol use, divorce, mental and physical illness (including AIDS), child abuse and neglect, incarceration, even death. Some skipped-generation families (grandparents raising grandchildren) are temporary arrangements while parents are completing their education, on military or business assignment, recovering from illness, or serving a short jail term. Whether brief or permanent, almost all skipped-generation families begin with trauma for children, parents, and grandparents.

A common refrain among grandparents who are parenting again is "I just feel so tired all the time. It keeps me from being the kind of grandparent I would like to be."

The challenges for these caregivers are unique and sometimes overwhelming. Few adults in their later years plan to be caring for children—especially children who may be traumatized, deeply unhappy, or suffering from chronic health conditions—while they themselves are experiencing some of the more difficult aspects of growing older. For grandparents, shortages of time and money, declining health, unfamiliarity with existing community resources (especially in the fields of medical care and education), and confusing legal problems often combine with grief and guilt about their child's inability to parent.

Contrary to popular belief, not all of these grandparents are elderly. Some are in their thirties, with children still at home; some are of the so-called sandwich generation, caring for children and grandchildren in addition to aging parents. Many must continue to hold jobs to provide adequately for grandchildren. A common refrain among grandparents who are parenting again is "I just feel so tired all the time. It keeps me from being the kind of grandparent I would like to be."

Older grandparents fear that they will become ill, disabled, or die and no one will be available to care for their grandchildren. They also worry that they will not be able to afford appropriate medical care if their grandchildren become ill or disabled. One half of the children living in homes with two grandparents (no parent present) have no health insurance (Bryson & Casper 1999).

Exploring Grandparenting Issues in Workshops

Parenting the Second Time Around is a manual that explores grandparenting issues in a workshop series. The manual contains invaluable material for six two-hour workshops on the following topics:

1. It Wasn't Supposed to Be Like This—Identifying and reflecting on ambivalent feelings about changing roles, finding helpful community resources

2. Getting to Know You—Exploring child development, individual differences, journaling

3. Rebuilding a Family—Examining adult-child interactions, grief and loss, relating to your adult child, solution-based problem solving

4. Discipline Is Not a Dirty Word, But It May Look Different Today—Covering characteristics of effective discipline, establishing a discipline style, addressing high-risk behaviors

5. Protecting and Planning for Your Grandchild's Future—Dealing with legal issues, including custody, visitation, and child support

6. Standing Up for Grandparents'/Grandchildren's Rights—Encouraging advocacy, negotiating systems, connecting with community programs

The 300-page manual features workshop outlines with handouts and supplementary material for the leaders.

From J. Birckmayer, J. Cohen, I. Jensen, D. Variano, & G. Wallace, *Parenting the Second Time Around* (Ithaca, NY: Cornell University, 2001). Available from The Resource Center, Cornell University, P.O. Box 3884, Ithaca, NY 14852; telephone 607-255-2080; online: www.cce.cornell.edu/store/customer/home. php?cat=271&page=3.

Raising grandchildren sometimes isolates grandparents, regardless of age, from their peers, often leaving them depressed and lonely. The situations that bring about a grandchild-grandparent household may also create physical or psychological problems for children. Helping children feel secure and loved, while simultaneously dealing with special needs and challenging behaviors, is an enormous task for parents and can be an overwhelming responsibility for grandparents.

Grandparents parenting the second time around need social support as well as up-to-date information about effective parenting and available community services. The early childhood program in which their grandchild is enrolled may be in the best position to offer help.

Early childhood educators can

• **listen empathically to grandparents.** Introduce them to others in similar situations, or suggest workshops and community meetings about common concerns.

• **encourage grandparents to avail themselves of community resources.** Introduce them to food banks and clinics. Help them to stay well. Notify them of immunization (especially flu) clinics, Al-Anon meetings, and recreational events and exercise. Let them know it is good for their grandchildren to see them as active participants in community life.

• **provide information about where to obtain good legal services.** Legal concerns of custody and guardianship are serious issues for grandparents raising grandchildren. Help keep children from losing the security their grandparents may provide because legal guardianship has not been established.

• **gather information about community organizations or resources for children with special needs.** It may be particularly difficult for grandparents to recognize that children suffering from attention deficit disorder (ADD) or attention deficit hyperactivity disorder (ADHD) are not deliberately "misbehaving." Refer grandparents to national support groups such as Children and Adults with Attention Deficit Disorders (ChADD) and the Attention Deficit Disorder Association (ADDA). Both organizations offer families good information and practical advice and are available online (www.chadd.org and www.add.org).

An early childhood program can address grandparents' needs for information and social support by offering workshops designed especially for them. The Cooperative Extension Service has developed manuals with suggested outlines for meetings around topics of particular interest for grandparents. Resources can be obtained from local county extension offices or often online (for example, at www.fcs.uga.edu/extension/cyf_pubs.php/parent#parent or http://parenting.wsu.edu/relative/links.htm). If information is not available locally, a manual for grandparenting workshops is available (see "Exploring Grandparenting Issues in Workshops").

Effective workshop sessions require a skilled and experienced leader who can keep discussion on track. It is also important to allow unstructured time for informal discussion and socializing. Grandparents can be invaluable resources for each other, and friendships often develop while sharing common concerns.

An early childhood program can address grandparents' needs for information and social support by offering workshops designed especially for them.

In addition to offering special workshops for grandparents, early childhood programs can take the following specific and helpful steps:

• **Use the word** *families* instead of *parents* on bulletin boards and in newsletters and notices.

• **Use black print** (initial capitals followed by lower case letters) on white paper or printed material for families. Choose fonts that are readable and at least a 12-point type. This is helpful to people with impaired vision.

• **Prepare for questions** like George's in our introductory example. Ask grandparents how they would like you to respond when children ask, "Where's Kyle's mommy?" Respect confidentiality. If Kyle's grandmother wants you to say, "His mommy is away on a trip," but you know she is in jail or in a substance abuse program, you can answer, "Kyle's grandma says his mommy is away, so she's taking care of Kyle right now."

• **Look for ways to include grandparents** by focusing on their special skills or strengths. Grandparents may feel out of place in a group of young families, even when the age difference may not be great. Reading, singing, storytelling, and cooking are obvious areas to explore, but grandparents may surprise you with expertise in puppetry, folk dancing, gardening, or bird watching.

• **Be sensitive to the comfort needs** of all adult visitors by providing adult-size chairs for classroom visits or meetings. Arthritis can develop at any age, and an adult with swollen hands can have difficulty engaging with a child using child-size puzzles, scissors, and games with small parts.

• **Plan holiday celebrations with care.** Perhaps Mothers Day and Fathers Day can become People We Love days.

• **Display pictures and posters** of various family constellations, including some with grandparents as primary caregivers.

• **Model roles other than Mommy and Daddy** in the dramatic play corner. Ask to join the children's play as a grandpa or an aunt or a cousin.

• **Introduce assistive devices,** such as walkers or canes, in the classroom for children to explore, use, and discuss.

• **Include figures of many adults** (including older people) in the block play accessories.

• **Examine puzzles and other games** to be sure they represent many different family structures.

• **Consider the language in poetry, songs, and books** you share with children. Be aware of the negative impact a nursery rhyme such as the following can have on a sensitive child who lives with a grandparent:

> There was an old woman who lived in a shoe
> She had so many children she didn't know what to do
> She gave them some broth without any bread
> And whipped them all soundly and sent them to bed.
> There was an old lady who swallowed a fly...
> Perhaps she'll die.

• **Include, read, and discuss books** dealing with all kinds of families and family issues. Many books about grandparents seem to emphasize pleasant, leisurely visits; gardening; or dealing with disability and death; but there are others to be found. See "Children's Books about Family Relationships for Grandparents and Grandchildren to Share" for a list of some of our favorite books. (A longer list appears online in Beyond the Journal at www.journal.naeyc.org/btj.)

Early childhood educators are in ideal positions to provide substantial support and assistance to grandparent-/relative-headed families. Teachers may be the first or only nonfamily adults to see that a child is exhibiting aggressive, withdrawn, or depressed behaviors after circumstances necessitate a move in with grandparents.

Clear communication and strong partnerships between teaching staff and grandparents can result in strategies to reduce a child's fears and foster healthy development and feelings of self-worth. Working as partners, all adults can think of specific words and phrases for explanations that meet a child's needs and level of understanding.

While books are no substitute for spontaneous, loving conversations, they do often provide openings for discussion. Consider establishing a lending library of children's books dealing with a wide variety of family issues, from divorce and the death of pets to coping with a parent's alcoholism (see "Good Books about Grandparents and Grandchildren").

Teachers can help grandparents choose and use books appropriately. They also can encourage grandparents to share children's reactions to books and discussions and together brainstorm further steps to provide reassurance and comfort. By developing partnerships with grandparents raising children, early childhood educators can support the growth of stronger families.

References

Bryson, K., & L.M. Casper. 1999. Coresident grandparents and grandchildren. Table 2. *Current Population Reports,* Special Studies (May). Washington, DC: U.S. Census Bureau.

Simmons, T., & J. Dye. 2003. Grandparents living with grandchildren: 2000. *Census 2000 Brief* (October). Online: www.census.gov/prod/2003pubs/c2kbr-31.pdf.

JENNIFER BIRCKMAYER, MA, has been a senior extension associate with the Department of Human Development at Cornell University in Ithaca, New York, for 40 years. During that time she has been a teacher, trainer, speaker, and author.

JAN COHEN, MEd, is executive director of Cornell University Cooperative Extension of Otsego County, New York. She has worked in the field of education and human services for more than 20 years. She is the author of "Help for Grandparents of Children with Developmental Disabilities," a six-workshop curriculum published by the New York State Office for Aging.

ISABELLE DORAN JENSEN, MS, is an extension resource educator for human development with Cornell Cooperative Extension of Ontario County, New York. She has worked with grandparent/caregiver relatives since 1991 and has been recognized with several awards from the National Extension Association of Family and Consumer Sciences.

DENYSE ALTMAN VARIANO, RN, MPS, is the senior extension resource educator in charge of human development programming for Cornell Cooperative Extension of Orange County, New York. Denyse is the administrator for the Relatives as Parents Program in Orange County.

The Dynamics of Families Who Are Homeless

Implications for Early Childhood Educators

KEVIN J. SWICK

F amily homelessness has emerged as a serious global problem (Stronge, 2000). Over the past 25 years in the United States, the makeup of the homeless population has changed significantly. As De Angelis (1994) reports:

The landscape of homelessness has changed since the early 1980s, when nearly all homeless people were men. Today, families—typically women with two children under age 5 make up 30 percent of the homeless population. (p. 1)

Some scholars (e.g., Bassuk, 1991) suggest that families may constitute 40 to 50 percent of the homeless.

Thus, the focus of this article is on articulating the various dynamics of families who are homeless, what this means for the early childhood education profession, and what strategies we can employ to effectively support homeless families with young children.

The Changing Concepts of Homelessness

Various government and private agencies have different concepts of homelessness. The U.S. federal government defines homeless individuals as:
those who lack a fixed, regular, and adequate nighttime residence; have a primary nighttime residence that is

- a supervised publicly or privately operated shelter designed to provide temporary living accommodations (including welfare hotels, congregate shelters, and transitional housing for the mentally ill);
- an institution that provides a temporary residence for individuals intended to be institutionalized; or
- a public or private place not designed for, or ordinarily used as, a regular sleeping accommodation for human beings. (cited in Heflin, 1991, p. 1)

Regarding children and youth, the McKinney-Vento Homeless Education Assistance Act, Section 725 (as cited in National Coalition for the Homeless, 1999) states,

"Homeless children and youths ..."

a) means individuals who lack a fixed, regular, and adequate nighttime residence (within the meaning of section 103(a)(1); and

b) includes—

(i) children and youths who are sharing the housing of other persons due to loss of housing, economic hardship, or a similar reason; are living in motels, hotels, trailer parks, or camping grounds due to the lack of alternative adequate accommodations; are living in emergency or transitional shelters; are abandoned in hospitals; or are awaiting foster care placement;

(ii) children and youths who have a primary nighttime residence that is a public or private place not designed for or ordinarily used as a regular sleeping accommodation for human beings (within the meaning of section 103(a)(2)(c);

(iii) children and youths who are living in cars, parks, public spaces, abandoned buildings, substandard housing, bus or train stations, or similar settings; and

(iv) migratory children (as such term is defined in section 1309 of the Elementary and Secondary Education Act of 1995) who qualify as homeless for the purposes of this subtitle because the children are living in circumstances described in clauses (i) through (iii). (p. 8)

The concept of homelessness continues to change, as many families that are not technically defined as homeless have all of the attributes of being homeless. For example, it is common among many families that are chronically poor to double- or triple-up with each other in order to survive, financially. In nations with high rates of poverty, it is common for three or more families to live in very small areas (Bellamy, 2003).

Women and children now represent up to one-half of the homeless population in many cities (National Coalition for the Homeless, 1999). When families with older children and adolescents are included in the count, over 50 percent of the homeless population is families (Shane, 1996). Vissing and Diament (1997) indicate that the problem is likely to be more serious than the statistics indicate; many adolescents who are homeless avoid the label, fearing the stigma it may give them with their peers, and so may not be represented in the statistics. Furthermore, many children in foster care are "housing displaced"; that is, no longer able to live in their home of origin (Toth, 1997). Another dynamic in this complex situation is that a large number of working families live on the edge of homelessness, due to low-paying jobs and high expenses (Heyman, 2000).

Homelessness of children and youth is particularly tragic. Estimates indicate that 1 to 3 million children and adolescents in the United States are homeless (National Coalition for the Homeless, 1999). The impact of child and family homelessness on society is even greater when one considers the resultant problems being passed from one generation to the next. As Vissing (1996) notes, children learn what they observe, and when their most consistent experiences are within chronically poor, powerless, and homeless situations, they are bound to acquire many of the attitudes that go with being powerless.

Family homelessness is not necessarily a factor of socioeconomic status. Even middle- and upper-income mothers and children are not immune from homelessness. Physical, sexual, and psychological abuse destroys the family system of many economically advantaged women and children (Shane, 1996). Women may escape from an abusive home environment to protect themselves and/or their children, or they may be forcibly evicted by their spouse or friend (Peled, Jaffe, & Edleson, 1995).

Indeed, many people now become homeless because of abuse, natural disasters, and other trauma. The widening income gap between the poor and the rich and the increasing cost of raising children are also key factors (Coontz, 1995). Furthermore, war, famine, and disease have led to dramatic increases in family homelessness throughout the world (Bellamy, 2003).

Diverse and Unique Situations of Homeless Families

The situations that lead to homelessness for families and children/adolescents range from leaving an abusive relationship, eviction for failure to make rent payments, running away from parents, or being displaced because of unsafe housing (Bassuk, 1991; Heyman, 2000).

Families that are homeless are distinct from individuals who are homeless. For example, De Angelis (1994) and Bassuk, Browne, and Buckner (1996) report that homeless families typically have much lower levels of substance abuse and mental health problems than do homeless individuals. It is also noteworthy that homeless women with children are usually homeless for shorter periods and are more actively engaged in strategies to empower themselves (Morris, 1998). They are also more likely to be employed and less likely to engage in antisocial behavior (Edin & Lein, 1997).

Homeless mothers also have unique situations. Some homeless mothers have all their children with them; some have one child with them and have placed the others with a relative or friend (many shelters will not accept adolescents); in

some cases, the children have been placed in the state's custody (Dail, 1990).

In yet other cases, the children may be in foster care (Shane, 1996; Toth, 1997) or in the state reform system (Ayers, 1997). Inclusion of these populations of "society's children" in homeless statistics would certainly increase the number of people classified as homeless. Also, "housed" children—who have a place to go home to, but who basically live on the streets without any adult supervision are often in worse condition than many homeless children (Berck, 1992).

Dail (1990) and Edin and Lein (1997) explicated the characteristics of women who are homeless, showing the diversity of these situations: 50 percent are between 17 and 25 years of age; a majority have never married, or are separated, divorced, or widowed; more than 50 percent have completed high school; and 75 percent have been employed at some point in their life (Buckner, Bassuk, & Zima, 1993).

As Dail (1990) suggests, the etiology of family homelessness is based in three areas of difficulty:

- A crisis, often of a violent nature, in a relationship with a male
- A prior crisis in the family of origin—sexual abuse, abandonment, parental death, or chronic neglect
- A consistent problem with mental illness and/or drug abuse.

While the situation of each homeless mother is unique, abuse, severe depression, chemical dependency, illiteracy, and chronic poverty are common contributing factors (Nunez, 1996).

The particular situation and complexities a homeless family faces will determine the type of services and assistance they need. For example, a middle class homeless mother who is seeking shelter from an abusive spouse may need a combination of short-term services with counseling for longer range needs. More intensive services are likely to be needed for the chronically poor and persistently homeless family (Wasson & Hill, 1998).

Early childhood educators can empower homeless mothers by building on their strengths. For example, homeless women with children appear to be more proactive than homeless women in general, and more so than chronically poor women who are not homeless (De Angelis, 1994). It appears that women who seek shelter and other support services for their children are more connected with sources of support in the community (Bassuk, 1991; Swick & Graves, 1993).

Success stories of homeless women and their children in attaining more self-sufficiency indicates that paying attention early on to homelessness in young families is crucial (Shane, 1996). In contrast, the prevalence of many poor "housed" families that live in violent and abusive environments indicates a pathology of isolation and neglect (Bassuk, Browne, & Buckner, 1996). Evidence suggests that homeless women with children "are the most likely to have finished high school and to have the lowest average of adult arrests" (De Angelis, 1994, p. 1). It also has been noted that homeless mothers are more likely to be gainfully employed than homeless women in general (Bassuk, Browne, & Buckner, 1996).

The observation that many housed but chronically poor women with children are more symptomatic of dysfunction than are classified homeless mothers (particularly those mothers with children in shelters or transitional housing) highlights the need for reconceptualizing "homelessness" within a broader context. The research suggests that American society has a large number of "hidden homeless families" that need the intensive services being provided for some homeless families (Swick, 1997).

Implications for Early Childhood Professionals: Relating and Responding to Family Homelessness

Early childhood professionals seeking to support homeless families should: 1) develop an ecological understanding of family homelessness; 2) develop responsive and supportive attitudes and behaviors; 3) create an inviting and validating center or school culture; 4) engage parents and families in all aspects of their children's learning and development; and 5) empower parents and families through adult education, job enhancement, and related family literacy (Nunez, 1996; Nunez & Collignon, 2000; Swick, 1997).

Develop an Ecological Understanding of Family Homelessness. The ecological framework theory emphasizes the influence of actions and events on people, and the transactive nature of the different "systems" in which people live (Bronfenbrenner, 1979). A basic construct of this perspective is that human development and learning are the result of dynamic interactions between people and their environment.

Three important elements can help early childhood professionals better understand the dynamic nature of family homelessness:

- The individual's system influences and is influenced by his or her interactive involvement in the various contexts of life. For example, comprehensive job support and training services, provided within a homeless shelter program, can improve mothers' job prospects (Nunez, 1996).
- Each system plays a role in the evolving life of human beings. As noted by Swick and Graves (1993), homeless families resolve their stressors most effectively when all systems are supportive and empowering.
- Whatever happens within and between systems influences people's functioning (Bronfenbrenner, 1979). For example, Powell (1998) indicates that quality child care affects parents' self-confidence and thus creates new possibilities for the family.

Develop Responsive and Supportive Attitudes and Behaviors. Swick and Graves (1993) emphasize that early childhood professionals need to first develop positive and supportive perspectives and behaviors toward families. They note four key elements of this process:

- Nurture and renew positive, supportive, and responsive attitudes and relationship patterns with parents and families.
- Seek to understand parent and family situations from the parental view first, so that you have the family's idea of what is important.
- Recognize and value the role of the parent and family.
- Model positive attitudes and behaviors to parents and families.

Create an Inviting and Validating Center or School Culture. "Homeless students and their parents develop their 'schema' of what schools are through direct experiences, including the messages they receive related to access and participation in social and educational activities" (Swick, 2000, p. 165).

Early childhood programs can foster an inviting atmosphere for homeless families by:

- Providing immediate and friendly access to basic human services
- Treating everyone in the center or school with respect, and making sure their ideas are represented in the fabric of the program
- Involving homeless families in shaping program goals and strategies, allowing them to take on ownership of the program
- Providing comprehensive services (such as adult education and family literacy practices), and being sure these services are family-friendly.

Engage Parents and Families in All Aspects of Their Children's Learning and Development. As Powell (1998) suggests, early childhood professionals need to develop and continually refine an "engagement, participatory" stance in relation to the involvement of homeless families. Quint (1994) notes that educators should begin this process during their initial contact with parents and families. Find out what parents believe is key to minimizing the stressors affecting them and their children. One school invites parents and children to list their top concerns about their lives and then integrates these issues into the plans for helping the families (Nunez, 1996).

Another important construct is that of engaging parents in positively relating to their children (Anooshian, 2000). Positive parent-child relations serve as a buffer to many stressors that otherwise can impede the learning and functioning of children and families (Stronge, 2000).

An extension of the parent-child relationship lies in the partnership between parents and teachers; in particular, home learning activities can empower the entire family (National Coalition for the Homeless, 1999). This partnership process can begin with early childhood educators providing critical home learning resources and community support in shelters and libraries.

It is also important that parents and families have regular opportunities to "educate" professionals about needed literacy and other support resources. Simple items like paper and pens, a quiet place to study, help for parents to understand the material being studied, and guidance on strategies parents can use to help their children are essential.

Empower Parents and Families Through Adult Education, Job Enhancement, and Related Family Literacy.
The most empowering element in caring for homeless families is to strengthen parental competence and confidence. As Nunez and Collignon (2000) note, "The surest way to support homeless children's education is to support their parents" (p. 115). As parents complete GEDs, high school diploma programs, postsecondary education, and related job skills training, children receive additional emphasis and modeling of the value of education. Furthermore, parents' increased economic and educational skills can lead to an improved quality of life for the family (Swick, 1997). Of course, such services need to be secondary to assistance in meeting families' emergency needs.

Empowerment Strategies for Supporting Homeless Families

Empowerment interventions should focus on supporting homeless families in resolving issues and stressors they see as impeding their functioning (Nunez, 1996). Two examples will illustrate how this empowerment process helps many homeless families address the difficulties they face.

Quint (1994) tells how one school used an on-site family service scheme to help one mother attain permanent housing along with a job, providing stability for her family. The school counselor and a social worker guided the mother in her interactions with the job placement staff and helped her successfully negotiate the housing agency process. They also provided essential follow-up support so that the gains could be sustained and expanded.

Toth (1997) describes how the placement of a foster child who had been in four homes in one year with a stable family altered the child's attitudes toward life in a powerful way. The family eventually adopted the child, thus providing the security and continuity the child needed to gain a sense of competence. The child's school performance improved, and he also benefited from more positive peer relations and increased self-esteem.

Here are three further examples of how early childhood programs can nurture families toward more positive living:

- A preschool center for homeless children and their families ensures that all of the children have a special place at the center where they can develop their sense of security and love. Parents are also helped to feel valued and special.
- An early childhood program for families in abusive situations helps each parent to learn how to take pride in themselves and their children. Parents are encouraged to make and display collages of the things they value the most in their lives. Each parent also develops a plan to strengthen themselves to be more nurturing, positive, and supportive in their relations with their child.
- An elementary school uses a "buddy" program to match children who are new to the school with caring peer mentors. Many of the children in this particular school are homeless or at-risk, and several of them eventually become mentors themselves. The "buddy" activities

focus on helping children feel secure, important, and connected to their new school. Teachers and staff also act as mentors, often in informal ways with the parents.

Two additional and very important strategy areas are 1) helping families develop trust in each other and in their relations in the community, and 2) helping homeless families form mutually supportive relationships (Pipher, 1996; Swick, 2000).

Promoting trust among families further strengthens their social and emotional skills (Swick, 1997). Early childhood educators can model trusting relations with parents and children, providing a supportive environment in which parents learn about having positive and trusting relations with their children. One parent who participated in a focus group for homeless mothers said, "This program has really helped me turn my trust issues toward the positive, helping me see the best in myself and, thus, in my child."

Families who are homeless also need to have mutually supportive and responsive relations with each other, thereby enabling them to view each other in positive ways (Swick, 2000). Early childhood educators can support families in this process by:

- Encouraging families to recognize and support each other's strengths
- Complimenting parents on their positive interactions with their children
- Including parent-child social learning activities in every aspect of the program
- Encouraging families to use appropriate conflict resolution strategies
- Nurturing in families the importance of open and continuing communication with each other.

Early childhood educators can positively affect the lives of children and families who are homeless or in other high-risk situations. By understanding the dynamics of what homeless families experience, we can be more responsive to the challenges impeding their functioning. For example, family literacy and adult education strategies have been successful in empowering parents, both educationally and economically. Providing basic services like child care and transportation can make a powerful difference in how families work and interact in the world. Educators need to realize just how powerful we can be in using the early years of the family's life as a time to strengthen them—thus preventing homelessness or other "housing-distressed" situations, or helping families gain the power to resolve their homeless situation.

References

Anooshian, L. (2000). Moving to educational success: Building positive relationships for homeless children. In J. Stronge & E. Reed-Victor (Eds.), *Educating homeless students: Promising practices*. Larchmont, NY: Eye on Education.

Ayers, W. (1997). *A kind and just parent: The children of juvenile court.* Boston: Beacon Press.

Bassuk, E. (1991). Homeless families. *Scientific American, 265,* 66–74.

Bassuk, E., Browne, A., & Buckner, J. (1996). Single mothers and welfare. *Scientific American, 275*(4), 60–67.

Bellamy, C. (2003). *The state of the world's children 2002.* New York: United Nations Children's Fund.

Berck, J. (1992). *No place to be: Voices of homeless children.* Boston: Houghton Mifflin.

Buckner, J., Bassuk, E., & Zima, B. (1993). Mental health issues affecting homeless women: Implications for intervention. *Journal of Orthopsychiatry, 63*(3), 385–399.

Bronfeubrenner, U. (1979). *The ecology of human development and learning.* Cambridge, MA: Harvard University Press.

Coontz, S. (1995). The American family and the nostalgia trap. *Phi Delta Kappan, 76*(1), K-1–K-20.

Dail, P. (1990). The psychosocial context of homeless mothers with young children: Program and policy implications. *Child Welfare, 69*(4), 291–307.

De Angelis, T. (1994). Homeless families: Stark reality of the 90's. *American Psychological Association Monitor, 1,* 38.

Edin, K., & Lein, L. (1997). *Making ends meet: How single mothers survive welfare and low-wage work.* New York: Russell Sage Foundation.

Heflin, L. (1991). *Developing effective programs for special education students who are homeless.* Reston, VA: Council for Exceptional Children. (ERIC Document Reproduction Service No. ED 339 167).

Heyman, J. (2000). *The widening gap: Why America's working families are in jeopardy and what can be done about it.* New York: Basic Books.

Morris, J. (1998). Affiliation, gender, and parental status among homeless persons. *The Journal of Social Psychology, 138*(4), 241–271.

National Coalition for the Homeless. (1999). *Why are people homeless? NCH Fact Sheet #1.* Washington, DC: Author.

Nunez, R. (1996). *The new poverty: Homeless families in America* New York: Insight Books, Plenum Press.

Nunez, R., & Collignon, K. (2000). Supporting family learning: Building a community of learners. In J. Stronge & E. Reed-Victor (Eds.), *Educating homeless students: Promising practices* (pp. 115–134). Larehmont, NY: Eye on Education.

Peled, E., Jaffe, P., & Edleson, J. (Eds.). (1995). *Ending the cycle of violence: Community responses to children of battered women.* Thousand Oaks, CA: Sage.

Pipher, M. (1996). *The shelter of each other: Rebuilding our families.* New York: G.P. Putnam's Sons.

Powell, D. (1998). Reweaving parents into the fabric of early childhood programs. *Young Children, 53*(5), 60–67.

Quint, S. (1994). *Schooling homeless children.* New York: Teachers College Press.

Shane, P. (1996). *What about America's homeless children?* Thousand Oaks, CA: Sage.

Stronge, J. (2000). Educating homeless children and youth: An introduction. In J. Stronge & E. Reed-Victor (Eds.), *Educating homeless students: Promising practices* (pp. 1–20). Larchmont, NY: Eye on Education.

Swick, K. (1997). Strengthening homeless families and their young children. *Dimensions of Early Childhood, 25*(2), 29–34.

Swick, K. (2000). Building effective awareness programs for homeless students among staff, peers, and community members. In J. Stronge & E. Reed-Victor (Eds.), *Educating homeless students: Promising practices.* Larchmont, NY: Eye on Education.

Swick, K., & Graves, S. (1993). *Empowering at-risk families during the early childhood years.* Washington, DC: National Education Association.

Toth, J. (1997). *Orphans of the living: Stories of America's children in foster care.* New York: Simon & Schuster.

Vissing, Y. (1996). *Out of sight, out of mind: Homeless children and families in small-town America.* Lexington, KY: The University Press of Kentucky.

Vissing, Y., & Diament, J. (1997). Housing distress among high school students. *Social Work, 42*(1), 31–42.

Wasson, R., & Hill, R. (1998). The process of becoming homeless: An investigation of female-headed families living in poverty. *Journal of Consumer Affairs, 32*(2), 320–332.

KEVIN J. SWICK is Professor, Early Childhood Education, College of Education, University of South Carolina, Columbia.

From *Childhood Education,* Vol. 80, no. 3, Spring 2004, pp. 116–120. Copyright © 2004 by Association for Childhood Education International. Reprinted by permission of the authors and the Association for Childhood Education International.

UNIT 3

Supporting Young Children's Development

Unit Selections

Key Points to Consider

- How does a strong background in child development assist teachers when working with infants and toddlers?

- Why has childhood obesity become such an epidemic in our country today?

- What are some of the special needs and challenges when working with young boys? How can teachers best meet their needs?

- What are some of the less prominent needs of children that are just as important as acquiring academic skills?

Student Web Site

www.mhcls.com/online

Internet References

Further information regarding these websites may be found in this book's preface or online.

American Academy of Pediatrics
  www.aap.org
Canada's Schoolnet Staff Room
  http://www.schoolnet.ca/home/e/
Classroom Connect
  http://www.classroom.com/login/home.jhtml
The Council for Exceptional Children
  http://www.cec.sped.org/index.html
Early Learning Standards: Full Report
  http://www.naeyc.org/resources/position_statements/positions_2003.asp
Early Learning Standards: Executive Summary
  http://www.naeyc.org/resources/position_statements/creating_conditions.asp
Make Your Own Web page
  http://www.teacherweb.com
National Resource Center for Health and Safety in Child Care
  http://nrc.uchsc.edu
Online Innovation Institute
  http://oii.org

Care for our youngest citizens—infants and toddlers—requires caregivers to bring a special set of characteristics to the setting. Veteran infant/toddler researchers J. Ronald Lally and Peter Mangione write "The Uniqueness of Infancy Demands a Responsive Approach to Care." In this article J. Ronald Lally and Peter Mangione provide an overview of the developmental needs of infants and outline what caregivers must do to respond to these needs.

It has been a little over 10 years since the first major research on early brain development began to emerge. Since that time hundreds of articles on the importance of early brain stimulation have been written. Some have prompted the development of programs such as Baby Einstein as well as a whole series of commercial materials. Others reinforce what parents for centuries have known: young children need a variety of active learning experiences to stimulate their minds and bodies. Pat Wingert and Martha Bryant provide an up-to-date look at early brain development in their article "Reading Your Baby's Mind."

One of my challenges this year was deciding which of the many excellent articles on educating boys I should choose for this book. After many readings, I selected Peg Tyre's "The Trouble With Boys" from *Newsweek*. Education of boys is one of the hot topics this year, and I reviewed many articles for this edition. There are schools moving to same-sex classrooms and adopting programs that cater to the educational needs of boys. This comes after almost two decades of attention placed on improving test scores, particularly in math and science, for girls. Boys now are receiving greater attention, and none too soon. The U.S. Department of Education recently announced more relaxed guidelines for single-sex classes or schools. When schools offer single-sex classes, enrollment must be voluntary and the programs must be re-evaluated every two years. The classes must also have an important objective, and a "substantially equal coeducational class" in the same subject must also be provided.

Issues related to the health of young children continued to emerge this year. I have included an article that reflects the new interest in children's health and well-being. As with the previous edition of *Annual Editions: Early Childhood Education*, there were numerous articles on childhood obesity. Childhood obesity has become conspicuous; on practically every visit to a fast food restaurant, one hears a child order a meal by its number on the menu because they are so familiar with the selections there. Obesity also becomes evident on the playground where children just sit on the sidelines not wanting to participate with their peers because of their poor body image. In "What Can We Do To Prevent Childhood Obesity?", Julie Lumeng provides many suggestions for educators to follow that will help children develop appropriate eating habits and develop an active lifestyle. Parents and educators must work together to promote healthy living. Teachers should also participate in healthy living activities. Only then will our society begin to realize that a lifestyle that includes good nutrition and exercise is one of the best ways to lead a long and healthy life.

The Uniqueness of Infancy Demands a Responsive Approach to Care

Infants have a built-in plan for how they will learn. They start to pursue their course work even in the womb and, when born, are ready, interested, and actively engaged in study. For those who are asked to develop curricula and lesson plans for infants, it would be a great mistake to do too much planning without paying close attention to the infant's built-in curriculum.

J. Ronald Lally and Peter Mangione

Development is a continuous process through which a child gradually grows and changes. But as early childhood professionals we need to keep in mind that each developmental period has its own challenges and opportunities. As brain development research has reached the general public, most of us have become aware of the infant period as an important time when neural pathways that influence learning and development are formed.

The rapid development of the brain during the early years does not mean that infancy is the most important period in life. Each period is important. Although optimum attention to infants' development helps them become resilient, it is not an inoculation against negative experience in subsequent periods. Infancy, however, is distinctly important. It is a unique period that calls for unique responses from adults.

The ways infants think, feel, and function differ significantly from the ways of children and adults in other periods of life. The developmental periods of preschool, middle childhood, adolescence, adulthood, and aging are unique as well. Each period of life has its special challenges, issues, and developmental milestones, calling for different responses, attention, and care.

This article focuses on children in the first two years of life. It points out the unique aspects of this period, and makes recommendations for the ways infants need to be approached and treated. We propose that infants should be treated differently from preschoolers and older children with regard to approaches to readiness for school, guidance and discipline, selection of curriculum content, the learning milieu, and the relationship of teachers to children.

In this article we use the terms *genetic programming* and *genetic wiring* to indicate that infants follow common developmental paths and have strong inborn drives to learn and develop. Experience plays a necessary and important role, but

infants follow these common developmental paths even though their early experiences vary greatly. We use the term *infant care teacher* to recognize that in infant care settings, the adult simultaneously teaches and cares for the child.

The term *caregiver* refers to all adults who are in a caring relationship with infants, regardless of the setting.

The Unique Make-up of Infants

There are four main areas in which infants and toddlers differ from older children.

1. The intensity of infants' inborn inclination to learn and develop in particular areas

All humans are internally driven to learn and develop, but this internal drive functions in slightly different ways and degrees at different points in life. Where content of learning is concerned, infants' internal drives are much more specific than those of older children.

Babies have their own learning agenda. For example, infants and toddlers are genetically programmed to learn language, to become more skillful in their small muscle and large muscle functioning, to construct knowledge about the functioning of people and things in the world around them, to seek out significant relationships through which they can be nurtured and protected, and to use relationships to learn appropriate and inappropriate ways of relating to others. Infants actively pursue and engage in learning in these content areas. Selma Fraiberg says, with regard to an infant's inclination to master learning language, "It's a little bit like having God on our side" (Fraiberg, Shapiro, & Cherness 1980, 56).

Adults who want to help infants and toddlers learn need to understand this learning agenda and find ways to facilitate and build on it rather than supplant it. The need to motivate infants' interest in learning is fundamentally different from the need to motivate older children. For example, the impulse to master algebra or ice skating or reading is not necessarily present in an older child's developmental trajectory. Interest in these topics comes from group socialization and an introduction by adults, coupled with the more generalized genetic programming to learn that all humans have.

Where content of learning is concerned, infants' internal drives are much more specific than those of older children. Babies are perfectly motivated to seek out the skills and relationships that will help them survive and prosper.

For the older child, selecting and presenting topics for mastery as well as motivating the child to pursue mastery in those areas are appropriate actions to be taken by teachers and other helping adults and peers. Without this introduction the child may not become aware of the pleasure and usefulness of certain content. But for the infant, there is no need for adults to present specific topics for mastery or to provide the motivation to learn.

Babies are perfectly motivated to seek out the skills and relationships that will help them survive and prosper. They have been genetically wired to do so. In a video about her infant/toddler care approach, Magda Gerber wisely proclaims, "Nobody knows better about what a baby needs than that baby" (1988). Without special attention and adaptations to the uniqueness of infants' inborn curriculum, the curriculum clarity of the infant would be missed, and mastery motivation already in place would simply be thwarted or ignored. For an adult to usurp this decision-making process is inappropriate. The adult role in infants' learning is facilitative, not directive. It is only as the child grows and topics of learning are less genetically programmed that the adult role comes to involve more guided activities and instruction. As school readiness, language and literacy development, and numeracy initiatives move downward toward infancy, it is important to discourage generalizing pedagogical practices with older children for use with infants.

2. The holistic nature of infant learning

The second unique aspect of the infancy period is the holistic way in which infants learn. Infants take in information continuously, naturally, and fluidly. They pick up from their actions, interactions, and observations all kinds of information through which they build knowledge and skills in all areas of development. One interaction can teach many things. They make no distinctions between physical, emotional, intellectual, social, and language lessons. Lessons in all domains are processed almost simultaneously and each interaction is mined for all its information, not just that which is intended or focused on by those with whom infants interact.

Because infants learn in this holistic way, adults need to take a more organic approach to infant learning than with learning by older children. Structuring lessons for 15 to 20 minutes on a particular content area—for example, language or shapes—will almost always result in the adult missing the larger learning experience in which the infant is perpetually engaged. The infant receives information from every domain simultaneously no matter which one we may wish to emphasize. Thus plans to help with infant learning are best created in ways that reflect this awareness.

A teacher may think that crafting a special lesson on seriation or colors will result in specific learning, but infants don't segregate their lessons into topic areas. Unless the teacher has considered all the potentials for learning in the interaction, the lesson learned may wind up being nothing to do with colors. Instead, learning will center on a part of the interaction that is more important to the infant whose focus at the time may be the texture of the materials used to display color, the emotional tone in the interaction, or perception of the style adults use to introduce something new to someone.

The infant receives information from every domain simultaneously no matter which one we may wish to emphasize. As they grow toward seven months of age, infants turn their attention to exploring through movement, manipulation, and visual inspection.

In high school it is appropriate for teenagers to focus narrowly on solving a problem in algebra class and put other messages coming into their heads on the back burner, so to speak. For the infant, narrow focusing is an impossible task. Even with the best of intentions, this is misguided pedagogy. Babies follow their natural inclination to process everything about what is in front of them and never focus narrowly unless compelled.

3. Infants' rapid move through three major developmental stages in their first two years

During the first six to eight months of life, most infants focus their attention and behavior on developing a sense of security. On the larger stage of seeking security, nurturance, and protection, infants play out their explorations of the world around them and a growing knowledge of themselves as individuals with separate identities.

As they grow toward seven months of age, infants turn their attention to exploring through movement, manipulation, and visual inspection. Although still needing and seeking security, they do so through the lens of exploration. No longer do they constantly seek to be given to or held or immediately gratified by their trusted caregiver. Captivated by the exciting world out in front of them, they now want to move out into and manipulate the world.

Active Partnerships

From all that early childhood educators know about how children learn best, we recognize that infants must have a hand in selecting what they learn. The infant should be an active partner in selecting curriculum content. The curriculum should be dynamic enough to flow and change daily based on the infant's changing interests and needs. In this way, curriculum is responsive to and respectful of what infants bring to and want from these early learning experiences.

Infants see themselves as active explorers, no longer physically bound to the trusted adult but on their own for brief periods. They seem to be practicing independence, motivated by a powerful urge to explore but still quite dependent on the trusted adult being there when needed. The seven-month-old looks to the infant care teacher to validate his explorative bursts by showing confidence in his developing competence and providing security on new terms.

During this new exploratory stage, adults need to make a switch in how they care for the infant and alter the ways they provide security and relate to the child's growing sense of self. If children in this stage of infancy enjoy a safe, secure environment, are allowed to use the caregiver as a base of security from which they can journey back and forth for emotional refueling, and see their caregivers providing eye contact, they prosper. When caregivers simply continue relating to the children as if they remained in the first developmental stage, children learn that their natural urge to explore is seen as problematic and think that those who care for them don't believe in their developing sense of competence.

As children move to the third stage of infancy—starting around 16 months of age—their focus changes again. For the rest of their infancy, they seem to be consumed by issues of *me* and *mine*, notions of *good* and *not so good,* and distinctions of self from other. Their need for security and their drive to explore are subsumed under an almost consuming preoccupation with the pursuit of a definition of self. Interactions and negotiations with others lead to learning about themselves as independent, dependent, and interdependent beings. Sixteen-month-old infants explore not only the environment around them but also their power to choose how, what, and when they explore. At this stage they frequently resist the suggestions of those who provided their security when a choice is involved. They start to get a clearer understanding about distinctions between self and other, begin to feel the power of self to both choose and resist, and then at the end of the stage move toward learning early lessons about taking responsibility for their actions.

Here again the adult must make a switch in relating to the child. Providing security becomes an issue of setting boundaries to help children learn the rules of social behavior while letting each child know the adult is still there for him or her when boundaries are breached.

This rapid movement of the infant through three significant developmental stages and the need for the adult to be responsive to developmental shifts and the bumpy transitions between stages makes the work of the infant care teacher challenging. Just when a teacher seems to be getting things right with regard to a child, the child's major orientation shifts and the teacher is called on to adjust.

Curriculum planning, implementation, and supportive materials should not only anticipate developmental stages but also allow for individual variations in learning styles and temperaments. These elements need to be broad enough in scope to respond to all developmental domains simultaneously. Infancy's uniqueness, once again, needs to be considered.

4. Development of a first sense of self

In contrast to preschoolers and school-age children, infants are developing a first sense of self during their first two years. How they are treated and what they are allowed and expected to do and not to do are incorporated into the infant's developing self. Three-year-olds can take a stand, resist eating food they don't like, judge someone as mean or unfair. Infants can't. Instead, they take in the ways they are treated as examples of how things are, thinking, "This is the way people express emotions," "These are the things people get yelled at for," "These are the ways to approach people," and "This is how my inborn curiosity is accepted."

Children build a first sense of self through their interactions: "I am a person who is liked, encouraged, given choices, protected, listened to, or I am not." Infants pick up their definition of self by perceiving how they are treated by those who care for them. This distinction between the infant, in the process of developing a first sense of self, and the older child, acting from a newly formed sense of self, has many implications for care.

Infant care teachers must understand that they are taking part in the creation of a baby's first sense of self, that they are molding and shaping the way babies see themselves. The baby is innocent, trusting, and unguarded and takes in as the necessary information to build a sense of self the messages from those giving her care. Thus, the infant care teacher's job carries with it a great degree of responsibility in influencing the way the child defines *self*. Creating a warm, caring, subjective relationship with the infant is more than nice; it significantly contributes to a child's positive sense of self. As noted Reggio Emilia pedagogist Carlina Rinaldi (2006) describes, "Learning and loving are not so separate as we once thought."

Implications for Infant Care Teachers

These four areas of uniqueness—genetic wiring, holistic learning, rapidly changing developmental perspectives, and development of a child's first sense of self—make the infancy period different from all other age periods. This uniqueness makes it incumbent upon adults who care for infants to treat them differently from older children. Because the infant is genetically programmed for specific learning, the role of the adult in supporting learning is one of respect for and responsiveness to the child's lessons rather than generating lessons for the child. Because early learning is holistic, plans to facilitate infants' learning need to be holistic. Because security, exploration, and identity formation manifest themselves differently during the infancy period, the way adults respond to these needs must fit with the child's developmental stage.

Infants are just becoming aware of themselves as individuals and are unable to pick, choose, and judge the appropriateness of messages they receive from others. Adults need to be particularly sensitive to their role in the infant's shaping of self, respectful of the uniqueness of infancy, and responsive to infants' particular way of functioning.

What Is and Isn't Responsive Care?

In general, infant care practice in the United States reflects a picture of curriculum extremes. One approach often used suggests that very young children only need safe environments and tender, loving care, and that specific attention to learning is inappropriate. Another common approach suggests that for infants to grow and develop cognitively they must be stimulated intellectually by adult-developed and -directed lessons and activities, carefully preplanned and then programmed into an infant's day. Both views fall short of meeting the needs of infants.

Loving care is an important base for learning but only half of what is needed. Adult-generated lessons violate the child's learning expectations. Most learning theorists and cognitive specialists affirm that infant interest needs to play a significant role in guiding teachers' selection of learning experiences, materials, and content (Shonkoff & Phillips 2000). Therefore, curriculum plans should focus not on games, tasks, and activities, but on ways to best create a social, emotional, and intellectual climate that supports child-initiated learning and imitation and builds and sustains positive relationships among adults and children. For example, in the area of language learning, spontaneously and responsively talking with infants is more effective in producing rich language than planning and sequencing language lessons (Hart & Risley 1995).

The infant care teacher's job carries with it a great degree of responsibility in influencing the way the child defines *self*.

Attention to children's interests, curiosity, and motivation is the place to begin curriculum planning. Then the environment must be seen as a crucial part of the curriculum, provoking interest and encouraging and supporting infants' learning agendas. And the stage for a responsive curriculum must be set by establishing program policies that create a climate for learning.

Planning the Responsive Curriculum

Curricula and lesson plans for infants must center on their needs and interests and guide the development of environments,

selection of materials, and supportive interaction styles that are responsive to infants' needs and interests. Plans should engender respect for the competencies that infants bring to each interaction and reflect children's need for relationship-based experiences.

Responsive curriculum planning focuses on finding strategies to help infant care teachers search for, support, and keep alive children's internal motivation to learn and spontaneous explorations of people and things that are naturally of interest and important to them. Planning to work responsively with infants can begin with the study of the specific infant children in care. Each child's unique thoughts, feelings, needs, and interests are a significant part of the equation in developing plans. Records of each child's interests and skills should be kept to guide adults in creating the role they will take in each child's learning.

Adaptation and change are an expected and critical part of the planning process. Once an interaction with a child or small group of children begins, an infant care teacher is ready to adapt his or her plans and actions to meet the momentary and long-term needs and interests of each child. Good plans always include a number of alternative strategies and approaches.

Lesson plans, appropriately developed, include strategies to broaden infant care teachers' understanding of and deepen their relationship with each child served. In addition, plans specify content and materials. Good plans (1) reflect activities that orient the caregiver to the role of facilitator of learning rather than the role of teacher and (2) assist the infant care teacher in reading the cues each infant projects.

Conclusion

In a responsive curriculum a good portion of the work has to do with infant care teachers preparing themselves and the environment so that infants can learn, not figuring out what to teach infants. Then, program planning involves exploring ways to help infant care teachers attune themselves to each infant they serve and learn from the individual infant what he or she needs, thinks, and feels. Regardless of what daily plans look like, positive learning relies on a curriculum and lesson planning that includes

- attending to the development of a safe and interesting place for learning;
- selecting appropriate materials for meeting the individual needs and interests of the children served;
- organizing learning and care in small groups;
- developing management policies that maximize children's sense of security in care and continuity of connection with their caregivers;
- building ways to optimize program connections with children's families; and
- grounding caregivers in the cognitive, social, and emotional experiences in which infants and toddlers are naturally interested.

As we construct programs, let's keep the infant foremost in our minds. Let's ensure that our first goal is meeting infant needs for intimate, nurturing relationships through which a child can have safe, interesting experiences. Carlina Rinaldi's words remind us that "infants and toddlers should be the primary focus of reference for constructing services" (1991). If we let these words be our guide, we will help facilitate the development of motivated, powerful, competent, emotionally healthy, and intellectually curious children.

Program planning involves exploring ways to help infant care teachers attune themselves to each infant they serve.

References

Fraiberg, S., V. Shapiro, & D.S. Cherness. 1980. Treatment modalities. In *Clinical studies in infant mental health: The first year of life,* ed. S. Fraiberg. New York: Basic.

Gerber, M. 1988. *Respectfully yours: Magda Gerber's approach to professional infant/toddler care.* Video. Produced by J. Ronald Lally. Sacramento: California Department of Education.

Hart, B., & R.R. Risley. 1995. *Meaningful differences in the experiences of young American children.* Baltimore, MD: Brookes.

Rinaldi, C. 1991. Quality infant/toddler care. Presentation at the annual conference of the National Association for the Education of Young Children, Denver.

Rinaldi, C. 2006. *New perspectives in infant/toddler care.* DVD. Produced by J. Ronald Lally. Sacramento: California Department of Education.

Shonkoff, J.P., & D.A. Phillips, eds. 2000. *From neurons to neighborhoods: The science of early childhood development.* A report of the National Research Council. Washington, DC: National Academies Press.

J. RONALD LALLY, EdD, is codirector of the Center for Child and Family Studies at WestEd, an educational research and development laboratory in San Francisco. For many years he taught at Syracuse University, chaired its Department of Child and Family Studies, and directed the Family Development Research Program. He is a founder of *Zero to Three* and a recipient of the 2004 California Head Start Association Founder's Award.

PETER MANGIONE, PhD, is codirector of WestEd's Center for Child and Family Studies. He has worked extensively in the fields of child development, early childhood education, family support services, research and evaluation design, and public policy, and helped to make the Program for Infant/Toddler Caregivers a national model for training early childhood practitioners.

Reading Your Baby's Mind

**New research on infants finally begins to answer
the question: what's going on in there?**

PAT WINGERT AND MARTHA BRANT

Little Victoria Bateman is blond and blue-eyed and as cute a baby as there ever was. At 6 months, she is also trusting and unsuspecting, which is a good thing, because otherwise she'd never go along with what's about to happen. It's a blistering June afternoon in Lubbock, Texas, and inside the Human Sciences lab at Texas Tech University, Victoria's mother is settling her daughter into a high chair, where she is the latest subject in an ongoing experiment aimed at understanding the way babies think. Sybil Hart, an associate professor of human development and leader of the study, trains video cameras on mother and daughter. Everything is set. Hart hands Cheryl Bateman a children's book, "Elmo Pops In," and instructs her to engross herself in its pages. "Just have a conversation with me about the book," Hart tells her. "The most important thing is, do not look at [Victoria.]" As the two women chat, Victoria looks around the room, impassive and a little bored.

After a few minutes, Hart leaves the room and returns cradling a lifelike baby doll. Dramatically, Hart places it in Cheryl Bateman's arms, and tells her to cuddle the doll while continuing to ignore Victoria. "That's OK, little baby," Bateman coos, hugging and rocking the doll. Victoria is not bored anymore. At first, she cracks her best smile, showcasing a lone stubby tooth. When that doesn't work, she begins kicking. But her mom pays her no mind. That's when Victoria loses it. Soon she's beet red and crying so hard it looks like she might spit up. Hart rushes in. "OK, we're done," she says, and takes back the doll. Cheryl Bateman goes to comfort her daughter. "I've never seen her react like that to anything," she says. Over the last 10 months, Hart has repeated the scenario hundreds of times. It's the same in nearly every case: tiny babies, overwhelmed with jealousy. Even Hart was stunned to find that infants could experience an emotion, which, until recently, was thought to be way beyond their grasp.

And that's just for starters. The helpless, seemingly clueless infant staring up at you from his crib, limbs flailing, drool oozing, has a lot more going on inside his head than you ever imagined. A wealth of new research is leading pediatricians and child psychologists to rethink their long-held beliefs about the emotional and intellectual abilities of even very young babies. In 1890, psychologist William James famously described an infant's view of the world as "one great blooming, buzzing confusion." It was a notion that held for nearly a century: infants were simple-minded creatures who merely mimicked those around them and grasped only the most basic emotions—happy, sad, angry. Science is now giving us a much different picture of what goes on inside their hearts and heads. Long before they form their first words or attempt the feat of sitting up, they are already mastering complex emotions—jealousy, empathy, frustration—that were once thought to be learned much later in toddlerhood.

They are also far more sophisticated intellectually than we once believed. Babies as young as 4 months have advanced powers of deduction and an ability to decipher intricate patterns. They have a strikingly nuanced visual palette, which enables them to notice small differences, especially in faces, that adults and older children lose the ability to see. Until a baby is 3 months old, he can recognize a scrambled photograph of his mother just as quickly as a photo in which everything is in the right place. And big brothers and sisters beware: your sib has a long memory—and she can hold a grudge.

Babies yet to utter an INTELLIGENT SYLLABLE are now known to feel a range of COMPLEX EMOTIONS like envy and empathy.

The new research is sure to enthrall new parents—See, Junior *is* a genius!—but it's more than just an academic exercise. Armed with the new information, pediatricians are starting to change the way they evaluate their youngest patients. In addition to tracking physical development, they are now focusing much more deeply on emotional advancement. The research shows how powerful emotional well-being is to a child's future health. A baby who fails to meet certain key "emotional milestones" may have trouble learning to speak, read and, later, do well in school. By reading emotional responses, doctors have begun to discover ways to tell if a baby as young as 3 months is showing early signs of possible psychological disorders, including depression, anxiety, learning disabilities and perhaps autism. "Instead of just asking if they're crawling or sitting, we're asking more questions about how they share their world with their caregivers," says Dr. Chet Johnson, chairman of the American Academy of Pediatrics' early-childhood committee. "Do they point to things? When they see a new person, how do they react? How children do on social and emotional and language skills are better predictors of success in adulthood than motor skills are." The goal: in the not-too-distant future, researchers hope doctors will routinely identify at-risk kids years earlier than they do now—giving parents crucial extra time to turn things around.

One of the earliest emotions that even tiny babies display is, admirably enough, empathy. In fact, concern for others may be hard-wired into babies' brains. Plop a newborn down next to another crying infant, and chances are, both babies will soon be wailing away. "People have always known that babies cry when they hear other babies cry," says Martin Hoffman, a psychology professor at New York University who did the first studies on infant empathy in the 1970s. "The question was, why are they crying?" Does it mean that the baby is truly concerned for his fellow human, or just annoyed by the racket? A recent study conducted in Italy, which built on Hoffman's own work, has largely settled the question. Researchers played for infants tapes of other babies crying. As predicted, that was enough to start the tears flowing. But when researchers played babies recordings of their own cries, they rarely began crying themselves. The verdict: "There is some rudimentary empathy in place, right from birth," Hoffman says. The intensity of the emotion tends to fade over time. Babies older than 6 months no longer cry but grimace at the discomfort of others. By 13 to 15 months, babies tend to take matters into their own hands. They'll try to comfort a crying playmate. "What I find most charming is when, even if the two mothers are present, they'll bring their own mother over to help," Hoffman says.

Part of that empathy may come from another early-baby skill that's now better understood, the ability to discern emotions from the facial expressions of the people around them. "Most textbooks still say that babies younger than 6 months don't recognize emotions," says Diane Montague, assistant professor of psychology at LaSalle University in Philadelphia. To put that belief to the test, Montague came up with a twist on every infant's favorite game, peekaboo, and recruited dozens of 4-month-olds to play along. She began by peeking around a cloth with a big smile on her face. Predictably, the babies were delighted, and stared at her intently—the time-tested way to tell if a baby is interested. On the fourth peek, though, Montague emerged with a sad look on her face. This time, the response was much different. "They not only looked away," she says, but wouldn't look back even when she began smiling again. Refusing to make eye contact is a classic baby sign of distress. An angry face got their attention once again, but their faces showed no pleasure. "They seemed primed to be alert, even vigilant," Montague says. "I realize that's speculative in regard to infants … I think it shows that babies younger than 6 months find meaning in expressions."

This might be a good place to pause for a word about the challenges and perils of baby research. Since the subjects can't speak for themselves, figuring out what's going on inside their heads is often a matter of reading their faces and body language. If this seems speculative, it's not. Over decades of trial and error, researchers have fine-tuned their observation skills and zeroed in on numerous consistent baby responses to various stimuli: how long they stare at an object, what they reach out for and what makes them recoil in fear or disgust can often tell experienced researchers everything they need to know. More recently, scientists have added EEGs and laser eye tracking, which allow more precise readings. Coming soon: advanced MRI scans that will allow a deeper view inside the brain.

When infants near their first birthdays, they become increasingly sophisticated social learners. They begin to infer what others are thinking by following the gaze of those around them. "By understanding others' gaze, babies come to understand others' minds," says Andrew Meltzoff, a professor of psychology at the University of Washington who has studied the "gaze following" of thousands of babies. "You can tell a lot about people, what they're interested in and what they intend to do next, by watching their eyes. It appears that even babies know that … This is how they learn to become expert members of our culture."

Meltzoff and colleague Rechele Brooks have found that this skill first appears at 10 to 11 months, and is not only an important marker of a baby's emotional and social growth, but can predict later language development. In their study, babies who weren't proficient at gaze-following by their first birthday had much less advanced-language skills at 2. Meltzoff says this helps explain why language occurs more slowly in blind children, as well as children of depressed mothers, who tend not to interact as much with their babies.

In fact, at just a few months, infants begin to develop superpowers when it comes to observation. Infants can easily tell the difference between human faces. But at the University of Minnesota, neuroscientist Charles Nelson (now of Harvard) wanted to test how discerning infants really are. He showed a group of 6-month-old babies a photo of a chimpanzee, and gave them time to stare at it until they lost interest. They were then shown another chimp. The babies perked up and stared at the new photo. The infants easily recognized each chimp as an individual—they were fascinated by each new face. Now unless you spend a good chunk of your day hanging around the local zoo, chances are you couldn't tell the difference between a roomful of chimps at a glance. As it turned out, neither could babies just a few months older. By 9 months, those kids had lost the ability to tell chimps apart; but at the same time, they had increased their powers of observation when it came to human faces.

Nelson has now taken his experiment a step further, to see how early babies can detect subtle differences in facial expressions, a key building block of social development. He designed a new study that is attempting to get deep inside babies' heads by measuring brain-wave activity. Nelson sent out letters to the parents of nearly every newborn in the area, inviting them to participate. Earlier this summer it was Dagny Winberg's turn. The 7-month-old was all smiles as her mother, Armaiti, carried her into the lab, where she was fitted with a snug cap wired with 64 sponge sensors. Nelson's assistant, grad student Meg Moulson, began flashing photographs on a screen of a woman. In each photo, the woman had a slightly different expression— many different shades of happiness and fear. Dagny was given time to look at each photo until she became bored and looked away. The whole time, a computer was closely tracking her brain activity, measuring her mind's minutest responses to the different photos. Eventually, after she'd run through 60 photos, Dagny had had enough of the game and began whimpering and fidgeting. That ended the session. The point of the experiment is to see if baby brain scans look like those of adults. "We want to see if babies categorize emotions in the ways that adults do," Moulson says. "An adult can see a slight smile and categorize it as happy. We want to know if babies can do the same." They don't have the answer yet, but Nelson believes that infants who display early signs of emotional disorders, such as autism, may be helped if they can develop these critical powers of observation and emotional engagement.

Halfway across the country, researchers are working to dispel another baby cliché: out of sight, out of mind. It was long believed that babies under 9 months didn't grasp the idea of "object permanence"—the ability to know, for instance, that when Mom leaves the room, she isn't gone forever. New research by psychologist Su-hua Wang at the University of California, Santa Cruz, is showing that babies understand the concept as early as 10 weeks. Working with 2- and 3-month-olds, she performs a little puppet show. Each baby sees a duck on a stage. Wang covers the duck, moves it across the stage and lifts the cover. Sometimes the duck is there. Other times, the duck disappears beneath a trapdoor. When they see the duck has gone missing, the babies stare intently at the empty stage, searching for it. "At 2½ months," she says, "they already have the idea that the object continues to exist."

A strong, well-developed ability to connect with the world— and with parents in particular—is especially important when babies begin making their first efforts at learning to speak. Baby talk is much more than mimickry. Michael Goldstein, a psychologist at Cornell University, gathered two groups of 8-month-olds and decked them out in overalls rigged up with wireless microphones and transmitters. One group of mothers was told to react immediately when their babies cooed or babbled, giving them big smiles and loving pats. The other group of parents was also told to smile at their kids, but randomly, unconnected to the babies' sounds. It came as no surprise that the babies who received immediate feedback babbled more and advanced quicker than those who didn't. But what interested Goldstein was the way in which the parents, without realizing it, raised the "babble bar" with their kids. "The kinds of simple sounds that get parents' attention at 4 months don't get the same reaction at 8 months," he says. "That motivates babies to experiment with different sound combinations until they find new ones that get noticed."

A decade ago Patricia Kuhl, a professor of speech and hearing at the University of Washington and a leading authority on early language, proved that tiny babies have a unique ability to learn a foreign language. As a result of her well-publicized findings, parents ran out to buy foreign-language tapes, hoping their little Einsteins would pick up Russian or French before they left their cribs. It didn't work, and Kuhl's new research

shows why. Kuhl put American 9-month-olds in a room with Mandarin-speaking adults, who showed them toys while talking to them. After 12 sessions, the babies had learned to detect subtle Mandarin phonetic sounds that couldn't be heard by a separate group of babies who were exposed only to English. Kuhl then repeated the experiment, but this time played the identical Mandarin lessons to babies on video- and audiotape. That group of babies failed to learn any Mandarin. Kuhl says that without the emotional connection, the babies considered the tape recording just another background noise, like a vacuum cleaner. "We were genuinely surprised by the outcome," she says. "We all assumed that when infants stare at a television, and look engaged, that they are learning from it." Kuhl says there's plenty of work to be done to explain why that isn't true. "But at first blush one thinks that people—at least babies—need people to learn."

So there you have it. That kid over there with one sock missing and smashed peas all over his face is actually a formidable presence, in possession of keen powers of observation, acute emotional sensitivity and an impressive arsenal of deductive powers. "For the last 15 years, we've been focused on babies' abilities—what they know and when they knew it," says the University of Washington's Meltzoff. "But now we want to know what all this predicts about later development. What does all this mean for the child?"

Some of these questions are now finding answers. Take shyness, for instance. It's long been known that 15 to 20 percent of children are shy and anxious by nature. But doctors didn't know why some seemed simply to grow out of it, while for others it became a debilitating condition. Recent studies conducted by Nathan Fox of the University of Maryland show that shyness is initially driven by biology. He proved it by wiring dozens of 9-month-olds to EEG machines and conducting a simple experiment. When greeted by a stranger, "behaviorally inhibited" infants tensed up, and showed more activity in the parts of the brain associated with anxiety and fear. Babies with outgoing personalities reached out to the stranger. Their EEG scans showed heightened activity in the parts of the brain that govern positive emotions like pleasure.

Just because your baby is MORE PERCEPTIVE than you thought doesn't mean she'll be DAMAGED if she cries for a minute.

But Fox, who has followed some of these children for 15 years, says that parenting style has a big impact on which kind of adult a child will turn out to be. Children of overprotective parents, or those whose parents didn't encourage them to overcome shyness and childhood anxiety, often remain shy and anxious as adults. But kids born to confident and sensitive parents who gently help them to take emotional risks and coax them out of their shells can often overcome early awkwardness. That's an important finding, since behaviorally inhibited kids are also at higher risk for other problems.

Stanley Greenspan, clinical professor of psychiatry and pediatrics at George Washington University Medical School, is one of the leaders in developing diagnostic tools to help doctors identify babies who may be at risk for language and learning problems, autism and a whole range of other problems. He recently completed a checklist of social and emotional "milestones" that babies should reach by specific ages (graphic). "I'd like to see doctors screen babies for these milestones and tell parents exactly what to do if their babies are not mastering them. One of our biggest problems now is that parents may sense intuitively that something is not right," but by the time they are able to get their child evaluated, "that family has missed a critical time to, maybe, get that baby back on track."

So what should parents do with all this new information? First thing: relax. Just because your baby is more perceptive than you might have thought doesn't mean she's going to be damaged for life if she cries in her crib for a minute while you answer the phone. Or that he'll wind up quitting school and stealing cars if he witnesses an occasional argument between his parents. Children crave—and thrive on—interaction, one-on-one time and lots of eye contact. That doesn't mean filling the baby's room with "educational" toys and posters. A child's social, emotional and academic life begins with the earliest conversations between parent and child: the first time the baby locks eyes with you; the quiet smile you give your infant and the smile she gives you back. Your child is speaking to you all the time. It's just a matter of knowing how to listen.

With **T. TRENT GEGAX, MARGARET NELSON, KAREN BRESLAU, NADINE JOSEPH AND BEN WHITFORD**

The Trouble with Boys

They're kinetic, maddening and failing at school. Now educators are trying new ways to help them succeed.

Peg Tyre

Spend a few minutes on the phone with Danny Frankhuizen and you come away thinking, "What a *nice* boy." He's thoughtful, articulate, bright. He has a good relationship with his mom, goes to church every Sunday, loves the rock band Phish and spends hours each day practicing his guitar. But once he's inside his large public Salt Lake City high school, everything seems to go wrong. He's 16, but he can't stay organized. He finishes his homework and then can't find it in his backpack. He loses focus in class, and his teachers, with 40 kids to wrangle, aren't much help. "If I miss a concept, they tell me, 'Figure it out yourself'," says Danny. Last year Danny's grades dropped from B's to D's and F's. The sophomore, who once dreamed of Stanford, is pulling his grades up but worries that "I won't even get accepted at community college."

44%—The number of male undergraduates on college campuses; 30 years ago, the number was 58%.

His mother, Susie Malcom, a math teacher who is divorced, says it's been wrenching to watch Danny stumble. "I tell myself he's going to make something good out of himself," she says. "But it's hard to see doors close and opportunities fall away."

What's wrong with Danny? By almost every benchmark, boys across the nation and in every demographic group are falling behind. In elementary school, boys are two times more likely than girls to be diagnosed with learning disabilities and twice as likely to be placed in special-education classes. High-school boys are losing ground to girls on standardized writing tests. The number of boys who said they didn't like school rose 71 percent between 1980 and 2001, according to a University of Michigan study. Nowhere is the shift more evident than on college campuses. Thirty years ago men represented 58 percent of the undergraduate student body. Now they're a minority at 44 percent. This widening achievement gap, says Margaret Spellings, U.S. Secretary of Education, "has profound implications for the economy, society, families and democracy."

With millions of parents wringing their hands, educators are searching for new tools to help tackle the problem of boys. Books including Michael Thompson's best seller "Raising Cain" (recently made into a PBS documentary) and Harvard psychologist William Pollack's definitive work "Real Boys" have become must-reads in the teachers' lounge. The Gurian Institute, founded in 1997 by family therapist Michael Gurian to help the people on the front lines help boys, has enrolled 15,000 teachers in its seminars. Even the Gates Foundation, which in the last five years has given away nearly a billion dollars to innovative high schools, is making boys a big priority. "Helping underperforming boys," says Jim Shelton, the foundation's education director, "has become part of our core mission."

The problem won't be solved overnight. In the last two decades, the education system has become obsessed with a quantifiable and narrowly defined kind of academic success, these experts say, and that myopic view is harming boys. Boys are biologically, developmentally and psychologically different from girls—and teachers need to learn how to bring out the best in every one. "Very well-meaning people," says Dr. Bruce Perry, a Houston neurologist who advocates for troubled kids, "have created a biologically disrespectful model of education."

Thirty years ago it was girls, not boys, who were lagging. The 1972 federal law Title IX forced schools to provide equal opportunities for girls in the classroom and on the playing field. Over the next two decades, billions of dollars were funneled into finding new ways to help girls achieve. In 1992, the American Association of University Women issued a report claiming that the work of Title IX was not done—girls still fell behind in math and science; by the mid-1990s, girls had reduced the gap in math and more girls than boys were taking high-school-level biology and chemistry.

'Often boys are treated like defective girls,' says Thompson.

Some scholars, notably Christina Hoff Sommers, a fellow at the American Enterprise Institute, charge that misguided

Elementary School

Boys start off with lower literacy skills than girls, and are less often encouraged to read, which only widens the gap.

■ Girls ages 3 to 5 are **5%** more likely than boys to be read to at home at least three times a week.

■ Girls are **10%** more likely than boys to recognize words by sight by the spring of first grade.

■ Boys ages 5 to 12 are **60%** more likely than girls to have repeated at least one grade.

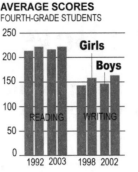

AVERAGE SCORES
FOURTH-GRADE STUDENTS

■ Girls' reading scores improve **6%** more than boys' between kindergarten and third grade.

■ First- to fifth-grade boys are **47%** more likely than girls to have disabilities such as emotional disturbances, learning problems or speech impediments.

■ Fourth-grade girls score **3%** higher on standardized reading tests than boys.

■ Fourth-grade girls score **12%** higher on writing tests than boys.

Figure 1

Sources: U.S. Department of Education, Centers for Disease Control

---

feminism is what's been hurting boys. In the 1990s, she says, girls were making strong, steady progress toward parity in schools, but feminist educators portrayed them as disadvantaged and lavished them with support and attention. Boys, meanwhile, whose rates of achievement had begun to falter, were ignored and their problems allowed to fester.

Standardized tests have become common for kids as young as 6.

Boys have always been boys, but the expectations for how they're supposed to act and learn in school have changed. In the last 10 years, thanks in part to activist parents concerned about their children's success, school performance has been measured in two simple ways: how many students are enrolled in accelerated courses and whether test scores stay high. Standardized assessments have become commonplace for kids as young as 6. Curricula have become more rigid. Instead of allowing teachers to instruct kids in the manner and pace that suit each class, some states now tell teachers what, when and how to teach. At the same time, student-teacher ratios have risen, physical education and sports programs have been cut and recess is a distant memory. These new pressures are undermining the strengths and underscoring the limitations of what psychologists call the "boy brain"—the kinetic, disorganized, maddening and sometimes brilliant behaviors that scientists now believe are not learned but hard-wired.

When Cris Messler of Mountainside, N.J., brought her 3-year-old son Sam to a pediatrician to get him checked for ADHD, she was acknowledging the desperation parents can feel. He's a high-energy kid, and Messler found herself hoping

for a positive diagnosis. "If I could get a diagnosis from the doctor, I could get him on medicine," she says. The doctor said Sam is a normal boy. School has been tough, though. Sam's reading teacher said he was hopeless. His first-grade teacher complains he's antsy, and Sam, now 7, has been referring to himself as "stupid." Messler's glad her son doesn't need medication, but what, she wonders, can she do now to help her boy in school?

For many boys, the trouble starts as young as 5, when they bring to kindergarten a set of physical and mental abilities very different from girls'. As almost any parent knows, most 5-year-old girls are more fluent than boys and can sight-read more words. Boys tend to have better hand-eye coordination, but their fine motor skills are less developed, making it a struggle for some to control a pencil or a paintbrush. Boys are more impulsive than girls; even if they can sit still, many prefer not to—at least not for long.

Thirty years ago feminists argued that classic "boy" behaviors were a result of socialization, but these days scientists believe they are an expression of male brain chemistry. Sometime in the first trimester, a boy fetus begins producing male sex hormones that bathe his brain in testosterone for the rest of his gestation. "That exposure wires the male brain differently," says Arthur Arnold, professor of physiological science at UCLA. How? Scientists aren't exactly sure. New studies show that prenatal exposure to male sex hormones directly affects the way children play. Girls whose mothers have high levels of testosterone during pregnancy are more likely to prefer playing with trucks to playing with dolls. There are also clues that hormones influence the way we learn all through life. In a Dutch study published in 1994, doctors found that when males were given female hormones, their spatial skills dropped but their verbal skills improved.

Middle School

Coming of age in a culture that discourages bookishness, boys are more likely to fall victim to drugs and violence.

■ Eighth-grade girls score an average of **11 points** higher than eighth-grade boys on standardized reading tests.

■ Eighth-grade girls score **21 points** higher than boys on standardized writing tests.

■ Between 1993 and 2003, the number of ninth-grade boys who skipped school at least once a month because they didn't feel safe increased **22%.**

■ Boys between the ages of 5 and 14 are **200%** more likely to commit suicide than girls.

■ Ninth-grade boys are **78%** more likely than girls to get injured in a fight at least once a year.

■ Between the ages of 5 and 14, boys are **36%** more likely to die than their female counterparts.

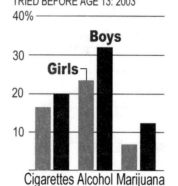

DRUG USE BY GENDER
TRIED BEFORE AGE 13: 2003

Figure 2

In elementary-school classrooms—where teachers increasingly put an emphasis on language and a premium on sitting quietly and speaking in turn—the mismatch between boys and school can become painfully obvious. "Girl behavior becomes the gold standard," says "Raising Cain" coauthor Thompson. "Boys are treated like defective girls."

Two years ago Kelley King, principal of Douglass Elementary School in Boulder, Colo., looked at the gap between boys and girls and decided to take action. Boys were lagging 10 points behind girls in reading and 14 points in writing. Many more boys—than girls were being labeled as learning disabled, too. So King asked her teachers to buy copies of Gurian's book "The Minds of Boys," on boy-friendly classrooms, and in the fall of 2004 she launched a bold experiment. Whenever possible, teachers replaced lecture time with fast-moving lessons that all kids could enjoy. Three weeks ago, instead of discussing the book "The View From Saturday," teacher Pam Unrau divided her third graders into small groups, and one student in each group pretended to be a character from the book. Classes are noisier, Unrau says, but the boys are closing the gap. Last spring, Douglass girls scored an average of 106 on state writing tests, while boys got a respectable 101.

Boys love video-games because when they lose, the defeat is private.

Primatologists have long observed that juvenile male chimps battle each other not just for food and females, but to establish and maintain their place in the hierarchy of the tribe. Primates face off against each other rather than appear weak. That same evolutionary imperative, psychologists say, can make it hard

for boys to thrive in middle school—and difficult for boys who are failing to accept the help they need. The transition to middle school is rarely easy, but like the juvenile primates they are, middle-school boys will do almost anything to avoid admitting that they're overwhelmed. "Boys measure everything they do or say by a single yardstick: does this make me look weak?" says Thompson. "And if it does, he isn't going to do it." That's part of the reason that videogames have such a powerful hold on boys: the action is constant, they can calibrate just how hard the challenges will be and, when they lose, the defeat is private.

When Brian Johns hit seventh grade, he never admitted how vulnerable it made him feel. "I got behind and never caught up," says Brian, now 17 and a senior at Grand River Academy, an Ohio boarding school. When his parents tried to help, he rebuffed them. When his mother, Anita, tried to help him organize his assignment book, he grew evasive about when his homework was due. Anita didn't know where to turn. Brian's school had a program for gifted kids, and support for ones with special needs. But what, Anita asked his teachers, do they do about kids like her son who are in the middle and struggling? Those kids, one of Brian's teachers told Anita, "are the ones who fall through the cracks."

It's easy for middle-school boys to feel outgunned. Girls reach sexual maturity two years ahead of boys, but other, less visible differences put boys at a disadvantage, too. The prefrontal cortex is a knobby region of the brain directly behind the forehead that scientists believe helps humans organize complex thoughts, control their impulses and understand the consequences of their own behavior. In the last five years, Dr. Jay Giedd, an expert in brain development at the National Institutes of Health, has used brain scans to show that in girls, it reaches its maximum thickness by the age of 11 and, for the next decade or more, continues to mature. In boys, this process is delayed by 18 months.

High School and Beyond

Many boys continue to fall behind girls in reading and writing proficiency, and fewer are going to college.

■ Boys are **33%** more likely than girls to drop out of high school.

■ Twelfth-grade girls score **16 points** higher than boys on standardized reading tests.

■ High-school boys are **30%** more likely to use cocaine than high-school girls.

AVERAGE TEST SCORES*
WRITING   READING

159   160
Girls
        289   292

Boys
140
        136
        282
        278

1998   2002   1980   2004
*TWELFTH-GRADE SCORES

■ Twelfth-grade girls score **24 points** higher than boys on standardized writing tests.

■ High-school girls are **36%** more likely to take Advanced Placement or honors biology than high-school boys.

■ **22%** more high-school girls are planning to go to college than boys.

■ The percentage of male undergraduates dropped **24%** from 1970 to 2000.

Figure 3

Middle-school boys may use their brains less efficiently than girls.

Middle-school boys may use their brains less efficiently, too. Using a type of MRI that traces activity in the brain, Deborah Yurgelun-Todd, director of the cognitive neuroimaging laboratory at McLean Hospital in Belmont, Mass., tested the activity patterns in the prefrontal cortex of children between the ages of 11 and 18. When shown pictures of fearful faces, adolescent girls registered activity on the right side of the prefrontal cortex, similar to an adult. Adolescent boys used both sides—a less mature pattern of brain activity. Teenage girls can process information faster, too. In a study about to be published in the journal Intelligence, researchers at Vanderbilt University administered timed tests—picking similar objects and matching groups of numbers—to 8,000 boys and girls between the ages of 5 and 18. In kindergarten, boys and girls processed information at about the same speeds. In early adolescence, girls finished faster and got more right. By 18, boys and girls were processing with the same speed and accuracy.

Scientists caution that brain research doesn't tell the whole story: temperament, family background and environment play big roles, too. Some boys are every bit as organized and assertive as the highest-achieving girls. All kids can be scarred by violence, alcohol or drugs in the family. But if your brain hasn't reached maturity yet, says Yurgelun-Todd, "it's not going to be able to do its job optimally."

Across the nation, educators are reviving an old idea: separate the girls from the boys—and at Roncalli Middle School, in Pueblo, Colo., administrators say, it's helping kids of both genders. This past fall, with the blessing of parents, school guidance counselor Mike Horton assigned a random group of 50 sixth graders to single-sex classes in core subjects. These days, when sixth-grade science teacher Pat Farrell assigns an earth-science lab on measuring crystals, the girls collect their materials—a Bunsen burner, a beaker of phenyl salicylate and a spoon. Then they read the directions and follow the sequence from beginning to end. The first things boys do is ask, "Can we eat this?" They're less organized, Farrell notes, but sometimes, "they're willing to go beyond what the lab asks them to do." With this in mind, he hands out written instructions to both classes but now goes over them step by step for the boys. Although it's too soon to declare victory, there are some positive signs: the shyest boys are participating more. This fall, the all-girl class did best in math, English and science, followed by the all-boy class and then coed classes.

One of the most reliable predictors of whether a boy will succeed or fail in high school rests on a single question: does he have a man in his life to look up to? Too often, the answer is no. High rates of divorce and single motherhood have created a generation of fatherless boys. In every kind of neighborhood, rich or poor, an increasing number of boys—now a startling 40 percent—are being raised without their biological dads.

Psychologists say that grandfathers and uncles can help, but emphasize that an adolescent boy without a father figure is like an explorer without a map. And that is especially true for poor boys and boys who are struggling in school. Older males, says Gurian, model self-restraint and solid work habits for younger ones. And whether they're breathing down their necks about grades or admonishing them to show up for school on time, "an older man reminds a boy in a million different ways that school is crucial to their mission in life."

A boy without a father figure is like an explorer without a map.

In the past, boys had many opportunities to learn from older men. They might have been paired with a tutor, apprenticed to a master or put to work in the family store. High schools offered boys a rich array of roles in which to exercise leadership skills—class officer, yearbook editor or a place on the debate team. These days, with the exception of sports, more girls than boys are involved in those activities.

'An older man reminds a boy that school is crucial to life,' says Gurian.

In neighborhoods where fathers are most scarce, the high-school dropout rates are shocking: more than half of African-American boys who start high school don't finish. David Banks, principal of the Eagle Academy for Young Men, one of four all-boy public high schools in the New York City system, wants each of his 180 students not only to graduate from high school but to enroll in college. And he's leaving nothing to chance. Almost every Eagle Academy boy has a male mentor—a lawyer, a police officer or an entrepreneur from the school's South Bronx neighborhood. The impact of the mentoring program, says Banks, has been "beyond profound." Tenth grader Rafael Mendez is unequivocal: his mentor "is the best thing that ever happened to me." Before Rafael came to Eagle Academy, he dreamed about playing pro baseball, but his mentor, Bronx Assistant District Attorney Rafael Curbelo, has shown him

another way to succeed: Mendez is thinking about attending college in order to study forensic science.

Colleges would welcome more applications from young men like Rafael Mendez. At many state universities the gender balance is already tilting 60-40 toward women. Primary and secondary schools are going to have to make some major changes, says Ange Peterson, president-elect of the American Association of Collegiate Registrars and Admissions Officers, to restore the gender balance. "There's a whole group of men we're losing in education completely," says Peterson.

For Nikolas Arnold, 15, a sophomore at a public high school in Santa Monica, Calif., college is a distant dream. Nikolas is smart: he's got an encyclopedic knowledge of weaponry and war. When he was in first grade, his principal told his mother he was too immature and needed ADHD drugs. His mother balked. "Too immature?" says Diane Arnold, a widow. "He was six and a half!" He's always been an advanced reader, but his grades are erratic. Last semester, when his English teacher assigned two girls' favorites—"Memoirs of a Geisha" and "The Secret Life of Bees" Nikolas got a D. But lately, he has a math teacher he likes and is getting excited about numbers. He's reserved in class sometimes. But now that he's more engaged, his grades are improving slightly and his mother, who's pushing college, is hopeful he will begin to hit his stride. Girls get A's and B's on their report cards, she tells him, but that doesn't mean boys can't do it, too.

With Andrew Murr, Vanessa Juarez,
Anne Underwood, Karen Springen and Pat Wingert

What Does It Mean to Educate the Whole Child?

In a democratic society, schools must go beyond teaching fundamental skills.

NEL NODDINGS

Public schools in the United States today are under enormous pressure to show—through improved test scores—that they are providing every student with a thorough and efficient education. The staled intention of No Child Left Behind (NCLB) is to accomplish this goal and reverse years of failure to educate many of our inner-city and minority children. But even if we accept that the motives behind NCLB are benign, the law seems fatally flawed.

Some critics have declared NCLB an unfunded mandate because it makes costly demands without providing the resources to meet them. Others point to its bureaucratic complexity; its unattainable main goal (100 percent of students proficient in reading and math by 2014); its motivationally undesirable methods (threats, punishments, and pernicious comparisons); its overdependence on standardized tests; its demoralizing effects; and its corrupting influences on administrators, teachers, and students.

All these criticisms are important, but NCLB has a more fundamental problem: its failure to address, or even ask, the basic questions raised in this issue of *Educational Leadership:* What are the proper aims of education? How do public schools serve a democratic society? What does it mean to educate the whole child?

The Aims of Education

Every flourishing society has debated the aims of education. This debate cannot produce final answers, good for all times and all places, because the aims of education are tied to the nature and ideals of a particular society. But the aims promoted by NCLB are clearly far too narrow. Surely, we should demand more from our schools than to educate people to be proficient in reading and mathematics. Too many highly proficient people commit fraud, pursue paths to success marked by greed, and care little about how their actions affect the lives of others.

Surely, we should demand more from our schools than to educate people to be proficient in reading and mathematics.

Some people argue that schools are best organized to accomplish academic goals and that we should charge other institutions with the task of pursuing the physical, moral, social, emotional, spiritual, and aesthetic aims that we associate with the whole child. The schools would do a better job, these people maintain, if they were freed to focus on the job for which they were established.

Those who make this argument have not considered the history of education. Public schools in the United States—as well as schools across different societies and historical eras—were established as much for moral and social reasons as for academic instruction. In his 1818 *Report of the Commissioners for the University of Virginia,* for example, Thomas Jefferson included in the "objects of primary education" such qualities as morals, understanding of duties to neighbors and country, knowledge of rights, and intelligence and faithfulness in social relations.

Periodically since then, education thinkers have described and analyzed the multiple aims of education. For example, the National Education Association listed seven aims in its 1918 report, *Cardinal Principles of Secondary Education:* (1) health; (2) command of the fundamental processes; (3) worthy home membership; (4) vocation; (5) citizenship; (6) worthy use of leisure; and (7) ethical character (Kliebard, 1995, p. 98). Later in the century, educators trying to revive the progressive tradition advocated open education, which aimed to encourage creativity, invention, cooperation, and democratic participation in the classroom and in lifelong learning (Silberman, 1973).

Recently, I have suggested another aim: happiness (Noddings, 2003). Great thinkers have associated happiness with such qualities as a rich intellectual life, rewarding human relationships, love of home and place, sound character, good parenting, spirituality and a job that one loves. We incorporate this aim into education not only by helping our students understand the components of happiness but also by making classrooms genuinely happy places.

Few of these aims can be pursued directly, the way we attack behavioral objectives. Indeed, I dread the day when I will enter a classroom and find *Happiness* posted as an instructional objective. Although I may be able to state exactly what students should be able to do when it comes to adding fractions, I cannot make such specific statements about happiness, worthy home membership, use of leisure, or ethical character. These great aims are meant to guide our instructional decisions. They are meant to broaden our thinking—to remind us to ask why we have chosen certain curriculums, pedagogical methods, classroom arrangements, and learning objectives. They remind us, too, that students are whole persons—not mere collections of attributes, some to be addressed in one place and others to be addressed elsewhere.

In insisting that schools and other social institutions share responsibility for nurturing the whole child, I recognize that different institutions will have different emphases. Obviously, schools will take greater responsibility for teaching reading and arithmetic; medical clinics for health checkups and vaccinations; families for housing and clothing; and places of worship for spiritual instruction.

But needs cannot be rigidly compartmentalized. The massive human problems of society demand holistic treatment. For example, leading medical clinics are now working with lawyers and social workers to improve housing conditions for children and to enhance early childhood learning (Shipler, 2004). We know that healthy families do much more than feed and clothe their children. Similarly, schools must be concerned with the total development of children.

Democracy and Schools

A productive discussion of education's aims must acknowledge that schools are established to serve both individuals and the larger society. What does the society expect of its schools?

From the current policy debates about public education, one would think that U.S. society simply needs competent workers who will keep the nation competitive in the world market. But both history and common sense tell us that a democratic society expects much more: It wants graduates who exhibit sound character, have a social conscience, think critically, are willing to make commitments, and are aware of global problems (Soder, Goodlad, & McMannon, 2001).

In addition, a democratic society needs an education system that helps to sustain its democracy by developing thoughtful citizens who can make wise civic choices. By its very nature, as Dewey (1916) pointed out, a democratic society is continually changing—sometimes for the better, sometimes for the worse—and it requires citizens who are willing to participate and competent enough to distinguish between the better and the worse.

If we base policy debate about education on a serious consideration of society's needs, we will ask thoughtful questions: What modes of discipline will best contribute to the development of sound character? What kinds of peer interactions might help students develop a social conscience? What topics and issues will foster critical thinking? What projects and extracurricular activities might call forth social and personal commitment? Should we assign the task of developing global awareness to social studies courses, or should we spread the responsibility throughout the entire curriculum (Noddings, 2005b)?

In planning education programs for a democratic society, we must use our understanding of the aims of education to explore these questions and many more. Unfortunately, public policy in the United States today concentrates on just one of the *Cardinal Principles* proposed by NEA in 1918: "command of the fundamental processes." Although reading and math are important, we need to promote competence in these subjects while also promoting our other aims. Students can develop reading, writing, speaking, and mathematical skills as they plan and stage dramatic performances, design classroom murals, compose a school paper, and participate in establishing classroom rules.

If present reports about the effects of NCLB on the education of inner-city and minority children are supported by further evidence, we should be especially concerned about our democratic future. Wealthier students are enjoying a rich and varied curriculum and many opportunities to engage in the arts, whereas many of our less wealthy students spend their school days bent over worksheets in an effort to boost standardized test scores (Meier & Wood, 2004). Such reports call into question the notion that NCLB will improve schooling for our poorest students. Surely all students deserve rich educational experiences—experiences that will enable them to become active citizens in a democratic society.

All students deserve rich educational experiences that will enable them to become active citizens in a democratic society.

Life in a healthy democracy requires participation, and students must begin to practice participation in our schools. Working together in small groups can furnish such practice, provided that the emphasis is consistently on working together—not on formal group processes or the final grade for a product. Similarly, students can participate in establishing the rules that will govern classroom conduct. It is not sufficient, and it may actually

Aims of Education

The habits we form from childhood make no small difference, but rather they make all the difference.
—Aristotle

undermine our democracy, to concentrate on producing people who do well on standardized tests and who define success as getting a well-paid job. Democracy means more than voting and maintaining economic productivity, and life means more than making money and beating others to material goods.

The Whole Child

Most of us want to be treated as persons, not as the "sinus case in treatment room 3" or the "refund request on line 4." But we live under the legacy of bureaucratic thought—the idea that every physical and social function should be assigned to its own institution. In the pursuit of efficiency, we have remade ourselves into a collection of discrete attributes and needs. This legacy is strong in medicine, law, social work, business, and education.

Even when educators recognize that students are whole persons, the temptation arises to describe the whole in terms of collective parts and to make sure that every aspect, part, or attribute is somehow "covered" in the curriculum. Children are moral beings; therefore, we must provide character education programs. Children are artistically inclined; therefore, we must provide art classes. Children's physical fitness is declining; therefore, we must provide physical education and nutrition classes. And then we complain that the curriculum is overloaded!

We should not retreat to a curriculum advisory committee and ask, "Now where should we fit this topic into the already overloaded curriculum?" Although we cannot discard all the fragmented subjects in our present school system and start from scratch, we can and should ask all teachers to stretch their subjects to meet the needs and interests of the whole child. Working within the present subject-centered curriculum, we can ask math and science teachers as well as English and social studies teachers to address moral, social, emotional, and aesthetic questions with respect and sensitivity when they arise (Simon, 2001). In high school math classes, we can discuss Descartes' proof of God's existence (is it flawed?); the social injustices and spiritual longing in *Flatland*, Edwin Abbott's 1884 novel about geometry; the logic and illogic in *Alice's Adventures in Wonderland;* and the wonders of numbers such as ϕ and π.

For the most part, discussions of moral and social issues should respond to students' expressed needs, but some prior planning can be useful, too. When a math teacher recites a poem or reads a biographical piece or a science fiction story, when she points to the beauty or elegance of a particular result, when she pauses to discuss the social nature of scientific work, students may begin to see connections—to see a whole person at work (Noddings, 2005a). Teachers can also look carefully at the subjects that students are required to learn and ask, "How can I include history, literature, science, mathematics, and the arts in my own lessons?" This inclusion would in itself relieve the awful sense of fragmentation that students experience.

The benefits of a more holistic perspective can also extend beyond the academic curriculum and apply to the school climate and the issue of safety and security. Schools often tackle this problem the way they tackle most problems, piece by piece: more surveillance cameras, more security guards, better metal detectors, more locks, shorter lunch periods, more rules. It seems like a dream to remember that most schools 40 years ago had no security guards, cameras, or metal detectors. And yet schools are not safer now than they were in the 1960s and 1970s. We need to ask why there has been a decline in security and how we should address the problem. Do we need more prison-like measures, or is something fundamentally wrong with the entire school arrangement?

Almost certainly, the sense of community and trust in our schools has declined. Perhaps the most effective way to make our schools safer would be to restore this sense of trust. I am not suggesting that we get rid of all our security paraphernalia overnight, but rather that we ask what social arrangements might reduce the need for such measures. Smaller schools? Multiyear assignment of teachers and students? Class and school meetings to establish rules and discuss problems? Dedication to teaching the whole child in every class? Serious attention to the integration of subject matter? Gentle but persistent invitations to all students to participate? More opportunities to engage in the arts and in social projects? More encouragement to speak out with the assurance of being heard? More opportunities to work together? Less competition? Warmer hospitality for parents? More public forums on school issues? Reduction of test-induced stress? More opportunities for informal conversation? Expanding, not reducing, course offerings? Promoting the idea of fun and humor in learning? Educating teachers more broadly? All of the above?

> **If we base policy debate about education on a serious consideration of society's needs, we will ask thoughtful questions.**

We will not find the solution to problems of violence, alienation, ignorance, and unhappiness in increasing our security apparatus, imposing more tests, punishing schools for their failure to produce 100 percent proficiency, or demanding that teachers be knowledgeable in "the subjects they teach." Instead, we must allow teachers and students to interact as whole persons, and we must develop policies that treat the school as a whole community. The future of both our children and our democracy depend on our moving in this direction.

References

Dewey, J. (1916). *Democracy and education.* New York: Macmillan.

Jefferson, T. (1818). *Report of the commissioners for the University of Virginia.* Available: www.libertynet.org/edcivic/jefferva.html

Kliebard, H. (1995). *The struggle for the American curriculum.* New York: Routledge.

Meier, D., & Wood, G. (Eds.). (2004). *Many children left behind.* Boston: Beacon Press.

Noddings, N. (2003). *Happiness and education.* Cambridge, MA: Cambridge University Press.

Noddings, N. (2005a). *The challenge to care in schools* (2nd ed.). New York: Teachers College Press.

Noddings, N. (Ed.). (2005b). *Educating citizens for global awareness.* New York: Teachers College Press.

Shipler, D. K. (2004). *The working poor: Invisible in America.* New York: Alfred A. Knopf.

Silberman, C. E. (1973). *The open classroom reader.* New York: Vintage Books.

Simon, K. G. (2001). *Moral questions in the classroom.* New Haven, CT: Yale University Press.

Soder, R., Goodlad, J. I., & McMannon, T. J. (Eds.). (2001). *Developing democratic character in the young.* San Francisco: Jossey-Bass.

NEL NODDINGS resides in Ocean Grove, New Jersey and is **LEE L. JACKS** Professor of Education, Emerita, at Stanford University, Stanford, California; noddings@stanford.edu.

From *Educational Leadership,* September 2005, pp. 8–13. Reprinted by permission of the Association for Supervision and Curriculum Development. Copyright © 2005 by ASCD. All rights reserved. The Association for Supervision and Curriculum Development is a worldwide community of educators advocating sound policies and sharing best practices to achieve the success of each learner. To learn more, visit ASCD at www.ascd.org

What Can We Do to Prevent Childhood Obesity?

Julie Lumeng

Center for Human Growth and Development University of Michigan

Childhood obesity is a real and pressing public health problem in the United States. Moreover, the obesity epidemic is accelerating—even among babies and toddlers. Contrary to popular opinion, all the information available to date indicates that a child less than 3 years old who is overweight is no more likely to be overweight as a young adult than is a toddler who is not overweight. However, the same research indicates that an overweight 3-year-old child is nearly 8 times as likely to become an overweight young adult as is a typically developing 3-year-old (Whitaker, Wright, Pepe, Seidel, & Dietz, 1997). In other words, by the time a child is 3, she may be on the path to obesity in adulthood. If we assume that the weight status of a 3-year-old has taken some time to develop, we must conclude that factors predisposing children to overweight begin operating in children in the first 3 years of life.

What factors in the experience of infants and toddlers seem likely to account for childhood overweight? What evidence do we have to suggest that these factors do, in fact, influence obesity risk? If research findings are scarce (or shaky), what advice about preventing obesity can practitioners offer to parents and caregivers of babies and toddlers? What can we do at a public health and policy level to change our obesigenic (obesity-producing) environment? This article is an effort to answer these questions as fully as reliable research findings will allow. We will also define some terms that are used in medical discussions about childhood obesity; attempt to dispel some common misunderstandings about the causes of childhood obesity; and suggest some promising approaches for practice, research, and policy.

Definitions and Data

What is obesity in early childhood? *Obesity* is a term for excessive body fat. We measure body fat in anyone older than 24 months by calculating body mass index (BMI; weight in kilograms divided by the square of height in meters). Clinicians can plot a child's BMI on gender-specific charts provided by the National Center for Health Statistics (NCHS) of the Centers for Disease Control (CDC) (http://www.cdc.gov/growthcharts/). There are no BMI-for-age references or consistent definitions for overweight for children younger than 2 years. However,

nutrition programs such as the Special Supplemental Nutrition Program for Women, Infants and Children have used weight-for-length recommendations to determine overweight and thus program eligibility. Consequently, overweight in this age group is defined as at or above the 95th percentile of weight for length (Ogden, Flegal, Carroll, & Johnson, 2002). Thus, for the remainder of this discussion, we will use the term "overweight" to describe children aged 2 years to 18 years whose BMI falls at the 95th percentile or above.

> **An overweight 3-year-old child is nearly 8 times as likely to become an overweight young adult as is a typically developing 3-year-old.**

Why does BMI mean something different for adults than for children? Adults have stopped growing. Because an adult's height remains the same, one can look at the weight and height

At a Glance

- Rates of childhood obesity are increasing.
- Children less than 3 years old who are overweight are no more likely to be overweight in adulthood than are children who are not overweight, but 3-year-olds who are overweight are likely to be overweight in adulthood.
- Children learn many of their food preferences from their peers and from advertisements—not from their parents.
- Researchers have studied many possible factors in childhood obesity, such as genetics; the family's access to supermarkets and fresh, healthy foods; parents' attempts to limit when a child eats; and parents' attempts to make children eat more vegetables.

of an adult and calculate BMI in a straightforward fashion. But think about children. Who appears to be naturally "chubbier"—a healthy 3-year-old or a 5-year-old? The 3-year-old—because she is still losing her "baby fat." *All* children are naturally at their "skinniest" when they are between 4 and 6 years old. Then their BMI slowly increases. Compare a 10-year-old girl about to enter puberty to a 5-year old girl. The 10 year-old's BMI is higher, but that is as it should be, given her stage of development. In other words, different degrees of "adiposity" (fatness) are normal at different ages during childhood. Babies *should* be "fat"—but fat within the normal range on the NCHS weight-for-length charts. The 3-year-olds who are in the top 5% of the weight-for-length bell curve are much more likely to continue to be overweight into adulthood. And adults who are at the top end of the BMI bell curve are at increased risk for serious health problems.

Terminology aside, more of America's children are becoming overweight, and today's overweight children tend to be heavier than overweight children were in past years. These data are concerning for a number of reasons. First of all, the obesity epidemic is accelerating—even among our youngest children. For example, between 1976 and 2000, the prevalence of overweight in 6- to 23-month-old children increased from 7% to nearly 12%. Most of this increase occurred from 1990 to 2000. Among 2- to 5-year-old children, the prevalence of overweight more than doubled (from 5% to more than 10%), again with most of the increase between 1990 and 2000 (Ogden et al., 2002).

Even among very young children, we are seeing significant—and growing—racial disparities in the prevalence of overweight. The greatest increases in the prevalence of overweight between 1971 and 1994 occurred in children of black and Hispanic race/ethnicity (Ogden et al., 1997). Racial disparities with respect to overweight appear to grow and interact with socioeconomic status as children grow older. For example, in 1986, the prevalence of overweight among 12-year-old upper-income White girls and low-income African American and Hispanic boys of the same age was nearly identical—6.5%. By 1998, the prevalence of overweight in upper-income White girls was essentially unchanged at 8.7%, but had more than quadrupled among low-income African American and Hispanic boys, at 27.4% (Strauss & Pollack, 2001). Unfortunately, we do not yet understand the causes underlying these alarming racial and socioeconomic disparities in the prevalence of overweight among children.

Chubby Babies, Fat Adults?

As noted above, all of the information available to date indicates that a child who is overweight at less than 3 years of age is no more likely to be overweight as a young adult than is a child who is not overweight. However, a child who is overweight at 3 years or older is nearly 8 times as likely to be overweight as a young adult than is a 3-year-old who is not overweight (Whitaker et al., 1997). Why and how is overweight in early childhood tied to adult obesity? Not surprisingly, current hypotheses focus on genes and the environment.

Genetic factors that predispose to obesity in a family may already be expressing themselves in early childhood. Genetic factors related to obesity may include: metabolism rates, behavioral

predispositions to food preferences, eating behavior, and patterns of physical activity. Even among children younger than 3 years, a child with one parent who is obese is 3 times as likely to become an obese adult as is a child with two parents of normal weight. A child with two obese parents is more than 13 times as likely to become an obese adult as is a child with parents of normal weight (Whitaker et al., 1997). This phenomenon undoubtedly reflects a complex interplay of biology and behavior. In other words, as we have come to recognize that with respect to most aspects of child development, the old dichotomy of nature versus nurture represents an oversimplification of a complex issue.

We do know that the dramatic increase in the prevalence of overweight in the general population and among children since 1990 absolutely cannot be accounted for by genetic shifts in the population. Genetic changes simply do not occur this quickly. It *is* possible, however, that genetic predispositions toward certain behaviors (e.g., preferences for sweet or high-fat foods) vary within the population. When the environment changes, these genetic predispositions may be more apt to express themselves than formerly; the result is overweight or obesity. The overarching message? Our genes have not changed recently; our environment has. What does this conclusion tell us about the strong transmission of overweight risk from parent to child?

Parents' modeling of behavior and their shaping of a child's relationship to food have been areas of active research in child development for quite some time. Accounts in the lay press do not hesitate to hold parents responsible for childhood overweight. For example, recent articles in national newspapers have been headlined, "Overweight kids? You might deserve a big slice of the blame" (Lee, 2004), or "If parents can't say no, then their children won't learn to either" (Hart, 2003). Blaming parents for a problem that is growing more quickly—and at epidemic proportions—in disadvantaged minority populations than in the population as a whole immediately raises concerns about the validity of this conceptualization of the problem. If parents are generally and primarily to blame for the increased prevalence of child overweight since 1990, one or both of the following statements would have to be true: (a) Parenting practices as a whole have shifted dramatically in the last 15 years, and (b) low-income parents (especially mothers) have a reasonable chance of overcoming the influence of both food advertising that is targeted at their children and the economic conditions in which they live.

Who Influences Children's Eating Behavior?

If poor parenting is to blame for the growing prevalence of childhood obesity, then something must have changed since 1990 in the ways in which parents teach their children about food, set limits around food, and promote healthy eating habits. This assertion is difficult to support, for a variety of reasons. For example, if parents have a powerful influence over children's eating behavior and development of food preferences, then family members' food preferences should be very much alike. In fact, very little correlation exists between parent and child food preferences (even when the children have grown to be adults; Rozin, 1991). Parents are not very effective at transmitting preferences for foods to their children (a finding that will not surprise any parent or caregiver who has struggled to encourage a child to sample a new food!).

Today's overweight children tend to be heavier than overweight children were in past years.

Although parents have limited control over what children are willing to eat while sitting at the dinner table parents *do* control what food is in the cupboards. Given that obesity is more common in low-income minority populations, perhaps efforts should focus on encouraging low-income mothers with young children to stock the house with a range of healthy food options for their children. Unfortunately, this recommendation is problematic from a public health perspective. Consider, for example, the research finding that families who live closer to supermarkets are more likely to consume a healthier diet than are families who live further away, presumably because those living closer have readier access to a range of fresh and healthy foods (Morland, Wing, & Roux, 2002). However, the number of supermarkets per capita is nearly 6 times greater in White neighborhoods than it is in neighborhoods of primarily minority race/ethnicity (Morland, Wing, Roux, & Poole, 2002). The reasons for these stark disparities are undoubtedly complex, and not fully understood. These differences, however, would potentially be amenable to public policy intervention.

Where *do* children learn their food preferences? The bulk of the evidence suggests that even children as young as 2 years learn food preferences from their peer group. In one study, researchers in a preschool setting seated children who didn't like broccoli next to children who did. The broccoli eaters ate their green vegetable in full view of their broccoli-averse classmates. Over time, the children who hadn't liked broccoli began to eat it (Birch, 1980). In a more recent experiment, teachers in a preschool setting and peer models were put head-to-head to determine who was more likely to influence a child's food preferences. The children were significantly more powerful influences than the adults were (Hendy & Raudenbush, 2000).

Evolutionary biology suggests two principal reasons why peers may be more powerful than adults in shaping children's food preferences:

- *Young children's reluctance to sample new foods is biologically wired.* Reluctance to try new foods begins to emerge at around age 2 years and lessens as children approach school age. The unfamiliar foods that children are most reluctant to try are vegetables (Cooke, Wardle, & Gibson, 2003). That children become reluctant to sample new foods just as they are becoming mobile, independent explorers seems to be more than mere coincidence. It would be to the human species' survival advantage for its young to be reluctant to eat unfamiliar

plant life (e.g., vegetables): Plants can be poisonous. Instead of tasting any new item that they encounter, human children (in fact, nearly all mammals) determine what to eat by observing others around them.

- *Modeling eating behavior after peers may provide young children with some survival advantage.* A biological perspective suggests that the nutritional needs of the young human are more similar to those of other young humans than to those of full-grown adults. For example, because children's bodies are smaller than those of adults and to some extent less able to protect against infection, foods that adults can eat or drink safely in reasonable quantities could prove toxic to a young child (e.g., sushi, steak tartar, unpasteurized apple cider, and alcohol).

In brief, if nature had tried to equip children's brains with a preset system for recognizing which foods are safe to eat, a system that led children to imitate the behavior of the organisms most like themselves (i.e., other children), would clearly be the best design. This appears to be, indeed, the food-selection system that children use.

Unfortunately, advertisers seem to have recognized the power of peers to influence children's food preferences long before the rest of us. Anyone who has ever watched television recognizes that to sell food to children, advertisers use other children (e.g., "Mikey") or characters designed to appeal to and resonate with children. No cereal or candy company would ever attempt to sell a product to a child with a commercial featuring a firm (yet kind and gentle) adult model eating the product while enthusiastically explaining to the child how "yummy" it is. Paradoxically, this is exactly the method by which parents try to get children to eat healthy foods. Perhaps reframing our efforts at changing childhood eating behavior is in order. Food advertisements on television are powerful. Children's consumption of specific foods correlates with their having viewed advertisements for these foods. Obese children are more likely than are children of normal weight to recognize food advertisements on television (Halford, Gillespie, Brown, Pontin, & Dovey, 2004). Even children as young as 2 years are more likely to select a food that they recently saw advertised in a 30-second commercial embedded in a cartoon than are children who have watched the cartoon without the commercial (Borzekowski & Robinson, 2001). Unless the government can be convinced to provide sufficient funding to advertise vegetables, whole grains, and milk on television with the same vigor and enormous advertising budget of the junk-food industry, hawking healthy food to children through television may be an unreachable goal. However, children who attend preschool and child care are exposed to peers in eating situations every day. These interactions may be prime opportunities for promoting the transmission of healthy food preferences between and among children.

What Is the Right Way to Parent to Prevent Obesity?

Parents do exert some control over how their children learn to prefer healthy foods and regulate food intake. Therefore, professionals who work with the parents of young children should base their recommendations about nutrition and feeding on solid scientific evidence. Unfortunately, although professionals frequently give families advice on these topics, we have little data to back up our suggestions.

Although parents have limited control over what children are willing to eat . . . parents do control what food is in the cupboards.

For example, early childhood professionals and clinicians generally believe that young infants should be fed "on demand." (Whether or not parents actually accept and implement this advice is an unanswered question.) But although feeding an infant on demand may certainly promote a sense of security and help the infant to calm and self-regulate, we have no evidence to suggest that feeding a baby on demand has anything to do with her eventual ability to regulate appetite. Interestingly, at some point in the early childhood years, however, general professional opinion and advice seem to shift from feeding "on demand" to feeding at scheduled snack and mealtimes. We encourage parents to have a child wait until dinner for food, even if he or she is clearly hungry. The theory is that the child will then "have a good appetite" and will "eat a good dinner." On the other hand, some professionals advise parents to allow young children to "graze" on healthy foods all day long. They counsel parents to allow their child to eat a snack when they ask for one, with the thought that the child is learning to respond to his hunger cues accurately. Feeding children when they say that they are hungry, these professionals and parents believe, will teach children that "we eat when we are hungry," not that "we eat because it is dinnertime."

Evidence to support either method of regulating food intake is scanty. Some data suggest that restricting children's access to palatable foods makes children like and want these foods even more over time (Birch, Zimmerman, & Hind, 1980) and promotes overeating when the restricted foods are actually available (Fisher & Birch, 1999). The more that mothers control how much, what, and when children eat at age 5 years (regardless of the child's weight status at that age), the more likely the child is to eat without being hungry (i.e., to be insensitive to hunger cues and therefore apt to overeat) by age 9 years (Birch, Fisher, & Davison, 2003). These data suggest that parents who set strict limits on their young children's eating may actually promote obesity. This information might, therefore, prompt professionals to instruct mothers *not* to restrict the amount, timing, or content of children's meals. However, such advice runs directly counter to how much of the general public views the cause of today's childhood obesity epidemic—lax, inconsistent parenting with little limit-setting.

Similar confusion exists concerning strategies to get children to eat more vegetables. Simply encouraging parents to put vegetables on the dinner table each evening does not result in children's becoming more familiar with a food and therefore more likely to eat it. Children must actually taste a vegetable repeatedly before they begin to like it (Birch, McPhee, Shoba, Pirok, & Steinberg, 1987). If simply prompting a child to "take one bite" could make a typical child easily and pleasantly take a bite of a disliked vegetable, parenting (and obesity prevention) would certainly be a much simpler endeavor than it is. Unfortunately, as we have seen, children have an inherent reluctance to sample new vegetables, and parental modeling, as described above, has limited power to overcome this reluctance. If these methods fail, parents often then resort to rewarding the child for trying one bite of the vegetable. Most commonly, parents will tell a child that she may not leave the table, or may not have dessert, or may not have any more servings of a preferred food until the target vegetable is sampled. Unfortunately, it seems that these methods of reward actually result in a decreased preference for the target vegetable over time—certainly not the desired outcome (Birch, Marlin, & Rotter, 1984).

Synthesis of the Research to Date

Do we have evidence that any feeding practices in the first few years of life influence obesity risk? It is relatively well-accepted among researchers that breast-feeding reduces the risk of obesity (Hediger, Overpeck, Kuczmarski, & Ruan, 2001), although questions remain concerning whether this correlation is simply due to the presence of confounders, such as the general health consciousness of mothers who breast-feed (Parsons, Power, & Manor, 2003). If one accepts that a relationship exists between breast-feeding and lowered risk of obesity, one should note that breast-feeding in infancy has not been found to be associated with protection against overweight among children of preschool age in all populations. Among low-income children, for example, the relationship between breast-feeding and protection against overweight is present only in white children—not in black or Hispanic children (Grummer-Strawn & Mei, 2004). The reason for this discrepancy remains unclear. Researchers are also debating whether or not the timing of a baby's introduction to solid foods is associated with an increased risk of child overweight. Most recent research seems to indicate that introduction of solid foods before 4–6 months does not seem to be associated with infant weight status, at least at 12 months of age. We have no data about timing of solid food introduction and weight status at age 3 years or later. The use of food as a reward (for example, to avert a tantrum) has been associated with children's increased preference for the food that has been used as a reward (Birch et al., 1980). However, the children of mothers who report that they use food as a reward do not seem, as a group, to be particularly obese (Baughcum et al., 2001).

Because of the high prevalence of obesity among children living in poverty, several researchers have studied the feeding practices of low-income mothers of young children. However, efforts to relate children's weight status at 11 to 24 months of age to self-reported maternal feeding practices in low-income populations have not uncovered any clear associations. Baughcum and her colleagues (2001) found that low-income mothers of children who were overweight did not report being more concerned about their infant's hunger, being less aware of their infant's hunger and satiety cues, feeding their infant more on a schedule, being more likely to use food to calm their infant, or having less social interaction during feeding than did low-income mothers of children of normal weight. However, low-income obese mothers in this study were more likely to be concerned about their baby's being underweight than other mothers. Given their concern, obese mothers may have been more apt to overfeed their babies, and thereby place them at greater risk for overweight. Regardless of the weight status of child or mother, low-income mothers are more likely to be concerned about their child's hunger than are higher-income mothers (Baughcum et al., 2001). Low-income mothers said that they found it difficult to withhold food from a child who said he or she was hungry, even if the child had just finished a meal.

Results from the same authors for children 23 to 60 months of age provide equally confusing information for the practitioner who wants to provide straightforward advice to a family. The researchers found that obese mothers and low-income mothers were more likely to engage in what professionals consider age-inappropriate feeding practices than were non-obese or upper-income mothers (Baughcum et al., 2001). For example, low-income toddlers and preschoolers were more likely than upper-income young children to eat in front of the TV or walking around the living room rather than having a meal at a table with a place setting. Lower-income mothers said that they had less difficulty feeding their children than did higher-income mothers, but low-income mothers reported a tendency to push their children to eat more. However, none of these frowned-upon feeding practices were associated with increased risk of overweight at age 5 years.

Some data suggest that restricting children's access to palatable foods makes children like and want these foods even more over time.

In summary, we find no evidence from mothers' reports that overweight children experience a different feeding style from their mothers than do non-overweight children. Although lower-income mothers do feed their young children differently than do upper-income mothers, we have no evidence that these different feeding practices are actually related to an increased risk of child overweight. In other words, the fact that a low-income mother chooses to have unstructured mealtimes, encourages her child to eat more, allows her child to have a bottle during the day, or will feed the child herself if the child does not want to eat, may reflect sociocultural differences between lower-income and upper-income parents in their beliefs about feeding practices. Professionals have no basis on which to make a value judgment about these practices as they pertain to child overweight outcomes.

What *Should* Professionals Recommend to Parents?

We have reviewed the research on young children's eating behavior and parental feeding practices (with a particular focus on low-income minority children) and their relationship to childhood overweight. We have found an absence of robust research to guide us in advising parents about how to prevent childhood overweight. What advice *should* professionals give to parents of young children about feeding practices? Research suggests four guidelines for practice:

1. *Acknowledge the limits of parental influence in the face of an obesigenic environment.*

Especially when working with disadvantaged parents, acknowledge that although parents influence their children's eating and will do the best job they can to prevent obesity in their child, individual parents are constantly battling a myriad of societal and biological influences on their child's eating behavior.

2. *Empower parents to advocate for systemic change.*

Parents are in a prime position to advocate for change in their children's child-care and preschool settings with regard to the foods served and the mealtime atmosphere. Parents are also important voices in advocating for more and safer playgrounds in their neighborhoods so that children can get exercise outdoors.

3. *Refrain from urging parents to change their feeding practices when we have little scientific evidence to suggest that these are actually "wrong."*

Although allowing a child to walk around all day with a bottle of juice is certainly problematic from an oral health perspective, professionals tend to frown on other feeding practices without compelling evidence that these practices increase children's risk of poor health outcomes. For example, telling a mother to have structured mealtimes rather than allowing her young child to "graze" has little basis in science, and may only serve to alienate a mother from the health care provider. She is likely to be feeding her child as her mother fed her, and as her cultural and socioeconomic peers feed their children.

4. *Advocate, advocate, advocate.*

Although working with individual families to reduce their child's risk for overweight is important, advocating for change on a public health and policy level is critical. Providing low-income families in both urban and rural areas with ready access to fresh and palatable fruits and vegetables would be an important change for the better. Increasing the availability of healthy, tasty, and inexpensive fast food could also make a big difference in children's health. Although an upper-income working family can find palatable (albeit expensive) rather healthy take-out food in some communities, cost and availability preclude this option for most low-income families. Yet few low-income mothers have the time or energy after a long day at work to take public transportation (which doesn't exist in many communities) with several children in tow to buy fresh food at a supermarket (which may not exist in the vicinity of many low-income families' homes), and then cook while the children vie for her attention. Because many low-income families do not feel safe allowing their children to play outside in their home neighborhoods, it is important to ensure that, along with healthy meals and snacks, children get adequate opportunity for physical activity in child-care, preschool, school, and after-school programs. Of course our long-term goal should be safe child- and family-friendly communities with ample sources of affordable, healthy food to purchase and accessible resources for information and physical exercise (including community gardening).

In Conclusion

The early childhood professional can play a critical role in stemming the tide of childhood overweight. However, this role may not play out in the home of the individual family as much as it may in the Early Head Start or Head Start classroom or the community meeting hall. Preventing childhood overweight will, as the saying goes, take a village.

References

Baughcum, A., Powers, S., Johnson, S., Chamberlin, L., Deeks, C., Jain, A., et al. (2001). Maternal feeding practices and beliefs and their relationships to overweight in early childhood. *Journal of Developmental & Behavioral Pediatrics, 22*(6), 391–408.

Birch, L. (1980). Effects of peer models' food choices and eating behaviors on preschoolers' food preferences. *Child Development, 51,* 489–496.

Birch, L., Fisher, J., & Davison, K. (2003). Learning to overeat: Maternal use of restrictive feeding practices promotes girls' eating in the absence of hunger. *American Journal of Clinical Nutrition, 78*(2), 215–220.

Birch, L., Marlin, D., & Rotter, J. (1984). Eating as the "means" activity in a contingency: Effects on young children's food preference. *Child Development, 55,* 432–439.

Birch, L., McPhee, L., Shoba, B., Pirok, E., & Steinberg, L. (1987). What kind of exposure reduces children's food neophobia? *Appetite, 3,* 353–360.

Birch, L., Zimmerman, S., & Hind, H. (1980). The influence of social affective context on the formation of children's food preferences. *Child Development, 51*(3), 856–861.

Borzekowski, D., & Robinson, T. (2001). The 30-second effect: An experiment revealing the impact of television commercials on food preferences of preschoolers. *Journal of the American Dietetic Association, 101*(1), 42–46.

Cooke, L., Wardle, J., & Gibson, E. (2003). Relationship between parental report of food neophobia and everyday food consumption in 2–6-year-old children. *Appetite, 41*(2), 205–206.

Fisher, J., & Birch, L. (1999). Restricting access to palatable foods affects children's behavioral response, food selection, and intake. *American Journal of Clinical Nutrition, 69,* 1264–1272.

Grummer-Strawn, L., & Mei, Z. (2004). Does breastfeeding protect against pediatric overweight? Analysis of longitudinal data from the Centers for Disease Control and Prevention Nutrition Surveillance System. *Pediatrics, 113*(2), e81–e86.

Halford, J., Gillespie, J., Brown, V., Pontin, E., & Dovey, T. (2004). Effect of television advertisements for foods on consumption in children. *Appetite, 42*(2), 221–225.

Hart, B. (2003, November 16). If parents can't say no, then their children won't learn to either. *Chicago Sun-Times,* p. 36.

Hediger, M., Overpeck, M., Kuczmarski, R., & Ruan, W. (2001). Association between infant breastfeeding and overweight in young children. *Journal of the American Medical Association, 285,* 2453–2460.

Hendy, H., & Raudenbush, B. (2000). Effectiveness of teacher modeling to encourage food acceptance in preschool children. *Appetite, 34,* 61–76.

Lee, E. (2004, May 30). Overweight kids? You might deserve a big slice of the blame. *Atlanta Journal-Constitution,* p. 1A.

Morland, K., Wing, S., & Roux, A. D. (2002). The contextual effect of the local food environment on residents' diets: The atherosclerosis risk in communities study. *American Journal of Public Health, 92*(11), 1761–1768.

Morland, K., Wing, S., Roux, A. D., & Poole, C. (2002). Neighborhood characteristics associated with the location of food stores and food service places. *American Journal of Preventive Medicine, 22,* 23–29.

Ogden, C., Flegal, K., Carroll, M., & Johnson, C. (2002). Prevalence and trends in overweight among US children and adolescents, 1999–2000. *Journal of the American Medical Association, 288,* 1728–1732.

Ogden, C., Troiano, R., Briefel, R., Kuczmarski, R., Flegal, K., & Johnson, C. (1997). Prevalence of overweight among preschool children in the United States, 1971 through 1994. *Pediatrics, 99*(4), e1.

Parsons, T., Power, C., & Manor, O. (2003). Infant feeding and obesity through the life-course. *Archives of Disease in Childhood, 88*(9), 793–794.

Rozin, P. (1991). Family resemblance in food and other domains: The family paradox and the role of parental congruence. *Appetite, 16,* 93–102.

Strauss, R., & Pollack, H. (2001). Epidemic increase in childhood overweight. *Journal of the American Medical Association, 286*(22), 2845–2848.

Whitaker, R., Wright, J., Pepe, M., Seidel, K., & Dietz, W. (1997). Predicting obesity in young adulthood from childhood and parental obesity. *New England Journal of Medicine, 337,* 869–873.

UNIT 4

Educational Practices

Unit Selections

Key Points to Consider

- What is causing the pressure to push the curriculum down from the primary grades into preschool? How can teachers of young children resist that pressure?
- What are some of the pros and cons of retaining a child in the early grades?
- Make a brief list of the components of developmentally appropriate practice that you believe are vital.
- How can teachers and parents assist young children as they move from preschool to kindergarten?
- What are some of the best design features of a preschool classroom where you have worked or observed?
- Why are transition grades not the best way to educate children?
- Why is the ability to make choices a crucial skill to learn in the early years?
- Describe some of the negative effects of testing on young children.
- How do you rate the playground of a preschool where you have observed or worked?

Student Web Site

www.mhcls.com/online

Internet References

Further information regarding these websites may be found in this book's preface or online.

Child Welfare League of America (CWLA)
http://www.cwla.org

In the overview for Unit 1 the intense pressure on first graders was discussed. I am struck with the increasing push to have young children do things at an earlier and earlier age even though life expectancy keeps increasing. Children born today have an excellent chance of living into their 90s and beyond. There is no need to rush to acquire skills that can easily be learned when the child is older, especially at the expense of valuable lifelong lessons that are best learned when children are young. How to get along with others, to make choices, to negotiate, to develop a sense of compassion, and to communicate needs are all skills that require introduction and practice during the preschool years. The article "Back to Basics" by Jill Englebright Fox focuses on the importance of developmentally appropriate play experiences for young children. The basics in this case are a solid foundation in understanding how things work, the many opportunities to explore and manipulate materials, and opportunities for creative expression.

The passage of No Child Left Behind legislation by Congress in 2002 has many implications for early childhood care and educational practices. As academic assessment and accountability measures are implemented, the impact on children's play is becoming quite clear. Young children are spending more time preparing for and taking tests and less time in developmental play. In the article, "Stop the Insanity!: It Takes a Team to Leave No Child Behind," Butzin contends that teaching *is* rocket science. It requires committed individuals who are well prepared to deal with a variety of development levels and needs as appropriate learning experiences are planned for all children. Good teaching does make a difference and children deserve no less than adults who truly are passionate about being with young children on a daily basis. Teaching cannot be viewed as a great profession for someone who wants their summers off.

Both Francis Wardle in "Rethinking Early Childhood Practices" and Vera Estok in "One District's Study on the Propriety of Transition-Grade Classrooms" gives careful consideration to a variety of common practices in programs for young children. Teachers often put great thought and time into preparing lesson plans, but give little attention to developing the daily schedule, to grouping children, or to recommending children for a transitional grade. Effective teachers must make research-based decisions. Any teacher who carefully studied the research would not support transitional grades. We must take our cues from those in the medical community: read and follow the research.

The word "transition" is used a different way in the next article. In "Successful Transition to Kindergarten: The Role of Teachers and Parents," the author provides ways teachers and parents can help young children make the major transition to kindergarten. For some children, kindergarten is their first experience with formal schooling. For many others it means a different school, classroom, and teacher than they had during their preschool years. With this new experience comes many different expectations. As I sent my youngest child off to his first year of college I thought about the many ways he was prepared for this major transition. First year orientation, welcome week, and parents' weekend were all carefully planned to assist the new students with adjusting to college. But we do little to help five-year-olds who are also making a major change in their life. It is time for preschool teachers, kindergarten teachers and families to collaborate to insure a smooth progression to the next learning experience.

Another implication of No Child Left Behind is an alarming increase in the number of children, particularly boys, who are retained in the early grades. The reasons most frequently cited for retention is to motivate failing students to try harder and raise their self-esteem. Yet research shows that retention has the opposite effect; achievement does not increase, and so self-esteem suffers. With schools under pressure to meet higher annual yearly progress goals, teachers are recommending more and more young children for retention. While retention is not proving to be an effective approach to low achievement or emotional problems, neither is social promotion. The issues involved in retaining young children are discussed in "Second Time Around."

In "Making the Case for Play Policy: Research-Based Reasons to Support Play-Based Environments," the author addresses the need to protect children's right to play as an avenue of cognitive, emotional, and academic growth. The reader should also recognize that, to benefit growth and development, play needs to be channeled and supported. Teachers are encouraged to provide appropriate props and materials to foster the type of play that extends learning.

The last article in this unit deals with how to create a positive outdoor experience for young children. "Essential Contributions from Playgrounds," summarizes the benefits of time children spend on playgrounds. The authors describe important aspects of playground design, supervision, and equipment that go into making a safe and appropriate outdoor play environment. They conclude with specific recommendations for early childhood educators to ensure that the playground meets children's physical, social, emotional, and intellectual development.

Back to Basics

Play in Early Childhood

JILL ENGLEBRIGHT FOX, PH.D.

K yle plays with blocks and builds a castle. Tony and Victoria play fire station and pretend to be firefighters. Kenzo and Carl play catch with a ball. Children playact with playmates in the playhouse. Playgroups on the playground choose players to play ball. As an early childhood professional, you probably use the word "play" a hundred times per day.

Research indicates that children learn best in an environment which allows them to explore, discover, and play. Play is an important part of a developmentally appropriate child care program. It is also closely tied to the development of cognitive, socio-emotional, and physical behaviors. But what exactly does it mean to play and why is play so important for young children?

What Is Play?

Although it is simple to compile a list of play activities, it is much more difficult to define play. Scales, et al., (1991) called play "that absorbing activity in which healthy young children participate with enthusiasm and abandon" (p. 15). Csikszentmihalyi (1981) described play as "a subset of life . . . an arrangement in which one can practice behavior without dreading its consequences" (p. 14). Garvey (1977) gave a useful description of play for teachers when she defined play as an activity which is: 1) positively valued by the player; 2) self-motivated; 3) freely chosen; 4) engaging; and 5) which "has certain systematic relations to what is not play" (p. 5). These characteristics are important for teachers to remember because imposing adult values, requirements, or motivations on children's activities may change the very nature of play.

According to *Webster's Desk Dictionary of the English Language,* the word play has 34 different meanings. In terms of young children and play, the following definitions from Webster's are useful:

- light, brisk, or changing movement (e.g., to pretend you're a butterfly)
- to act or imitate the part of a person or character (e.g., to play house)
- to employ a piece of equipment (e.g., to play blocks)
- exercise for amusement or recreation (e.g., to play tag)

- fun or jest, as opposed to seriousness (e.g., to play peek-a-boo or sing a silly song)
- the action of a game (e.g., to play duck-duck-goose)

Why Is Play Important?

According to Fromberg and Gullo (1992), play enhances language development, social competence, creativity, imagination, and thinking skills. Frost (1992) concurred, stating that "play is the chief vehicle for the development of imagination and intelligence, language, social skills, and perceptual-motor abilities in infants and young children" (p. 48).

Garvey (1977) states that play is most common during childhood when children's knowledge of self, comprehension of verbal and non-verbal communication, and understanding of the physical and social worlds are expanding dramatically.

Fromberg (1990) claims that play is the "ultimate integrator of human experience" (p. 223). This means that when children play, they draw upon their past experiences–things they have done, seen others do, read about, or seen on television–and they use these experiences to build games, play scenarios, and engage in activities.

Children use fine and gross motor skills in their play. They react to each other socially. They think about what they are doing or going to do. They use language to talk to each other or to themselves and they very often respond emotionally to the play activity. The integration of these different types of behaviors is key to the cognitive development of young children. According to Rogers and Sawyer (1988), "until at least the age of nine, children's cognitive structures function best in this unified mode" (p. 58). Because children's play draws upon all of these behaviors, it is a very effective vehicle for learning.

Play and Cognitive Development

The relationship between play and cognitive development is described differently in the two theories of cognitive development which dominate early childhood education–Piaget's and Vygotsky's.

Piaget (1962) defined play as assimilation, or the child's efforts to make environmental stimuli match his or her own concepts. Piagetian theory holds that play, in and of itself, does not necessarily result in the formation of new cognitive structures. Piaget claimed that play was just for pleasure, and while it allowed children to practice things they had previously learned, it did not necessarily result in the learning of new things. In other words, play reflects what the child has already learned but does not necessarily teach the child anything new. In this view, play is seen as a "process reflective of emerging symbolic development, but contributing little to it" (Johnsen & Christie, 1986, p. 51).

In contrast, Vygotskian theory states that play actually facilitates cognitive development. Children not only practice what they already know, they also learn new things. In discussing Vygotsky's theory, Vandenberg (1986) remarks that "play not so much reflects thought (as Piaget suggests) as it creates thought" (p. 21).

Observations of children at play yield examples to support both Piagetian and Vygotskian theories of play. A child who puts on a raincoat and a firefighter's hat and rushes to rescue his teddy bear from the pretend flames in his playhouse is practicing what he has previously learned about firefighters. This supports Piaget's theory. On the other hand, a child in the block center who announces to his teacher, "Look! When I put these two square blocks together, I get a rectangle!" has constructed new knowledge through her play. This supports Vygotsky's theory.

Whether children are practicing what they have learned in other settings or are constructing new knowledge, it is clear that play has a valuable role in the early childhood classroom.

Play—Indoors and Out

Early childhood teachers have long recognized the value of play in programs for young children. Unfortunately, teachers often fail to take advantage of the opportunities play provides for observing children's development and learning. Through such observations teachers can learn about children's social interactions, cognitive and language abilities, motor skills, and emotional development.

Frost (1992) recommends that observing children at play be a daily responsibility for early childhood professionals. Regular observations provide teachers with assessment information for identifying children with special needs, planning future play experiences, evaluating play materials, determining areas of strength and weakness for individual children, planning curriculum for individual children, reporting to parents, and checking on a child's on-going progress. The increased use of authentic assessment strategies is making observations of children's play more commonplace in early childhood classrooms.

Hymes (1981) recommends that children have two classrooms—one indoors and one outdoors. The outdoor play environment should be used as an extension of the indoor classroom. It should be a learning environment as carefully planned as the indoor activity centers and should encourage motor and social skills as well as help children refine existing cognitive structures and construct new ones. Used in this way, the outdoor play environment provides a basis for observational assessment in all areas of development.

Fox (1993) researched the practicality of observing young children's cognitive development during outdoor play. Her observations of four- and five-year-old children during outdoor play found examples of addition and subtraction, shape identification, patterning, one-to-one correspondence, number sense, sequencing of events, use of ordinal numbers, knowledge of prepositions, and identification of final and initial consonants. Fox's outdoor observations also found multiple examples of problem-solving, creative thinking, social competence, language use, and gross and fine motor skills. Although outdoor observations do not replace classroom assessment, they can provide valuable information for teachers of young children. As Fox stated, "These observations can be performed unobtrusively, without intruding upon the children's activities and without placing children in a stressful testing situation" (p. 131).

Parten's Five Types of Play

Play for young children assumes many different forms. Mildred Parten (1932) was one of the early researchers studying children at play. She focused on the social interactions between children during play activities. Parten's categories of play are not hierarchical. Depending on the circumstances, children may engage in any of the different types of play. Parten does note, however, that in her research with two- to five-year-olds, "participation in the most social types of groups occurs most frequently among the older children" (p. 259).

"Extra playtime allows children to become involved in more complex and productive play activities"

- **Onlooker behavior**—Playing passively by watching or conversing with other children engaged in play activities.
- **Solitary independent**—Playing by oneself.
- **Parallel**—Playing, even in the middle of a group, while remaining engrossed in one's own activity. Children playing parallel to each other sometimes use each other's toys, but always maintain their independence.
- **Associative**—When children share materials and talk to each other, but do not coordinate play objectives or interests.
- **Cooperative**—When children organize themselves into roles with specific goals in mind (e.g., to assign the roles of doctor, nurse, and patient and play hospital).

How Much Should Children Play?

Indoors and outdoors, children need large blocks of time for play. According to Christie and Wardle (1992), short play periods may require children to abandon their group dramatizations or constructive play just when they begin to get involved. When this happens a number of times, children may give up on more sophisticated forms of play and settle for less advanced forms that can be completed in short periods of time. Shorter play periods reduce both the amount and the maturity of children's play, and many important benefits of play, such as persistence, negotiation, problem solving, planning, and cooperation are lost. Large blocks of time (30 to 60 minutes, or longer) should be scheduled for indoor and outdoor play periods. Christie and Wardle remind teachers that extra playtime does not result in children becoming bored. Instead, it prompts children to become involved in more complex, more productive play activities.

The Teacher's Role

The early childhood teacher is the facilitator of play in the classroom. The teacher facilitates play by providing appropriate indoor and outdoor play environments. Safety is, of course, the primary concern. Age and developmental levels must be carefully considered in the design and selection of materials. Guidelines for selecting safe and appropriate equipment for outdoor play environments are available through the U.S. Consumer Product Safety Commission's Handbook for Public Playground Safety and the Playground Safety Manual by Jambor and Palmer (1991). Similar guidelines are also available for indoor settings (Torelli & Durrett, 1996; Caples, 1996; Ard & Pitts, 1990). Once appropriate environments and materials are in place, regular safety checks and maintenance are needed to ensure that the equipment is sound and safe for continued play.

Teachers also facilitate play by working with children to develop rules for safe indoor and outdoor play. Discussion about the appropriate use of materials, the safe number of participants on each piece of equipment, taking turns, sharing, and cleaning up provides the children with information to begin their play activities. These discussions need to be ongoing because some children may need frequent reminders about rules and because new situations may arise (e.g., new equipment).

By providing play materials related to thematic instruction, early childhood teachers can establish links between the children's indoor and outdoor play and their program's curriculum.

Thematic props for dramatic play can be placed in the dramatic play center or stored in prop boxes and taken outside to extend the dramatic play to a new setting. An art center in the outdoor play environment may encourage children to explore the possibilities of using leaves, twigs, pebbles, and sand in their three-dimensional art productions. Painting easels and water tables may also be moved outside periodically for children's use during outdoor play periods. Finally, a collection of books stored in a wagon to be taken outside during play time may offer some children a needed alternative to more active play.

As facilitators of children's play, teachers should closely observe children during play periods not only for assessment purposes, as stated earlier, but also to facilitate appropriate social interactions and motor behaviors. It is important that children be the decision-makers during play, choosing what and where to play, choosing roles for each player, and choosing how play will proceed. Occasionally, however, some children will need adult assistance in joining a play group, modifying behavior, or negotiating a disagreement. Careful observation will help the teacher to decide when to offer assistance and what form that assistance should take.

Conclusion

Although play is a difficult concept to define, it is very easy to recognize. Children actively involved in play may be engaged in a variety of activities, independently, with a partner, or in a group. Because play is closely tied to the cognitive, socio-emotional, and motor development of young children, it is an important part of developmentally appropriate early childhood programs.

JILL ENGLEBRIGHT FOX, PH.D., is an assistant professor of early childhood education at Virginia Commonwealth University. She taught kindergarten and first grade in the Texas public schools for eight years, and is currently an active member of the International Play Association-USA. Her research interests focus on play and aesthetic development in young children, and professional development schools.

Stop the Insanity! It Takes a Team to Leave No Child Behind

Who says learning always has to be drudgery? Sarah Butzin, the founder of the Institute for School Innovation, proposes "triangulated learning" as a way to give children time to play and develop, even as they pursue high standards.

SARAH M. BUTZIN

What has happened to common sense in this era of No Child Left Behind? What makes anyone believe that talking louder makes a deaf man hear? Albert Einstein reputedly defined insanity as doing the same thing over and over and expecting different results.

Yet that is what I see happening in elementary schools today. In response to high-stakes testing and higher standards for even the most challenging students, schools have responded by talking louder. They haven't changed the way they teach. Instead, they push more papers in front of the kids, keep them off the playground, and take away music and art. Here in Florida, they make kids repeat third grade if they can't keep up (an estimated 43,000 failed in 2003) and send them to summer reading "camps" to cram in a little more knowledge.

Everything we know about human nature and child development should tell us to pause. Children need time to play and time to develop at a natural pace. Every parent knows that not all infants learn to walk by age 1 and talk by age 2. Neither do all first-graders learn to read at the stroke of midnight on their sixth birthday. Young children need security and encouragement, not pressure and humiliation if they can't keep up.

Yet at the same time, there is a legitimate need for rigorous academic standards, high expectations, and reliable assessments to gauge each child's progress so that he or she is not left behind. The stakes are indeed high. Children of the 21st century absolutely need much higher literacy and mathematical skills than their grandparents. The world has been transformed through technology and global competition.

So how do you lay a foundation for solid academic skills without killing childhood? One thing is certain. One teacher working solo with a classroom of 20 to 30 children cannot do it in one year—actually 180 school days. And when you subtract all the non-instructional school time, including getting to know the children and playing catch-up from the previous grade, that 180 days really translates to about 100 days. In essence, one teacher has a little over three months to teach to high standards in reading, writing, math, science, and social studies.

What's the solution? Add more days to the school year? Reduce class size? Buy more computers and newer textbooks? Pay for after-school tutors and summer reading camps? Nope, those ideas have all been tried, and they don't work. Plus, they are very expensive remedies. There is another option, which I call "triangulated learning." It takes a team approach to instruction and gives teachers the time and techniques to meet higher standards without stifling young children's natural desire to play and explore. Children can work at their own pace in diversified classrooms, using a variety of learning modes that best meet their individual learning styles. They can be challenged without being coerced.

And there are benefits for teachers as well. They become less isolated and stop taking the blame for the failure of the system. It's not their fault. Teachers are being asked to do the impossible—meet higher standards using the old grade school system in which one teacher is expected to do it all and pass the kids along through first grade, second grade, third grade, and so on. By the time children reach fifth grade, it's not surprising that large numbers of them have fallen by the wayside, especially if they lack a support system at home.

For the past 15 years, I've been working on developing a triangulated learning system that incorporates best practices from the past along with newer innovations such as computers and the Internet. It's really a system of "retro-techno" teaching. In 2003–04 there were over 15,000 students and over 450 teachers involved.

Triangulation is a metaphor for strength. A triangulated learning system taps the power of three to meet higher standards for more kids. Here's how it works.

Three core subjects. The three R's are still the critical elements for future success. The fundamental role of the elementary school is to lay the foundation for these basic skills. Thus the academic focus of the triangulated system is on reading, writing, and mathematics. This is not to say that science, social studies, and the arts are not important. They are in fact enhanced in this system by being incorporated into daily station work, as well as being explicitly taught. More on that later.

Three-teacher expert teams. Teachers work in teams of three so that each teacher can focus on one of the core subjects. Higher standards and more challenging students have made the generalist teacher's role very difficult to maintain. Today's teachers must become expert in a core subject. Teaching reading is rocket science, and a casual survey course in reading methods no longer suffices. Highly qualified teachers need advanced and in-depth training in reading, writing, and mathematics.

Three-grade clusters. In the triangulated model, cluster teachers work across three grade levels, K–2 or 3–5. Multi-age groupings are especially effective, although grade-specific classes work as well. Teachers in a triangulated system have access to a broader range of materials and methods and thus can break free from arbitrary grade-level confinements. A third-grader has access to fifth-grade materials, and vice versa. Teachers in a triangulated system need not fear overstepping their boundaries and incurring the wrath of the next grade's teacher for "jumping ahead."

Three-classroom rotations. Students rotate to the subject classrooms in their cluster for three 60- to 90-minute periods. One of the classrooms serves as their cluster home base. The home base teacher is responsible for the science and social studies lessons for those students. Students also go to special areas (art, music, and physical education) as normally scheduled.

Three + three learning stations. There are six learning stations in each of the three subject classrooms to provide self-paced practice through different learning modes. After the teacher presents a brief whole-group lesson, students move to the stations to practice and apply the lesson concept in a variety of ways. The six stations are:

- a Teacher Station for small-group tutorials or enrichment;
- a Computer Station for integrated instructional software and Internet explorations;
- a Textbook Station for written work;
- a Challenge Station for learning activities in a game like format;
- an Imagination Station for artistic and creative expression; and
- a Construction Station for hands-on learning.

In addition to these six basic stations, many classrooms add supplemental stations for science and social studies activities. This is especially true in schools using 90-minute rotations.

Three years of continuous progress. Triangulated learning takes "looping" to a new level. One year (180 days) is not enough time to get to know every student's strengths and weaknesses and to discover what turns each one on to learning. In the triangulated system, students have a different home base teacher each year but the same three subject teachers for the three years they are in the cluster. In other words, the third-grade teacher who is the reading specialist for the cluster will get a new third-grade group each year for home base, but her initial third-graders will return to her in fourth and fifth grades for reading. This design also reduces the lag time at the beginning of each new year, as the cluster teachers already know two-thirds of their students.

Three learning modes. Triangulated learning uses 1) technology, 2) hands-on learning, and 3) paper-and pencil activities to engage students in challenging work. High-quality instructional software that is integrated with lesson objectives adds motivation, individual self-paced learning, and immediate feedback. Hands-on learning adds developmentally appropriate tasks for young children maturing into the abstract phase of learning. And traditional printed text and paper-and-pencil work still have their value.

Making the transition to triangulated learning takes commitment and effort. It requires support from the top down. Triangulated learning works best when teachers have appropriate materials, training, and coaching to help them move from isolated, solo teaching to teaching in a team context, identifying as a specialist, and using computers and active learning strategies. The history of education reform is strewn with the wreckage of wonderful models that have come and gone because teachers learned a theory and method but lacked the follow-up coaching and resources to sustain the new approach.

Teachers making the transition to triangulated learning will need more than good ideas. They need effective software and materials for the technology and hands on stations. They need to learn how to function as part of a team and to communicate effectively with their cluster peers. They need standards-based curriculum planning guides to help them coordinate instruction with their cluster teammates and to align topics across the three grade levels in their cluster. And most important, teachers need to learn classroom management techniques that are appropriate to self-regulated, multidimensional classrooms where children are active learners.

In 1995 I founded the Institute for School Innovation (ISI), a private nonprofit organization, to create a learning community of innovative educators and to support teachers with research-based materials, training, and coaching. ISI disseminates Project CHILD (Changing How Instruction for Learning is Delivered), which is a vehicle to help schools get started with triangulated learning. At ISI we continue to draw from the expertise of the hundreds of CHILD teachers with whom we work. They help us upgrade the CHILD materials so that we can continue to offer teacher-created station activities along with updated software correlation guides and lesson-planning guides that are aligned with state standards. We also host an annual conference and offer support groups for CHILD teachers to share ideas and help one another. You can learn more on our website at www.ifsi.org.

And does it work? By all measures, triangulated learning beats self-contained teaching across the board. Since I first developed the system at Florida State University in 1988, numerous independent studies have documented the success of CHILD students in reading, writing, and mathematics. We've even followed their progress into middle school. Their test scores are consistently higher than those of traditional students, their behavior is better, and parent enthusiasm is very high.

But most important, we have ample evidence to suggest that we are creating a wonderful classroom climate that engages children. They look forward to coming to school, they are eager to participate, and they feel good about their accomplishments. They even have time to play!

Sarah M. (Sally) Butzin is president and executive director of the Institute for School Innovation, Tallahassee, Fla. She is the developer of Project CHILD (Changing How Instruction for Learning is Delivered), previously called Computers Helping Instruction and Learning Development. She can be reached at sbutzin@ifsi.org.

Uniquely Preschool

To prepare children for authentic learning, early childhood education must bolster basic cognitive and social-emotional competencies.

ELENA BODROVA AND DEBORAH J. LEONG

W hat should education for young children be about? At a time when zeal for testing has inadvertently led to an overemphasis on acquiring academic content and skills, it is tempting to focus preschool and early elementary teaching on mastering these skills. But early education for the whole child cannot be reduced to teaching facts and skills. As Russian educator Alexander Zaporozhets cautioned,

> Optimal educational opportunities for a young child to reach his or her potential and to develop in a harmonious fashion are not created by accelerated ultra-early instruction aimed at shortening the childhood period—that would prematurely turn a toddler into a preschooler and a preschooler into a first-grader. What is needed is just the opposite—expansion and enrichment of the content in the activities that are uniquely "preschool." (1978, p. 88)

Although voiced in 1978, this warning against inappropriate acceleration of the curriculum seems appropriate today. Zaporozhets was a colleague and student of Lev Vygotsky and a lifelong advocate for high-quality preschool programs that address the needs of the whole child. In advocating "activities that are uniquely 'preschool,'" Zaporozhets was referring to Vygotsky's belief that in the preschool years, children need to acquire a set of fundamental cognitive, linguistic, and social-emotional competencies that shape their minds for further learning—not just academic learning, but all learning. These skills include oral language, deliberate memory, focused attention, and self-regulation. Such skills not only shape the way we learn to read and answer math problems but also influence how we resolve a conflict with a neighbor or kick a soccer ball. Vygotskians believe that children do not automatically acquire these underlying skills; they require explicit instruction by teachers or parents. As education consultants, we have seen the way skillful teachers of young children help their students acquire these crucial competencies, laying a foundation for academic learning without overemphasizing academics before children are ready.

From Reactive Thinking . . .

To understand the importance of these underlying skills, consider the mind of the preschool child. Vygotskians, like many other psychologists, describe the thinking of 2- and 3-year-old children as dominated by sensation and perception. Preschool children's thinking is *reactive*: They react to the most salient characteristic or the first thing that comes to their minds, whether or not it is important to the situation (Vygotsky, 1956). For example, when you ask preschool children to "get up, wash your hands, and sit down at the table," most children react to either the first direction or the last direction. Many just do what the other children are doing. When children see a toy that they want, they often grab it, regardless of who else is playing with the toy. Such reactions represent an immediate response to what children see and feel rather than a premeditated act.

Their reactive thinking also keeps young children from doing what Vygotsky called "learning on demand." Preschool children's ability to learn depends on repetition or on an experience being personally meaningful. Children can remember information only when it is presented in a repetitive and exciting way—such as the letter A jumping out of a box and dancing around over and over again—or when the information is of special interest to them, such as the month of their birthday. Vygotskians argue that this is why young children easily remember the names of dinosaurs or Pokémon characters but take much longer to learn their phone numbers or the letters of the alphabet.

. . . To Learning on Demand

One of the key aspects that distinguish formal schooling from preschool is that post-preschool students are able to learn on demand. They can expend mental effort to learn information just because the teacher tells them to learn it, even if it is not particularly interesting or salient. When a teacher gives an elementary class a list of spelling words, for example, students are expected to put effort into learning the words; the teacher will not repeat the information multiple times or use a lot of gimmicks to make the task fun. To succeed in school, a child must make this transition from learning that "follows the child's own agenda" to learning that "follows the school agenda" (Vygotsky, 1956, p. 426). One of the milestones of the preschool age is the development of intentionality in all areas—from physical behaviors to social interactions to problem solving. From the Vygotskian perspective, the major goal of preschool education for the whole child is to transform a child who is wholly reactive into one who is wholly intentional.

Ideally, in preschool, children move from reactive thinking to the ability to think *before* they act. Being able to reflect and draw on past experience makes it possible for young children to engage in thoughtful behaviors.

In a study conducted in Alexander Zaporozhets's lab, a teacher read "Little Red Riding Hood" to 3-, 4-, and 5-year-old children while an EEG device measured the children's brain waves (as described in Bodrova & Leong, 2003b). The first time they heard the story read aloud, all the children showed signs of anxiety, indicated by changes in their brain waves, at the part where the wolf jumped out to eat Red Riding Hood. The second time they heard the story, the 3-year-olds showed signs of anxiety at this same point in the story; the 5-year-olds, however, showed signs of nervousness earlier. As soon as the teacher read the part where Red Riding Hood starts on the wrong path through the woods, the pattern of the 5-year-olds' brain waves changed because the children had already begun to anticipate the wolf. The 5-year-olds' reactions to the story were influenced by their memories of the story, meaning they were less reactive and more thoughtful than the younger children. According to Vygotsky, older children's mental functioning is no longer dominated by immediate perception but is influenced by memory.

As children become more thoughtful, learning becomes more efficient and less frustrating for both students and teachers. Teachers spend more time on task and less time trying to get students to pay attention. Students can regulate themselves to participate in activities; they do not depend on "teacher regulation" to stay involved. Students are also better able to learn from previous social experiences, so that mastering social skills becomes easier. By contrast, children who do not develop the ability to regulate their attention and their behaviors before they enter kindergarten face a higher risk of falling behind academically (Blair, 2002).

The Role of Preschool

How can early childhood teachers help children develop the ability to act with forethought and intention, which will help them learn in later grades? The teacher's role is especially important; unfortunately, children today have fewer opportunities to learn to regulate themselves because many of the activities that they engage in work counter to developing thoughtful, deliberate action. Television, computer games, even the kinds of toys that children play with tend to emphasize behaviors that lead to more reactive thinking. One 5-year-old told his mom as she tried to play his computer game, "If you could just stop thinking and keep pressing the buttons as fast as you can, Mario would live a lot longer!"

From the Vygotskian perspective, early childhood teachers can foster the development of self-regulation in three ways: by helping children develop mature intentional play, by modifying existing activities to support cognitive skills, and by minimizing or eliminating activities that are counterproductive to developing such skills. Following are examples of these strategies that we have seen at work in preschool classrooms.[1]

Scaffolding Intentional Play

Mature intentional play is dramatic play in which children act out specific roles and plan their play (Elkonin, 1978; Vygotsky, 1977). Children describe the pretend scenario in advance and decide who will play what role and what will happen. They have to solve social problems when they have differing ideas about how play should proceed, as shown in this exchange:

Marcia: Let's pretend we're going on an airplane. We have to get tickets, take our passports, and then we go through security and get on the plane. I'll be the mom, and I'll have my baby.

Kim: I don't want to be a mom. I want to be the pilot. I'll take your ticket, and then I'll fly the airplane. You'll sit in the plane and eat.

Marcia: OK, you're the pilot, but then you help with the babies.

To play their parts, children need to remember the many actions that are going to occur; they practice the underlying skills of deliberate memory, focused attention, and self-regulation in this kind of play. In our work in classrooms, we have found that teachers need to incorporate support for this kind of play (Bodrova & Leong, 2003a). Young children need guidance to get the play going, to discuss play, and to act out what was planned.

Modifying Preschool Activities

A second way to foster self-regulation is to modify existing activities. For example, early childhood teachers regularly read books aloud and ask questions about the story to teach listening comprehension skills. By modifying this activity, a teacher can use a read-aloud to foster self-regulation.

Preschool teacher Sungu Hwang has children retell the story after he reads it aloud. The students sit in a circle and pass a "talking stick" to one another in turn, each child ending his or her comment with the words "and then. . . ". The talking stick ensures that children take turns, giving them practice in self-regulation. Repeating "and then . . ." helps them remember that the next person must add on to the story. During the first retelling, Mr. Hwang keeps the book open to the pictures to provide support; after a few readings, students recall the story on their own.

Minimizing Counterproductive Activities

The third way to promote self-regulation is to identify and modify classroom settings that work against the development of these competencies. In our experience, we have found that both extremely chaotic classrooms and extremely teacher-directed classrooms are counterproductive to developing self-regulation and other underlying skills in children. Classrooms where children flit from activity to activity support reactive behavior. But when all the instruction is whole-group, students become too teacher-regulated.

One preschool teacher we observed in rural Iowa noticed that her students were most likely to get out of control as they

Aims of Education

What is the use of transmitting knowledge if the individual's total development lags behind?

—Maria Montessori

transitioned from playtime in classroom centers to a group read-aloud. When she simply told students to clean up and come sit on the carpet, many returned to their play instead of cleaning up; the teacher found herself continually "policing" cleanup and leading children one at a time to the carpet to start the read-aloud. She realized that excess teacher regulation and the amount of time some children had to sit waiting were making this transition chaotic, so she modified the routine to encourage self-regulation. Now as playtime ends, the teacher plays a tape of the song "Down By the Bay." Students know to start putting their toys away as soon as they hear the line "Did you ever see a bear?" They know when they hear the phrase "llamas eating pajamas" that the song will end soon and that they need to hurry and finish. This teacher now looks forward to cleanup time as an opportunity for students to practice self-regulation.

Preschool environments like these that nurture foundational cognitive skills are not incompatible with nurturing academic skills. Including underlying cognitive, linguistic, and social-emotional competencies in our definition of what is needed to educate the whole child will help educators build the skills children need to be active, lifelong learners. Preschool educators should view academic skills and concepts as valuable tools in the process of developing these essential competencies—not as the end goal of preschool education.

Note

1. Some examples are composites of practices we have seen in several classrooms. All names are pseudonyms.

References

Blair, C. (2002). School readiness. *American Psychologist, 57*(2), 111–127.

Bodrova, E., & Leong, D. (2003a). Chopsticks and counting chips. *Young Children, 58*(3), 10–17.

Bodrova, E., & Leong, D. J. (2003b). Learning and development of preschool children from the Vygotskian perspective. In V. Ageyev, B. Gindis, A. Kozulin, & S. Miller (Eds.), *Vygotsky's theory of education in cultural context.* New York: Cambridge University Press.

Elkonin, D. (1978). Psychologija igry [The psychology of play]. Moscow: Pedagogika. Selected chapters of this book are available in English in the January/February 2005 and March/April 2005 issues of the *Journal of Russian and East European Psychology.*

Vygotsky, L. S. (1956). Obuchenije i razvitije v doshkol'nom vozraste [Learning and development in preschool children]. In *Izbrannye psychologicheskije trudy* (pp. 204–205). Moscow: RSFSR Academy of Pedagogical Sciences.

Vygotsky, L. S. (1977). Play and its role in the mental development of the child. In M. Cole (Ed.), *Soviet developmental psychology.* White Plains, NY: M. E. Sharpe.

Zaporozhets, A. V. (1978). Printzip razvitiya v psichologii [*Principles of development in psychology*]. Moscow: Pedagogika.

ELENA BODROVA is a Senior Researcher at Mid-continent Research for Education and Learning in Aurora, Colorado; 303-632-5610; ebodrova@mcrel.org. **DEBORAH J. LEONG** is Professor of Psychology at Metropolitan State College of Denver in Golden, Colorado; 303-279-5589; leongd@mcsd.edu.

Rethinking Early Childhood Practices

FRANCIS WARDLE, PH.D

All professions have a canon of beliefs and practices. Some of these come from research and best practices; many simply develop and are passed on without critical examination. The early childhood field is no exception. Not only should any "self-renewing" profession continually re-examine itself on a regular basis, but, in this period of postmodern thought, we have the opportunity to carefully evaluate many beliefs that our profession accepts as the truth.

Critical theory is one way to examine our common beliefs and practices. Critical theory is, "an umbrella term for a range of perspectives . . . (that) all assume knowledge is socially constructed . . . From a critical theory perceptive, therefore, no universal truths or set of laws or principals can be applied to everyone." (Ryan & Glieshaber, 2004, p. 45) However, this article does not suggest we simply deconstruct our profession from one specific point of view for several reasons. First, a critical theory critique presupposes our current early childhood practices come from some kind of logic and order—one of power and oppression. Secondly, the power orientation creates straw arguments: in early childhood education an attack on developmentally appropriate practice (DAP) (Hatch, Bowman, Jortlan, Morgan, Hart, Soto, Lubeck & Hyson, 2002; Lubeck, 1998.). As you will see in this article, many early childhood practices should be more DAP, not less (particularly because, in spite of the view of many critics, most of our early childhood programs are not DAP) (Dunn & Kontos, 1997). Finally, when I teach my qualitative methods graduate classes I strongly advise students against threats to theoretical validity—the temptation to force or morph all data into an existing and popular theoretical orientation (Burke, 1997). It's not hard to make 'the data fit'.

The question, of course, is where have our practices come from? Critical theorists say from research on white, middle class students, and from dead white men (Ryan & Grieshaber, 2004). I believe they have largely developed as a downward extension of school practices (Wardle, 2003). It seems to me, historically, that our approach to everything regarding young children—building design, playgrounds, health/safety, bus safety, scheduling, curriculum, etc., can be characterized as a reaction against the traditional home, farm and village upbringing, and a belief that school is better and early school is even better (Johnson, Christie & Wardle, 2005).

Same-Age Grouping

Part of the history of U.S. public schools is the one-room schoolhouse, which was characterized by vertical grouping of children, with older children assisting younger ones as they themselves learned about service and caring for others. But in 1843 Horace Mann returned from visiting the Prussian military, and decided the regimented, same-age grouping would be an improvement (Wiles & Bondi, 1998).

While same-age grouping has dominated K–12 schools, it is slowly becoming the norm in most early childhood programs. Many Head Start programs, for example, have children grouped by "older 4s" and "younger 4s". The pedagogical rationale for this approach is to target curricula content and instruction to specific age groups. However, the arguments against same-age grouping of children in early childhood programs are overwhelming:

The tremendous diversity within age groups, due to gender; race/ethnicity social-economic status, experience, and exceptionality (special needs and gifted) make curriculum targeting well neigh impossible.

The reduced size of most US families (Berger, 2005) requires that children have multiage experiences in their early childhood programs.

Vygotsky argues learning takes place when an 'expert' assists the learner to learn within his zone of proximal development; and the best expert is often a child who is slightly more advanced than the learner (Berk & Winsler, 1995).

Piaget argues that one of the best ways for a child to learn is when a child is 'forced' to expand his existing schemas to match overwhelming evidence from the environment. One of the best ways to expose a child to this evidence is by interacting with a child who is one level higher than the learner (Brainerd, 1978).

It would seem that, along with language, race/ethnicity and income, age differences are forms of diversity we should expose our children to.

Character education curricula in early childhood programs stress a sense of caring and responsibility (Wardle, 2004). One of the best ways to develop these values is to have children practice helping, caring for, and protecting younger, more vulnerable children. The result may be fewer issues with bullying and harassment in the later school years.

The Importance of a Daily Schedule

A regular, daily schedule teaches children a needed sense of security, especially children from low-income and minority homes. Almost all early childhood textbooks and research articulate this belief. For example, "Daily routines form the framework for a young child's day; some children depend on them for a sense of security. . . . But no matter what type of schedule the early childhood program follows, there are certain routines that should occur daily" (Gonzalez-Mena, 2001, p. 262). And, according to Gordon & Browne, (2004), "Children are more secure in a place that has a consistent schedule; they can begin to anticipate the regularity of what comes next and count on it" (p. 367) "Routines are the framework of programs for young children. A routine is a constant; each day certain events are repeated, providing continuity and a sense of order. Routines are reassuring to children, and they take pride in mastering them" (Gordon & Browne, 2004, p. 366).

The argument for this canon goes something like this: "Children need regular routines to enable them to develop a sense of security in a predictable environment". And, of course, the more "unstructured" their home life, the more they need structure and routine in a program. Argument against this fixation on routine include:

Research has shown time and again that the most important form of security for young children is a consistent, warm, responsive, long-term relationship with a caregiver (Bowlby, 1969; Honig, 2002; Lally, 1998). Yet there is an embarrassing dearth of suggestions in the literature about ways to achieve this important relationship, which requires providing caregivers with adequate salaries, benefits, and working conditions. Is our fixation on schedules and routines due to the inability to provide consistent and long-term care with one provider?

Children have no sense of time as adults' know it. Certainly the sequence of activities provides important mental scripts that children use in cognitive and language development (Berger, 2005). Many argue that one reason for schedules is to teach children about time, and the behaviors needed to function in an adult world fixated on schedules. Members of one of my early childhood classes argued vehemently that children who don't follow a strict timetable would not be able to function effectively in the adult world. After I pointed out that each of them were late for class, they dropped the argument!

Children from less structured, more chaotic environments desperately need time to fully complete important projects they are personally and socially invested in, without being interrupted by a more powerful adult. Research suggests that children who lack a sense of control over their learning eventually reduce commitment to on-task behavior (Johnson, Christie & Wardle, 2005). Thus it would seem to me that all children, but particularly children from unstructured environments, need programs that encourage them to pursue projects and interactions until they decide they are finished.

The new brain research has reinforced the need for stimulation, change, challenge, involvement, and meaningful learning (Shore, 1997), which is often much easier to achieve with a less structured schedule, and more difficult to achieve with more structure. Structure begets bored children, frustrated teachers, and stressful transitions.

Learning is continuous. Young children learn in continuous ways, relating new learning to past experiences and accomplishments. Children learn best when a project, idea, or activity veers off into new and different directions, "emerging" into new and exciting learning (Dewey, 1938).

The American workplace is less and less structured by traditional routines, and more often organized by projects, flextime, team activities, and self-directed problem solving. Early childhood programs need to develop workers who can structure their own time, and who do not feel confused when work demands require varied and flexible schedules.

Meals Must be Provided at Regular Intervals

One of the areas where early childhood programs insist on a schedule is eating. While this is often dictated by the reality of the kitchen schedule, catering service, and use of the cafeteria, we also seem to deeply believe that children should be fed "on schedule". However, it is fairly well established that infants should be fed, "on demand".

Most of us will stop off at a store to pick up a snack when we get hungry, and go to the refrigerator when we cannot last till the next full meal. Why not allow children to do the same? Does our meal schedule—and the accompanying need for children to clean off their plate before they get desert—contribute to our child obesity problem? After all, if a child thinks they won't get food until a specific time (or maybe, if they won't get it till very late at home), they might "stuff themselves" so they won't get hungry. Providing healthy snacks in a refrigerator in the classroom for children to eat when they are hungry might be a good idea.

Sleep-Time Should be Scheduled

The biggest struggle my wife and I had with our children's child care was naptime. We insisted our children not have a nap because when they did they would not get tired until 11 at night. At the opposite end of the spectrum, some teachers complain that parents keep their children up so late that they fall asleep before naptime. Maybe early childhood programs should provide a quiet area away from the noise and activity of the classroom, where children can lie down when they get tired.

A Curriculum is at the Center of All Good Educational Programs

According to Diane Trister Dodge and Toni Bickart (2003), "Curriculum and assessment drive our work with young children every day. If we do them well we achieve positive outcomes for children. Good input means good output" (p. 28). The No Child Left Behind Act and the Head Start outcomes have refueled this belief in the veracity of a curriculum. A curriculum is, "a plan for learning" (Wiles & Bondi, 1998), and most are driven by specific outcomes—those that some expert has decided are needed to reach the next rung on the educational ladder (usually developmentally inappropriate kindergarten entry-level skills). Several questions, however, must be asked:

Does, in fact, input result in output? Is the educational model so simple, mechanical, linear, and businesslike? Doesn't this kind of model deny any sense of inner direction, child-center learning, and spirituality and soul? (Steiner, 1926).

Does following the prescribed rungs of the ladder develop the kind of people we want? There are many examples of famous people who did not follow these rungs: Einstein, Erikson, Bill Gates, home-schooled students, and the very successful graduates of the free schools in the 1960s and 1970s. A mother told me a story of her daughter who dropped out of high school. When she finally decided to go to college she negotiated with the college to take the first two semesters on a trial basis—without ever getting a high school diploma or GED. Not only did she pass with flying colors, she is now a pediatrician!

Who develops the plan, and how do they know what is best for our children? John Dewey (1938) talked a lot about basing curricula of children's own experiences, interests, and aspirations.

Why do we not trust children and teachers to collaborate with parents to develop their own curricular? This reliance on a curriculum is a strong indictment against the professionalism of teachers; it's also obviously a deep belief that children will not learn what is needed without a curriculum-by-numbers approach.

What happens if the plan is wrong? More specifically, what happens if the plan misses important outcomes, such as teaching a second language beginning in preschool, focusing extensively on the epidemic of childhood obesity, spending more time and energy on emotional, and social development and conflict resolution, and integrating effective diversity education? Are we developing a bunch of fat, asocial citizens who cannot relate to others, who are intolerant of differences, and who cannot compete in the global marketplace because they only speak English, but who can read, write, and work on a computer at home?

Minority Students are Unsuccessful Due to a Eurocentric Approach to Education

Multiculturalists insist that the failure of minority children in our educational programs is because these programs are Eurocentric—developed to work only for the white children. Early childhood multiculturalists have fully embraced this cannon (Ramsey, 1998; York, 2003). Clearly, there is a tragic achievement gap between white and Asian students on the one hand, and Native American, Black and Hispanic students on the other hand. But is this gap due solely to an Eurocentric approach?

Asian children as a group, who are clearly a minority, not only do as well as white children, but in some cases do better (Thernstrom & Thernstrom, 2003).

Picture young Mayan children in their ragged clothes and bare feet writing in small slate tablets with subs of chalk in a 'school'—a four-post structure with a laminar (corrugated iron) roof. These little children learned their lesson enthusiastically. The fact the building was primitive and lacked resources, the instructor white, and the material Eurocentic, did not bother them. They were motivated to learn because their parents were learning with them, and because they were starved for basic literacy instruction.

We must admit that, while we have children in this country from a variety of cultural backgrounds, all of them are American—especially African American, Native American, and Hispanic families that have been here for generations. As such, these children and their families generally subscribe to the American values of competition, individualism, legal justice, materialism, gender differences, the value of education, and religious freedom.

The fact a disproportionate number of minorities are placed in special education is, I believe, more of a function of the U.S. deficit approach to disabilities (IDEA), than a Eurocentric idea. After all, far fewer students in Europe are diagnosed with special needs than the U.S., and more boys, including white boys (the ultimate symbol of white privilege) are in special education (Berger, 2005).

The strongest statistical correlation with school success is income (Hout, 2002). The problem is that minority families are statistically more represented in the low-income category. Schools in low-income areas tend to have fewer resources, less experienced teachers, and more discipline problems (Hout, 2002)

School success is largely dependent on family support of education. I have proposed what I call a three-legged-stool model of school success: home, school and community. Each leg must provide the optimal stimulation, support, structure and expectations needed. The seat connects all 3 legs together, in a unified manner, much like Bronfenbrenner's mesosystem (1979). Without the seat the stool falls; without open, supportive two-way communication between home, school and community, the minority child will not succeed.

Is a Eurocentric approach really bad for our minority children? Many claim that because DAP is Eurocentric it is a detrimental to minority children (Lubeck, 1998; Ramsey 1998; York, 2003). But a DAP approach calls for adjusting the curriculum to meet individual needs, working closely with families and the community, responding to "the whole child", and considering cultural and linguistic diversity (Bredekamp & Copple, 1997). How is this bad? As our population becomes more and more diverse we need a more DAP approach, and a less standards-based approach (Wardle & Cruz-Janzen, 2004).

Further, our very approach to special needs, linguistic diversity, and the right of each individual child to succeed in our schools is 'based on this country's Eurocentric belief in individual rights, educational opportunity, and legal justice. The academic divide is a tragedy in a society that depends heavily on its schools to provide equal opportunity. We must solve this dilemma. To do so, we must challenge our orthodoxies about the causes of the problem.

The Calendar Activity

In 1996 I was asked by Partners of the Americas to build a play ground for a low income crèche in Brazil (Wardle, 1999). While I was checking out the site I toured the dingy classrooms. There were no books, building blocks, or paints. There was no housekeeping area or place for the children to nap, and the kitchen was very poorly equipped. But they did have a calendar proudly affixed to the wall (with names and numbers in Portuguese, of course). Recently in a graduate psychology class I discussed with my students that, according to Piaget, preoperational children cannot possibly do the calendar activity in a meaningful way (Wardle, 2001). Then a kindergarten teacher asked me the obvious question: why do we teach this activity? And it seems like we teach it all over the world!

I have already discussed that children's ideas of time are based on activity—what we do—not the passage of time. Further, in today's world it's extremely easy to know the date by checking a watch, computer or newspaper. Important concepts of such as past, present and future, sequence, repetition, can all be taught in much more effective ways.

Universal ECE Standards Will Improve the Image of Our Profession

Clearly our profession is not well regarded by much of the public: Many see us as "just babysitters"; the teaching profession still perpetuates the notion that school starts at kindergarten. I recently met a Head Start education manager who believes the new outcomes are very positive, "because now we are not just babysitters". And many colleges prefer to graduate teachers with an elementary education degree with a few ECE classes tacked on, rather than a full ECE degree (Silva & Johnson, 1999). Others deeply believe if it's something that any parent can do, then it can't be that difficult.

When the public's view of the counseling profession plummeted after the 'free love' approach of many therapists during the sixties, counseling organizations quickly established professional codes of ethnics and developed training standards for their field. The early childhood profession is doing the same thing, creating codes of ethics (NAEYC, 1989, 1992, 1998), codifying a ladder of professional development, and professing the value of standards. Head Start now requires college degrees for teachers; the No Child Left Behind act requires degrees for public school paraprofessionals.

But this will not increase the status of the early childhood profession. First, professionals must be paid like professionals and get the kind of benefits professionals deserve. In France ECE teachers are paid the same as regular teachers, have the same professional requirements, are paid the same benefits, and have the same number of paid in-service and further education classes each year (and, of course, paid substitutes) (Hurless, 2004). Secondly, in my mind one of the things that perpetuate the public's low view of our profession is a total lack of ethical behavior. And I'm not talking about teachers. From my personal experience in Head Start, corporate child care, and early childhood leadership groups, I have come to realize that members at the top of our profession do not follow the ethical standards that we ask of our teachers.

And, as we are discovering with K-12 standards, the negatives of standards for the early childhood field far outweighs any positives. These include:

Children who cannot achieve the standards are viewed as failures or placed in special education.

All the schools resources—space, energy professional support, money—are focused 100 percent toward the standards.

Everything else is secondary: special education, emotional/mental health, school climate, diversity, anti-obesity efforts, working with parents, etc.

The standards are not DAP. A central component of DAP is individual differences (Bredekamp & Copple, 1997). Declaring that every child should be reading at a third grade level denies this individual difference.

The entire concept of standard implies lack of a standard. While we are trying to change the stigma of children with special needs, we are creating a stigma that children who cannot meet a standard are somewhat abnormal. In some states, for example, special education students are still required to take each of the standardized tests.

There are many instances where important learning activities are being withheld from children because they have performed poorly on a standardized test. This includes withholding recess, physical education, computers, and extra classes such as music and art. These activities are the very thing these children desperately need; yet they are being withheld to improve their scores in literacy, math, and science.

Since we teach to the standards and their tests, an area that is not tested is simply unimportant. Thus art, music, dance, social development, emotional development, character education, conflict resolution, and physical education are shortchanged.

Conclusion

All professions develop a canon of beliefs and practices that are passed from generation to generation. Unfortunately, if these canons are not carefully examined, we can end up perpetuating harmful practices in the name of professional behavior. This article highlighted areas important for careful examination, and most importantly areas where a change of approach might be beneficial to the children in early childhood programs.

References

Berger, K. (2005). *The developing person. Through the lifespan.* (6th ed.). New York, NY: Worth Publisher.

Berk, L.E. & Winsler, A. (1995). *Scaffolding children's learning: Vygotsky and early childhood education.* Washington, DC: NAEYC.

Bowlby, J. (1969). Attachment. *Vol.1 of attachment and loss.* New York: Basic Books.

Brainerd, C.J. (1978). *Piaget's theory of Intelligence.* Englewood Cliffs, NJ: Prentice-Hall.

Bredekamp, S., & Copple, C. (1997). *Developmentally appropriate practice* (rev. ed.). Washington, DC: NAEYC.

Bronfenbrenner, U. (1979). *The ecology of human development.* Cambridge, MA: Harvard University Press.

Burke, J. R. (1997). Examining the validity structure of qualitative research. *Education,* 118 (2), 282–293.

Dodge, D.T., & Bickart, T. (2003). Curriculum, assessment, and outcomes. Putting them all in perceptive. *Children and Families,* XVII (1), 28–31.

Dewey, J. (1938). *Education and experience.* New York, NY: McMillan.

Dunn, L., & Kontos, S. (1997). Research in review: What we have learned about developmentally appropriate practice. *Young Children,* 52(4), 4–13

Gonzalez-Mena, J. (2001). Foundations. *Early Childhood education in a diverse society.* (2nd ed.) Mountain View, CA: Mayfield.

Gordon, A.M. & Browne, K.W (2004). *Foundations in early childhood education.* (6th ed.) Clifton Park, NJ: Delmar Learning.

Hatch, A. Bowman, B., Jor'dna, J., Morgan, Hart, C., Soto, J, Lubeck, S., and Hyson, M. (2002). Developmentally appropriate practice: Continuing the dialogue. *Contemporary Issues in Early Childhood,* 3, 439–57.

Honig, A.S. (2002). The power of positive attachment. *Scholastics Early Childhood Today.* (April), 32–34.

Hout, M. (2002). Test scores, education, and poverty. In J.M. Fish (Ed.) *Race and Intelligence: Separating Science from Myth* (329–354). Mahwah, NJ: Lawrence Erlbaum Associates.

Hurless, B.R. (Sept, 2004). Early childhood education in France. A personal perspective. *Beyond the Journal: Young Children on the Web.* Retrieved, Oct, 2004.

Johnson, J., Christie, J., & Wardle, F. (2005). *Play, development, and early education.* Boston, MA: Allyn and Bacon.

Lally, J.R. (1998). Brain research, infant learning and child care curriculum. *Child Care Information Exchange* (May/June), 46–48.

Lubeck, S. (1998). Is developmentally appropriate practice for everyone? *Childhood Education,* 74 (5) 283–92.

National Association for the Education of Young Children (1989, 1992, 1998). *Code of ethnical conduct and statement of commitment: Guidelines for responsible behavior in early childhood education.* (Rev. ed.). Brochure. Washington, DC: Author.

Ramsey, PG. (1998). *Teaching and learning in a diverse world: Multicultural education for young children.* (2nd ed) New York, NY: Teachers College Press.

Ryan, S., & Grieshaber, S. (2004). It's more than child development: Critical theories, research, and teaching young children. *Young Children,* 59 (6), 44–52.

Shore, R. (1997). *Rethinking the brain. New insights into early development.* New York, NY: Families and Work institute.

Silva, D.Y., & Johnson, J.E. (1999). Principals' preference for the N-3 certificate. *Pennsylvania Educational Leadership,* 18 (2), 71–81.

Steiner, R. (1926). *The essentials of education.* London: Anthroposophical Publishing Co.

Thernstrom, A., & Thernstrom, S. (2003). *No excuses: Closing the racial gap in learning.* New York, NY: Simon and Schuster.

Wardle, F. (1999). The story of a playground. *Child Care Information Exchange,* 128 (July/Aug), 28–30.

Wardle, F. (2001). Developmentally appropriate math: How children learn. *Children and Families. XVII* (2), 14–15.

Wardle, F. (2003). Introduction to early childhood education: A multidimensional approach to child-centered care and learning. Boston, MA: Allyn and Bacon.

Wardle, F. (2004). Character education: Seeing a bigger picture. *Child Care Information Exchange.* 160 (Nov/Dec.) 41–43.

Wardle, F., & Cruz-Janzen, M. I. (2004), *Meeting the needs of multiethnic and multiracial children in schools.* Boston, MA: Allyn and Bacon.

Wiles, J. & Bondi, J. (1998). *Curriculum development: A guide to practice* (5th ed.) Upper Saddle River, NJ: Merrill.

York, S. (2003). *Roots and Wings: Affirming culture in early childhood programs* (Rev. ed). St. Paul, MN: Redleaf Press.

Francis Wardle, Ph.D., teaches for the University of Phoenix (Colorado) and is the executive director for the Center for the Study of Biracial Children. He has just published the book with Marta Cruz Jansen, *Meeting the Needs of Multiethnic and Multiracial Children,* available from Allyn & Bacon, www.ablongman.com.

One District's Study on the Propriety of Transition-Grade Classrooms

VERA ESTOK

The end of the school year brought the usual cheers from the children, a flurry of exchanging phone numbers, and promises to kweep in touch. As a pre-first teacher, I too cheered, traded phone numbers, and promised to keep in touch with my colleagues.

Our task...was to review the district's pre-first classrooms, in which kindergartners considered developmentally unprepared for first grade attend an extra-year transitional program.

During the previous six months, my fellow teachers and I had become close partners in reviewing our program's approach to individualized education and the use of sound early childhood practice. We had served on a committee formed by Springfield (Ohio) Local Schools to align our district philosophy with developmentally appropriate practice to meet the individual needs of young children. Our task—now completed—was to review the district's pre-first classrooms, in which kindergartners considered developmentally unprepared for first grade attend an extra-year transitional program.

We began our six-month journey by comparing our practices with those advocated by NAEYC (Bredekamp 1987; Bredekamp & Copple 1997). Many questions arose. Committee members wanted to know what had prompted the district's adoption of pre-first 23 years earlier. They were also interested in what research shows about the academic achievement and self-esteem of children placed in pre-first classrooms. We wondered where professional organizations stand on pre-first programs. Finally, all of us wanted to examine existing alternatives, those that would best align our early childhood classes with current best practices. This article outlines the process followed by our district's teachers and administrators to improve our early childhood program.

History of Pre-first Programs

Pre-first classrooms were first introduced in the United States in the 1940s as reading readiness programs for children who lacked necessary skills for formal reading instruction (Harris

1970). Each pre-first classroom had a low teacher-child ratio, a flexible curriculum, and an interactive environment with learning centers (Horm-Wingerd, Carella, & Warford 1993; Patton & Wortham 1993). In the late 1970s, with pressure mounting for more academic emphasis in kindergarten and first grade and reliance on standardized testing for promotion and placement, interest in pre-first programs was renewed. In response to this emphasis on academics, Springfield Local Schools added a pre-first classroom. The implementation of the new class

Views on Grade Retention

"When individual children do not make expected learning progress, neither grade retention nor social promotion are used; instead, initiatives such as more focused time, individualized instruction, tutoring, or other individual strategies are used to accelerate children's learning."

—NAEYC

"Delaying children's entry into school and/or segregating them into extra-year classes actually labels children as failures at the outset of their school experience. These practices are simply subtle forms of retention. Not only is there a preponderance of evidence that there is no academic benefit from retention in its many forms, but there also appear to be threats to the social-emotional development of the child subjected to such practices."

—NAECS/SDE

"Students recommended for retention but advanced to the next level end up doing as well as or better academically than non-promoted peers. Children who have been retained demonstrate more social regression, display more behavior problems, suffer stress in connection with being retained, and more frequently leave high school without graduating."

—NAECS/SDE

Sources: From NAEYC position statement on developmentally appropriate practice, online pp. 16–17: www.naeyc.org/about/positions/pdf/PSDAP98.PDF and NAECS/SDE position statement on kindergarten entry and placement, online pp. 4 and 10: www.naeyc.org/about/positions/pdf/Psunacc.pdf

was featured in *Changing to a Developmentally Appropriate Curriculum—Successfully* (Uphoff 1989).

Today, some school districts still initiate pre-first classes as intervention programs for children who, regardless of chronological age, are considered "unready" or "immature" for placement in a regular first grade. Generally, the purpose of an additional year of instruction is to allow children to mature and develop those skills necessary for success in a regular first grade curriculum (Smith & Shepard 1987). An assumption of pre-first grade placement is that participating children will experience academic success and demonstrate higher levels of achievement than would have been possible if they had gone straight to first grade. Some studies (for example, Bohl 1984) support transitional programs based on a maturational theoretical perspective by considering them a "gift of time."

What the Research Shows

The committee weighed the research information carefully. We realized that transitional placement—a decision that requires an additional year of school life—should not be taken lightly. We turned our attention toward finding research that would support pre-first's success at promoting children's higher academic achievement and greater self-esteem.

Our investigation found the use of transition programs questionable (Shepard & Smith 1989). Gredler (1984) suggests it is counterproductive to wait for children to mature.

Academic Achievement

Three studies offer an extended and in-depth analysis of academic achievement of children in transitional programs. Shepard and Smith (1989); Mantzicopoulos and Morrison (1991); and Ferguson, Jimerson, and Dalton (2001) used recognized testing and screening measures and a host of variables to compare children in transitional classes with peers who had been promoted to first grade. The carefully designed studies show little or no improvement in achievement between children who attended extra-year programs and their peers who moved into first grade. Moreover, when placement in a transitional program did improve/increase academic achievement, the benefits prove to be short-lived. In all three studies the differences between test scores of children in transitional classes and comparison groups diminished and were nonexistent by the end of fourth grade.

Self-esteem

While objective measures of the cognitive functioning of children are highly developed, measuring social and emotional functioning is less exact, lacking comparable reliability and validity. Still, Sandoval and Fitzgerald (1985) and Rihl (1988) document a negative or insignificant difference in the self-concept and emotional development of children assigned to extra-year classrooms.

When placement in a transitional program did improve/increase academic achievement, the benefits were found to be short-lived.

Examination of the research was beginning to sway the committee toward an alternative to the pre-first program that would solidify our early childhood program, but what would that be? We concluded that professional organizations might offer some guidance.

What Professional Organizations Recommend

In 1987, following the release of its position statement on developmentally appropriate practice, NAEYC noted that tracking young children into ability groups is developmentally *inappropriate* practice (Bredekamp 1987). David Elkind, NAEYC past president, calls transitional classes simply "another programmatic strategy for dealing with the mismatch between children and first grade curriculum" (1987, 175). More recently, NAEYC has recommended, "Children who fall behind [should] receive individualized support, such as tutoring, personal instruction, focused time on areas of difficulty, and other strategies to accelerate learning progress" (Bredekamp & Copple 1997, 176).

Now that we knew what was needed to enhance our program, implementing a full-day kindergarten program was the next step.

The National Association of Early Childhood Specialists in State Departments of Education (NAECS/SDE) also finds transitional classes unacceptable. The NAECS/SDE states in a position paper that "all children should be welcomed into regular heterogeneous classroom settings and not be segregated into transitional programs following kindergarten" (1987, 10). In a newer, revised position statement, NAECS/SDE points out, "Reducing class size, making the curriculum less abstract and therefore more related to children's conceptual development, insisting that only the most appropriately trained, competent, child-oriented teachers are placed in kindergarten programs, and assuring every child access to a high-quality prekindergarten program are among better means to achieving the educational goal of success for all students" (2000, 14).

Our committee turned to our own state board of education for more guidance. Following a longitudinal study, the Ohio Department of Education concluded that kindergarten and first grade classrooms need developmentally appropriate programs to address children's diverse needs (Ohio Department of Education 1992). The study offers three ways to accomplish this task: (1) implement a preschool program in public schools, (2) establish Chapter 1 reading services, and (3) expand alternate-day and half-time kindergartens to full-day programs. Of the three suggestions, extension to a full-day kindergarten program is reported to reduce grade retention rates and produce the fewest remedial placements. This was the new direction we had been seeking.

We encourage any district that still has a pre-first in its early childhood program to analyze the appropriateness of such classes and find better ways to educate young children.

Implementing Our Plan

Now that we knew what was needed to enhance our program, implementing a full-day kindergarten program was the next step. As is almost always the case, financing proved to be the most difficult part of the project. Knowing what the addition of full-day kindergarten could mean in the growth of our district, our administrative staff pulled together. They tightened the budget by eliminating the pre-first program and asked the high school and middle school to make as many cuts as they could. State funds already allocated to our district were redirected toward funding the project.

At the final school board meeting of the school year, board members were so impressed with our commitment and dedication to the project that they gave unanimous approval for full-day kindergarten. It would be implemented the next school year.

Will the addition of a full-day kindergarten experience provide added support to the children in our school system? Our committee did its homework well, and we are confident that we are following guidelines to ensure that every child has a successful school experience. We encourage any district that still has a pre-first in its early childhood program to analyze the appropriateness of such classes and find better ways to educate young children.

I am no longer a pre-first teacher but a kindergarten teacher eagerly waiting to join in as children cheer for the new school year.

References

Bohl, N. 1984. A gift of time: The transition year. *Early Years* (January): 14.

Bredekamp, S., ed. 1987. *Developmentally appropriate practice in early childhood programs serving children from birth through age 8.* Exp. ed. Washington, DC: NAEYC.

Bredekamp, S., & C. Copple, eds. 1997. *Developmentally appropriate practice in early childhood programs.* Rev. ed. Washington, DC: NAEYC.

Elkind, D. 1987. *Miseducation: Pre-schoolers at risk.* New York: Knopf.

Ferguson, P., S. Jimerson, & M. Dalton. 2001. Sorting out successful failures: Exploratory analyses of factors associated with academic and behavioral outcomes of retained students. *Psychology in the Schools* 38 (4): 327–41.

Gredler, G.R. 1984. Transition classes: A viable alternative for the at-risk child? *Psychology in the Schools* 21: 463–70.

Harris, A.J. 1970. *How to increase reading ability.* 5th ed. New York: David McKay.

Horm-Wingerd, D., P. Carella, & S. War-ford. 1993. Teacher's perceptions of the effectiveness of transition classes. *Early Education and Development* 4 (2): 130–38.

Mantzicopoulos, D., & P. Morrison. 1991. Transitional first grade referrals. *Journal of Educational Psychology* 90 (1): 122–33.

NAECS/SDE (National Association of Early Childhood Specialists in State Departments of Education). 1987. Unacceptable trends in kindergarten entry and placement. Position statement. ERIC ED 297 856.

NAECS/SDE. 2000. Still unacceptable trends in kindergarten entry and placement. Position statement. Online: www.naeyc. org/about/positions/pdf/Psunacc.pdf and http://naecs.crc.uiuc. edu/position/trends2000.html

Ohio Department of Education, Division of Early Childhood Education. 1992. *Effects of pre-school attendance and kindergarten schedule: Kindergarten through grade 4. A longitudinal study.* 1992. ERIC ED 400 038.

Patton, M., & S. Wortham. 1993. Transition classes, a growing concern. *Journal of Research in Childhood Education* 8 (1): 32–40.

Rihl, J. 1988. *Pre-first: A year to grow. A follow-up study.* ERIC ED 302 332.

Sandoval, J., & P. Fitzgerald. 1985. A high school follow-up of children who were nonpromoted or attended a junior first grade. *Psychology in the Schools* 22: 164–70.

Shepard, L.A., & M.L. Smith. 1989. Effects of kindergarten retention at the end of the first grade. *Psychology in the Schools* 16 (5): 346–57.

Smith, M.L., & L.A. Shepard. 1987. What doesn't work: Explaining policies of retention in the early grades. *Phi Delta Kappan* 69: 129–34.

Uphoff, J. 1989. *Changing to a developmentally appropriate curriculum—successfully.* Rosemont, NJ: Programs for Education.

VERA ESTOK, ME, is a full-day kindergarten teacher with Springfield Local Schools in Holland, Ohio. Vera taught pre-first classes for six years and has four years of experience in a variety of kindergarten classrooms.

Successful Transition to Kindergarten: The Role of Teachers & Parents

PAM DEYELL-GINGOLD

While new kindergartners are worrying about whether or not anyone will be their friend and if they'll be able to find the bathroom, their preschool teachers are wondering if they've succeeded at preparing their small students for this big transition. In recent years the role of kindergarten has changed from an extension of preschool to a much more academic environment because of new standards in the public schools that "push back" academic skills to earlier grades.

How can we ensure that our students make a smooth transition? Are our students mature enough? What can we do to make them "more" ready? This article will explore the skills that constitute kindergarten "readiness," how preschool teachers can collaborate with parents and kindergarten teachers to make the process more rewarding for all, and activities to help prepare children for what will be expected of them in kindergarten.

The Transition Process

Children go through many transitions throughout their lives, but one of the most important transitions is the one from a preschool program to kindergarten. "During this period behavior is shaped and attitudes are formed that will influence children throughout their education" (PTA and Head Start, 1999). Children's transitions are most strongly influenced by their home environment, the preschool program they attend, and the continuity between preschool and kindergarten (Riedinger, 1997).

In 1995, Head Start and the Parent Teacher Association (PTA) began a plan to create a partnership between the two organizations in order to create effective transition practices and to promote continuity in parent and family involvement in the schools. Three pilot programs were studied to determine "best practice" in kindergarten transition, and to foster the continued strong involvement of families in their children's education. They worked with elementary schools to create parent-friendly environments and to develop strategies that lessen the barriers to involvement (Head Start & PTA, 1999). Even Start, a federal program for low-income families implemented to improve educational opportunities for children and adults, also helps parents to work with the school system to help their children succeed. Their research found that parents felt that the way in which Even Start focuses on the family strengths rather than weaknesses and allows the families to identify their own needs, empowered them more than anything else to help them to support their children in school (Riedinger, 1997).

Kindergarten Readiness

A 1998 study by the National Center for Early Development & Learning of nearly 3,600 kindergarten teachers nationwide indicated that 48 percent of children have moderate to serious problems transitioning to kindergarten. Teachers are most often concerned about children's skills in following directions, academics, and working independently. There seems to be a discrepancy between the expectations of teachers and the actual skills of kindergarten children. Therefore, a need for kindergarten teachers to collaborate with both parents and preschool teachers exists (Pianta & Cox, 1998). School readiness is more than a matter of academics, though. As reported in a National Education Goals Panel in 1998; "The prevailing view today, however, is that readiness reflects a range of dimensions, such as a child's health and physical development, social and emotional development, approaches to learning, language and communication skills, and cognitive and general knowledge" (California Department of Education, 2000).

Historically, kindergarten was a "children's garden": a place to interact for the first time with a group of agemates, and to learn basic skills through play. Today, because of increasing numbers of working mothers, single-parent families, and strict welfare regulations, many children begin having group experiences in a child care program or family child care home at a much earlier age. Together with the concern that America's children are not getting adequate education to compete in a global market, our schools began to make the transition from the children's garden to "curriculum escalation" (Shepard & Smith, 1988) and "academic trickle-down" (Cunningham, 1988). While the trend towards focusing on academic skills continues at a fast pace, early childhood professionals argue for a more integrated curriculum that addresses the developmental needs of each child.

Social Adjustment

Although academics may be becoming increasingly more important, research shows that social skills are what most affect school adjustment (Ladd & Price, 1987; Ladd, 1990). Preschool teachers should not feel pressured into teaching academics beyond what is developmentally "best practice" (Bredekamp & Copple, 1997) but should continue to focus on social and emotional development. Children who have been rejected by their peers in kindergarten tend to have poor school performance, more absences, and negative attitudes towards school that last throughout their school years. "Three particular social skills that are known to influence children's peer acceptance: play behavior, ability to enter play groups, and communication skills" (Maxwell & Eller, 1994).

Play Behavior and Communication Skills

Specific behaviors that cause rejection by fellow students include things like rough play, arguing, upsetting things in class, trying to get their own way, and not sharing. Children who exhibit these behaviors also tend to be less independent and less cooperative than their peers. Most children prefer playing with others who are polite, caring, and attentive. Preschool teachers and parents need to teach young children social skills, especially how to enter social groups. For example, children who say, "Looks like that's a fun game, can I play?" are more likely to be accepted than those who shove others aside and whine, "I want a turn!"

Another important social skill is the ability to participate in complicated fantasy games and take part in making up and extending the story. Children who lack sufficient experience playing with agemates may feel frustrated at not being able to keep up with the capabilities of their classmates. "A generous amount of guided social experience with peers prior to kindergarten helps children do well in this new world" (Maxwell & Eller, 1994). Some children need assistance to learn how to play make-believe. A teacher can help model this by giving verbal cues like, "You be the mommy, and I'll be your little girl. Can I help you make dinner, Mommy?" Some children need reminders to keep them focused on their roles. Others may need help to read the emotions on people's faces. "Look at Nick's face. He is sad because you pulled the hat away from him." Because young children do not have a large enough vocabulary to express themselves, teachers can help them find words to express their feelings such as, "You're feeling frustrated. Let's go find a puzzle with fewer pieces."

Communication skills, such as being able to take part in a conversation, listen to others, and negotiate are also important. For example, children who speak directly to peers, are attentive to others in the group, and respond to the initiations of others tend to be liked by the other children. Disliked children are more likely to make irrelevant comments, reject the initiations of other children without reasons or explanations, and often make comments without directing them to anyone (Maxwell & Eller, 1994). Part of a teacher's task is to quietly remind children to look at the person they're talking to, and listen to what another child is saying.

Immaturity and Redshirting

A common practice when dealing with children who are not socially mature is to keep them out of school for a year, in the hope that "readiness will emerge." In academic circles this is referred to as "redshirting," a term borrowed from college athletics. However, "Research shows that redshirts are not gaining an academic advantage, and the extra year does not solve the social development problems that caused initial concern" (Graue, 1994). Parents who are told that their children need to stay home for a year should ask for the reasons.

"Developmentally appropriate practice is less common in kindergarten, and primary teachers face many constraints and pressures that teachers of younger children are not yet experiencing in the same intensity [although preschool appears to be next in line for "pushdown" curriculum]." (Jones, Evans, & Rencken, 2001). "If we think inclusively we have to problem-solve in ways to accommodate the incredible diversity presented by the characteristics of kindergartners. ... Redshirting and retention are outmoded tools that should be replaced by more appropriate practices. One step in the right direction is collaboration between preschool and elementary school educators" (Graue, 1994). A second step is to have parents understand what experiences can help their child have a successful transition.

Learning About Classroom Styles

In collaborating with kindergarten teachers, preschool teachers and parents need to visit the school and pay close attention to details that may affect their students in kindergarten. "When teachers and parents agree on a philosophy of education, children usually adjust more easily" (Maxwell & Eller, 1994). Children feel more secure in their new environment if they feel that their parents support the teacher and the school.

The first step may be either a meeting with the kindergarten teacher or a class field trip to the elementary school. "Observe kindergarten classrooms to identify teaching styles, classroom management techniques, and routines. Also try to identify skills that are needed to be successful in participating in the kindergarten classroom" (Karr-Jelinek, 1994).

In her research, Karr-Jelinek used a checklist of what parents (and teachers) should look for in a kindergarten classroom, to see if their children—both normally developing and with special needs—are ready for the classroom they visit (Karr-Jelineck, 1994):

- How many steps are given at a time in directions?
- What types of words are children expected to understand?
- How does each individual child compare to the other children?
- How long are children expected to sit still in a group?
- How often do children speak out of turn or move around when they should be sitting?
- How much independence is expected?
- What type of work is being done? (small groups, seatwork, etc.)
- Where might my special needs students need extra help?
- What kind of special information can I pass along to the teacher about each child?

Although expectations vary by teacher and school district, by the time children reach kindergarten they should be able to listen to a story in a group, follow two or three oral directions, take turns and share, follow rules, respect the property of others, and work within time and space constraints. They need to learn the difference between work and play, knowing when and where each is appropriate. "Most five-year-olds can express themselves fluently with a variety of words and can understand an even larger variety of words used in conversations and stories" (Nurss, 1987).

Many kindergartens make use of learning centers, small group instruction, and whole group language activities. However, others use "structured, whole group paper-and-pencil activities oriented to academic subjects, such as reading and mathematics. The curriculum in these kindergartens often constitutes a downward extension of the primary grade curriculum and may call for the use of workbooks, which are part of a primary level textbook series. Many early childhood professionals have spoken out on the inappropriateness of such a curriculum" (Nurss, 1987).

Preparing Parents for the Transition

High-quality preschool programs encourage parent involvement in the home and in the classroom. Volunteering to read during story time, to share cultural traditions, or to be a lunch guest are all ways for parents to feel that they are a part of their child's school life. According to the National PTA, parent and family involvement increases student achievement and success. If preschool teachers can make parents feel welcome helping in the classroom, they will be more likely to remain involved in their child's future education.

Many parents worry about their children entering elementary school because of their own negative school experiences. They may feel intimidated by teachers and uncomfortable showing up at school events—even for orientation and enrolling their children in school (Reidinger, 1997). Parents' expectations of how well children will do in school influence children's performance. It appears that parents who expect success may provide more support, encouragement and praise, which may give their children more self-esteem and confidence. The most important thing is that children who believe in their own abilities have been found to be more successful in school (Dweck, 1991).

To assist parents, preschool teachers can arrange visits to the school and take parents along on the kindergarten field trip. They can ask for children to be paired with a kindergarten "buddy" who can take them around, while parents meet with the teacher or go to the office to register their child. A study done by Rathbun and Hauskin (2001) showed that the more low-income students that were enrolled in a school, the less parental involvement there was. Involving low-income families in the schools may help to break the cycle of poverty of future generations.

One way to really help the family with transition is to empower the parents to act as advocates for their children. Parent meetings and newsletters can help parents learn how to work with school staff, learn about volunteer opportunities at school, as well as how to prepare their child at home for kindergarten. They may need some advice on how to help their children and themselves cope with anxieties related to transitions from preschool to kindergarten.

Preparing Children for Transition

In the last few weeks of summer, children start getting excited about going to kindergarten, and are apprehensive at the same time. It is important for parents to treat the child's entrance into kindergarten as a normal occurrence and not build up the event in children's minds. An important way to provide continuity for the child is to find preschool classmates or other children who will be in their kindergarten class. According to research, children who have a familiar peer in a new group setting have fewer problems adjusting to new environments (Howes, 1988).

Transition Activities for Parents and Children

The more you discuss this transition in a matter-of-fact way, the more comfortable children will become. Encourage parents to prepare their child for kindergarten with the following:

- Visit the school so the children can meet the kindergarten teacher and see what kindergarten is really like. Try to arrange for them to see more than one type of classroom activity, such as seatwork time and free choice time.
- Show them where the bathroom and cubbies are located.
- Find out what lunchtime will be like. If the children are going to be getting a school lunch, they may have to learn how to open new kinds of containers.
- Read books about kindergarten.
- Answer children's questions in a straight forward way about what they will do in kindergarten. Tell them they

will listen to stories, do counting activities, have group time, and play outside.

- Explore how long the kindergarten day is and what the daily routine will be like. They will want to know what will be the same as preschool and what will be different.

Kindergarten Readiness Is . . .

A Child Who Listens

To directions without interrupting
To stories and poems for five or ten minutes without restlessness

A Child Who Hears

Words that rhyme
Words that begin with the same sound or different sounds

A Child Who Sees

Likeness and differences in pictures and designs
Letters and words that match

A Child Who Understands

The relationship inherent in such words as up and down, top and bottom, little and big
The classifications of words that represent people, places and things

A Child Who Speaks and Can

Stay on the topic in class discussions
Retell a story or poem in correct sequence
Tell a story or relate an experience of her own

A Child Who Thinks and Can

Give the main idea of a story
Give unique ideas and important details
Give reasons for his opinions

A Child Who Adjusts

To changes in routine and to new situations without becoming fearful
To opposition or defeat without crying or sulking
To necessity of asking for help when needed

A Child Who Plays

Cooperatively with other children
And shares, takes turns and assumes his share of group responsibility
And can run, jump, skip, and bounce a ball with comparative dexterity

A Child Who Works

Without being easily distracted
And follows directions And completes each task
And takes pride in her work

*Adapted from Howlett, M.P. (1970, February 18). Teacher's edition: My Weekly Reader Surprise, Vol. 12, Issue 20.

- If the children are going to a school that presents more diversity than they are familiar with, talk honestly with them about racial and ethnic differences and disabilities.
- If children are going to be taking the schoolbus for the first time, you will need to discuss schoolbus safety rules.
- Reassure children that they will be picked up from school every day just as they are in preschool.
- Check to make sure your pre-kindergarten children are capable of basic kindergarten "readiness" skills. (See sidebar at left.)

Conclusion

The transition from preschool to kindergarten can be a stressful time for both children and parents. However, if preschool teachers can facilitate collaboration between parents and kindergarten and familiarize children with the workings of kindergarten, it will be a smoother process. Parents need to try to find a developmentally appropriate class for their child by observing different classrooms and talking to teachers about educational philosophies. Preschool teachers, with their knowledge of different learning styles and the temperaments of their students, can help everyone with this important transition.

References

Bredekamp, S. & Copple, C. (1997). *Developmentally appropriate practice for early childhood programs*. Revised edition. Washington, DC: NAEYC.

California Dept of Ed., (2000). *Prekindergarten learning and development guidelines*. Sacramento, CA.

Cunningham, A. 1988. Eeny, meeny, miny, moe: Testing policy and practice in early childhood. Berkeley, CA: National Commission on Testing and Public Policy In Graue, E (2001, May) What's going on in the children's garden today? *Young Children*.

Dweck, C.S. (1991). Self-theories and goals: their role in motivation, personality and development. In *Nebraska symposia on motivation*, Vol. 36, ed. by R. Dienstbier, 199–235, Lincoln: University of Nebraska Press. [In Maxwell, Eller, 1994]

Graue, E. (2001, May) What's going on in the children's garden today? *Young Children*, pp. 67–73.

Howes, C. (1988). Peer interaction of young children. Monographs of the Society for Research in Child Development 53 (2. Serial No. 217). In Maxwell, K. and Eller, C. (1994, September) Children's Transition to Kindergarten, *Young Children*.

Howlett, M.P. (1970, February 18). Teacher's edition: *My Weekly Reader Surprise*, Vol. 12, Issue 20.

Jones, E., Evans, K., & Rencken, K. (2001) *The Lively Kindergarten*, NAEYC publications.

Karr-Jelinek, C. (1994). *Transition to kindergarten: Parents and teachers working together*. Educational Resources Information Center.

Ladd, G.W., 1990. Having friends, keeping friends, making friends and being liked by peers in the classroom: Predictors of children's early school adjustment? *Child Development* (61) 1081–100.

Ladd, G.W., & J.M. Price. 1987. Predicting children's social and school adjustment following the transition from preschool to kindergarten. *Child Development*, (58) 1168–89.

Maxwell, K. & Eller, S. (1994, September). Children's transition to kindergarten. *Young Children*, pp.56–63.

National PTA & National Head Start Association. (1999). *Continuity for success: Transition planning guide*. National PTA, Chicago, IL. National Head Start Association, Alexandria, VA.

Nurss, J. 1987, *Readiness for Kindergarten*, ERIC Clearinghouse on Elementary and Early Childhood Education, Urbana, IL; BBB16656.

Pianta, R. & Cox, M. (1998). Kindergarten Transitions. Teachers 48% of Children Have Transition Problems. *NCEDL Spotlights Series*, No. 1, National Center for Early Development & Learning: Chapel Hill, NC.

Rathbun, A. & Hauskin, E. (2001). How are transition-to-kindergarten activities associated with parent involvement during kindergarten? Paper presented at the Annual meeting of the American Educational Research Foundation: Seattle, WA.

Riedinger, S. (1997), *Even Start: Facilitating transitions to kindergarten*. Dept. of Education: Washington, DC: Planning and Evaluation Service.

Shepard, I.A. & M.I. Smith. (1988) Escalating academic demand in kindergarten: counterproductive policies. *The Elementary School Journal*, (89) 135–45. In Maxwell, K. and Eller, C. (1994, September) Children's Transition to Kindergarten, Young Children.

PAM DEYELL-GINGOLD is a graduate student in Human Development at Pacific Oaks College. She works as master teacher at Head Start, teaches child development classes for Merced Community College, and is a freelance writer and anti-bias curriculum enthusiast. Her home is in the Sierra foothills near Yosemite National Park, California.

Second Time Around

If repeating a grade doesn't help kids, why do we make them do it?

Susan Black

Making students repeat a grade hasn't worked for 100 years, so why is it still happening? And why do government officials, school leaders, and teachers persist in recommending retention as a remedy for low student achievement—even when researchers call it a failed intervention?

Linda Darling-Hammond, executive director of Columbia University's National Center for Restructuring Education, Schools, and Teaching, has a one-word answer: assumptions. Many schools, she says, operate on the assumption that failing students motivates them to try harder, gives them another chance to "get it right," and raises their self-esteem.

Those claims aren't true, Darling-Hammond maintains. The widespread trust in retention is uncritical and unwarranted, she says. It ignores several decades of research showing that, for most children, retention:

- Fails to improve low achievement in reading, math, and other subjects.
- Fails to inspire students to buckle down and behave better.
- Fails to develop students' social adjustment and self-concept.

Darling-Hammond concedes that grade retention might benefit some students in the short term, but in the long term, holding students back puts them at risk. More often than not, students who are retained never catch up academically. Many eventually drop out, and some end up in the juvenile justice system.

The belief that students, as well as their parents, are to blame for low achievement plays into most retention decisions. But teachers and principals seldom accept their share of blame for inept instruction, lackluster lessons, low expectations, and other school factors that contribute to students' academic disengagement and behavior problems, Darling-Hammond says.

As a result, most retained students are just recycled. But as Darling-Hammond points out, simply giving students more of what didn't work the first time around is an exercise in futility.

Teachers' Power to Retain

It's easy to see why teachers believe retention works. But it's less easy to understand why schools allow teachers to hold so much power over this practice.

Gwendolyn Malone, a fifth-grade teacher in Virginia and president of her local teachers union, writes in *NEA Today* that retention offers students the chance to "refresh, relearn, and acquire new skills," as well as to gain self-confidence and become good students. She urges schools to "nip problems in the bud by retaining students early in their school careers"—as early as kindergarten and first grade.

Malone believes the threat of retention is an incentive for students to study so they'll be promoted with their same-age classmates. Weak students who are promoted, she says, end up feeling ashamed, angry, and defensive about their so-called deficiencies.

In most schools, classroom teachers determine which students will pass or fail. At the end of the 2003–04 school year, for instance, one New York City teacher identified 17 of her 28 third-graders for retention. The high numbers didn't trouble her—although she told a reporter that "there would be no fourth grade if all struggling children were held back."

Shane Jimerson of the University of California-Santa Barbara says teachers play a key role in deciding which students will be retained, even though most teachers are unfamiliar with research that casts a dubious light on this practice. School psychologists should study the research and present it to school staffs, Jimerson recommends, and they should head teams consisting of counselors, teachers, and administrators who will make pass/fail decisions.

But before they make those decisions, he says, team members should know these research findings:

- Retaining elementary-age students may provide an achievement "bounce," but gains tend to be slight and temporary; once the bounce tapers off, students either level off or again fall behind their classmates.
- Retaining kindergarten and first-grade students as a preventive intervention is no better for students than retaining them in upper grades.
- Retaining students without providing specific remedial strategies and attending to students' risk factors has little or no value.

Team decision making might help avoid a problem RMC Research Corporation's Beckie Anderson has identified. She reports that teachers often retain students to avoid criticism from teachers in the next grade for promoting poorly prepared students. Many principals, it turns out, are quietly complicit in this practice by giving teachers complete authority over retention decisions.

A Troubling Process

Over the years I've watched a number of schools, both rural and urban, retain more students each year, especially in kindergarten, first grade, and ninth grade. Many of the schools I've studied now hold back 30 to 40 percent of their youngest students, but a handful of schools retain close to 50 percent.

And many of the teachers and principals I've interviewed think of retention as standard practice. A first-grade teacher told me, "By November, I know which half of my class will pass and which half will fail."

The retention ritual doesn't begin in earnest until April or May, however, when teachers submit a list of students for retention to their principals, who generally approve their recommendations.

Here's how one such decision played out a few weeks before the close of school in 2004. A third-grade teacher called in a 10-year-old boy's mother to discuss retention, and I sat in on the conversation. The teacher admitted that the boy—I'll call him Ryan—was "quite smart," especially in science and math. But, she insisted, Ryan, who is small for his age, needed another year to "grow into third grade."

The mother balked—Ryan had already repeated first grade for the same reason—but the teacher overruled her objection. The principal was nowhere to be seen, and neither were the school's counselor or psychologist.

At the end of the meeting the teacher brought a signed form to the office, and Ryan was officially retained. I thought of Lorrie Shepard and Mary Smith's 1989 book *Flunking Grades* in which they write that "teachers consistently underplay the extent of conflict with parents over the decision to retain and underestimate the degree of parents' active resistance or passive but unhappy compliance."

Teachers may believe retention does no harm, but Anderson says researchers' interviews with children who were held back in elementary school tell a different story. More than 25 percent of the children were too ashamed to admit that they had failed a grade. Almost without exception, the retained children said staying back made them feel "sad," "bad," and "upset," and they thought repeating a grade was "punishment."

When I met with Ryan over the summer, he told me, "I'll never be smart in school. I'm only smart at things we don't do in school—like inventing mazes and drawing." When I asked why he thought he had to repeat third grade he replied, without hesitation, "I got in lots of trouble for not walking on the red line." In this school, I learned, teachers drill students on walking silently and ramrod straight on a narrow red line that runs the length of the school's corridor.

Retention's Long Reach

According to best estimates, nearly 2.5 million students are retained each year in U.S. schools, with the highest rates found among boys—especially minorities, special education students, and those who come from low-income families and live in the inner city.

University of Wisconsin-Madison's Robert Hauser, who recorded national retention rates for the National Research Council, found that 25 percent of 6- to 8-year-olds and 30 percent of 9- to 11-year-olds have been retained at least once. By ages 15 to 17, retention rates for black and Hispanic students are 40 to 50 percent, compared with 35 percent for white students.

Retention rates in some metropolitan schools are even higher. In Baltimore, for instance, a nine-year study shows that 41 percent of white students and 56 percent of black students were retained by grade three, and up to a third of those students were retained again before entering middle school.

Schools often retain students on the basis of a shortsighted belief that repeating a grade will give kids a boost that will last through 12th grade. It's true that retention reaches far into students' futures, but often the long-term effects are devastating. Jimerson's studies show that students who are retained once are 40 to 50 percent more likely to drop out than promoted students. Retaining students twice doubles their chances of dropping out, raising the risk to 90 percent.

Retention is a *predictor* of dropping out, not a *cause*, he says. Achievement, behavior, and home and school environments also factor into the equation. Still, retained students run a high risk of developing problems with self-esteem, social and emotional adjustment, peer relations, and school engagement—and such problems substantially increase the likelihood of giving up on school.

A Better Plan

But if retention isn't working, neither is promoting students who aren't learning. As Darling-Hammond puts it. "The negative effects of retention should not become an argument for social promotion."

The solution, say Richard Allington and Sean Walmsley, authors of *No Quick Fix*, requires whole-school reform, beginning with the school's "institutional ethos."

In schools with an adversarial climate (teachers against parents and students), Allington and Walmsley found that two out of three children were retained, assigned to transitional classes, or placed in special education. But schools with a respectful and professional climate retained only 1 or 2 percent of their students.

How can school leaders halt runaway retention? Darling-Hammond recommends four strategies:

1. Teach teachers how to instruct all students according to the ways they learn.
2. Redesign schools to give students more intensive learning opportunities through multiage classes, cross-grade grouping, and block scheduling.
3. Give struggling students support and services as soon as they're needed.
4. Use student assessments to monitor and adjust teaching content and strategies.

For his part, Jimerson suggests "constructive discussions" on prevention and intervention techniques that keep students from failing in the first place. In addition, he recommends:

1. Train school psychologists to be well-informed about retention research and serve as advocates for children as soon as they show problems learning.
2. Promote students' social competence as a counterpart to academic competence.
3. Establish protective factors, such as parent involvement programs and school-community partnerships that offer support to needy children.
4. Sponsor high-quality preschool programs that focus on child development.

These researchers layout a tough mission for schools. But perhaps the toughest job will be confronting and dismantling ungrounded assumptions about retention.

Selected References

Allington, Richard, and Sean Walmsley. *No Quick Fix*. New York: Teachers College Press/International Reading Association, 1995.

Anderson, Beckie. "Retention in the Early Grades: A Review of the Research." Learning Disabilities Online, Winter 1998; www.ldonline.org/ld_indepth/legal_legislative/retention_ in_early_grades.html.

Darling-Hammond, Linda. "Alternatives to Grade Retention." *The School Administrator Web Edition*, August 1998; www.aasa.org/publications/sa/1998_08/Darling-Hammond.htm.

Hauser, Robert, and others. "Race-Ethnicity, Social Background, and Grade Retention." Paper presented at the Laboratory for Student Success at Temple University, October 2000.

Jimerson, Shane. "A Synthesis of Grade Retention Research: Looking Backward and Moving Forward." *The California School Psychologist*, 2001; www.education. ucsb.edu/jimerson/retention/CSP_RetentionSynthesis 2001.pdf.

Jimerson, Shane, and others. "Grade Retention: Achievement and Mental Health Outcomes." National Association of School Psychologists, July 2002; www.nasponline.org/pdf/graderetention.pdf.

Jimerson, Shane, and others. "Winning the Battle and Losing the War: Examining the Relation between Grade Retention and Dropping out of High School." *Psychology in the Schools*, 2002; www.education.ucsb.edu/jimerson/retention/PITS_DropoutRetention 2002.pdf.

Malone, Gwendolyn, and Philip Bowser. "Debate: Can Retention Be Good for a Student" *NEA Today*, 1998. www.nea.org/neatoday/9803/debatehtml.

Shepard, Lorrie and Mary Smith. *Flunking Grades: Research and Policies on Retention*. London: Folmer Press, 1989.

SUSAN BLACK, an *ASBJ* contributing editor, is an education researcher in Hammondsport, N.Y.

Making the Case for Play Policy

Research-Based Reasons to Support Play-Based Environments

Dolores A. Stegelin

> Play is a child's life and the means by which he comes to understand the world he lives in.
>
> —Susan Isaacs,
> *Social Development in Young Children*

Contemporary early childhood classrooms are complex places where the opportunities for play are few. The need for effective play policy has never been greater. We early childhood professionals know that physically and mentally engaging, play-based activity is essential for overall healthy child development. But these days we often find ourselves defending play-based curriculum and instructional approaches to families, administrators, even colleagues.

This article can help teachers and directors become eloquent and effective advocates of play-based early learning environments. It defines play and play policy and discusses distinct research areas that support play policy and practice for physical, cognitive, social, and emotional development within diverse early childhood settings. Also presented are three anecdotal examples of current challenges to play-based curriculum. I hope the information serves as a useful tool for developing strategies for organizing a play policy effort.

Defining Play and Play Policy

Play research has many important dimensions, and play policy is an untapped and fertile area for research (Stegelin 2002b). An appropriate definition of play is necessary for effective play policy development and implementation. Definitions of play emerge from three perspectives: (1) the exploratory and open-ended nature of play; (2) the intrinsic, evolutionary, and synergistic nature of play; and (3) the developmental aspects of play (Anderson 1998).

The *exploratory nature* of play has been studied extensively (Pellegrini & Perlmutter 1989; O'Neill-Wagner, Bolig, & Price 1994; Bolig et al. 1998) and is captured in this definition:

"Play is an essential part of every child's life and vital to his/her development. It is the way children *explore* the world around them and develop practice skills. It is essential for

physical, emotional, and spiritual growth; for intellectual and educational development; and for acquiring social and behavioral skills" (Hampshire Play Policy Forum 2002, 1). Play

---

Explaining a Literacy Approach to a Family

Ms. Ruhnquist is a veteran child care director of a large for-profit preschool center that provides comprehensive services for more than 100 children. Ms. Ruhnquist has a master's degree in educational administration and a bachelor's in child development. Well-organized and attentive to detail, she is respected for her understanding of early childhood development, her engaging style of family and staff interactions, and her business skills.

Today, as she enrolls four-year-old Mariah, the parents ask her about the center's approach to "teaching reading." Somewhat surprised, she listens attentively and then asks what their main concern is.

"Well, we want Mariah to know the alphabet and be able to read when she starts kindergarten. We want her to be ahead of the others and ready for higher academic work. Do you use a recognized reading curriculum?"

Ms. Ruhnquist explains that the center uses a nationally recognized early childhood curriculum that focuses on all aspects of a child's development, including language development.

"We use a play-based, child-directed approach that focuses on developing autonomy and self-reliance," she says. "In terms of language development, we have a literacy center, lots of books, and we encourage the exploration of reading and writing in six different learning centers. We focus on storytelling, exploration of different kinds of books and literature, and on phonemic awareness. But we do not teach reading per se. We believe that helping Mariah learn to love books and gain confidence in her own abilities will help her be ready for the early reading experiences in kindergarten. If you'd like to observe the classroom and talk to Mariah's teacher, you're welcome to do so before finalizing her enrollment."

The parents observe the classroom and complete Mariah's enrollment but make it clear they will be watching her progress in prereading skills.

and exploration behaviors are characteristic behaviors of both young humans and primates and are observable in a variety of contexts that include specific conditions, such as availability of toys and objects for manipulation and freedom from excessive anxiety. Play behaviors are often preceded by exploration, so it is important that the environment encourages exploration.

The *evolutionary and intrinsic* nature of play is reflected in the creative aspect of play that is open-ended, unpredictable, unique, and "comedic" or imbued with "surprise" (Salthe 1991). From the child's perspective, the opportunity to play is an invitation that turns into a "self-fueled, synergistic, inherently rewarding, but not necessarily rewarded process called play" (Anderson 1998, 103). The resulting patterns of play activity lead to a summative experience known as "fun" (Anderson 1998). Thus, a definition of play should include the *intrinsic, evolutionary, synergistic,* and *motivating* aspects of play.

Play behaviors are often preceded by exploration, so it is important that the environment encourages exploration.

The *developmental* aspects of play include the more predictable structures of play associated with children's social, cognitive, language, physical, and creative development from infancy through the primary years. At every stage of development, play activity takes on some degree of predictability but still allows for spontaneous, fluid, repetitive, and turn-taking behaviors. The responsibility of the early childhood professional and the policy advocate is to provide appropriate contexts in which these predictable and developmental behaviors can occur, as delineated in the Hampshire play policy statement (2002) above.

In summary, play policy advocates can use the following essential features to define play:

- Play requires specific *conditions of safety and psychological security* that are essential for the child to engage in relaxed, open-ended, and exploratory behaviors.
- Play includes *exploratory behaviors* that involve manipulation of objects, toys, and other materials, and this exploratory nature of play often precedes actual focused play behavior.
- Play is an important *evolutionary behavior* that is essential for healthy development to occur across all areas: social, cognitive, language, physical, and creative.
- Play is behavior that *sustains the healthy development of the individual* and the larger sociocultural fabric of society and reflects the contexts in which the child lives (home, community, and the larger society).

Linking Play to Play Policy

Many contemporary play policy initiatives have originated in the United Kingdom, while systematic play research has been done in the United States and other parts of the world. Effective play

---

Defending Learning Centers to the Assistant Principal

Mr. Hemminger, a first-year kindergarten teacher, graduated top of his class with a bachelor's degree in early childhood education. He impresses everyone with his enthusiasm, eagerness to learn about new teaching approaches, and obvious delight in working with five-year-olds.

Mr. Hemminger advocates and models a highly interactive, hands-on approach to learning, and his classroom is known for creative expression, high levels of family involvement, and a learning environment that invites everyone to come in, observe, and participate. The classroom includes five learning centers, small-group cooperative-learning opportunities, and a high level of child-initiated planning and assessment of learning experiences.

Mr. Hemminger is guided by state and local school curriculum guidelines, content expectations, and assessment procedures. He uses many different assessment strategies, including observation, work sampling, portfolios, and periodic testing.

During Mr. Hemminger's first evaluation, the assistant principal asks about his use of center-based learning. "Isn't that for preschool children? There have been some complaints by other teachers about the noise level in this classroom. Is there some way you can tone it down a bit? Shouldn't the children be doing more seat work, silent reading, and worksheets? After all, they'll soon be taking a standardized test."

Mr. Hemminger explains that he has specific learning objectives and outcomes in mind for all daily activities. He points out that research supports active, exploratory learning at the kindergarten level. He is so confident in his center-based approach to teaching that he says he is not concerned about testing outcomes in the spring. "The children are learning *and* they are having fun. I believe that if they are involved in the planning of the day's activities, have a chance to create hypotheses and then explore them, and have daily interactions with their peers, they will learn much more than they would in isolation or in completing seat work."

"Well, we'll see how it goes this year," says the assistant principal. "I'll be noting the noise level and the way your children perform in April."

---

policy is founded on clear articulation of what is meant by play and a commitment to respond to children's needs and wishes (PLAYLINK 2001). But what is a play policy? According to Play Wales (2002), a play policy is a statement of both an organization's current play provision and its aspirations for change and development. Play policy usually includes the following important criteria (PLAYLINK 2001; Play Wales 2002):

- the objectives of play and play-related services and activities;
- the connection between acceptable levels of risk and healthy play;

- an assumption of inclusive play settings for all children (ethnic and developmental diversity);
- the criteria for evaluating a quality play environment;
- the essential and inherent aspect of play as part of a child's cultural life; and
- the need to create and integrate play opportunities in the general environment.

Effective play policy is founded on clear articulation of what is meant by play and a commitment to respond to children's needs and wishes.

Using Manipulatives and Other Play-Based Approaches in First Grade

Mrs. Alvarez is an experienced primary teacher in a large public school system. She has twice been named Teacher of the Year at the elementary school and is now working toward a master's degree in elementary education.

Today, during unit meetings, three other first grade teachers want to know why Mrs. Alvarez does not use the rigorous math and science curriculum recommended by the school district. The new curriculum is heavily teacher-directed, uses daily worksheets and drills, and requires standardized testing every nine weeks.

Mrs. Alvarez says, "You know, I really thought about making a change this year. The new textbooks are attractive, and in some ways the curriculum seems easier in terms of planning and teaching. But then I thought about how much my students really look forward to math and science and how well they have done the past several years on the school district's end-of-the-year tests. I decided that even though it takes more time and resources, I really believe in a hands-on approach to learning.

"Besides," she adds, "six-year-olds need time and space to explore, suggest activities, make up their own hypotheses, and feel their ideas really do count. My math and science activities require the children to think, work together, and record their own answers. I like the opportunities for creative thinking, for students to think for themselves and to move around and take charge of their time. For now, I'm going to keep using manipulatives.

"And yes," she says, "I know my classroom is louder and messier than most of yours, but so far the parents agree with my approach. I'm convinced that six-year-olds learn best with interactive, cooperative learning experiences."

Developing and implementing effective play policy takes time, commitment, and perseverance. Effective play policy at

the local, state, national, and international levels evolves over time and is the result of many attempts. The primary aim of play policy is to

- articulate and promote the importance of play for all children,
- recognize that all children have the right to play, as stated in the 1989 United Nations Convention on the Rights of the Child, and
- enable all children to have equal access to good quality play environments in their local communities. (Hampshire Play Policy Forum 2002)

Early childhood professionals involved in play policy development can use the above definitions of play and play policy to bolster their play policy rationales and to strengthen their role as advocates. Essential to policy development is the use of research-based information for integrating systematic play into child care, Head Start, preschool, and K–3 settings. Three critical research areas support the rationale for play-based environments.

Research Focus 1: Active Play and Health-related Indicators

The first area of research that addresses the critical need for play-based learning environments—especially physically active and vigorous play—is health related. The rapidly increasing rates of childhood obesity and weight-related health problems are exacerbated by physical inactivity and sedentary routines. Experts point to the prevalence of junk food marketed to children, too much television and other sedentary entertainment, and fewer families sitting down together to eat (American Heart Association 2005).

In addition, mental health research points out the link between physical exercise and the reduced incidence of anxiety, depression, and behavioral problems in young children (U.S. Department of Health and Human Services 1996). Physical activity through play alleviates stress and helps children learn to manage feelings and gain a sense of self-control (Aronson 2002; Sanders 2002). Therefore, integrated and physically demanding play requires the use of both mind and body (Larkin 2002).

Physical activity through play alleviates stress and helps children learn to manage feelings and gain a sense of self-control.

The Link between Physical Inactivity and Health Problems

Rates of childhood obesity in the United States and England have doubled since 1970 (Edmunds, Waters, & Elliott 2001; Elliott 2002). Even some infants and toddlers are being diagnosed as obese by their second or third birthdays. According to the American Heart Association (2005) the U.S. obesity epidemic is now affecting the youngest children, with more than 10 percent of two- to five-year-olds overweight—up from 7 percent in 1994. Childhood obesity is related to five critical health and psychosocial problems: (1) high blood pressure, (2) Type 2 diabetes, (3) coronary heart disease, (4) social rejection, and (5) school failure and dropout (Freedman et al. 2001).

Early childhood professionals and play advocates can bolster the case for physically active and play-based environments by citing current information from national and international entities. For example, in the United States the Centers for Disease Control and Prevention (CDC) assumes a preventive health stance, advocating for greater physical activity, balanced nutrition, and much more active life-styles. Because 25 percent of American children are obese and 61 percent of adults are overweight (Guo et al. 2002), it is difficult to overstate the dimensions of the problem. The CDC uses the Body Mass Index (BMI) with children as a predictor of adult obesity (Guo et al. 2002). Advocates for physically active play environments can use these facts to emphasize the seriousness of health issues for children in sedentary care and learning environments and stress the need for all types of play, both indoor and outdoor.

The Health Benefits of Physically Active Play

Daily schedules, play objects, and adult-child interactions can be contrasted in high- and low-quality early childhood settings to make advocacy points. For example, high-quality early childhood classrooms incorporate (1) daily schedules that routinely include active indoor and rough-and-tumble outdoor play (Rivkin 2000); (2) kinesthetic movement as part of concept learning; (3) integration of music, movement, and creative expression; and (4) adult-child interactions that model moderate to high levels of physical activity. In contrast, low-quality settings (1) do not have predictable schedules for indoor and outdoor play; (2) employ more passive and sedentary learning strategies such as television viewing or adult-directed teaching; (3) minimize opportunities for kinesthetic movement and learning; and (4) do not encourage creative expression through physical exercise, dance, and movement.

At the elementary school level, organized sports and physical education also provide play opportunities. Supporters of sports as a form of play suggest that sports contain many of the elements used to describe play (Frost, Wortham, & Reifel 2001). The policy issue of regular and scheduled outdoor recess in public schools is being studied, but research indicates that children need recess for a variety of reasons, including socialization opportunities, respite from attention to classroom tasks, a break that allows them to give maximum attention to their work once again, and the obvious benefits of physical activity to counter sedentary lifestyles and patterns of obesity (Pelligrini & Bjorklund 1996; Jarrett 2002).

In summary, play advocates can state the following health benefits of active play to bolster their play advocacy efforts:

- large muscle development through reaching, grasping, crawling, running, climbing, skipping, and balancing;

- fine motor skill development and eye-hand coordination as the child handles objects in play;
- increased metabolism and energy consumption through routine physical activity;
- decreased weight and heart-related problems;
- reduced levels of chronic stress; and
- increased feelings of success, self-control, and social competence. (Piaget 1962; Piaget & Inhelder 1969)

This research area may represent the most urgent rationale for physically active and rigorous play for all children. Teachers, parents, and administrators should place health concerns high on their priority list when developing play policy. What can be more important than the overall health of young children?

Research Focus 2: Brain Research—The Critical Link between Play and Optimal Cognitive and Physical Development

Brain research now documents observable differences in the quantity and quality of brain cell development between young children with stimulating and nonstimulating early learning experiences during the first 36 months of life. Children's play behaviors become more complex and abstract as they progress through childhood (Piaget 1962; Johnson, Christie, & Yawkey 1987). In very concrete terms, the recent flurry of research related to brain growth and development clearly supports and under-girds the necessity of active, physical, and cognitively stimulating play for *all* young children (Zwillich 2001).

Children's play behaviors become more complex and abstract as they progress through childhood.

Information gathered through new brain-imaging techniques is already playing a major role in how public policy decisions are made. Cognitive skills advance during problem solving with play materials, ideas, events, and people. This begins in infancy—for example, when a baby makes the startling discovery that shaking a rattle causes a sound reaction. Stimulating play environments facilitate progress to higher levels of thought throughout childhood. Functional magnetic resonance imaging (fMRI), positron emission tomography (PET), and other brain-scanning tools are for the first time providing meaningful insights into the way human brains change and develop during the early years of life (Zwillich 2001).

Neuroscientists point out that the connections between brain cells that underlie new learning become hard-wired if they are used repeatedly but can be diminished if they are not (Morrison 2004). However, caution is warranted here: we should not interpret brain research findings to label or place limits on children whose brains do not appear to be "normal" at very young ages. What is clear among the varied brain research findings is that younger children need (1) physical activity, (2) hands-on activities that develop large and fine motor skills, (3) opportunities for eye-hand coordination activities, (4) auditory and visually stimulating environments, and (5) consistent daily routines that actively engage the child both in the home and preschool environments.

Stimulating play environments facilitate progress to higher levels of thought throughout childhood.

Research Focus 3: The Link between Play, Early Literacy, and Social Competence

Research on play and its relationship to social and language development has been conducted for many years (for example, Parten 1932). Current research on early literacy outcomes shows a relationship between active, socially engaging play and early language and literacy development (Neuman & Roskos 1993; Owocki 1999; Morrow 2001). Social skills also grow through play experiences as the child moves from enjoying simple contact with another person to learning to cooperate, take turns, and play by the rules. Social skills, oral language development, and dramatic play go hand in hand. Children who are provided play opportunities in same-age and multi-age settings broaden their own understandings of the social world and of language diversity (Roskos et al. 1995).

Relationships between Social Play, Language, and Early Literacy Development

The growing emphasis on the teaching of early literacy skills in child care, Head Start, and other early learning settings stems from this important research linkage (Neuman & Roskos 1993). Play policy advocates can find much support in the research literature for social play as a significant contributor to early language development and later literacy indicators (Strickland & Strickland 1997; Christie 1998; Owocki 1999; Morrow 2001; International Reading Association 2002). A noted group of early literacy specialists (Neuman & Roskos 1993; Goldhaber et al. 1996; Morrow 1997; Strickland & Strickland 1997; Christie 1998; Morrow 2001) are documenting the significant effect of hands-on, socially engaging early literacy experiences on the literacy readiness and prereading skills of young children in preschool and kindergarten settings. Although not always regarded as "reading" in a formal sense, acquisition of these print-meaning associations is viewed as an important precursor to more skilled reading (Mason 1980; Goodman 1986).

Literacy props, especially developmentally appropriate books and writing tools, placed in learning centers *beyond* the traditional reading and meeting areas increase both the quality and quantity of early literacy play-based experiences.

Play advocates can argue for a "materials intervention" strategy that involves making play areas resemble the literacy environments that children encounter at home and in their communities (Christie 1998). Since not all families offer equal opportunities for young children to engage in rich literacy events, it is especially important that child care and other early learning settings provide these play-based experiences for equal access to literacy building skills. And children are more likely to engage in play-related reading and writing activities if available materials invite these types of activities (Morrow & Rand 1991; Vukelich 1991; Christie & Enz 1992).

Research shows that the following play-based activities in the early childhood setting promote social awareness and early literacy development:

- *Use of literacy props*—puppets, stuffed animals, dramatic-play items, books, markers, signs, paper of many types—along with adult modeling and encouragement, fosters greater print awareness, verbal expression, and social interactions (Christie & Enz 1992; Neuman & Roskos 1992; Goldhaber et al. 1996). Literacy props, especially developmentally appropriate books and writing tools, placed in learning centers *beyond* the traditional reading and meeting areas (such as block, puzzle and manipulative, dramatic play, and natural science) increase both the quality and quantity of early literacy play-based experiences (Goldhaber et al. 1996; Neuman & Roskos 1993). One study (Neuman & Roskos 1993) found a significant increase in book handling, reading, and writing choices by children (98% African-American and 2% Hispanic) after Head Start teachers set up and participated in a play "office" setting.

- *Integration of art activities* (such as painting, finger painting, and drawing) in the curriculum promotes writing and print awareness (Morrow 2001). Play in the visual arts is immediate and responsive rather than planned out and goal-directed (Johnson 1998); children learn to "invent" their own words, represent letters of the alphabet, and otherwise re-create their imaginary world through forms of printing and drawing.

- *Emphasis on environmental print* (such as labeling of blocks, learning centers, and materials within centers), along with print-rich learning environments (which include maps, newspapers, magazines, many types of books, and posters) encourages alphabet awareness, understanding that print has meaning, and the assimilation of new words in children's vocabularies (Morrow 2001).

- *Incorporation of poetry, songs, chants, storytelling, and sharing of big books* on a daily basis encourages children to verbalize their feelings, learn letter sounds (phonemic awareness) and words, and begin to understand written language through repetition with adults and peers. This is especially important for preschoolers who may have limited exposure to oral language, rituals, and storytelling at home (Morrow 2001; Stegelin 2002a).
- *Teachers should provide adequate time for children to play* and should be sensitive to matching authentic play-based literacy materials to the cultural and developmental characteristics of the children (Neuman & Roskos 1991; Christie & Wardle 1992).

In short, play policy advocates can find an abundance of current research on the positive effects of play-based early literacy experiences that increase the likelihood of positive outcomes in language and literacy development.

Research Linking Play to Social Competence

Much research-based evidence supports the common-sense notion that play with others is necessary for the development of social competence, and that it in turn has a direct relationship to success in school. In fact, a convincing body of evidence has accumulated to indicate that unless children achieve minimal social competence by about age six, they have a higher probability of being at risk in adolescent and adult development (McClellan & Katz 2001). Other studies (Hartup & Moore 1990; Ladd & Profilet 1996) suggest that a child's long-term social and emotional adaptation, academic and cognitive development, and citizenship are enhanced by frequent childhood opportunities to strengthen social competence.

Early childhood educators and play advocates alike should be able to articulate this critical relationship. In addition, we can cite specific studies that document important social outcomes. For example, in the area of pretend play, research (Piaget 1962; Fein 1981; Smilansky 1990; Nourot 1998) reveals that pretend and dramatic play strengthens the child's understanding of the real world and provides opportunities for imagination to develop. Sociodramatic play provides the matrix for understanding and representing the perspectives of others and for opportunities to compromise and to stand firm in one's beliefs and intentions (Nourot 1998).

Pretend and dramatic play strengthens the child's understanding of the real world and provides opportunities for imagination to develop.

Fabes and colleagues (2003) studied the role that young children's same-sex peer interactions play in influencing early school competence. In observing 98 young children (median age of 54.77 months), they found that patterns differed for boys and girls related to school outcomes and specific play interactions. This study invites follow-up research to determine more specific gender-related differences in play. Further, these studies show that informal interactions with peers in play situations foster the social competence behaviors necessary for learning and development.

Summary

All of us can become play advocates who influence play policy in varied settings such as child care, Head Start, and public school kindergarten and primary classrooms. Early childhood professionals wanting to become more active in play policy development can point to research-based evidence that active play leads to optimal outcomes for young children. There are clear positive outcomes in the following areas:

1. *Physical and mental health indicators* reflect a direct correlation between rigorous, physically active play and reduced levels of obesity, heart-related problems, and chronic stress.
2. *Cognitive development* is optimized through active, exploratory play, as evidenced through brain scans and research that document that active, stimulating play on a regular basis promotes optimal brain development in young children.
3. *Language and early literacy development* is enhanced through print-rich learning environments that engage children in active, reciprocal, and systematic interaction with their peers and supportive adults through books, writing experiences, manipulatives, and story-sharing routines.
4. *Social competence*, largely developed by age six, is best nurtured in young children through sociodramatic and pretend play with peers, social interactions in small group settings, and assimilation of routines and reciprocal engagement with peers and caring adults.

We make a strong case for the importance of play in early childhood education when we are able to cite research that strongly supports play and play-based environments. Play-based instructional strategies and environments are a widely discussed topic in the field these days. Many forces counter the play movement, promoting accelerated academic requirements at earlier ages, standardized testing, and accountability mandates, while also citing scheduling issues in elementary schools and safety factors. We early childhood professionals must be prepared to assume an advocacy role in the area of play policy. Parents, teachers, and administrators must be willing to speak up and speak out on behalf of the play needs of our children.

References

American Heart Association. 2005. *Heart disease and stroke statistics—2005 update*. Dallas, TX: Author. Online: www.americanheart.org/downloadable/heart/1103829139928HDSStats2005Update.pdf

Anderson, M. 1998. The meaning of play as a human experience. In *Play from birth to twelve and beyond*, eds. D. Fromberg & D. Bergen, 103–08. New York: Garland.

Aronson, S.S., ed., comp. with P. Spahr. 2002. *Healthy young children: A manual for programs.* 4th ed. Washington, DC: NAEYC.

Bolig, R., C.S. Price, P.L. O'Neill-Wagner, & S.J. Suomi. 1998. Reactivity and play and exploration behaviors of young Rhesus monkeys. In *Play and culture studies*, Vol. 1, ed. S. Reifel, 165–77. Greenwich, CT: Ablex.

Christie, J., & F. Wardle. 1992. How much time is needed for play? *Young Children* 47 (3): 28–32.

Christie, J.F. 1998. Play as a medium for literacy development. In *Play from birth to twelve and beyond*, eds. D. Fromberg & D. Bergen, 50–55. New York: Garland.

Christie, J.F., & B. Enz. 1992. The effects of literacy play interventions on preschoolers' play patterns and literacy development. *Early Education and Development* 3: 205–20.

Edmunds, L., E. Waters, & E. Elliott. 2001. Evidence-based management of childhood obesity: Evidence-based pediatrics. *British Medical Journal* 323 (7318): 916–9.

Elliott, V. 2002. Adult options for childhood obesity? Doctors say the high number of extremely overweight young people is serious enough to consider radical interventions. *American Medical News* 45 (20): 27.

Fabes, R.A., C.L. Martin, L.D. Hanish, M.C. Anders, & D.A. Madden-Derdich. 2003. Early school competence: The roles of sex-segregated play and effortful control. *Developmental Psychology* 39 (5): 848–59.

Fein, G.G. 1981. Pretend play in childhood: An integrative review. *Child Development* 52: 1095–1118.

Freedman, D., L. Khan, W. Dietz, S. Srivinasian, & G.S. Berenson. 2001. Relationship of childhood obesity to coronary heart disease risk factors in adulthood. *Pediatric* 108 (3): 712.

Frost, J.L., S.C. Wortham, & S. Reifel. 2001. *Play and child development.* Columbus, OH: Merrill/Prentice-Hall.

Goldhaber, J., M. Lipson, S. Sortino, & P. Daniels. 1996. Books in the sand box? Markers in the blocks? Expanding the child's world of literacy. *Childhood Education* 73 (2): 88–92.

Goodman, Y. 1986. Children coming to know literacy. In *Emergent literacy*, eds. W. Teale & E. Sulzby, 1–14. Norwood, NJ: Ablex.

Guo, S.S., W. Wu, W.C. Chulea, & A.F. Roche. 2002. Predicting overweight and obesity in adulthood from body mass index volume in childhood and adolescence. *Journal of Clinical Nutrition* 76 (3): 653–56.

Hampshire Play Policy Forum. 2002. *Hampshire play policy position statement.* Online: www.hants.gov.uk/childcare/playpolicy.html

Hartup, W.W., & S.G. Moore. 1990. Early peer relations: Developmental significance and prognostic implications. *Early Childhood Research Quarterly* 5 (1): 1–18.

International Reading Association. 2002. *What is evidence-based reading instruction?* Reading standards statement. Online: www.reading.org/advocacy/standards

Jarrett, O.S. 2002. Recess in elementary school: What does the research say? *ERIC Digest* EDO-PS-02-5.

Johnson, H.A. 1998. Play in the visual arts: One photographer's way-of-working. In *Play from birth to twelve and beyond*, eds. D. Fromberg & D. Bergen, 435–41. New York: Garland.

Johnson, J., J. Christie, & T. Yawkey. 1987. *Play and early childhood development.* Glenview, IL: Scott, Foresman.

Ladd, G.W., & S.M. Profilet. 1996. The Child Behavior Scale: A teacher-report measure of young children's aggressive, withdrawn, and prosocial behaviors. *Developmental Psychology* 32 (6): 1008–24.

Larkin, M. 2002. Defusing the "time bomb" of childhood obesity. *The Lancet* 359: (9310): 987.

Mason, J. 1980. When do children begin to read?: An exploration of four-year-old children's word reading competencies. *Reading Research Quarterly* 15: 203–27.

McClellan, D.E., & L.G. Katz. 2001. Assessing young children's social competence. *ERIC Digest* EDO-PS-01-2.

Morrison, G.M. 2004. *Early childhood education today.* 9th ed. Columbus, OH: Merrill/Prentice-Hall.

Morrow, L.M. 1997. *The literacy center.* York, ME: Stenhouse.

Morrow, L.M. 2001. *Literacy development in the early years.* 4th ed. Boston: Allyn & Bacon.

Morrow, L.M., & M.K. Rand. 1991. Preparing the classroom environment to promote literacy during play. In *Play and early literacy development*, ed. J.F. Christie, 141–65. Albany: State University of New York.

Neuman, S.B., & K. Roskos. 1991. Peers as literacy informants: A description of young children's literacy conversations in play. *Early Childhood Research Quarterly* 6: 233–48.

Neuman, S.B., & K. Roskos. 1992. Literacy objects as cultural tools: Effects on children's literacy behaviors in play. *Reading Research Quarterly* 27: 202–25.

Neuman, S., & K. Roskos. 1993. Access to print for children of poverty: Differential effects of adult mediation and literacy-enriched play settings on environmental and functional print tasks. *American Educational Research Journal* 30 (1): 95–122.

Nourot, P.M. 1998. Sociodramatic play—Pretending together. In *Play from birth to twelve and beyond*, eds. D. Fromberg & D. Bergen, 378–91. New York: Garland.

O'Neill-Wagner, P.L., R. Bolig, & C.S. Price. 1994. Do play activity levels tell us something of psychosocial welfare in captive monkey groups? *Communication and Cognition* 27: 261–72.

Owocki, G. 1999. *Literacy through play.* Portsmouth, NH: Heinemann.

Parten, M. 1932. Social participation among preschool children. *Journal of Abnormal and Social Psychology* 27: 243–69.

Pelligrini, A.D., & D.F. Bjorklund. 1996. The place of recess in school: Issues in the role of recess in children's education and development. *Journal of Research in Childhood Education* 11: 5–13.

Pelligrini, A., & M. Perlmutter. 1989. Classroom contextual effects of children's play. *Child Development* 25: 289–96.

Piaget, J. 1962. *Play, dreams, and imitation in childhood.* New York: Norton.

Piaget, J., & B. Inhelder. 1969. *The psychology of the child.* New York: Basic.

PLAYLINK. 2001. *Articulating play policy.* London, UK: Author.

Play Wales. 2002. *Defining play policy.* Cardiff, UK: Author.

Rivkin, M.S. 2000. Outdoor experiences for young children. *ERIC Digest* EDO-RC-007.

Roskos, K., J. Vukelich, B. Christie, B. Enz, & S. Neuman. 1995. *Linking literacy and play.* Newark, DE: International Reading Association.

Salthe, S.N. 1991. *Development and evolution: Complexity and change in biological systems.* Cambridge, MA: MIT Press.

Sanders, S.W. 2002. *Active for life: Developmentally appropriate movement programs for young children.* Washington, DC: NAEYC.

Smilansky, S. 1990. Sociodramatic play: Its relevance to behavior and achievement in school. In *Children's play and learning: Perspectives and policy implications*, eds. E. Klugman & S. Smilansky, 18–42. New York: Teachers College Press.

Stegelin, D.A. 2002a. *Early literacy education: First steps toward dropout prevention.* Clemson, SC: National Dropout Prevention Center, Clemson University.

Stegelin, D.A. 2002b. Play policy: A survey of online and professional literature. Unpublished paper presented to the Play, Policy, and Practice Forum, NAEYC Annual Conference, Nov. 20–23, New York, New York.

Strickland, D., & M. Strickland. 1997. Language and literacy: The poetry connection. *Language Arts* 74 (3): 201–05.

U.S. Department of Health and Human Services. 1996. *Physical activity and health: A report of the Surgeon General.* Atlanta, GA: Author, Centers for Disease Control and Prevention.

Vukelich, C. 1991. Learning about the functions of writing: The effects of three play settings on children's interventions and development of knowledge about writing. Unpublished paper presented at the National Reading Conference, December, Palm Springs, California.

Zwillich, T. 2001. Brain scan technology poised to play policy. Online: www.loni.ucla.edu/ thompson/MEDIA/RH/rh.html

DOLORES A. STEGELIN, PhD, is associate professor and program coordinator of early childhood education in the Eugene T. Moore School of Education at Clemson University in South Carolina. Active in policy research and professional activities for 20 years, Dee is the public policy chair for South Carolina AEYC and the author of two books and numerous articles.

Essential Contributions from Playgrounds

It Doesn't Just Happen!

JOHN A. SUTTERBY AND CANDRA D. THORNTON

May is a great month for discussing outdoor play and play environments. In the United States, Northeast and Midwest daily temperatures are finally becoming warm enough for comfortable outdoor play; in the South and West, May is generally the last month before the intense summer heat drives everyone indoors. Whether the space is a back-yard, a neighborhood park, a soccer field, a school playground, or a vacant lot, when given the opportunity children will play outside. And including playground equipment enhances their free play (McKenzie et al. 1997; Stratton, Marsh, & Moores 2000; Sallis et al. 2001; Sutterby, Brown, & Thornton 2004).

Good outdoor play, however, does not happen by chance. What was once taken for granted—that children get plenty of exercise and opportunities to play outdoors—is no longer true. Educators concerned about children's health and development can greatly enhance the quality of outdoor play by understanding the essential contributions of outdoor play and playgrounds.

Challenges to Outdoor Play

Outdoor play environments are the places where much of what it means to be a child happens—the freedom of movement, the excitement, and the total engagement of the senses. Unfortunately though, while most people support the concept of outdoor play, there are many challenges in providing children with outdoor play opportunities, including pressures for greater academic performance and fears for the safety of children. A comparison of time-log diaries written in 1981 and 1997 shows that as organized sports and structured after-school programs became increasingly available, children's free time headed toward extinction (Hofferth & Sandberg 2000).

Accountability

Loss of time for outdoor play can also be attributed to the No Child Left Behind education accountability movement and its accompanying high-stakes testing. Young children are being assigned greater amounts of homework while simultaneously being denied time for outdoor free play at school (Kralovec & Buell 2000; Kieff 2001; O'Hanian 2002; Castle & Ethridge 2003; Lynn-Garbe & Hoot 2004). A recent accounting documents more than 16 thousand schools within the United States that have removed recess from their daily schedules (Sindelar 2002).

School Safety

Schools are also concerned about potential injury and bullying on the playground, leading many to eliminate recess altogether. Some states are opting to replace recess with structured physical education classes despite research findings indicating that young children often do not relate well to structured activities and are actually less active during physical education classes than during outdoor free play (Sanders & Graham 1995; Sutterby, Brown, & Thornton 2004). The National Association for Sports and Physical Education recommends that schools provide both recess and physical education classes (NASPE 2001).

Home Safety

In addition to schools being fearful of potential safety negligence litigation, there is also a general societal fear of the world outside. While families face an ever-growing number of fears for their children, the greatest may be of letting them play outside alone (Sutterby 2004). A mother who describes this particular fear in her own family says, "My mother would tell us to go outside and play until dinnertime…. But I can't send my kids outside unless I go with them. If I'm making dinner, they have to stay inside and watch a video" (Gardner 2004, 14).

Crime, unsafe playgrounds, traffic, pollution, and insect-borne illnesses such as Lyme disease and West Nile virus keep parents on edge (Bar-Or 2000; Gordan-Larsen, McMurray, & Popkin 2000; Surface Transportation Policy Project 2003; Gardner 2004). As a result, children remain indoors day after day, watching television, playing video games, or surfing the Web.

Physical Benefits of Playgrounds

To deny children the opportunity to reap the many benefits of regular, vigorous physical activity is to deny them the opportunity to experience the joy of efficient movement, the health effects of movement, and a lifetime as confident, competent movers.

—David Gallahue,
Handbook of Research on the Education of Young Children

According to Keith Christianson and Jill Morgan (2003), the most beneficial type of play is the free, spontaneous movement possible only outside the confined spaces of homes, schools, and arcades. While the concept itself may be easily grasped by early childhood educators, a comprehensive understanding of specific benefits of outdoor play—particularly on playgrounds—can only be gained from research. Over the past decade, a number of researchers (e.g., Rivkin 1995; Pellegrini et al. 2002; Sibley & Etnier 2003; Frost et al. 2004) have focused not only on the traditional domains related to outdoor play, like physical performance, health, and fitness, but also on the impact outdoor play has on children's neurological development.

Outdoor play motivates and sustains the level of physical activity that is necessary for children to burn off excess calories and prevent weight gain.

At the most basic level, the critical issue related to outdoor play is physical activity. Today children's risk of obesity is epidemic, along with associated health hazards such as diabetes, high blood pressure, and psychological stress (Brown, Sutterby, & Thornton 2002a; Forest & Riley 2004). Much of this health risk can be attributed to an increase in caloric intake and sedentary living and a decrease in levels of physical activity. Outdoor play motivates and sustains the level of physical activity that is necessary for children to burn off excess calories and prevent weight gain (Brown, Sutterby, & Thornton 2002b). Moreover, physical activity reduces body fat without the risk of stunting growth that occurs with low-calorie diets (Loewy 1998; Bar-Or 2000).

Physical Development and Playground Equipment

Children develop important physical skills while playing on playground equipment. They participate in many types of new activities and engage in higher levels of physical challenge when they have these opportunities. Wide, open, and flat spaces better facilitate children's large motor skills, such as running and hopping. More complicated movements, such as climbing, seat swinging, brachiating (swinging from hold to hold by the arms), and balancing, however, are most effectively developed when children have access to play equipment.

Climbing

Humans climb for many reasons—wanting to reach a height for observation, to participate in chase games, or simply to challenge themselves—and anyone who has been around young children knows that they will climb just about anything, whether it is intended for climbing or not. Although playgrounds often contain equipment purposefully designed for climbing, we should assume that children will see the entire arrangement, including slides, barriers, and the exterior, as potentially climbable.

In a study of children's climbing skills, we found that movement patterns tightly correlate with time spent on climbing equipment. For example, as children become more proficient, they gradually lose the need to look at their feet and hands as they move upward. Instead, they begin to trust their own physical skills and feel comfortable shifting their visual focus to a distant goal. With repeated experiences children cease to move only one hand or foot at a time; rather, they adjust their hands and feet to move in coordination with each other, creating a smooth, efficient climbing motion.

In addition to experience, another determinant of children's proficiency is the type of climbing equipment. Playground components intended for climbing can be more or less challenging depending on the distance between rungs, the elements for movement, the height of equipment, and the type of hand- and footholds provided. Equipment at a steep incline or that lacks rigidity (e.g., a net climber) is much more challenging than low-rising stairs, for example. Further, the degree of equipment challenge affects the degree of climbers' skills. Children who are proficient or even advanced climbers on relatively low-challenge-level pieces of equipment revert back to novice climbing tendencies when approaching new and more difficult climbing tasks (Frost et al. 2004).

Swinging

Swings are some of the most popular pieces of playground equipment. Swings, slides, and merry-go-rounds allow children to move faster through space than they can physically propel themselves. These activities provide thrills as children experience the sensation of moving through the air. Swinging, sliding, and spinning are each important for developing balance, motor control, and sensory development (Langendorfer 1988; Yisreal 1998).

As children become more proficient, they gradually lose the need to look at their feet and hands as they move upward.

Our research into children's swinging has examined what children do on swings (Frost et al. 2004). Although swinging is often seen as a solitary activity, it is actually more frequently a social experience. It serves as a way for children to encourage interaction from adults, getting them to push as children swing. Children engage in dramatic play on swings and even challenge each other to participate in swinging competitions.

The development of swinging involves coordination of a number of skills. Children have to learn how to approach and access the swing; for young children this often means riding the swing on their stomachs until they are able to sit unsupported. Children must learn how to coordinate the use of legs, arms, and torso to pump the swings into motion. They also must learn how to exit the swing, which at the most advanced stage often involves jumping from the swing while still in the air (Frost et al. 2004).

One of the important physical benefits of swinging is its capability to either stimulate or relax the human nervous system. Rhythmic swinging relaxes and settles the child, and its most pronounced effect is rocking a child to sleep. In contrast, arrhythmic and vigorous swinging or motion can stimulate the central nervous system (e.g., dizziness after spinning in swings).

Brachiating

Overhead play equipment is controversial today. Overhead ladders, ring treks, track rides, and rings cause families and schools to fear for children's safety because of the high risk of fall injuries associated with the equipment. But by not providing children with opportunities to use overhead equipment, research is indicating that far more serious damage occurs. As early as the 1980s, studies were showing the alarming lack of upper body strength in American children. For example, 25 to 30 percent of boys and 60 percent of girls could not do a single pull-up (Pate et al. 1987). Given this finding, the high number of fall injuries associated with overhead equipment may be due more to children's poor upper-body strength—the result of not having overhead equipment in the first place—rather than to the equipment itself.

Not only do overhead components develop upper-body strength, the brachiation skill is also developed. Unlike climbing, which can be done in a wide range of environments, brachiation is a skill unique to playgrounds. "The skill that kids develop on the overhead ladder," say Hewes and Beckwith, "is called brachiation, and it is one of the very few experiences that are new to children on the playground" (1975, 123). Coordinated, rhythmic body motion combined with the upper-body strength necessary to successfully traverse an overhead ladder progresses through four stages: fundamental, practice, refining, and mastery (Frost et al. 2004).

One of the important physical benefits of swinging is its capability to either stimulate or relax the human nervous system.

The *fundamental stage* is a time of initial introduction to and exploration of the equipment. Progress to the practice stage happens after the fundamentals of navigating the apparatus are learned and are ready to be practiced. With repeated experience, the brachiating hand and body movements cease to be a challenge. Now the *refining stage* begins. No longer needing to concentrate on simply moving from rung to rung, children are able to focus on making their brachiation movements efficient: coordinating arm and leg timing, controlling side-to-side body motion, and using their legs for momentum. When children are able to traverse an overhead apparatus with "an economy of motion, displaying little to no extraneous movement, [plus] their bodies and legs move rhythmically and efficiently" (Frost et al. 2004, 111), then finally the *mastery stage* is reached.

Among early childhood educators, researchers, kinesiology experts, and government agencies, disagreement exists on the age at which children are capable of developing brachiation skills or when they possess the appropriate physiology to safely use overhead playground equipment. While age chronology is a good general predictor of ability, individual skills vary widely across age groups. Frost and colleagues (2004) recommend that playgrounds be designed to accommodate the various ranges of brachiation skill levels that may be present among any age or grade level.

Balancing

In addition to obesity and other health risks, the growing trend of sedentary lifestyles among children is generating concern among early childhood educators and child development experts. Because of a decrease in opportunities for outdoor play and experiences on balance-enhancing equipment on playgrounds, children are not developing adequate balance, coordination, or weight-bearing skills. Subsequently they are at a high risk of injury (Thornton & Sutterby 2004). Balance, like brachiation, is a physical skill best developed with outdoor play equipment. Good balance skills are achieved only through practice with gradually increasing levels of challenge on equipment like swings, moving bridges, merry-go-rounds, and balance beams with a range of widths and heights.

Because of a decrease in opportunities for outdoor play and experiences on balance-enhancing equipment on playgrounds, children are not developing adequate balance, coordination, or weight-bearing skills.

Neurological Benefits of Playgrounds

As technology improves and brain research becomes more and more precise, neurologists are able to get a better idea of what goes on in the human brain during various activities and during different phases of life. For instance, we now know that the brain contains a multitude of folds that mature at different, predictable times in a highly organized sequence (Wallis 2004). The first region to fully develop is located at the very back of the brain—the sensorimotor cortex, which contains neurons for sensory functions (e.g., vision, hearing, touch, and so on) and for spatial awareness (Wallis 2004). Healy (1997) found that the sensorimotor cortex does not develop independently; rather, its growth hinges upon large-scale physical movement such as running, hopping, jumping, and climbing.

The amount of physical movement that is possible only during outdoor play critically affects children's healthy brain development.

The brain folds continue to mature throughout childhood and into early adolescence. At roughly age 11 for girls and 12½ for boys, the final region of neural development begins—the prefrontal cortex (Wallis 2004). The neurons located within the prefrontal cortex are associated with logical reasoning, impulse control, and motor coordination (Gogtay et al. 2004). It is worth noting that a dominant component of both the first and last stages of brain development is movement. This fact strongly reinforces a point early childhood educators have been arguing since the days of Froebel, that children need to be given frequent opportunities to freely move their bodies. In large measure, the amount of physical movement that is possible only during outdoor play critically affects children's healthy brain development.

Standardization and Accessibility

Creating play environments that meet all of children's physical and neurological needs requires careful design and planning.

Recommendations for Playground Design

Consider children's experience and skill, not just chronological age, when making decisions about playground equipment.

Provide opportunities for daily recess or outdoor movement to help fight the childhood obesity epidemic.

Be a careful observer of children's outdoor play. Teachers and parents can learn a great deal about their children's physical and mental development through outdoor play. Further, given the wide variation of skill levels within age groups, be careful to match the abilities of children with the challenges of equipment.

Make play spaces creative and interesting enough in this electronic age to maintain children's interest. Creating an outdoor play environment is more than just placing equipment in the middle of a space. Playgrounds require attention to all aspects of children's play, including social play, dramatic play, and games.

As children's play and opportunities to play change, so also do children's play environments. Playground design has been slowly evolving over the past decade. Currently, the field is in what some playground experts have dubbed the "standardization era." As implied in the name, standardization era playgrounds are typified by large, standard structures with linked equipment pieces (for example, slides and climbers), strategically placed within fall-zones; resilient materials such as wood chips, pea gravel, or rubber surfacing cover the ground to reduce potential injuries from falls. Most commonly, these playgrounds are manufactured by certified playground equipment fabricators, put in place by certified playground installers, and inspected by certified playground inspectors (Sutterby & Frost In press). Expectations regarding the safety of playground equipment are set and are closely monitored by the American Society for Testing and Materials (ASTM) and the Consumer Product Safety

---

Actions to Support Outdoor Play

Become an advocate for outdoor play. In many states groups are working toward requiring schools to offer recess to children. The following organizations hold this goal and provide information, research, and ways to contact local people interested in outdoor play advocacy: the International Play Association (IPA)—www.ipausa.org; the National Association for Sport and Physical Education (NASPE)—www.aahperd.org/naspe; the Association for Childhood Education International (ACEI)—-www.acei.org; the National Recreation and Parks Association (NRPA)—www.nrpa.org; the National Association of Elementary School Principals (NAESP)—www.naesp.org; and the National Association for the Education of Young Children (NAEYC)—www.naeyc.org.

Make outdoor activity safer through traffic calming. Safe playgrounds are important but so are safe neighborhoods where families feel secure about allowing their children to go outdoors. High traffic speeds in neighborhoods prohibit children's walking and bicycle riding as well as outdoor play.

In Salt Lake City, efforts are under way to make walking safer through better crosswalks and orange flags that make pedestrians more visible to motorists. In Oakland, California, a Walk-a-Child-to-School Day promotes pedestrian activities (Surface Transportation Policy Project 2004).

Enlist the support of school administrators and families to send a clear message that recess is an important part of the school day. School administrators should not assume that children have time to play outdoors after school; discouraging or eliminating recess may eliminate the only time children have for outdoor play. School administrators are key in setting policy that ensures play areas are safe and supervised. Schools and communities exploring their own playground development will find the Web site www.kaboom.org useful for contacts and resources.

Commission (CPSC) as well as the International Playground Equipment Manufacturers Association (IPEMA).

In addition to safety requirements, passage of the Americans with Disabilities Act has led to major changes in playground design. The United States Access Board Final Rule in reference to playgrounds describes three important elements to make playgrounds accessible: approach, ability to enter, and use.

Approach is the means by which people can get from the parking lot or surrounding area to the playground itself; for most playgrounds this is a concrete sidewalk. The second element is the *ability to enter* the play area. The requirement calls for at least part of the playground surfacing to be made of a material considered accessible and the curbs holding in the surfacing material to not limit accessibility. Examples of accessible surfacing materials include poured rubber surfacing and wood fiber that is uniform enough to support wheelchair users. Finally, use requires that there be access to different types of play events on the playground. This means that a variety of equipment needs to be placed at ground level and that large structures must include transfer platforms, ramps, or climbers to allow access by children with disabilities (Hendy 2001).

Standardization and regulation of playground development have some benefits as these installations typically are much more accessible than previous playground designs and have important safety improvements. On the other hand, standardization has had unintended consequences, with elements such as swings eliminated because they cannot fit on smaller playgrounds. In addition, sand, which is an important sensory material, has been replaced as a common ground cover because it is not accessible. Hopefully, future advances in playground design and landscape architecture will uncover ways to make it possible for these creative elements to be found again on every playground.

Conclusions

As academic pressure increases in schools and the world outside the home appears more frightening, it is important to remember that playground free play has many benefits for children that are available in no other place. Increasing evidence from research on brain development (Frost, Wortham, & Reifel 2004) shows that reducing play opportunities for children has serious negative consequences, while creating enriching and challenging environments encourages overall healthy growth for children.

It is important to remember that playground free play has many benefits for children that are available in no other place.

References

Bar-Or, O. 2000. Juvenile obesity, physical activity, and lifestyle changes. *The Physician and Sports Medicine* 28 (11): 51–58.

Brown, P., J.A. Sutterby, & C.D. Thornton. 2002a. Combating childhood obesity with physical play opportunities. *Today's Playground* (1) 6: 10–11.

Brown, P., J.A. Sutterby, & C.D. Thornton. 2002b. Positive effects of play for children with diabetes. *Today's Playground* (2) 3: 10–11.

Castle, K., & E. Ethridge. 2003. Urgently needed: Autonomous and effective early childhood teacher educators. *Journal of Early Childhood Teacher Education* 24 (2): 111–18.

Christianson, K., & J. Morgan. 2003. To help children with disabilities, design by types of activities, not types of equipment. *Parks and Recreation* 38 (4): 50–54.

Forest, C., & A. Riley. 2004. Childhood origins of adult health: A basis for life-course health policy. *Health Affairs* 23 (5): 155–64.

Frost, J., P. Brown, J. Sutterby, & C. Thornton. 2004. *The developmental benefits of playgrounds.* Olney, MD: Association for Childhood Education International.

Frost, J., S. Wortham, & S. Reifel. 2004. *Play and child development.* Upper Saddle River, NJ: Merrill/Prentice Hall.

Gallahue, D. 1993. Motor development and movement skill acquisition in early childhood education. In *Handbook of research on the education of young children*, ed. B. Spodek, 24–41. New York: Macmillan.

Gardner, M. 2004. Changing habits, expanding waistlines. *Christian Science Monitor* 96 (238): 14.

Gogtay, N., J. Giedd, L. Lusk, K. Hayachi, D. Greenstein, C. Vaituzis, T. Nugent, D. Herman, L. Clasen, A. Toga, J. Rapaport, & P. Thompson. 2004. Dynamic mapping of human cortical development during childhood through early adulthood. *Proceedings of the National Academy of Sciences* 101 (21): 8174–79.

Gordan-Larsen, P., R. McMurray, & B. Popkin. 2000. Determinants of adolescent physical activity and inactivity patterns. *Pediatrics* 105 (6). Online: www.pediatrics.org/cgi/content/full/105/6/e83.

Healy, J. 1997. *Failure to connect: How computers affect our children's minds—For better and worse.* New York: Simon & Schuster.

Hendy, T. 2001. The Americans With Disabilities Act insures the right of every child to play. *Parks and Recreation* 36 (4): 108–18.

Hewes, J., & J. Beckwith. 1975. *Build your own playground.* Boston: San Francisco Book Co.

Hofferth, S., & J. Sandberg. 2000. Changes in American children's time, 1981–1997. Ann Arbor: University of Michigan Population Studies Center.

Kieff, J. 2001. The silencing of recess bells. Annual theme issue. *Childhood Education* 77 (5): 319–20.

Kralovec, E., & J. Buell. 2000. *The end of homework: How homework disrupts families, overburdens children, and limits learning.* Boston: Beacon Press.

Langendorfer, S. 1988. Rotating, spring rocking, and see-saw equipment. In *Where our children play: Elementary school playground equipment,* eds. L. Bruya & S. Langendorfer, 107–31. Reston, VA: American Association for Health, Physical Education, Recreation and Dance.

Loewy, M. 1998. Suggestions for working with fat children in schools. *Professional School Counseling* 1 (4): 18–23.

Lynn-Garbe, C., & J. Hoot. 2004. Weighing in on the issue of childhood obesity. *Childhood Education* 81 (2): 70–76.

McKenzie, T., J. Sallis, J. Elder, C. Berry, P. Hoy, P. Nader, M. Zive, & S. Broyles. 1997. Physical activity levels and prompts in young children at recess: A two-year study of a bi-ethnic sample. *Research Quarterly for Exercise and Sport* 68 (3): 195–202.

NASPE (National Association for Sport and Physical Education). 2001. *Recess in elementary schools.* Reston, VA: Author.

O'Hanian, S. 2002. *What ever happened to recess and why are our children struggling in kindergarten?* New York: McGraw-Hill.

Pate, R., J. Ross, T. Baumgartner, & R. Sparks. 1987. The modified pull-up test. *Journal of Physical Education, Recreation and Dance* 58 (9): 71–73.

Pellegrini, A., K. Kato, P. Blatchford, & E. Baines. 2002. A short-term longitudinal study of children's playground games across the first year of school: Implications for social competence and adjustment to school. *American Educational Research Journal* 39 (4): 991–1015.

Rivkin, M. 1995. *The great outdoors: Restoring children's right to play outdoors.* Washington, DC: NAEYC.

Sallis, J., T. Conway, J. Prochaska, T. McKenzie, S. Marshall, & M. Brown. 2001. The association of school environments with youth physical activity. *American Journal of Public Health* 91 (4): 618–20.

Sanders, S., & G. Graham. 1995. Kindergarten children's initial experiences in physical education: The relentless persistence of play clashes with the zone of acceptable responses. *Journal of Teaching in Physical Education* 14: 372–83.

Sibley, B., & J. Etnier. 2003. The relationship between physical activity and cognition in children: A meta-analysis. *Pediatric Exercise Science* 15: 243–56.

Sindelar, R. 2002. *Recess: Is it needed in the 21st century?* ERIC Clearinghouse. Online: http://ceep.crc.uiuc.edu/poptopics/recess.html.

Stratton, G., I. Marsh, & J. Moores. 2000. Promoting children's physical activity in primary school: An intervention study using playground markings. *Ergonomics* 43 (10): 1538–46.

Surface Transportation Policy Project. 2003. American attitudes toward walking and creating better walking communities. Online: www.transact.org/report.asp?id=205.

Surface Transportation Policy Project. 2004. *Mean Streets 2004: How far have we come?* Online: www.transact.org/report.asp?id=235.

Sutterby, J. 2004. Fear of outdoor play: An analysis of the West Nile crisis in South Texas. Paper presented at the Annual Conference of the National Association for the Education of Young Children, Anaheim, California.

Sutterby, J., P. Brown, & C.D. Thornton. 2004. Physical activity levels during free play and physical education. Paper presented at the annual conference of the American Educational Research Association, San Diego, California.

Sutterby, J., & J. Frost. In press. Play environments: Indoors and out. In *Handbook of Early Childhood Education*, eds. B. Spodek & O. Saracho. Mahweh, NJ: Erlbaum.

Thornton, C.D., & J. Sutterby. 2004. Balance beams: Developing balance skills on the playground. *Today's Playground* 4 (6): 8–10.

Wallis, C. 2004. What makes teens tick. *Time*, May 10.

Yisreal, L. 1998. Fast facts on: Developmental disabilities—Sensory integration therapy. Institute for Human Development, University of Missouri–Kansas City. Online: www.moddrc.com/Information-Disabilities/FastFacts/SensoryIntegration.htm.

JOHN A. SUTTERBY, PHD, is an assistant professor at the University of Texas at Brownsville/Texas Southmost College. He is a coauthor of *The Developmental Benefits of Playgrounds* with Joe Frost, Pei-San Brown, and Candra Thornton.

CANDRA D. THORNTON, PHD, is an assistant professor of early childhood education at Auburn University in Alabama. She is actively involved in research, writing, and consulting on various topics concerning children's play.

UNIT 5

Guiding and Supporting Young Children

Unit Selections

Key Points to Consider

- How can teachers establish a more child-friendly environment in their classroom?
- Why is emotional stability so important to develop during the preschool years?
- Is it possible to prevent disruptive behavior before it occurs?
- How can a teacher build positive relationships with children?
- What are the ramifications of corporal punishment, which is allowed in 23 states, on children?

Student Web Site

www.mhcls.com/online

Internet References

Further information regarding these websites may be found in this book's preface or online.

Future of Children
   http://www.futureofchildren.org
Busy Teacher's Cafe
   http://www.busyteacherscafe.com
Tips for Teachers
   http://www.counselorandteachertips.com
You Can Handle Them All
   http://www.disciplinehelp.com

Early childhood teaching is all about problem-solving. Just as children work to solve problems, so do their teachers. Every day, teachers make decisions about how to guide children socially and emotionally. In attempting to determine what could be causing a child's emotional distress, teachers must take into account a myriad of factors. They consider physical, social, environmental, and emotional factors, in addition to the surface behavior of a child. Whether it is an individual child's behavior or interpersonal relationships, the pressing problem involves complex issues that require careful reflection and analysis. Even the most mature teachers spend many hours thinking and talking about the best ways to guide young children's behavior: What should I do about the child who is out of bounds? What do I say to parents who want their child punished? Are the needs of boys and girls handled equally well in my classroom?

The first article in this unit, "From Policing to Participation: Overturning the Rules and Creating Amiable Classrooms," begins with a frank examination and discussion by a number of teachers at three child care centers. The staff had the goal of transforming their role as a police officer for the many rules—some of which had no logical basis—to a child centered behavior

and guidance policy. In the article the teachers reexamine long standing practices and rules, make changes in the physical environment of their classrooms, and describe some of the changes they witnessed in child behavior. The reader will find him or herself reexamining the rules and practices at programs where they may work.

As teachers of young children our goal should be to prevent behavior problems from occurring in the first place. The authors of "Emotional Security in the Classroom: What Works for Young Children," set a proactive tone by providing teachers with an overview of the importance of children feeling secure about themselves and their place in life. Children who believe they are accepted and respected in the classroom feel confident and are able to develop genuine relationships with their peers and teachers. Teachers who have a limited number of disruptive children in their class are those teachers who take precautionary steps to establish firm rules, establish a supportive environment, and help children learn about consequences of their behavior.

Determining strategies of guidance and discipline is important work for an early childhood teacher. Because the teacher-child relationship is foundational for emotional well-being and social competence, guidance is more than applying a single set of guidance techniques. Instead of one solitary model of classroom discipline strictly enforced, a broad range of techniques is more appropriate. It is only through careful analysis and reflection that teachers can look at children individually, assessing not only the child but the impact of family cultures as well, and determine what is appropriate and effective guidance.

Unfortunately, there are teachers who do not work to develop a positive environment in the classroom and resort to physical punishment when children need behavior guidance. In "Unprotected in the Classroom," Ferraro and Weinreich discuss the continued use of corporal punishment in our schools. In the United States twenty-three states allow school personnel to use "reasonable corporal punishment" to discipline children, even as young as kindergarten. Reflect on memories of classroom discipline you witnessed or received as a student while you were in school. What effect do you think this discipline had on you or your fellow classmates? Think about the guidance techniques that are most effective in a classroom.

Children crave fair and consistent guidelines from caring adults in their world. They want to know the consequences of their behavior and how to meet the expectations of others.

When the expectations are clear and the students see a direct relation between their behavior and the consequences they begin to develop the self control that will be so important as they move through life. In Unit One there are a number of articles on the importance of preschool education. For one of the most striking differences between high quality preschool programs and mediocre programs the reader can review the findings from the High/Scope Perry Preschool Project. When children had the opportunity to make choices and be responsible for their choices they were better able to make wise decisions later in life. More of the students who did not participated in a quality preschool program as four years olds dropped out of school, became involved in juvenile crime or were arrested as adults. Quality preschool programs offer children many opportunities to make decisions about everything from colors of paint to use to activities in which they will participate. Reasonable consequences that are a direct result of the behavior in which the child engaged are much more effective for guiding behavior than corporal punishment.

Effective guidance techniques go hand in hand with effective teaching strategies. An excellent teacher has a large repertoire of skills to best use when needed.

From Policing to Participation

Overturning the Rules and Creating Amiable Classrooms

> We were playing outside after a rainy day, and there was a huge mud puddle the size of a large table and of course a rule about no playing in the mud—children get dirty. The children played around the perimeter of the puddle, digging with shovels and throwing rocks in and watching them splash. Then some started tapping their toes in the water. We thought, "Well that's OK, they're wearing boots." Then they were up to their ankles in water. We were really hesitant but thought, "What's the big deal? It's only mud." But then we were anxious: "They are going to be really dirty, what will the parents say?" Before we knew it, they were jumping off the bench into the mud puddle, tumbling over each other. They were covered in mud. We were all standing back, kind of white-knuckling it and thinking, "Oh, should we let them?" We decided yes, and went to get the camera.

CAROL ANNE WIEN

How did the staff of three child care centers transform their work lives from continuous policing and correction of young children to a pedagogy in which they and the children participate together in constructing richly lived events? How were they able to let children engage in such wild activities as playing in a fresh mud puddle? Their experience shows that, contrary to common sense, aggression, accidents, and the stress of constantly enforcing rules are all reduced and transformed when many rules are eliminated by staff in a collaborative process.

The process of reexamining and then removing multiple rules for children's behavior permitted fuller participation in the life of the centers and led to an overall transformation of power relationships: both teachers and children gained more power to affect what happened in the programs. While reexamining the rules was not the only thoughtful process undertaken by the teachers, it seemed to be especially powerful in opening up practice toward more expansive living. Simultaneously, teachers reexamined the physical environments (organization of time space) and the ways these contributed to a stressful atmosphere that generated aggression. As Karyn Callaghan comments, "The whole question of letting go of power just flies in the face of [established] practice."

The Children and Families Served

The three centers are all nonprofit sites—one with 63 children on a university campus, one (42 children) in a workplace setting, and the other (32 children) in a high school. In the latter, eight children have special needs and another 16 are considered to have general developmental delays. All three centers are inclusive settings with resource-teacher consultants for children with special needs. Staff are qualified early childhood educators, and the centers accept early childhood education students in practicum placements. As an example of diversity, in one center 40 percent of the families served use English as a second language in their homes, with 10 percent being newly arrived immigrants. Cultures and languages of the families include Mandarin and its dialects, as well as Spanish and Portuguese. The centers serve many single-parent families and families with two parents on shift work.

Established Practice in the Centers

In all three centers the established, conventional practice was rule based, yet staff felt they had few rules and no problems as a result. Safety for young children was the highest priority, with rules often designed to prevent harm to children. However, in creating the rules the educators did not consider the possibility that harm might come to the children and teachers in other ways as a consequence of these rules. Callaghan noted, "Safety, you can justify any rule with safety."

Another justification was government requirements, that is, the authority of the official regulating body. Sometimes these regulations were real; sometimes they were assumed to exist by the teachers but in fact did not. Teacher anxiety over responsibility for young children's lives is clear. Rules proliferated out of fear for the safety of the young and vulnerable charges.

Bobbie-Jo described how her center had been "very structured." For example, "we had pictures of three faces" defining how many children were permitted in a location, and "children were not allowed to take toys [from one play area to another]."

Brenda, at another center, said, "You always had to go down the slide feet first, and you always had to sit up going down the slide." Laurie noted that in the center serving many children with special needs, staff were "stopping things from happening all day long." For instance, only four children were allowed in the water play area, so any additional children who tried to join the play would be redirected to another activity.

With tightly defined spaces for every activity, teachers acted as traffic officers, directing children to available spots. The time segments for activities were brief, play spaces rigorously defined, and play areas small and tight. In one center, for instance, two separate playrooms each had precisely the same interest areas, all of them small.

To give an idea of the tone at the centers during their rule-governed regimes, here is a partial list of what children could and could not do. One center discovered they had 26 rules for outdoor play, including this sampling:

No swinging from the slide.
No crashing riding toys.
Only run in one direction.
No sitting on balls.
No using big brooms.
No banging on shed.
No licking the door.

Another center found that it had many indoor rules, including such specifics as the order for eating lunch and other rules such as

No blowing on food.
No other toys used with playdough.
No toys traveling around the room from area to area.
Sit in the same seat for lunch every day.

When I asked the educators to define a *rule* in such practice,

Melita said, "Something necessary to keep control."
"And control is conceived as?"
Several teachers responded, "Children obeying, children doing as they are told."
Brenda added, "It was a comfort for teachers to know there was a rule in place and everything would run smoothly."
"Ah, you believed that this control would in fact work! *[chorus of yeses]* But in fact it didn't, because people were policing all the time!"

The amount of energy teachers spent on enforcing the rules to govern the children was immense and highly stressful. Laurie said, "The energy the staff were expending on policing the center, redirecting children, and giving time-out was just so draining." She described the block area at her center:

Children would go in, and things would start flying, blocks would get knocked over, kids would get pushed, and there would be yelling and screaming. Half the time you would not want the block center open because you couldn't deal with it. It was so loud. That whole half of the room would get really crazy. The noise level would go

up, and then children would start bouncing off each other and teachers would start pulling out their hair. You could make a comedy movie of it.

Reexamining the Rules

How did changes to practice begin? Callaghan offered workshops for the early childhood community in which the match between values and practices was examined. Influenced by interpretations of the Reggio Emilia approach (Malaguzzi 1996; Cadwell 1997; Hendrick 1997; Edwards, Gandini, & Forman 1998), she invited teachers to explore their images of children, and she gently questioned some scenarios observed in the community, such as

Children told what position to lie in on their cots.
No toys allowed from home.
Weekly themes planned for the entire year without considering children's interests.

Callaghan asked, "If we believe that children are unique and to be respected, and yet we are making children finish all the food on their plates before they get to have a drink, or there are designated times when they can go to the washroom, then what must the view really be?" The notion of a regulated child forced to follow prescribed institutional scripts for living had not occurred to those attending the workshop.

The invitation to consider the contrast between the rule-based scenarios seen in their centers and the lovely images of children to which the teachers gave lip service prompted Bobbie-Jo to challenge teachers at her center to rethink their rules. This process was difficult. When they tried to discuss their rules as a group, individuals reacted so strongly to one another's rules, laughing and making faces, that they had to make a rule not to be judgmental about rules. The teachers described so many rules that the group could not deal with all of them in one session.

The amount of energy teachers spent on enforcing the rules to govern the children was immense and highly stressful.

A decision to have a second meeting with a focus on one area only—outdoor play—allowed the staff to note 26 teacher-generated rules for children's play. This was many more than they *thought* they had, but these rules had never been written down. Bobbie-Jo noted, "Individually we had only a few rules, but when you put all those rules together, for a child there were a lot of different rules because staff had different expectations."

Collaboratively, the teachers decided on three criteria for a rule: Did it [the behavior targeted by the rule] harm the child? Did it harm others? Did it damage property? With the criteria in mind, the group began to examine the rules. Someone noticed that play areas were closed when parents picked up children. Did this rule meet the criteria? No. The teachers asked, "So why do we have that area closed?"

Applying the criteria to their rules opened up the process of discarding rules. On the outdoor playground, for example, the 26 rules were reduced to five:

Riding toys are for riding.
Riding toys stay off the climber.
Sand in the sandbox.
Safe bike riding.
Hockey sticks stay down.

Bobbie-Jo provided an example of the process of questioning that could lead to rule reduction. One day a child brought in a new action figure and told Bobbie-Jo about it. A teacher interrupted, saying:

"That needs to go in his cubby."

"Wait a minute. Why?"

"Because it's not his show-and-tell day."

"Let's put this in adult perspective. Suppose on the weekend you got engaged. You come in with your engagement ring and want to show everybody, and I say to you, 'Whoa, whoa, it's not your day. But you can put that in your locker.' It's the same thing."

"OK, he can keep it in here [the class], as long as he shares it with everybody."

"I can go along with that as long as I can have a turn with your jewelry when you're done."

Bobbie-Jo argued that there are many toys to share in centers but "not everything is for sharing." "If it's not OK for me to borrow another adult's jewelry, watch, or sweater, I don't think it's OK for us to expect children to share their things."

Teachers worried that welcoming play materials from home would not work, and they called Bobbie-Jo to come and see how upset children were the first few times such toys were brought into class. Gradually, it became easier to permit items from home to be part of classroom life. Melita said, "It really reduced stress. You are not in power struggles with children." Brenda added that "parents really appreciate it too," not having to struggle over telling a child to leave a precious item behind. Children's self-investment in their belongings shows an attachment to their identity, and separating from something that contributes to identity is emotionally difficult.

We asked ourselves, "Why are we doing this? Why are only four children allowed in water play? How is that promoting children's development?"

Two months after the initial workshop, Bobbie-Jo, the first to stimulate a reexamination of rules in her center, presented the experience at a local teacher network meeting. After handing out a revised list of new and reduced rules, Bobbie-Jo said, "They thought it was completely crazy. They said, 'I would like to see you come and do that at our center!'" Removing rules seemed counterintuitive.

Laurie said of her center, "We started to abandon the rules and then understood their impact on both children and teachers."

We were dealing with 'behavior' on a regular basis. We asked ourselves, 'Why are we doing this? Why are only four children allowed in water play? How is that promoting children's development?'"

The teachers began allowing as many children as wished to to come to the water play area and found that the focus of the teachers became one of negotiating and developing children's social skills for entering play. The teachers made the water table more accessible, pulling it away from the wall so children could crowd all around it. The playdough table too went from having three places to many places. The staff focus became "giving children the skills to learn to enter the situation," such as problem-solving how to find another place to play.

Overall, the teachers in all three centers found that eliminating rules reduced stress. In addition, Callaghan was struck by the process of *negotiating* rules when incidents arose, with teachers asking each other, "What do you think about this?" Children were invited to join the discussions when teachers asked, "Do we need a rule about this?" Of interest is the fact that the changes and their consequences were consistent across the three centers and that the changes appeared quickly, over months, not years.

Changes in the Physical Environments

Reducing the rules in a setting, and experiencing positive change as a result, also led to explorations of the organization of the physical environment. Laurie described how the aforementioned block area in her center was reorganized and enlarged (from 4 by 6 feet to 10 by 20 feet) with much better results for the children. Teachers also found ways to permit block structures to remain standing, rather than insisting on tidying up each day, so children could return later and continue building. This meant redesigning the layout for cots at nap time, but teachers did this now that their priority was children's activity rather than adult convenience. The impact of the change astonished the teachers. Laurie noted,

The mania in the block area just started to die down. Children began to interact in a much nicer way. There was less fighting because there was more room. Children were not bumping into each other.

There were more materials available. There were fewer rules about what you could and couldn't do, and therefore the teachers, instead of having to stand over the children and police them, could go in and participate. They could build with the children. They could draw, take photographs, go get other materials. There was lot more spontaneous interaction.

Surprisingly, it was also much quieter. In addition, teachers in this center found the incidence of accidents and aggression decreasing. A government requirement calls for all centers to complete accident reports for any injuries. One year, among 12 children there were 42 injury incidents—33 accidental and 9 due to aggression (hitting, spitting, biting, tripping, and so forth). The next year, after the center had reduced its rules, incidents were reduced considerably among the same 12 children, with aggressive acts down by 50 percent. Total incidents were 25, of which 21 were due to accidents, four to aggression. While many factors affect accident rates, the teachers' perception was that the reduction resulted from the changes in pedagogy. This was both remarkable to them and corroborated their sense that the changes they made resulted in much more positive environments for children. The entire emotional tone of their center is more positive.

Teachers' priority was children's activity rather than adult convenience.

Many things were happening simultaneously. The examination of rules, teachers' surprise at their numbers, and the subsequent reduction created new degrees of freedom for both children and teachers to act spontaneously. This process stood out as momentous in its impact on changing practice. Other changes included a softening of the environment, such as creating conversation areas, adding Monet prints and flowers to bathrooms, and inviting parents to contribute family photos. Brenda said, "I love the fact that each of the three centers is different."

Consequences of Changes in Pedagogy for the Children

The biggest effect of rule reduction was that settings became quieter and calmer with less fuss about enforcing minor rules. With less monitoring to do and calmer children, staff could participate more fully, engaging with children in their activities. The teachers developed greater interest in following the children's lead, such as permitting them to interact fully and vigorously with a mud puddle in springtime.

Brenda made a videotape showing children deeply engaged in block play, woodworking, playing with Legos, and dramatic play in the loft. Half an hour into the video, children are still playing in the same areas. Laurie commented, "When children made their own choices, the time spent at activities increased." Concentration spans for self-initiated activity became long and sustained.

The children began to generate their own rules and to involve themselves in self-governing, a process Vygotsky long ago showed as necessary to the development of will power (1976; [1930–1935] 1978). For example, at Bobbie-Jo's center a group of boys made a space for hockey on the small playground, with rules about how to swing the hockey stick ("Not off the ground"). They made a net and demarcated their area with pylons. Such opportunities to generate rules for group activities make people feel they belong to the social group. Feelings of belonging are essential to any notion of community, and to the commitment of members to that community.

From Rule-driven, Clock Driven Practice to Values-based, Responsive Pedagogy

The teachers felt several things happened simultaneously. As they let go and gave more control to the children, the children learned that the adults thought of them as capable. By reorganizing the environments into more expansive spaces and reducing the number of rules, staff began to see new possibilities for practice. Several teachers joked about their previous focus on time and efficiency: "I remember always looking at the clock, thinking, 'OK, let's go, let's go' [laughing]; how many kids can you get to pee in five minutes?"

Previously, children were lucky if they had 15 or 20 minutes in an area. It was often 20 minutes of play, 5 minutes of tidying up, 5 minutes of transition, and then play in a new area. A teacher noted, "Time was a rule." Time was a rule that could not be broken. Time as a production schedule, and teachers as keepers of the schedule (Wien 1995), produced policing to maintain the schedule. With the changes in stance, practice was more relaxed, less clock driven.

Callaghan saw teachers taking ownership of their practice. They wondered, "What do I like?" and "What's driving me crazy?" and saw possibilities for changing to practices that they preferred, chose, and assessed for themselves. We might say the teachers removed themselves from the established scripts for institutional routine and were inventing practice to fit their own contexts.

All the teachers found that the changes reduced stress. The energy of policing, correcting, and giving time-out was exhausting for teachers; it created negative energy, tearing at the emotional well-being of staff and children. Laurie said, "That energy is now turned into facilitating social interaction among children, exploring their interests, and actually talking to children." With staff chatting with and observing children more, the children are receiving more positive attention and, according to the teachers, "there are fewer behavior problems to deal with."

The teachers have noticed increased calm among the children and a sense of emotional satisfaction. For example, after the vigorous mud-puddle play, the wet and dirty children had to be cleaned up, and their clothes washed and dried before parents arrived. Melita said: "It was the calmest, most easygoing change and cleanup ever. I couldn't believe it. They sat and helped each other. It was amazing, and we noticed that, as we were right in the middle of it."

Resistance to Change

All the teachers note the role of resistance in the process of change. Laurie said, "When I entered practice in 1984 or '85, I was very much a controlling sort of teacher. I was very consistent, [thinking] this is the fastest, most convenient way we could get it all done." She added that after the radical change in her practice, it was interesting to look back on the way she had been. The teachers agreed that it is difficult to think there are better ways to function as early childhood educators.

Bobbie-Jo commented that when she began as supervisor, one teacher said, "You're that Reggio girl, and don't think for a minute you are going to do that here!" Whatever interpretations people make of the term *Reggio*, advocates of the Reggio approach note that they first create their practice out of whatever provocations stimulate a sense of ownership and participation in their own teaching. "Of course we're not going to force you to do anything," Bobbie-Jo responded to the teacher and proceeded to talk with staff about their view of children and what they wished to see in the center. She described how an especially resistant staff person was later overheard telling visiting teachers the results of following the children's lead: "I can't believe what a difference this has made. I am no longer stressed when I go home."

Teachers Taking Ownership of Their Teaching Practice

What happened and how did it happen? From the teacher educator's perspective, Callaghan believes a crucial moment in changing practice was beginning with teachers' images of children. "To start with the view of the child is pivotal." Making this positive image of children explicit permits a conscious investigation of whether the pedagogy of teachers supports their images of children. When teachers see mismatches between their newly explicit image of what children can do and their teaching practices, they begin to see openings for doing something differently that better honors their values.

Once the reexamination of established practice had begun, possibilities for teachers' participation in creating their own pedagogy opened up. Teachers asked, "What's possible?" or "Do you think we could _____?" Bobbie-Jo noted that "the adults are doing exactly what we are doing with the children. We are asking the children, 'What are the possibilities on this? What can happen? Make your theories. Let's try it out. Let's revisit that.' "

What has happened is a change in teacher stance. There is a new disposition to think in terms of possibilities, to invent in response to context—an aspect of good constructivist teaching (Forman 2002). Laurie commented that this change requires redefining what it means to be a good teacher and that expectations for job performance also have to change.

These teachers are no longer "keepers of the routine" (Wien 1995), programming according to the production schedule, but partners with children. If teachers take control of their own practice, and of assessing the match between their values and their pedagogy, then teaching becomes not performing a job to someone else's criteria, but instead living in responsiveness to children and families and sharing a broad sense of possibilities about all the ways to participate together. Something about the change is profoundly democratic, if democracy is conceived as full creative participation of all members of the community.

Conclusion

The emotional tone of the three centers has changed from surveillance in order to enforce the rules and schedule to one of positive, even joyful participation. There is a release of energy, a "raising of windhorse" (to borrow a phrase of the Shambhala Buddhists)—a new, positive energy. Callaghan says, "You can taste it when you walk into a center. You just feel there is this life there." Bobbie-Jo adds, "You can feel it, the energy rising; it is just so exciting."

Vecchi (2002, 56) reminds us of Gregory Bateson's phrase "the pulsing of life," as one element relates to another and both change in response. Part of what makes rising energy so exciting is that the changes are occurring collaboratively for the group. Callaghan describes the changes as occurring "within the context of a real community of learners. We were coming together regularly and sharing these stories, bringing in documentation, bringing these lists of rules, and there was a fabulous sharing in the community."

There are now three more centers in their second year of reorganizing their practice, and six others have joined the project to begin the work. In her former practice, Brenda notes, she "couldn't wait to get out at the end of the day," whereas "working this [new] way is like being on vacation."

References

Cadwell, L. 1997. *Bringing Reggio Emilia home: An innovative approach to early childhood education.* New York: Teachers College Press.

Edwards, C., L. Gandini, & G. Forman, eds. 1998. *The hundred languages of children: The Reggio Emilia approach to early childhood education—Advanced reflections.* Rev. ed. Greenwich. CT: Ablex.

Forman, G. 2002. Constructivist teaching. Presentation at the conference of the Canadian Association for Young Children, Montreal.

Hendrick, J., ed. 1997. *First steps toward teaching the Reggio way.* Upper Saddle River, NJ: Prentice Hall.

Malaguzzi, L., ed. 1996. *The hundred languages of children: Narrative of the possible.* Catalogue to the exhibit. Reggio Emilia, Italy: Reggio Children.

Vecchi, V. 2002. *Theater curtain.* Reggio Emilia, Italy: Reggio Children.

Vygotsky, L. 1976. The role of play in development. In *Play—Its role in development and evolution*, eds J. Bruner, A. Jolly, & K. Sylva. New York: Penguin.

Vygotsky, L.S. [1930–1935] 1978. *Mind in society: The development of higher psychological processes,* eds. and trans. M. Cole, V. John-Steiner, S. Scribner, & E. Souberman. Cambridge, MA: Harvard University Press.

Wien, C.A. 1995. *Developmentally appropriate practice in 'real life': Stories of teacher practical knowledge.* New York: Teachers College Press.

Four early childhood educators and two professors took part in the discussions that form the basis for this article:

CAROL ANNE WIEN, PH.D., is an associate professor in the Faculty of Education at York University in Toronto, Canada. She is the author of a forthcoming book, *Early Childhood Teachers Negotiating Standardized Curriculum*, from Teachers College Press.

KARYN CALLAGHAN, ECE, C., M.ED., is a professor of early childhood education at Mohawk College in Hamilton, Ontario, and originator/coordinator of the Artists at the Centre project, which brings artists to centers exploring the Reggio Emilia approach.

BOBBIE-JO GRAMIGNA, ECE, C., is supervisor at Templemead, Umbrella Family and Child Centers in Hamilton, Ontario. She previously taught at a workplace child care center and was a mentor to colleagues sharing an interest in Reggio Emilia.

BRENDA GARDINER, ECE, C., is assistant director and head preschool teacher at McMaster Children's Center in Hamilton, Ontario, which began exploring the Reggio approach in 1999 and joined Artists at the Centre.

LAURIE JEANDRON, ECE, C., is an instructor in early childhood education at Mohawk College in Hamilton, Ontario. As former supervisor of Scott Park Children's Centre, she collaborated with a team to create an environment to support children's interests.

MELITA VEINOTTE, ECE, C., R.T., is an early childhood educator at Templemead, an Umbrella Family and Child Center in Hamilton, Ontario. She taught at Scott Park Children's Center when it began to explore the Reggio approach.

This research was supported by the Hamilton Community Foundation. For more information on the Artists at the Centre project, visit www.artistsatthecentre.ca.

Heading Off Disruptive Behavior

How Early Intervention Can Reduce Defiant Behavior—and Win Back Teaching Time

HILL M. WALKER, ELIZABETH RAMSEY, AND FRANK M. GRESHAM

More and more children from troubled, chaotic homes are bringing well-developed patterns of antisocial behavior to school. Especially as these students get older, they wreak havoc on schools. Their aggressive, disruptive, and defiant behavior wastes teaching time, disrupts the learning of all students, threatens safety, overwhelms teachers—and ruins their own chances for successful schooling and a successful life.

In a poll of AFT teachers, 17 percent said they lost four or more hours of teaching time per week thanks to disruptive student behavior; another 19 percent said they lost two or three hours. In urban areas, fully 21 percent said they lost four or more hours per week. And in urban secondary schools, the percentage is 24. It's hard to see how academic achievement can rise significantly in the face of so much lost teaching time, not to mention the anxiety that is produced by the constant disruption (and by the implied safety threat), which must also take a toll on learning.

But it need not be this way in the future. Most of the disruption is caused by no more than a few students per class[1]—students who are, clinically speaking, "antisocial." Provided intervention begins when these children are young, preferably before they reach age 8, the knowledge, tools, and programs exist that would enable schools to head off most of this bad behavior—or at least greatly reduce its frequency. Schools are not the source of children's behavior problems, and they can't completely solve them on their own. But the research is becoming clear: Schools can do a lot to minimize bad behavior—and in so doing, they help not only the antisocial children, they greatly advance their central goal of educating children.

In recent decades, antisocial behavior has been the subject of intense study by researchers in various disciplines including biology, sociology, social work, psychiatry, corrections, education, and psychology. Great progress has been made in understanding and developing solutions for defiant, disruptive, and aggressive behavior (see Burns, 2002). The field of psychology, in particular, with its increasingly robust theories of "social learning" and "cognition," has developed a powerful empirical literature that can assist school personnel in coping with, and ultimately preventing, a good deal of problematic behavior. Longitudinal and retrospective studies conducted in the United States, Australia, New Zealand, Canada, and various western European countries have yielded knowledge on the long-term outcomes of children who adopt antisocial behavior, especially those who arrive at school with it well developed (see Reid et al., 2002). Most importantly, a strong knowledge base has been assembled on interventions that can head off this behavior or prevent it from hardening (Loeber and Farrington, 2001).

To date, however, this invaluable knowledge base has been infused into educational practice in an extremely limited fashion. A major goal of this article (and of our much larger book) is to communicate and adapt this knowledge base for effective use by educators in coping with the rising tide of antisocial students populating today's schools. In our book, you'll find fuller explanations of the causes of antisocial behavior, of particular forms of antisocial behavior like bullying, and of effective—and ineffective—interventions for schools. And all of this draws on a combination of the latest research and the classic research studies that have stood the test of time.

In this article, we look first at the source of antisocial behavior itself and ask: Why is it so toxic when it arrives in school? Second, we look at the evidence suggesting that early intervention is rare in schools. Third, we look at a range of practices that research indicates should be incorporated into school and classroom practice. Fourth, in the accompanying sidebars we give examples of how these practices have been combined in different ways to create effective programs.

I. Where Does Antisocial Behavior Come from and What Does That Mean for Schools?

Much to the dismay of many classroom teachers who deal with antisocial students, behavior-management practices that work so well with typical students do not work in managing antisocial behavior. In fact, teachers find that their tried and true behavior-management practices often make the behavior of antisocial students much worse. As a general rule, educators do not have a thorough understanding of the origins and developmental course of such behavior and are not well trained to deal with moderate to severe levels of antisocial behavior. The older these students become and the further along the educational track they progress, the more serious their problems become and the more difficult they are to manage.

How can it be that behavior-management practices somehow work differently for students with antisocial behavior patterns? Why do they react differently? Do they learn differently? Do they require interventions based on a completely different set of learning principles? As we shall see, the principles by which they acquire and exercise their behavioral pattern are quite typical and predictable.

Frequent and excessive noncompliance in school (or home) is an important first indicator of future antisocial behavior.

One of the most powerful principles used to explain how behavior is learned is known as the Matching Law (Herrnstein, 1974). In his original formulation, Herrnstein (1961) stated that the rate of any given behavior matches the rate of reinforcement for that behavior. For example, if aggressive behavior is reinforced once every three times it occurs (e.g., by a parent giving in to a temper tantrum) and prosocial behavior is reinforced once every 15 times it occurs (e.g., by a parent praising a polite request), then the Matching Law would predict that, on average, aggressive behavior will be chosen five times more frequently than prosocial behavior. Research has consistently shown that behavior does, in fact, closely follow the Matching Law (Snyder, 2002). Therefore, how parents (and later, teachers) react to aggressive, defiant, and other bad behavior is extremely important. The Matching Law applies to all children; it indicates that antisocial behavior is learned—and, at least at a young enough age, can be unlearned. (As we will see in the section that reviews effective intervention techniques, many interventions—like maintaining at least a 4 to 1 ratio of praising versus reprimanding—have grown out of the Matching Law.)

First Comes the Family. . .

Antisocial behavior is widely believed to result from a mix of constitutional (i.e., genetic and neurobiological) and environmental (i.e., family and community) factors (Reid et al., 2002). In the vast majority of cases, the environmental factors are the primary causes—but in a small percentage of cases, there is an underlying, primarily constitutional, cause (for example, autism, a difficult temperament, attention deficit/hyperactivity disorder [ADHD], or a learning disorder). Not surprisingly, constitutional and environmental causes often overlap and even exacerbate each other, such as when parents are pushed to their limits by a child with a difficult temperament or when a child with ADHD lives in a chaotic environment.

Patterson and his colleagues (Patterson et al., 1992) have described in detail the main environmental causes of antisocial behavior. Their model starts by noting the social and personal factors that put great stress on family life (e.g., poverty, divorce, drug and alcohol problems, and physical abuse). These stressors disrupt normal parenting practices, making family life chaotic, unpredictable, and hostile. These disrupted parenting practices, in turn, lead family members to interact with each other in negative, aggressive ways and to attempt to control each others' behavior through coercive means such as excessive yelling, threats, intimidation, and physical force. In this environment, children learn that the way to get what they want is through what psychologists term "coercive" behavior: For parents, coercion means threatening, yelling, intimidating, and even hitting to force children to behave. (Patterson [1982] conducted a sequential analysis showing that parental use of such coercive strategies to suppress hostile and aggressive behavior actually increased the likelihood of such behavior in the future by 50 percent.)

For children, coercive tactics include disobeying, whining, yelling, throwing tantrums, threatening parents, and even hitting—all in order to avoid doing what the parents want. In homes where such coercive behavior is common, children become well-acquainted with how hostile behavior escalates—and with which of their behaviors ultimately secure adult surrender. This is the fertile ground in which antisocial behavior is bred. The negative effects tend to flow across generations much like inherited traits.[2]

By the time they are old enough for school, children who have developed an antisocial profile (due to either constitutional or environmental factors) have a limited repertoire of cooperative behavior skills, a predilection to use coercive tactics to control and manipulate others, and a well-developed capacity for emotional outbursts and confrontation.

. . .Then Comes School

For many young children, making the transition from home to school is fraught with difficulty. Upon school entry, children must learn to share, negotiate disagreements, deal with conflicts, and participate in competitive activities. And, they must do so in a manner that builds friendships with some peers and, at a minimum, social acceptance from others (Snyder, 2002). Children with antisocial behavior patterns have enormous difficulty accomplishing these social tasks. In fact, antisocial children are more than twice as likely as regular children to initiate unprovoked verbal or physical aggression toward peers, to reciprocate peer aggression toward them, and to continue aggressive behavior once it has been initiated (Snyder, 2002).[3]

From preschool to mid-elementary school, antisocial students' behavior changes in form and increases in intensity. During the preschool years, these children often display aversive behaviors such as frequent whining and noncompliance. Later, during the elementary school years, these behaviors take the form of less frequent but higher intensity acts such as hitting, fighting, bullying, and stealing. And during adolescence, bullying and hitting may escalate into robbery, assault, lying, stealing, fraud, and burglary (Snyder and Stoolmiller, 2002).

Although the specific form of the behavior changes (e.g., from noncompliance to bullying to assault), its function remains the same: Coercion remains at the heart of the antisocial behavior. As children grow older, they learn that the more noxious and painful they can make their behavior to others, the more likely they are to accomplish their goals—whether that goal is to avoid taking out the trash or escape a set of difficult mathematics problems. An important key to preventing this escalation (and therefore avoiding years of difficult behavior) is for adults to limit the use of coercive tactics with children—and for these adults to avoid surrendering in the face of coercive tactics used by the child. This has clear implications for school and teacher practices (and, of course, for parent training, which is not the subject of this article).

Frequent and excessive noncompliance in school (or home) is an important first indicator of future antisocial behavior. A young child's noncompliance is often a "gate key" behavior that triggers a vicious cycle involving parents, peers, and teachers. Further, it serves as a port of entry into much more serious forms of antisocial behavior. By treating noncompliance effectively at the early elementary age (or preferably even earlier), it is possible to prevent the development of more destructive behavior.

II. Early Intervention is Rare

How many children are antisocial? How many are getting help early? To study the national incidence of antisocial behavior among children, researchers focus on two psychiatric diagnoses: oppositional defiant disorder and conduct disorder. Oppositional defiant disorder, the less serious of the two, consists of an ongoing pattern of uncooperative, angry behavior including things like deliberately trying to bother others and refusing to accept responsibility for mistakes. Conduct disorder is characterized by severe verbal and physical aggression, property destruction, and deceitful behavior that persist over time (usually one or more years). Formal surveys have generally indicated that between two and six percent of the general population of U.S. children and youth has some form of conduct disorder (Kazdin, 1993). Without someone intervening early to teach these children how to behave better, half of them will maintain the disorder into adulthood and the other half will suffer significant adjustment problems (e.g., disproportionate levels of marital discord and difficulty keeping a job) during their adult lives (Kazdin, 1993). (It is worth noting that on the way to these unpleasant outcomes, most will disrupt many classrooms and overwhelm many teachers.) When we add in oppositional defiant disorder (which often precedes and co-occurs with conduct disorder), estimates have been as high as 16 percent of the U.S. youth population (Eddy, Reid, and Curry, 2002).

In contrast, school systems typically identify (through the Individuals with Disabilities Education Act [IDEA]) slightly less than one percent of the public school population as having emotional and behavioral problems. Further, the great tendency

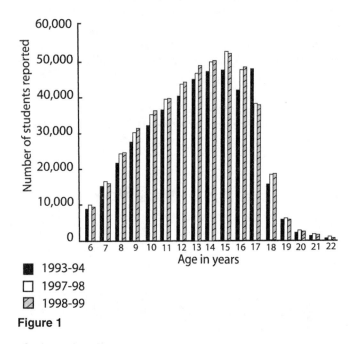

Students with Emotional Disturbance Served by Age, Selected School Years

■ 1993–94
□ 1997–98
▨ 1998–99

Figure 1

of schools is to identify these behavioral problems quite late in a child's school career.

The figure above provides a stark example of this practice, which is more typical than not in today's public school systems. Walker, Nikiosha, Zeller, Severson, and Feil (2000) examined the number of K–12 students in the 1993–94, 1997–98, and 1998–99 school years who were certified as emotionally disturbed (the IDEA category that captures antisocial students). As the figure shows, the number of students certified as emotionally disturbed peaks around age 15 (approximately 50,000 cases) during the 1997–98 and 1998–99 school years. Similarly, the older data, from the 1993–94 school year, show the peak in referrals spread over the ages 14, 15, and 17. These results suggest that a large number of students, who were no doubt in need of supports and services for emotional disturbance in their elementary and middle school years, were not referred, evaluated, or served under special education.[4] Only in adolescence, when their behavior problems had become so intractable and difficult to accommodate, were many of these students finally identified and served. This practice of delayed referral is the polar opposite of what research clearly shows is necessary.

Our society's social, cultural, and economic problems are spilling over into our schools. They are greatly complicating schools' central task of educating students safely and effectively. But the research is clear and growing: Even though many children and youth come from and return to chaotic, coercive home environments on a daily basis, they can still acquire sufficient behavioral control to succeed in school—and to allow classmates to learn in an orderly environment.

We have substantial knowledge about how to divert at-risk children, youth, and families from destructive outcomes.[5] We believe the problem is not one of knowing what to do, but of convincing schools to effectively use research-based intervention programs over the long term.

The remainder of this article is devoted to providing educators with guidelines and programs for early intervention that greatly reduce antisocial behavior. There are no magic bullets in the material presented herein. Dealing with the antisocial student population is difficult, frustrating, and, because schools tend to intervene too late, often without identifiable rewards. However, of all those who suffer from conditions and disorders that impair school performance, these students are among those with the greatest capacity for change—particularly when they first start school.

III. What can Schools Do?

Schools are not the source of children's antisocial behavior, and they cannot completely eliminate it. But schools do have substantial power to prevent it in some children and greatly reduce it in others.

First, and in some ways most importantly, schools can help by being academically effective. The fact is, academic achievement and good behavior reinforce each other: Experiencing some success academically is related to decreases in acting out; conversely, learning positive behaviors is related to doing better academically. Kellam and his colleagues (1994), for example, showed experimentally that gains in first-grade academic achievement, as measured by standardized achievement tests, resulted in substantially reduced levels of aggression, according to behavior ratings by their teachers. And, confirming what common sense tells us, Caprara, Barbaranelli, Pastorelli, Bandura, and Zimbardo (2000) found that positive behaviors (like cooperating, sharing, and consoling) among very young children contributed to their later academic achievement.

Second, schools can, to a large and surprising extent, affect the level of aggression in young boys just by the orderliness of their classrooms. An intriguing longitudinal study dramatically illustrates the role of this variable in the development or prevention of aggressive behavior from first grade to middle school (Kellam, Rebok, Ialongo, and Mayer, 1994). After randomly assigning students to first-grade classrooms, researchers found that nearly half of the classrooms were chaotic and the remainder were reasonably well-managed. Of the boys in the study who began schooling in the top quartile of aggressive behavior (as rated by their teachers), those assigned to orderly classrooms had odds of 3:1 in favor of being highly aggressive in middle school. However, those boys assigned to chaotic classrooms had odds of 59:1 for being highly aggressive in middle school. This seminal finding suggests that poor classroom management by teachers in grade one is a huge, but preventable, factor in the development of antisocial behavior—and, conversely, that effective classroom management can have an enormous long-term positive effect on behavior. Thus, working closely with first-grade teachers (and, presumably, other early-grade teachers) on their behavior management can yield substantial future benefits for students and their schools by offsetting destructive outcomes.

Aggressive first-grade boys assigned to orderly classrooms had odds of 3:1 in favor of being highly aggressive in middle school. Those assigned to chaotic classrooms had odds of 59:1 for being highly aggressive in middle school.

But to some extent, this just begs the larger question: How can schools and their teachers create and sustain orderly classrooms? We summarize here the key findings and conclusions from 40 years of research. First, we present a three-tiered intervention model that matches the extent of children's behavioral problems to the power (and, therefore, cost) of the programs implemented. Second, we offer tools that can accurately and effectively identify students as young as kindergarten (and, in daycare or preschool settings, even at-risk three-year-olds can be identified) who are likely to become school behavior problems (and, later in life, delinquents and even adult criminals). Third, we review five techniques that, in combination, are at the heart of preventing antisocial behavior. Fourth, we describe specific programs with substantial and growing records of effectiveness that successfully incorporate all of the above into entirely doable, economical, and feasible school interventions. These programs can be purchased by schools from a variety of for-profit publishers and non-profit child and family services organizations. Some are inexpensive; the more expensive interventions tend to be individualized to meet the needs of highly aggressive children. All of the programs described in this article can be funded with either IDEA resources or school improvement funds. Programs for antisocial children, such as those described here, can also be funded in partnership with mental health agencies and/or through grants available through the Safe and Drug Free Schools division of the U.S. Department of Education. (See box, Funding Early Interventions.)

A. Three Levels of Intervention

Research has shown that the best way to prevent antisocial behavior is actually to start with an inexpensive school-wide intervention and then add on more intensive interventions for the most troubled kids. Building on work done by the U.S. Public Health Service, Hill Walker and his colleagues developed a model with three progressively more intensive levels of intervention to address challenging behavior within schools (Walker, Horner, Sugai, Bullis, Sprague, Bricker, and Kaufman, 1996). This model has proved to be very popular among educational researchers and has been broadly adopted by practitioners as a way to select and coordinate interventions. It is sometimes referred to in educational forums as "the Oregon Model." However, this approach is clearly a matter of public domain and is not owned by anyone. The three levels of intervention are known as "universal," "selected," and "indicated." Each is briefly described below.

"Universal" interventions are school or classroom practices that affect all students. Examples of universal interventions relevant to behavior are classwide social skills training and well-enforced school discipline codes. (Outside of education, the polio vaccination is an example of a "universal intervention.") It may seem odd to implement a program for all students when most teachers can easily identify children who have, or are developing, antisocial behavior. But schoolwide programs accomplish three things. First, they improve almost all students' behavior—and most students, even if they don't qualify as troublemakers, still need some practice being well-behaved. Second, universal interventions have their greatest impact among students who "are on the margins"—those students who are just beginning to be aggressive or defiant. Sometimes, systematic exposure to a universal intervention will be sufficient to tip them in the right direction. Third, the universal intervention offers a foundation that supports the antisocial students throughout the day by reinforcing what they are learning in their more intensive selected and indicated interventions; these latter interventions are more efficient and have a greater impact when they are applied in the context of a prior, well-implemented, universal intervention.

Approximately 80 to 90 percent of all students will respond successfully to a well-implemented universal intervention (Sugai et al., 2002). Once the school environment is orderly, the antisocial students pop up like corks in water. These students have "selected" themselves out as needing more powerful "selected" interventions that employ much more expensive and labor-intensive techniques. The goal with these students is to decrease the frequency of their problem behaviors, instill appropriate behaviors, and make the children more responsive to universal interventions (Sugai et al., 2002). While selected interventions typically are based in the school, to be their most effective they often require parental involvement. Nevertheless, even when parents refuse to participate, selected interventions still have positive effects and are well worth the effort.

The vast majority of antisocial students will start behaving better after being involved in universal and selected interventions, but schools can expect that a very small percentage of antisocial students (about one to five percent of the total youth population) will not. These are the most severe cases—the most troubled children from the most chaotic homes—and they require extremely intensive, individualized, and expensive interventions. These interventions, called "indicated," are typically family focused, with participation and support from mental health, juvenile justice, and social service agencies, as well as schools. Most non-specialized schools will find that running such an intervention is beyond their capacity. It's for such students that alternative education settings are necessary.

This three-tiered intervention model offers a structure that educators can use when they are reviewing and trying to coordinate programs. It ensures that all students' needs will be met efficiently—each child is exposed to the level of intervention that his behavior shows he needs. This is a very cost-effective model for schools because interventions become much more expensive as they become more specialized.

But it all begins with effective early screening.

B. Early Screening and Identification of Potentially Antisocial Students

Many fields have well-established practices to identify problems early and allow for more effective treatments. For instance, in medicine, routine screening procedures such as prostate-specific antigen (PSA) tests to detect prostate cancer, mammograms to detect breast cancer, and Papanicolaou (Pap) tests to detect the early states of cervical cancer have been routine for years. Unfortunately, similar proactive, early identification approaches are not commonly used to identify children with, or at risk of developing, antisocial behavior.

But research shows that early identification is absolutely critical: Children who have not learned appropriate, non-coercive ways to interact socially by around 8 years of age (the end of third grade) will likely continue displaying some degree of antisocial behavior throughout their lives (Loeber and Farrington, 1998). We also know that the longer such children go without access to effective and early intervention services (particularly after the age of 8), the more resistant to change their behavior problems will be (Gresham, 1991) and the more expensive it will be to induce the change.

Yet, as discussed previously, schools offer special education services to just one percent of students, though two to 16 percent manifest some form of antisocial behavior—and virtually no special education services are provided before students become adolescents. The technology (usually simple normed checklists and observation instruments, as described below) for identifying such children is gradually becoming more accurate for children at younger and younger ages (Severson and Walker, 2002).

A particularly valuable approach to screening is known as "multiple gating" (Loeber, Dishion, and Patterson, 1984). Multiple gating is a process in which a series of progressively more precise (and expensive) assessments or "gates" are used to identify children who need help with their behavior. One such screening procedure is the Systematic Screening for Behavior Disorders (SSBD) (Walker and Severson, 1990).

This screening procedure offers a cost-effective, mass screening of all students in grades one to six in regular education classrooms. The SSBD is made up of a combination of teacher nominations (Gate 1), teacher rating scales (Gate 2), and observations of classroom and playground problem behavior (Gate 3). It was nationally standardized on 4,500 students for the Gate 2 measures and approximately 1,300 students for the Gate 3 measures. It represents a significant advance in enabling the systematic and comprehensive screening of behavioral problems among general education students (Gresham, Lane, and Lambros, 2002). The major advantage of the SSBD is first, its ease of use, and second, its common set of standards for teachers to use in evaluating students' behavior; these standards remove most of the subjectivity that is endemic to the referral process commonly used in schools (Severson and Walker, 2002). If all schools employed universal screening (and backed it up with effective early interventions), an enormous amount of defiant and destructive behavior could be prevented—and innumerable teaching hours could be preserved.

Researchers have found that teachers do tend to praise their regular students for good behavior, but they tend not to seize opportunities to praise antisocial students when they are behaving well.

C. Key Features of Effective Interventions

When dealing with well-established antisocial behavior, a combination of the following techniques is usually required in order to successfully bring about behavior change: (1) a consistently enforced schoolwide behavior code, (2) social-skills training, (3) appropriately-delivered adult praise for positive behavior, (4) reinforcement contingencies and response costs, and (5) time-out (see Wolf, 1978). Each of these techniques is briefly explained below.

Over the past three decades, an extensive body of research has developed on the effectiveness of these techniques for preventing and remediating problem behavior within the context of schools. Studies of the use of these techniques show that positive strategies (appropriate praise, social-skills training, providing free-time privileges or activities) are generally sufficient for developing and maintaining the appropriate behavior of most students. However, students with challenging behavior often also require sanctions of some type (e.g., time-out or loss of privileges) in order to successfully address their problems. Extensive research clearly shows that, to be most effective, intervention programs or regimens incorporating these techniques should be applied across multiple settings (classrooms, hallways, playgrounds, etc.), operate for a sufficient time period for them to work, and should involve teachers and parents in school-home partnerships whenever possible.

No single technique applied in isolation will have an enduring impact. Used together, however, they are effective—especially for antisocial students age 8 or younger. Assembling these techniques into feasible and effective daily routines can be done by individual teachers in well-run schools. But it is difficult, time-consuming, and fraught with trial and error. Among the fruits of the past several decades of research on this topic is a group of carefully developed and tested programs that integrate these techniques into entirely doable programs that don't overly distract teachers from their main job: teaching. Several are briefly described in this and the following section.

1. A Well-Enforced Schoolwide Behavior Code

A schoolwide behavior code creates a positive school climate by clearly communicating and enforcing a set of behavioral standards. The code should consist of 5 to 7 rules—and it's essential to carefully define and provide examples of each rule. Ideally, school administrators, teachers, related services staff,

students, and parents should all be involved in the development of the code. But writing the code is just the first step. Too often, teachers and others complain, a behavior code is established—and left to wither. To be effective, students must be instructed in what it means, have opportunities to practice following the rules, have incentives for adhering to it (as described in the third and fourth techniques), and know that violating it brings consequences.

One excellent, inexpensive program for teaching the schoolwide behavior expectations reflected in a code is called Effective Behavior Support (EBS). The principal features of EBS are that all staff (administrative, classroom, lunchroom, playground, school bus, custodial, etc.) recognize and abide by the same set of behavioral expectations for all students. The behavior expectations are explicitly taught to students and they are taught in each relevant venue. In groups of 30 to 45, students are taken to various parts of the school (e.g., the bus loading zone, cafeteria, main hallway, gym, and classrooms) to discuss specific examples of behaviors that would, and would not, meet the behavior expectations. Once they have learned the expectations, they are motivated to meet them by earning rewards and praise for their good behavior.

2. Social Skills Training

As discussed earlier, many antisocial students enter school without adequate knowledge of—or experience with—appropriate social skills. These skills must be taught, practiced, and reinforced. This is the purpose of social skills training. Skills

---

Funding Early Interventions

With the research reviewed here, building support for the idea of early interventions should not be difficult—but finding funds could be if you don't know where to look. One source is Title I. Schools in which at least 40 percent of the students are poor should look into using the schoolwide provision of Title I to fund universal interventions. Under Title I schoolwide, you can combine several federal, state, and local funding streams to support school improvement programs. Insofar as students are identified as emotionally disturbed, their interventions can be funded by IDEA. The federal government also provides funding to reduce behavior problems through the Safe and Drug Free Schools and Communities Act. In this case, state education agencies receive funds to make grants to local education agencies and governors receive funds to make complementary grants to community-based organizations. Schools can also partner with mental health agencies, enabling services to be covered by insurance such as Medicaid and the State Children's Health Insurance Program. Plus, most states have funding streams that could support the programs described in this article. (For more information on funding, see chapter two of *Safe, Supportive, and Successful Schools: Step by Step*, available from Sopris West for $49; order online at www.sopriswest.com/swstore/product.asp?sku=872)

taught include empathy, anger management, and problem solving. They are taught using standard instructional techniques and practiced so that students not only learn new skills, but also begin using them throughout the school day and at home. While the training is vital for antisocial students, all students benefit from improving their social skills—especially students "on the margin" of antisocial behavior. Social skills curricula are typically taught in one or two periods a week over the course of several months and in multiple grades.

3. Adult Praise

Adult praise (from teachers, parents, or others) is a form of focused attention that communicates approval and positive regard. It is an abundantly available, natural resource that is greatly underutilized. Researchers have found that teachers do tend to praise their regular students for good behavior, but they tend not to seize opportunities to praise antisocial students when they are behaving well (Mayer & Sulzer-Azaroff, 2002). This is indeed unfortunate because praise that is behavior specific and delivered in a positive and genuine fashion is one of our most effective tools for motivating all students and teaching them important skills. Reavis et al. (1996) note that praise should be immediate, frequent, enthusiastic, descriptive, varied, and involve eye contact. We would also suggest that the ratio of praise to criticism and reprimands be at least 4:1—and higher if possible. Although antisocial students may not immediately respond to praise because of their long history of negative interactions with the adults in their lives, when paired with other incentives (such as the type of reward system described below), the positive impact of praise will eventually increase.

4. Reinforcement Contingencies and Response Costs

Rewards and penalties of different sorts are a common feature of many classroom management strategies. Research shows that there are specific "best" ways to arrange these reinforcements to effectively motivate students to behave appropriately. These strategies are called individual reinforcement contingencies, group reinforcement contingencies, and response costs. Individual contingencies are private, one-to-one arrangements between a teacher or parent and a student in which specified, positive consequences are made available dependent ("contingent") upon the student's performance. Earning a minute of free time for every 10 or 15 math problems correctly solved, or attempted, is an example of an individual contingency.

Group contingencies are arrangements in which an entire group of individuals (e.g., a class) is treated as a single unit and the group's performance, as a whole, is evaluated to determine whether a reward is earned, such as an extra five minutes of recess. (Note: A group can fail to earn a reward, such as an extra five minutes of recess, but should not be penalized, such as by losing five minutes of the normal recess.) This strategy gets peers involved in encouraging the antisocial student to behave better. For example, if the antisocial student disrupts the class, instead of laughing at his antics, other students will encourage him to quiet down so that they can all earn the reward. To make it easier to keep track of students' behavior, reinforcement contingencies are often set up as point systems in which students must earn a certain number of points within a certain time period in order to earn a reward.

"Response costs" are a form of penalty that is added to the package of contingencies when working toward a reward is not quite enough to change students' behavior. Teachers can increase the effectiveness of contingencies by adding a response cost so that good behavior earns points and bad behavior subtracts points—making it much harder to earn a reward. (Response costs are the basis for late fees, traffic tickets, penalties in football, foul shots in basketball, and other sanctions in public life.)

5. Time-Out

Time-out is a technique of last resort in which students are removed for just five to 15 minutes from situations in which they have trouble controlling their behavior and/or their peers' attention is drawn to their inappropriate behavior. We recommend both in-classroom time-out for minor infractions and out-of-classroom time-out (the principal's office or a designated time-out room) for more serious infractions. Students should be given the option of volunteering for brief periods of time-out when they temporarily cannot control their own behavior, but teachers should *never* physically try to force students into time-out. Finally, *in-class* time-out should be used sparingly and should *not* be used with older students. Older students who need to be removed from a situation can be sent to the principal's office or another "cool-down" room instead of having an in-class time-out.

The research foundation for these techniques is quite strong and the empirical evidence of their effectiveness is both persuasive and growing. For the past 40 years, researchers in applied behavior analysis have worked closely with school staff and others in testing and demonstrating the effectiveness of these techniques within real world settings like classrooms and playgrounds. Literally hundreds of credible studies have documented the effectiveness of each of these techniques—as well as combinations of them—in remediating the problems that antisocial children and youth bring to schooling. The research has also surfaced guidelines for the effective application of the techniques in school contexts (Walker, 1995).

IV. Effective Programs for Preventing Antisocial Behavior

In spite of huge advances in our knowledge of how to prevent and treat antisocial behavior in the past decade, the Surgeon General's Report on Youth Violence indicates that less than 10 percent of services delivered in schools and communities targeting antisocial behavior patterns are evidence-based (see Satcher, 2001). As these children move through schools without effective intervention services and supports, their problems are likely to become more intractable and ever more resistant to change. This is simply not necessary. Effective, manageable programs exist.

Effective programs require an upfront investment of time and energy, but they more than "pay for themselves" in terms of teaching time won back.

We highlight three promising interventions—Second Step, First Step to Success, and Multisystemic Therapy—as examples of, respectively, universal, selected, and indicated interventions. The coordinated implementation of these or similar programs can make a remarkable difference in the orderliness of schools and classrooms and in the lives of antisocial youth (not to mention the victims of their aggression).

Second Step, a social skills training program for K-9 students, is described in detail. It was recently rated as the number one program for ensuring school safety by a blue ribbon panel of the U.S. Department of Education. Evaluations of Second Step have found results ranging from decreases in aggression and disruption among 109 preschool and kindergarten children from low-income, urban homes (McMahon, 2000) to less hostility and need for adult supervision among over 1,000 second- to fifth-grade students (Frey, Nolen, Van Schoiack-Edstrom, and Hirschstein, 2001).

First Step, is an intensive intervention for highly aggressive K-3 students. Experimental studies with kindergartners have found great improvments in their overall classroom behavior and academic engagement, and substantial reductions in their aggression during implementation and over many years following the end of intervention (see Walker, Kavanagh, Stiller, Golly, Severson, and Feil, 1998; Epstein and Walker, 2002). Similarly, studies involving two sets of identical twins enrolled in regular kindergarten programs found that exposure to the program produced powerful behavior changes upon introduction of the intervention that were maintained throughout the program's implementation (Golly, Sprague, Walker, Beard, and Gorham, 2000). These types of positive effects have also been replicated by other investigators. The First Step program has been included in six national reviews of effective early interventions for addressing oppositional and/or aggressive behavior in school.

Multisystemic Therapy (MST) is a family-focused intervention conducted by a trained therapist. It is aimed at the most severely at-risk youth, those who have been or are about to be incarcerated, often for violent offenses. Very often, the student has already been assigned to an alternative education setting. The therapist teaches parents the skills they need to assist their antisocial child to function more effectively across a range of social contexts. Daily contact between the student and therapist is common in the early stages of MST and reduces to several times per week as the intervention progresses. Therapists periodically talk to teachers to find out about the children's behavior,

attendance, and work habits. Most importantly, teachers need to let therapists know when they perceive incremental improvements in the children's behavior—the therapists use this information to guide their work with the families. According to the Blueprints for Violence Prevention Project, MST has been found to reduce long-term rates of being re-arrested by 25 to 70 percent, to greatly improve family functioning, and to lessen mental health problems (Blueprints, 2003). (To find out if MST is available in your area, visit) www.mstservices.com

As the research clearly shows, these three programs have the potential to prevent countless acts of aggression and positively influence both school and family functioning. Disruptive student behavior will decrease and teaching time will increase, allowing all children to learn more. Office discipline referrals will decrease, freeing up school staff to address other school needs like supporting instruction. Effective programs do require an upfront investment of time and energy, but over the school year, and certainly over the school career, they more than "pay for themselves" in terms of teaching time won back.

An obvious subtext in the article has been that elementary schools—and especially K-3 teachers—must bear the burden of preventing antisocial behavior. This may come as a surprise since behavior problems seem so much more severe as children age. But if there's one uncontestable finding from the past 40 years of research on antisocial children, it's this: The longer students are allowed to be aggressive, defiant, and destructive, the more difficult it is to turn them around. While high schools can, and should, do what they can to help antisocial students control themselves, elementary schools can, and should, actually help antisocial children to become socially competent.

References

Blueprints for Violence Prevention (2003). Multisystemic Therapy online at www.colorado.edu/cspv/blueprints/model/programs/MST.html

Burns, B. (2002). Reasons for hope for children and families: A perspective and overview. In B. Murns & K.K. Hoagwood (Eds.), *Community treatment for youth: Evidence-based interventions for severe emotional and behavioral disorders* (pp. 1–15). New York: Oxford University Press.

Caprara, G., Barbaranelli, C., Pastorelli, C., Brandura, A., & Zimbardo, P. (2000). Prosocial foundations of children's academic achievement. *Psychological Science, 11*(4), 302–306.

Catalano, R., Loeber, R., & McKinney, K. (1999). School and community interventions to prevent serious and violent offending. *Juvenile Justice Bulletin.* U.S. Department of Justice, Office of Juvenile Justice and Delinquency Prevention, Washington, D.C.

Eddy, J.M., Reid, J.B., & Curry, V. (2002). The etiology of youth antisocial behavior, delinquency and violence and a public health approach to prevention. In M.R. Shinn, H.M. Walker, & G. Stoner (Eds.), *Interventions for academic and behavior problems II: Preventive and remedial approaches,* (pp. 27–51). Bethesda, Md.: National Association for School Psychologists.

Epstein, M. & Walker, H. (2002). Special education: Best practices and First Step to Success. In B. Burns & K. Hoagwood (Eds.), *Community treatment for youth: Evidence-based intervention for severe emotional and behavioral disorders* (pp. 177–197). New York: Oxford University Press.

Frey, K.S., Nolan, S.B., Van Schoiack-Edstrom, L., and Hirschstein, M. (2001, June). "Second Step: Effects on Social Goals and Behavior." Paper presented at the annual meeting of the Society for Prevention Research, Washington, D.C.

Golly, A., Sprague, J., Walker, H.M., Beard, K., & Gorham, G. (2000). The First Step to Success program: An analysis of outcomes with identical twins across multiple baselines. *Behavioral Disorders, 25*(3), 170–182.

Gresham, F.M. (1991). Conceptualizing behavior disorders in terms of resistance to intervention. *School Psychology Review, 20,* 23–36.

Gresham, F.M., Lane, K., & Lambros, K. (2002). Children with conduct and hyperactivity attention problems: Identification, assessment and intervention. In K. Lane, F.M. Gresham, & T. O'Shaughnessy (Eds.), *Children with or at risk for emotional and behavioral disorders* (pp. 210–222). Boston: Allyn & Bacon.

Grossman, D., Neckerman, M., Koepsell, T., Ping-Yu Liu, Asher, K., Beland, K., Frey, K., & Rivara, F. (1997). Effectiveness of a violence prevention curriculum among children in elementary school: A randomized, control trial. *Journal of the American Medical Association, 277*(20), pp. 1605–1611.

Herrnstein, R. (1961). Relative and absolute strength of response as a function of frequency of reinforcement. *Journal of the Experimental Analysis of Behavior, 4,* 267–272.

Herrnstein, R. (1974). Formal properties of the matching law. *Journal of the Experimental Analysis of Behavior, 21,* 486–495.

Kauffman, J. (1999). How we prevent emotional and behavioral disorders. *Exceptional Children, 65,* 448–468.

Kazdin, A. (1993). Adolescent mental health: Prevention and treatment programs. *American Psychologist, 48,* 127–141.

Kellam, S., Rebok, G., Ialongo, N., & Mayer, L. (1994). The course and malleability of aggressive behavior from early first grade into middle school: Results of a developmental epidemiologically-based prevention trial. *Journal of Child Psychology and Psychiatry, 35*(2), 259–281.

Loeber, D. & Farrington, D. (2001). *Child delinquents: Development, intervention and service needs.* Thousand Oaks, Calif.: Sage.

Loeber, R., Dishion, T., & Patterson, G. (1984). Multiple-gating: A multistage assessment procedure for identifying youths at risk for delinquency. *Journal of Research in Crime and Delinquency, 21,* 7–32.

Loeber, R. & Farrington, D. (Eds.). (1998). *Serious and violent juvenile offenders: Risk factors and successful interventions.* Thousand Oaks, Calif.: Sage.

Loeber, R. & Farrington, D.P. (2001) *Serious and violent juvenile offenders: Risk factors and successful interventions.* Thousand Oaks, Calif.: Sage.

Mayer, G.R. & Sulzer-Azanoff, B. (2002). Interventions for vandalism and aggression. In M. Shinn, H. Walker, & G. Stoner (Eds.), *Interventions for academic and behavior problems II: Preventive and remedial approaches* (pp. 853–884). Bethesda, Md.: National Association of School Psychologists.

McMahon, S.D., et al. (2000). "Violence Prevention: Program Effects on Urban Preschool and Kindergarten Children." *Applied and Preventive Psychology, 9,* 271–281.

Patterson, G. (1982). *A social learning approach, Volume 3: Coercive family process.* Eugene, Ore.: Castalia.

Patterson, G.R., Reid, J.B., & Dishion, T.J. (1992). *Antisocial boys.* Eugene, Ore.: Castalia.

Reavis, H.K., Taylor, M., Jenson, W., Morgan, D., Andrews, D., & Fisher, S. (1996). *Best practices: Behavioral and educational strategies for teachers.* Longmont, Colo.: Sopris West.

Reid, J.B., Patterson, G.R., & Snyder, J.J. (Eds.). (2002). *Antisocial behavior in children and adolescents: A developmental analysis and the Oregon Model for Intervention.* Washington, D.C.: American Psychological Association.

Satcher, D. (2001). *Youth violence: A report of the Surgeon General.* Washington, D.C.: U.S. Public Health Service, U.S. Department of Health and Human Services.

Severson, H. & Walker, H. (2002). Proactive approaches for identifying children at risk for sociobehavioral problems. In K. Lane, F.M. Gresham, & T. O'Shaughnessy (Eds.), *Interventions for children with or at-risk for emotional and behavioral disorders,* pp. 33–53. Boston: Allyn & Bacon.

Snyder, J. (2002). Reinforcement and coercion mechanisms in the development of antisocial behavior: Peer relationships. In J. Reid, G. Patterson, & L. Snyder (Eds.), *Antisocial behavior in children and adolescents: A developmental analysis and model for intervention,* pp. 101–122. Washington, D.C.: American Psychological Association.

Snyder, J. & Stoolmiller, M. (2002). Reinforcement and coercive mechanisms in the development of antisocial behavior. The family. In J. Reid, G. Patterson, & J. Snyder (Eds.), *Antisocial behavior in children and adolescents: A developmental analysis and model for intervention* (pp. 65–100). Washington, D.C.: American Psychological Association.

Sugai, G. & Horner, R., & Gresham, F. (2002) Behaviorally effective school environments. In M. Shinn, H. Walker, & G. Stoner (Eds.). *Interventions for academic and behavior problems II: Preventive and remedial approaches* (pp. 315–350). Bethesda, Md.: National Association of School Psychologists.

Walker, H.M. (1995). *The acting-out child: Coping with classroom disruption.* Langmont, Colo.: Sopris West.

Walker, H.M., Horner, R.H., Sugai, G., Bullis M., Spraque, J.R., Bricker, D. & Kaufman, M.J. (1996). Integrated approaches to preventing antisocial behavior patterns among school-age children and youth. *Journal of Emotional and Behavioral Disorders, 4,* 193–256.

Walker, H., Kavanagh, K., Stiller, B., Golly, A., Severson, H., & Feil, E. (1997). *First Step to Success: An early intervention program for antisocial kindergartners,* Longmont, Colo.: Sopris West.

Walker, H., Kavanagh, K., Stiller, B., Golly, A., Severson, H., & Feil, E. (1998). First Step: An early intervention approach for preventing school antisocial behavior. *Journal of Emotional and Behavioral Disorders, 6*(2), 66–80.

Walker, H. & Severson, H. (1990). *Systematic screening for behavioral disorders.* Longmont, Colo.: Sopris West.

Walker, H.M., Nishioka, V., Zeller, R., Severson, H., & Feil, E. (2000). Causal factors and potential solutions for the persistent under-identification of students having emotional or behavioral disorders in the context of schooling. *Assessment for Effective Intervention, 26*(1) 29–40.

Wolf, M.M. (1978). Social validity: The case for subjective measurement, or how applied behavior analysis is finding its heart. *Journal of Applied Behavior Analysis, 11,* 203–214.

HILL M. WALKER is founder and co-director of the Institute on Violence and Destructive Behavior at the University of Oregon, where he has been a professor since 1967. Walker has published hundreds of articles; in 1993 he received the Outstanding Research Award from the Council for Exceptional Children and in 2000 he became the only faculty member to receive the University of Oregon's Presidential Medal. Elizabeth Ramsey is a school counselor at Kopachuck Middle School in Gig Harbor, Wash., and a co-author of the Second Step program. Frank M. Gresham is distinguished professor and director of the School Psychology Program at the University of California-Riverside. He is co-author of the Social Skills Rating System and co-principal investigator for Project REACH. The Division of School Psychology in the American Psychological Association selected him for the Senior Scientist Award. Together, Walker, Ramsey, and Gresham wrote Antisocial Behavior in School: Evidence-Based Practices, on which this article is based.

Notes

1. In the AFT's poll, of the 43 percent of teachers who said they had students in their classes with discipline problems, more than half said the problems were caused by one to three students. Poll conducted by Peter D. Hart Research Associates, October 1995.

2. It is important to note that the kind of coercive interaction described is very different from parents' need to establish authority in order to appropriately discipline their children. This is accomplished through the clear communication of behavioral expectations, setting limits, monitoring and supervising children's behavior carefully, and providing positive attention and rewards or privileges for conforming to those expectations. It also means using such strategies as ignoring, mildly reprimanding, redirecting, and/or removing privileges when they do not. These strategies allow parents to maintain authority without relying on the coercion described above and without becoming extremely hostile or giving in to children's attempts to use coercion.

3. This unfortunate behavior pattern soon leads to peer rejection (Reid, Patterson and Snyder, 2002). When behaviorally at-risk youth are rejected and forsaken by normal, well-behaved peers, they often begin to form friendships amongst themselves. If, over several years (and particularly in adolescence), these friendships solidify in such a way that these youth identify with and feel like members of a deviant peer group, they have a 70 percent chance of a felony arrest within two years (Patterson et al., 1992).

4. Kauffman (1999) suggests that the field of education actually "prevents prevention" of behavioral disorders through well-meaning efforts to "protect" difficult children from being labeled and stigmatized by the screening and identification process.

5. Successful model programs have been reviewed and described extensively by Catalano, Loeber, and McKinney (1999), by Loeber and Farrington (2001), and by Reid and his colleagues (2002).

Building Positive Teacher-Child Relationships

M.M. OSTROSKY AND E.Y. JUNG

While busy greeting children and preparing for the day, the teachers heard Alan, a 4-year boy, crying in the hallway. Every morning, Alan cried very loudly and refused to come into the classroom from the bus. Mrs. Hannon, the lead teacher, found herself becoming very frustrated with Alan, and she told him to come to the classroom without asking why he was upset. During circle time, Alan repeatedly kicked his feet on the carpet and did not pay attention as Mrs. Hannon read a story to the group. Mrs. Hannon told Alan to stop kicking, but he continued kicking his feet in the air. Exasperated, Mrs. Hannon snapped at Alan, "Stop kicking, I have had enough. You are going to leave circle time. Go over there and sit on the chair. I am going to tell your mom about this." As Alan moved to the thinking chair, he began to cry. He was very mad at Mrs. Hannon and wished someone would "snuggle him" instead of yell at him.

What Are Positive Teacher-Child Relationships?

In early childhood settings, each moment that teachers and children interact with one another is an opportunity to develop positive relationships. Teachers can use a variety of strategies to build positive relationships with children. Teacher behaviors such as listening to children, making eye contact with them, and engaging in many one-to-one, face-to-face interactions with young children promote secure teacher-child relationships. Talking to children using pleasant, calm voices and simple language, and greeting children warmly when they arrive in the classroom with their parents or from the buses help establish secure relationships between teachers and children.

In early childhood settings, each moment that teachers and children interact with one another is an opportunity to develop positive relationships.

It is important for teachers to use developmentally and individually appropriate strategies that take into consideration children's differing needs, interests, styles, and abilities. For example, with infants and toddlers, teachers respond to their cries or other signs of distress. Teachers let children know they care about them through warm, responsive, physical contact such as giving pats on the back, hugging, and holding young children in their laps. For preschool children, teachers encourage mutual respect between children and adults by waiting until children finish asking questions before answering them, and by encouraging children to listen when others speak. In addition, teachers' use of positive guidance techniques (e.g., modeling and encouraging appropriate behavior, redirecting children to more acceptable activities, setting clear limits) helps children develop trusting relationships with their teachers.

It is important for teachers to use developmentally and individually appropriate strategies that take into consideration children's differing needs, interests, styles, and abilities.

In developing positive teacher-child relationships, it is important to remember to:

- Engage in one-to-one interactions with children
- Get on the child's level for face-to-face interactions
- Use a pleasant, calm voice and simple language
- Provide warm, responsive physical contact
- Follow the child's lead and interest during play
- Help children understand classroom expectations
- Redirect children when they engage in challenging behavior
- Listen to children and encourage them to listen to others
- Acknowledge children for their accomplishments and effort

Given the above information, if we "revisit" our hypothetical early childhood classroom, we might observe the following scenario:

During center time, Mrs. Hannon heard Alan crying, while she was helping another child with an art project.

Mrs. Hannon, realizing that she was again feeling very frustrated with Alan, decided that she needed to develop some new strategies when interacting with him. The next day, when Mrs. Hannon heard Alan coming toward the classroom, she went out into the hallway and bent down to his level, greeting him warmly and smiling at him. As Alan entered the classroom holding Mrs. Hannon's hand, he did not cry; he even smiled. During circle time, Alan listened to Mrs. Hannon read The Very Quiet Cricket, *and he responded when she had the class rub "their wings together" by flapping their arms up and down in response to the book's repeated phrase "Nothing happened, not a sound." At the end of the day as she considered all that had happened, Mrs. Hannon was pleased with how well the day went for Alan. She decided to look for resources on developing positive relationships with young children. She found that affectionate behaviors (such as smiles, pats, and hugs), a calm voice, and truly listening to young children help build positive relationships between teachers and children. She realized that she was often so busy managing the group of children that she missed the individual interactions with them. The next day, when Mrs. Hannon saw her students coming down the hall to enter her classroom, she stopped talking with her assistant teacher so she could greet each child with a warm smile and welcome. During circle time, instead of giving attention to children who were not listening, Mrs. Hannon praised children who were listening and engaged in story time. Also, when Ms. Gloria, the teaching assistant, did some finger plays with the children, Mrs. Hannon sat next to Alan. After the finger plays, Mrs. Hannon gave Alan a high five and told him what a great job he did following along with the finger plays. The tone in the classroom felt more positive, and Mrs. Hannon felt she was using her energy to help children become engaged in classroom activities and enjoy their time in the classroom rather than using her energy to constantly nag and attend to challenging behaviors.*

Why Are Positive Teacher-Child Relationships Important?

Research has suggested that teacher-child relationships play a significant role in influencing young children's social and emotional development. In studies of teacher-child relationships, children who had a secure relationship with their preschool and kindergarten teachers demonstrated good peer interactions and positive relationships with teachers and peers in elementary school. On the other hand, children who had insecure relationships with teachers had more difficulty interacting with peers and engaged in more conflict with their teachers. In addition, research has shown that teachers' interaction styles with children help children build positive and emotionally secure relationships with adults. For instance, teachers' smiling behaviors, affectionate words, and appropriate physical contact help promote children's positive responses toward teachers. Also, children whose teachers showed warmth and respect toward them (e.g., teachers

who listened when children talked to them, made eye contact, treated children fairly) developed positive and competent peer relationships. Moreover, children who had secure relationships with their teachers demonstrated lower levels of challenging behaviors and higher levels of competence in school.

> **Research has suggested that teacher-child relationships play a significant role in influencing young children's social and emotional development.**

Who Are the Children Who Have Participated in Research on Teacher-Child Relationships?

Research on teacher-child relationships has been conducted with children from culturally diverse families in child care settings, university preschools, family child care settings, Head Start programs, and kindergarten classrooms. Participants have included children from European American, African American, Hispanic, and Asian American families. However, no studies indicated whether children with disabilities were included. When developing relationships with young children, teachers should pay attention to the cultural, linguistic, and individual needs of the children. The importance of adapting strategies to meet the unique needs of the children and families in a teacher's care cannot be overstated.

Where Do I Find More Information on Implementing This Practice?

Practical information on teacher-child relationship can be found in journals such as *Young Children*. See the following articles and books for examples of how to develop positive teacher-child relationships:

Bredekamp, S., & Copple, C. (Eds.). (1997). *Developmentally appropriate practice in early childhood programs* (Rev ed.). Washington, DC: National Association for the Education of Young Children.

Center on the Social and Emotional Foundations for Early Learning. (2003). *Promoting the social-emotional competence of children. Training modules* [Online]. Champaign, IL: Author. Available: http://csefel.uiuc.edu/modules/facilitatorguide/facilitatorsguide1.pdf [2003, August 12].

Elicker, J., & Fortner-Wood, C. (1995). Adult-child relationships in early childhood programs. *Young Children, 51*(1), 69–78.

Kontos, S., Howes, C., Shinn, M., & Galinsky, E. (1995). *Quality in family child care and relative care.* New York: Teachers College Press.

Kontos, S., & Wilcox-Herzog, A. (1997). Teachers' interactions with children: Why are they so important? *Young Children, 52*(2), 4–12.

Spodek, B., & Saracho, O. N. (1994). *Right from the start: Teaching children ages three to eight.* Needham Heights, MA: Allyn & Bacon.

What Is the Scientific Basis for This Practice?

For those wishing to explore this topic further, the following researchers have studied teacher-child relationships in early childhood settings:

Birch, S. H., & Ladd, G. W. (1998). Children's interpersonal behaviors and the teacher-child relationship. *Developmental Psychology, 34*(5), 934–946.

Howes, C., & Hamilton, C. E. (1993). The changing experience of child care: Changes in teachers and in teacher-child relationships and children's social competence with peers. *Early Childhood Research Quarterly, 8*(1), 15–32.

Howes, C., Philips, D. A., & Whitebook, M. (1992). Thresholds of quality: Implications for the social development of children in center-based child care. *Child Development, 63*(2), 449–460.

Kontos, S. (1999). Preschool teachers' talk, roles, and activity settings during free play. *Early Childhood Research Quarterly, 14*(3), 363–383.

Pianta, R. C., Steinberg, M. S., & Rollins, K. B. (1995). The first two years of school: Teacher-child relationships and deflections in children's classroom adjustment. *Development and Psychopathology, 7*(2), 295–312.

Webster-Stratton, D., Reid, M. J., & Hammond, M. (2001). Preventing conduct problems, promoting social competence: A parent and teacher training partnership in Head Start. *Journal of Clinical Child Psychology, 30*(3), 238–302.

Zanolli, K. M., Saudargas, R. A., & Twardosz, S. (1997). The development of toddlers' responses to affectionate teacher behavior. *Early Childhood Research Quarterly, 12*(1), 99–116.

This What Works Brief was developed by the Center on the Social and Emotional Foundations for Early Learning. Contributors to this Brief were **M. M. Ostrosky** and **E. Y. Jung**.

Unprotected in the Classroom

The good news is that corporal punishment is declining in the U.S. schools . . . the bad news is that it's still allowed in 23 states.

PAUL FERRARO AND JOAN RUDEL WEINREICH

It's prohibited in prisons, the military, and mental institutions. Schools are the only public institutions in the United States where hitting another person is legally sanctioned, says the Center for Effective Discipline. In fact, along with Australia and Canada, the United States has the dubious distinction of being one of the very few industrialized nations that allow educators to intentionally inflict pain on students as a form of discipline.

Corporal punishment can occur anywhere and encompass everything from paddling to forced exercise to prohibiting use of the bathroom. According to the U.S. Department of Education's Office for Civil Rights, 301,016 students endured some type of physical punishment in the 2002–03 school year. That is a significant reduction from 20 or even 10 years ago, when more than 1 million schoolchildren faced physical pain at the hands of a faculty member.

The decrease is due largely to legislation in many states outlawing the practice. Currently, 27 states have laws banning corporal punishment, 19 of which were enacted within the past two decades. Two states, Ohio and Utah, also have bans, but the prohibition can be overruled by a school board or a parent.

It might appear as though positive gains have been made in banning corporal punishment. But with nearly half of the country allowing its educators to spank, strap, flog, cane, or otherwise humiliate and degrade schoolchildren, there is little to be upbeat about.

Ignorance about corporal punishment no doubt contributes to its continued existence. That appears to have been the case in 1996, when California legislator Mickey Conroy lobbied to reinstate corporal punishment. "Right now [students] can get away with just about anything without fear of punishment," the Republican was quoted as saying. Conroy's logic seemed to appeal to fellow party members, who pushed his bill from the education committee to the assembly floor. Their support waned, however, after a public hearing at which they saw shocking photos of the battered backsides of students. The bill ultimately died.

Such shock tactics still may be needed to persuade some school officials and state lawmakers that meting out physical punishments on unruly children is not an effective method of discipline. In fact, corporal punishment actually can have long-term negative effects on students and on society as a whole.

Why It's Wrong

Twenty-three states allow "reasonable corporal punishment" in schools. Unfortunately, "reasonable" is not defined in state law, allowing for interpretation according to the vagaries of the state or school district. In 1988, for example, the 5th U.S. Circuit Court of Appeals ruled in *Cunningham v. Beavers* that corporal punishment could be administered up to the point of "deadly force." The case involved two kindergarten girls in Jacksonville, Texas, who had been paddled with a wooden board; the U.S. Supreme Court declined to hear an appeal. (Incidentally, Texas schools led the nation in the number of paddling incidents in the 2002–03 school year, according to the Office for Civil Rights.)

Proponents of corporal punishment argue that it helps establish a scale of disciplinary actions. Corporal punishment, they reason, could be used for an offense too severe for detention, but not severe enough to warrant an expulsion. Yet with so many other methods available to address behavior (including reward systems, short-term suspension, and parental intervention), corporal punishment amounts to an admission of failure on the part of the teacher.

Corporal punishment is degrading. Nothing but humiliation and shame can come from forcing a child to bend over and receive a paddling—especially when it takes place in front of other students. Instead of focusing on the misbehavior, the teacher who paddles a student is not only causing immediate physical pain and suffering, but also may be breaking down the child's psychological defenses, leading to withdrawal, depression, and anxiety or to anger and rebellion.

Research has shown corporal punishment perpetuates a cycle of child abuse. Children who are paddled learn that abuse is justified if an adult deems it's necessary. They learn to solve their problems or express their anger and frustration through violence. When children see adults inflicting pain on other children, they learn to do the same to their smaller and weaker peers.

Worse, children can learn and ultimately mirror sexual deviancy as a result of corporal punishment. The practice of paddling has disturbing sexual undercurrents. Sadomasochistic tendencies or pure sexual excitement may lead a person to choose this method of punishment for certain students. The deviancy can become explicit when children sense the sexual pleasure the beater derives from the act.

Another argument for maintaining corporal punishment is that it creates continuity between home and school. Many parents use spanking to discipline their children. Laws that prohibit corporal punishment in school, proponents of the practice say, send mixed messages to children and diminish the value of the punishments they receive at home. While it's true that schools are being asked to take on more and more responsibilities traditionally left to the home, this is an area where educators should not be expected to tread.

The Unintended Outcomes

Some tout corporal punishment as an immediate and nonburdensome form of discipline that punishes only the guilty. Yet studies have shown that corporal punishment has ramifications extending beyond the school building.

The correlation between corporal punishment and larger societal problems seems clear. A 2002 study by Maryland-based anti-spanking advocate John Guthrow suggests that corporal punishment is a contributing factor in many of society's ills. (Guthrow's study also took a number of other factors into account, including state and local education spending, high school completion rate, percentage of births to unwed mothers, and poverty rate. The study is available online at www.nospank.net/guthrow.htm.)

Guthrow found, for instance, that corporal punishment is legal in eight of the 10 states with the highest murder rates. Louisiana, which has the highest murder rate in the country, is ranked sixth in the nation in percentage of students struck by educators. Of the states with the lowest murder rates in the nation, educators paddle children in only one. That state, Idaho, has the third lowest murder rate in the country and ranks 18th by percentage of students hit.

Of the states with the 10 highest graduation rates, educators use corporal punishment in only one. Nonpaddling states like Minnesota have relatively better test scores, lower dropout rates, lower poverty rates, and better health care than paddling states like Louisiana.

In short, states that permit the use of corporal punishment in public schools have more negative sociological outcomes than states that have prohibited this violence on schoolchildren.

Evidence also supports the argument that corporal punishment promotes violence and discrimination and creates a hostile school environment. Children find it more difficult to perform and succeed under such pressures. Feelings of anger, resentment, and fear are bottled up and not addressed, which takes a toll on student performance. And as Guthrow surmised in his study, "Once educational achievement suffers, other aspects of society suffer proportionately."

Not the Right Lesson

As with any controversial issue, each side can point to studies and statistics about corporal punishment. But putting all scientific data and findings aside, the primary concern of all educators should be the child's well-being, and that well-being is in jeopardy whenever an adult is allowed to physically harm a child.

On a practical level as well, corporal punishment is not effective. Children who are subjected to corporal punishment are likely to respond with negative behavior. Common sense, compounded by numerous convincing studies, dictates that violence does, in fact, breed violence. Most adults understand that communication is the best vehicle for resolving issues. In times of international conflict, precedent suggests that those involved join to discuss possible remedies. War is never the first suggestion, but rather a last resort. We should model that approach when we discipline children at home or at school.

When big sister Sara grabs little Tommy's toy, Tommy is never taught to hurt Sara and then retrieve the object of contention. Instead, responsible parents teach their children that words are always more effective. Likewise, teachers should nurture, encourage, and protect the children in their care. Violence against children can only poison the student-teacher relationship.

PAUL FERRARO (paulferraro@hotmail.com) is an elementary teacher at the Bi-Cultural Day School in Stamford, Conn. **JOAN RUDEL WEINREICH** (weinreichj@mville.edu) is an associate professor of education at Manhattanville College in Purchase, N.Y.

From *American School Board Journal*, November 2006, pp. 40–42. Copyright © 2006 by National School Boards Association. Reprinted by permission.

UNIT 6
Curricular Issues

Unit Selections

Key Points to Consider

- What are the steps teachers can take to plan using an emergent curriculum planning approach?

- Can teachers support prosocial development and if so, how?

- Is it appropriate for young children to use computers and if so, what is acceptable when it comes to young children and technology?

- What information should teachers be sending to parents about their children's early literacy experiences?

- How can teachers put writing before reading for learning to occur?

- What are some of the key essentials of early literacy instruction?

- Why is physical fitness so valuable in learning for young children? How can teachers foster a healthy lifestyle?

Student Web Site
www.mhcls.com/online

Internet References
Further information regarding these websites may be found in this book's preface or online.

Action for Healthy Kids
www.actionforhealthykids.org
Association for Childhood Education International (ACEI)
http://www.acei.org
Awesome Library for Teachers
http://www.neat-schoolhouse.org/teacher.html
Early Childhood Education Online
http://www.umaine.edu/eceol/
The Educators' Network
http://www.theeducatorsnetwork.com
The Family Involvement Storybook Corner
http://www.gse.harvard.edu/hfrp/projects/fine.html
Grade Level Reading Lists
http://www.gradelevelreadinglists.org
International Reading Association
http://www.reading.org
PE Central
http://www.pecentral.org

The Perpectual Preschool
http://www.ecewebguide.com
Phi Delta Kappa
http://www.pdkintl.org
Prospects: The Congressionally Mandated Study of Educational Growth and Opportunity
http://www.ed.gov/pubs/Prospects/index.html
Reggio Emilia
http://www.ericdigests.org/2001-3/reggio.htm
Teacher Quick Source
http://www.teacherquicksource.com
Teachers Helping Teachers
http://www.pacificnet.net/~mandel/
Tech Learning
http://www.techlearning.com
Technology Help
http://www.apples4theteacher.com

There is a major difference between eating frozen dinners every night vs. meals that have been prepared using the freshest local ingredients. The same holds true for planning curriculum. The generic one curriculum package fits all classrooms approach allows for little if any local flavor. Curriculum that is jointly developed by the teachers and students brings the best of the children's interest coupled with what is happening in their world together for meaningful, authentic learning. The first two articles in this unit provide an excellent overview to the use of an emergent curriculum for young children. Teachers who carefully observe and listen to their children and their local community will find plenty of possibilities for topics of investigation. Young children are most interested in authentic curriculum that is meaningful to their lives. The twelve days I spent visiting schools in China in October, 2006 provided a wonderful glimpse into how emergent curriculum is in full force in many Beijing preschools and kindergartens. The streets and building sites throughout the city are filled with construction cranes and cement trucks as the city prepares to host the 2008 Olympics. Inside the classrooms I saw the most extensive block structures I have ever seen. The children are living day to day with many cranes and steel girders. It is said 25% of the world's building cranes are located in China. Construction is everywhere and quite evident in the play of young Chinese children. We wouldn't want to eat frozen dinners every night for the rest of our lives; neither would we want to teach from a pre-packaged curriculum. Get out there and choose some local flavor and spice up the teaching and learning in your classroom.

Increasingly preschool teachers are becoming aware of the tremendous responsibility to plan learning experiences which are aligned with standards to allow children to develop a lifelong love of learning along with the necessary skills they will need to be successful. Standards help to guide teachers as they plan appropriate activities that will allow their students to gain the necessary skills to continue to learn as they move through school.

The "what's in it for me?" decade of the nineties has lead to the "service for others" decade as the 21st century starts. "Fostering Prosocial

Behavior in Young Children" by Kathy Preusse offers the reader an overview of prosocial development along with strategies for helping children develop prosocial or altruistic behavior. Helping and caring for others are natural behaviors that can easily be modeled by supportive adults while children are young. Learning these behaviors in the early childhood years allows children to grow into adults who are caring, compassionate, and tolerant of others.

The well respected journal *Zero to Three* is the source for "Early Literacy and Very Young Children." Author Rebecca Parlakian examines strategies to introduce young children to reading. Educating parents and teachers of infants and toddlers about the role they play in introducing children to the many aspects of learning to read is critical for future school success. Children who enter kindergarten having an understanding of the reading process have a distinct advantage over children who are not aware of the meanings of little black squiggles on the page. This article is followed by two other early literacy articles equally important. "Writing First" and "The Sweet Work of Reading" provide the reader with additional information on this important early childhood skill; the acquiring of communication skills. The articles include suggestions for shared book experiences, emergent writing, and conversations with children in a variety of settings.

This unit ends with articles addressing an important issue for teachers of young children. Healthy discussion can take place about each of the articles and the role of technology, math and science, social studies, physical fitness, and creativity. Beginning and veteran teachers alike need to be well versed in a variety of topics affecting young children.

A number of the articles in unit 6 provide opportunities for the reader to reflect on the authentic learning experiences available for children. How can they investigate, explore, and create while studying a particular area of interest? Make children work for their learning. This unit is full of articles addressing different curriculum areas. Active child involvement leads to enhanced learning. Suggestions for project-based activities in literacy, movement, and technology are also included. Again, the theme runs deep. Hands on = Minds on!

Professional organizations, researchers, and educators are reaching out to teachers of young children with a clear message that what they do in classrooms is extremely important for the children's future development and learning capabilities. Of course the early childhood community will continue to support a hands-on experiential based learning environment, but teachers must be clear in their objectives and have standards that will lead to future school success. Only when we are able to effectively communicate to others the importance of what we do and receive proper recognition and support for our work, will the education of young children be held in high regard. We are working toward that goal, but need adults who care for and educate young children to view their job as building a strong foundation for children's future learning. Think of early childhood education as the extremely strong and stable foundation for a building that is expected to provide many decades of active service to thousands of people. If we view our profession in that light we can see the importance of our jobs. Bring passion and energy to what you do with young children and their families and you will be rewarded ten times over. Enjoy your work for it is important.

The Plan

Building on Children's Interests

HILARY JO SEITZ

During outdoor playtime four-year-old Angela discovers a loose metal nut about half an inch in diameter. She shows the nut to her teacher.

> Angela: Look what I found. It looks just like the big one on our workbench.
> Teacher: Yes, it sure does, Angela. It's called a nut.
> Angela: I wonder where it came from.
> Teacher: Where do you think it may have come from?
> Angela: Well, actually it is the same as the ones in the workbench inside.
> Teacher: This nut looks very similar to the nuts and bolts inside. I think this nut might be bigger than the nuts and bolts we have inside.
> Angela: Maybe it came off of something out here.
> Teacher: What do you think it is from?
> Angela: Umm, I don't know—something out here.
> Teacher: Maybe you should check.
> Angela: Okay.

Holding the nut tight in her fist, Angela walks around, stopping to examine the play equipment, the tables, the parked trikes, and anything else she thinks might have a missing nut. She can find only bolts with nuts on the trikes. She spies a large Stop sign, puts her special treasure in her pocket so other children cannot see it, and sets up a roadblock for the busy trike riders so she can check the nuts and bolts on their trikes.

Edmund stops and asks her what she is doing, and she explains. Edmund says he needs to see the nut. When Angela shows it to him, he gets off his trike and starts helping her inspect the other trikes. They eventually find the one that is missing the nut. Other children, curious, crowd around.

While incidents such as this are common in early childhood settings, teachers may not listen for them, seize upon them, and build on them. When teachers do pay attention, these authentic events can spark emergent curriculum that builds on children's interests. This kind of curriculum is different from a preplanned, "canned" thematic curriculum model. In emergent, or negotiated, curriculum, the child's interest becomes the key focus and the child has various motivations for learning (Jones & Nimmo 1994).

The motivations are intrinsic, from deep within, meaningful and compelling to the child. As such, the experience is authentic and ultimately very powerful.

This article outlines a plan that teachers, children, and families can easily initiate and follow to build on children's interests. It is a process of learning about what a child or a class is interested in and then planning a positive authentic learning experience around and beyond that interest. Teachers, children, and parents alike are the researchers in this process. All continuously observe and document the process and review the documentation to construct meaning (Edwards, Gandini, & Forman 1998). Documentation is the product that is collected by the researchers. It may include work samples, children's photos, children's dialogues, and the teacher's written interpretations.

The Plan

"The Plan," as it became known in my classroom, is a simple four-step process of investigation, circular in nature and often evolving or spinning off into new investigations. (See diagram) The Plan consists of

1. **Sparks** (provocations)—Identify emerging ideas, look at children's interests, hold conversations, and provide experiences. Document the possibilities.
2. **Conversations**—Have conversations with interested participants (teachers, children, and parents), ask questions, document conversations through video recordings, tape recordings, teacher/parent dictation, or other ways. Ask "What do we already know? What do we wonder about? How can we learn more? What is the plan?"
3. **Opportunities and experiences**—Provide opportunities and experiences in both the classroom and the community for further investigation. Document those experiences.
4. **More questions and more theories**—Think further about the process. Document questions and theories.

In other words, teachers, children, and parents identify something of interest; we discuss what we know about it or what we

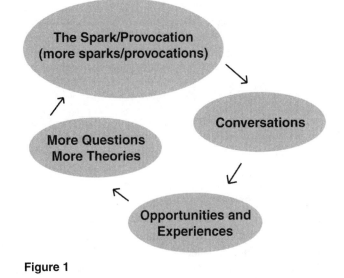

Figure 1

want to know about it; we experience it or have opportunities to learn about the idea; and then we discuss what we did and either ask more questions or make new theories. We document our understandings throughout the whole process.

The initial spark can come from anywhere or anything. For example, we might overhear children talking about the lawnmower at the park. The class, or sometimes a smaller group of children, then sits down and devises a plan with the help of interested adults.

Step 1: Sparks

Sparks can be things, phenomena, conversations—anything that provokes deeper thought. The sparks are what trigger a child (and adult) to want to know more, to investigate further. These sparks can occur at any time. They can be as simple as finding a pebble in one's shoe, grabbing an idea or story line from a book, or finding a nut on the playground. Young children have these sparks of interest all day long.

Sparks can be things, phenomena, conversations—anything that provokes deeper thought.

How Do Teachers See/Catch These Sparks?

I often hear teachers say, "How can I learn what the children are interested in?" or "How do we find out what the children want to know?" My response is always, Talk with the children, listen to them, and observe. For some teachers, it can be difficult to sit back and trust that ideas will naturally emerge. But once teachers become familiar with the process, they begin noticing how easily sparks appear.

Teachers in preschools, Head Start programs, and public school classrooms are expected to meet state standards or curriculum content goals. It is possible (although sometimes challenging) to integrate these standards and goals into emergent themes. Teachers who know and understand the "big picture" of standards and goals are more likely to *fit* a topic or emerging idea/plan into the curriculum. They document the process of The Plan (through photographs as well as descriptive narrative) to provide evidence of meeting standards and content goals.

Can We Provoke the Sparks?

Triggering sparks is sometimes helpful and can have exciting implications. Teachers can provoke children's thinking by suggesting ideas through stories, specific items, or experiences. Again, when a teacher is knowledgeable about standards and content goals, she knows when to provide appropriate sparks. For example, reading a book such as *If You Give a Moose a Muffin*, by Laura Numeroff, may trigger thinking and conversations about several different ideas (moose and what they eat and where they live, baking, puppet shows, painting, and others) as well as support literacy development. Owocki, in discussing teachable moments in literacy development, says, "Teachable moment strategies involve knowledgeably observing children and seeking out relevant opportunities to help them extend their understandings" (1999, 28).

Introducing an item into the classroom is another way of triggering sparks of thought. Watch children's eyes light up when you place a large beetle on a table or pluck an unfamiliar stringed instrument.

Finally, we can trigger sparks by offering experiences such as a neighborhood walk or a visit to the grocery store. Authentic experiences with meaningful things interest children (Fraser & Gestwicki 2001). The following is an excerpt of an observation from an early childhood classroom.

Teachers can provoke children's thinking by suggesting ideas through stories, specific items, or experiences.

A small group of four-year-olds and their teacher prepare to visit the park across the street. The teacher locks the gate and turns toward the children. She leans down and says, "Please stay on the sidewalk." Pointing to the nearby intersection, she adds, "We are going to walk over there to the crosswalk." The teacher holds hands with one child while the others pair off and walk behind her.

Kayla: What's a crosswalk?

José: It's over there.

Teacher: At the corner, we are going to walk inside the lines of the crosswalk. The lines show people where to walk. That way, cars know to stop. It is safer for us to cross in the crosswalk than in the middle of the street.

Tiana: My mom and me always cross over there by our car.

José: That's the middle of the street.

Michael (*motioning*): See that red sign? It says STOP, so you gotta stop at it.

As the small group negotiates the crosswalk and heads down the sidewalk on the other side of the street, José points out three more signs (a No Parking sign, a street name sign, and a Caution sign). The children are puzzled by the Caution sign and stop to try to figure it out.

The teacher documents this interest in street signs and crosswalks in writing and by drawing a sketch of the situation. Later, back in the classroom with the whole class, she brings up the subject of signs. The topic stirs interest and lots of conversation—triggering a new classroom investigation and the beginning of a new plan.

Step 2: Conversations and Writing a Plan

Formal meetings, built into the daily classroom routine, are ideal times for children, teachers, and family volunteers to have large group conversations about forming and writing a plan. In these routine meetings, children already know what to expect; they understand the process as well as the expectations. Our class meetings generally include a variety of fairly predictable experiences (reading stories, singing songs, conversations). Depending on the time of the meeting, we always discuss what has happened earlier or what is about to happen. While one teacher facilitates this meeting, another adult (teaching assistant or parent) writes down ideas, questions, and thoughts about the conversations. The adults later review this documentation to help plan and provide appropriate experiences.

Conversations also take place in settings such as activities or mealtimes. Small group conversations can be very meaningful to children and adults alike. Here is one snack time conversation:

Five girls, ages three and four, are seated at a small table, eating crackers. One child mentions going to the state fair the night before with her family. Two of the other children had been to the fair the previous week, so the teacher considers where to go with this spark of interest.

Kamie: It was cold at the fair, but the animals weren't cold
'cause they got fur on them.
Stacy: I touched the goats and the baby pig!
Kamie: Me too!
Karla: I went on a ride, but next time I'm gonna see the
animals.
Teacher: Where are the animals?
Stacy: They are in this big tent, and you gotta wait real long
to go inside. But you can put a penny or a dollar in the
machine to get food, then you can feed the goats and pigs.
Teacher: What do they eat?
Kamie: They eats lots of stuff.
Karla: Yeah, like rice and leaves.
Stacy: The pony has big teeth and a tongue. It gets your
hand sticky.
Teacher: Do all the animals eat the same food? (Kamie
nods yes.) Maybe we could go to the petting zoo and
feed the goats and sheep.
All the girls: Yes!
Teacher: Let's make a plan.

Karla and Stacy jump out of their seats to get a big sheet of paper and markers. Kamie reminds them to bring a clipboard too.

The teacher writes THE PLAN at the top of the paper. She prints the five girls' names under it. Then she begins writing a list, speaking the words at the same time she writes them.

1. Goats and pigs and ponies eat food.
2. What do they eat?

Karla: Where do they sleep? (The teacher makes this
No. 3.)

4. Go to library to get books.
5. Go to petting zoo and talk to zoo keeper.

The Plan is set and displayed on the wall. As a form of documentation, it is revisited frequently and adjusted to meet the needs of the children (Project Zero & Reggio Children 2001). Children, teachers, and families continuously reassess The Plan to guide inquiries. Often children and teachers add revisions to the plan.

Formal Planning

Teachers should also prepare a more formal lesson plan. This planning process works best when teachers, teaching assistants, and parents have opportunities to discuss ideas together. The teacher, who usually assumes the role of facilitator, needs to be prepared. She should know and understand standards and content goals; gather documentation, including photographs, observational records, and work samples; and guide the process of creating the formal plan.

The group discusses why the emerging ideas are important and how to further the investigations. Lesson plans should include the children's questions or inquiries as well as the teacher's; both are integrated into a formal plan.

Step 3: Opportunities and Experiences

Essential in a good plan is providing, facilitating, and initiating *meaningful* and *authentic* opportunities and experiences to help children further understand ideas. The word *meaningful* is the critical element here. Significant experiences create a sense of purpose for the child. John Dewey cautioned, "Attentive care must be devoted to the conditions which give each present experience a worthwhile meaning" (1938, 49).

One way to promote meaningful experiences is to find opportunities for authentic experiences that allow young children to see, negotiate, and participate in the real world. The experiences should be based on ideas that emerge from conversations or the written plan. For example, when the children initiated the conversation about street signs, their authentic experience of seeing and learning about street signs prompted a written plan for deeper understanding. The class began to take walks to explore different signs. Several children created a map showing where the street signs were located. Another group drew all the street signs they saw. Back in the classroom, everyone shared their information. Two children created signs and posted them in the classroom. There was a Stop sign and one that looked like a stop sign but read Quiet in the Library. At the sink, a yellow sign said Wash Hands.

One way to promote meaningful experiences is to find opportunities for authentic experiences that allow young children to see, negotiate, and participate in the real world.

The children also decided they needed road signs on the trike paths in the outdoor play area. Some confusion arose during this phase of the experience. Children began arguing about where signs should be placed and if they had to follow the direction on the signs. This discomfort led to the next phase of the plan (see Step 4).

Several content goals were acknowledged in the above experience. Children drew and created maps of a familiar setting; they practiced writing letters and putting together sounds; they used their knowledge of street signs to create classroom rules. In all, the children experienced authentic, meaningful learning.

Step 4: More Questions, More Theories

During this phase, the teacher carefully outlines the theories and documents new questions. As children raise new questions, they are forced to deepen their thinking about the situation. These thoughts become new sparks or provocations for future plans.

In the continuing sign investigation, the teacher called a large group meeting when the arguing about the trike signs and rules persisted. She posted a large piece of paper on the wall and said, "I noticed some confusion on the trike roads today. Jacob, tell me your plan with the signs." She was careful to focus the conversation on the plan rather than encouraging a blame game ("So-and-so went the wrong way"). Jacob expressed his concern of following the sign rules for safety. The teacher wrote

on the paper, "If we follow the street signs, we will stay safe." Kayla added another theory: "People who make the signs get to make the rules, but they have to write them out." Another child brought up additional safety issues, such as wearing helmets and keeping the trikes on the path. The children and teacher decided to post several signs on the roadway to direct traffic in a clockwise pattern.

Summary

Young children learn best through active participation and experience. When helped, allowed, and encouraged to follow an interest and construct a plan to learn more, children are empowered and become intrinsically motivated. They fully engage in the experience when it is their own (Jones & Nimmo 1994). Meaningful ideas are intrinsically motivating.

A caring, observant teacher can easily promote motivation by facilitating the planning process. As the four-step process described here becomes more familiar to children, teachers, and families, The Plan gets easier. Through collaboration, they document, reflect, and interpret ideas to form deeper meanings and foster lifelong learning.

References

Dewey, J. 1938. *Experience and education.* New York: Collier.

Edwards, C., L. Gandini, & G. Forman. 1998. *The hundred languages of children: The Reggio Emilia approach—Advanced reflections.* 2nd ed. Westport, CT: Ablex.

Fraser, S., & C. Gestwicki. 2001. *Authentic childhood: Experiencing Reggio Emilia in the classroom.* Albany, NY: Delmar.

Jones, E., & J. Nimmo. 1994. *Emergent curriculum.* Washington, DC: NAEYC.

Owocki, G. 1999. *Literacy through play.* Portsmouth, NH: Heinemann.

Project Zero & Reggio Children. 2001. *Making learning visible: Children as individual and group learners.* Reggio Emilia, Italy: Project Zero.

HILARY JO SEITZ, PhD, is an assistant professor at University of Alaska, Anchorage. She has worked in early childhood settings for the past 18 years as a teacher, administrator, and instructor.

One Teacher, 20 Preschoolers, and a Goldfish

Environmental Awareness, Emergent Curriculum, and Documentation

ANN LEWIN-BENHAM

Teaching preschoolers about the environment is hard. Many complex concepts are involved: the interactions among everything on the planet—air, land, water, and all living things; the systems that determine weather and climate, food supply, energy resources, and the quality of life for every plant and animal; systems operating on a planetary scale or in geologic time; the organisms living in a single water drop. Chemistry, geology, physics, and biology all intersect in discussions on the environment.

This article shares the experiences of one teacher in helping preschoolers learn about the environment. The article is based on my lifelong concerns for the environment, on my own experience helping children learn to take care of a goldfish in a preschool classroom, and on a composite of many different efforts—my own and other teachers'—helping children learn about the environment. It is also based on three of my own beliefs:

1. Most young children are eager to learn about the environment.
2. A teacher who lives an environmentally friendly life can be effective in teaching young children about the environment.
3. The emergent curriculum approach (Rinaldi 1992; Jones & Nimmo 1994), including documentation, is well suited for encouraging children to develop environmentally aware behavior.

These beliefs are reflected in this article through enthusiastic children, a teacher respectful of environmental concerns, and the success of the emergent curriculum in arousing and building on children's interests.

Social Constructivist Theory

The theoretical base for the use of an emergent curriculum is social constructivist theory. Briefly, we can infer from the theory that learning occurs when children are engaged in collaborative activity about something that deeply interests them and that the teacher's role is to collaborate with the children in their exploration so her knowledge can scaffold their understanding. "Learning and development emerge from the dynamic interaction of social and individual factors" (John-Steiner, Panofsky, & Smith 1994, 6). Today numerous psychologists and social theorists have confirmed

the idea, first proposed by Lev Vygotsky, that learning is a social process (Feuerstein, Klein, & Tannenbaum 1991; John-Steiner, Panofsky, & Smith 1994; Resnick & Hall 1998; Bronfenbrenner 2004).

Social constructivist theory is robustly practiced in the schools of Reggio Emilia, Italy. In these schools projects emerge through teacher collaboration with small groups of children. The projects are based on teachers' thoughtful listening to children's conversations to determine their deep interests and on subsequent focused talk with the children about these interests. The Reggio structure also involves a carefully designed classroom that functions as a "third teacher," and as such frees the teacher to engage in projects. Literature describing these schools and certain Web sites will acquaint those unfamiliar with the Reggio Emilia approach (see Jones & Nimmo 1994; Edwards, Gandini, & Forman 1998; Lewin-Benham 2006; visit the Web sites of NAREA and Reggio Children).

Ms. Putnam, 20 Children, and a Goldfish

Ms. Putnam, a preschool teacher, wanted to arouse children's concern for the environment and to inspire them to think and act in ecologically sound ways. An evolving chain of experiences about the environment emerged from the introduction of a goldfish to her class.

Projects are based on teachers' thoughtful listening to children's conversations to determine their deep interests and on subsequent focused talk with the children about these interests.

In September Ms. Putnam made five commitments. During the coming year she would:

- bring into the classroom things related to the environment.
- listen closely to children's conversations and observe their activities and explorations around the items, then use the children's interests as the basis for projects.

Emergent Curriculum

Rather than sets of lesson plans and objectives, emergent curriculum is a *process* that roughly follows these steps:

1. Select a topic that reflects interests expressed by children in their conversations or that you as their teacher suspect may be of high interest. Ms. Putnam brought a goldfish to school with the idea that the children's care of the fish might interest them in exploring environment-related subjects.
2. Brainstorm, alone or with colleagues, the many ways the experience could develop to ensure that the topic has rich "generative" (Perkins 1992, 92–95) potential. As it evolves, the project may or may not follow what you brainstormed.
3. Use something concrete—from the children, their families, or the teacher—to pique initial interest and to maintain it. The concrete "thing" may be children's own words as recorded by the teacher. Ms. Putnam used children's questions about the goldfish as the starter for many pursuits. Throughout the year she recorded, saved, and studied the children's conversations and kept using their words to arouse further interest.
4. Tape or take notes of the children's words as they react. Study their words to determine what *really* grabs their attention. You may let a day or more pass to heighten the children's anticipation and to allow yourself time to study their words.
5. Continue to bring the children's own words back to them: "On Monday you said the fish's water was really dirty. Joey said, 'It's full of poop.' Would you like to help me clean the fishbowl?"
6. Brainstorm what might happen before any new activity. Knowing she wanted to build environmental awareness, Ms. Putnam had a container available to save the dirty water. When the children asked why she was saving it, she asked, "What do you think we could do with this water?" Again she recorded and studied the children's answers, and brought back those that she had selected for their potential to spark environmental awareness.
7. Use children's words, some particular things they have made, or photo(s) taken during the process as the stimulus for the next steps.
8. Document the experience as each step happens. Record the story of the emerging project as *it emerges,* using children's words, photos of them, their drawings or other work, and a photojournalistic-type retelling. (See "Documentation." p. 31).

- use related vocabulary often and read aloud books on the environment twice weekly.
- keep parents informed so they could reinforce the topic at home.
- follow an emergent curriculum approach—teaching through small group projects, documenting the projects, and revisiting the documentation.

Where do subjects for in-depth projects come from? Miss Putnam knew that the information she needed for projects to emerge would come from a variety of sources: actively conversing with the children, listening to their conversations with each other to determine what they already knew and what else they wanted to know, and studying her notes on these conversations. Having decided to bring a goldfish to the classroom—because she believed it would be of great interest to the children—she brainstormed concepts that might emerge over time. Her list included the following areas:

- the ecosystem a goldfish requires
- energy sources for living things
- clean and unclean water
- waste disposal
- relationships between living things and the environment

The Goldfish Arrives

On the day Ms. Putnam brought the goldfish to school, Joey, the most active four-year-old in the class, spotted it immediately: "Ms. Putnam, what have we got?" She knew his enthusiasm would spread. During group time she asked Joey to describe what he had seen: "It's orange, and it's swimming, and . . ." jumping up and pointing, "it's THERE!"

Carefully, Ms. Putnam carried the bowl to the full class meeting. Immediately, an animated conversation ensued. Ms. Putnam made notes on the children's comments and, over the next few days, took photos of them observing the fish. After analyzing this information she determined which children were most interested in the goldfish. She created a documentation panel with the heading "Joey Discovered a New Fish" and two photos of children observing the fish, and she hung the panel in the classroom. Later she discussed the panel with the small group of children whom she had observed were most interested. Revisiting the panel with the children revealed more of their ideas because it sparked another conversation.

As the children and teacher discussed the panel, questions tumbled out:

- Where did the goldfish come from? The stream near the school?
- Where did you get the bowl?
- Can we feed the fish from our lunchboxes?
- How does it poop?
- Can I hold it?
- Will it have babies?
- Can I take it home?
- Will it get old and die?
- What do you do with a dead fish?

Like most children, the four-year-olds in Ms. Putnam's class are interested in everything around them. Even by age 4 they have had many experiences, and know more than adults may realize. They are naturally empathetic, know instinctively if living things feel sad or are hurt, and express their concern with words and hugs. Ms. Putnam felt certain she could focus their empathy on the

Documentation

Documentation is the process of recording children's thoughts and actions on a topic to maintain their focus and expand their interest. It works like this:

1. As an experience begins, create a large panel out of sturdy cardstock or illustration board. Write a question, repeat a child's comment, or make up a title as a headline for the panel. Include a photo, a drawing, or an object to show what sparked the project.
2. Continue to add information to the panel as the experience continues. Information can be key words from the teacher or children, a child's drawing, or a photo or series of photos of the children, even an object. The information should reflect a pivotal moment which led to next steps. Ms. Putnam added a photo of the full class at the first group meeting with the fishbowl in the center, one child's comment, and one question each from two other children. As the project continued, she added drawings of children's ideas for how to clean the fish bowl—one a theory, the other the process the class eventually adopted.
3. Whenever a panel is hung or words or photos are added, and before continuing the experience, gather the children who were involved, and read the panel to them (or have them "read"—retell—to you) what has happened thus far. This is called *revisiting*. Ms. Putnam and the small group revisited the panel at least once a day.
4. Add whatever photos and comments or questions bring the experience to a conclusion. In this case, Ms. Putnam added a series of photos—cleaning the fishbowl, discovering Big Eyes dead, everyone crying, and the fish's grave. At the end she added two children's questions which stimulated new projects: "What are we going to do with the dirty water?" and "What will happen to the dead fish?"

A finished documentation panel should convey what started the experience, how it developed and why, and its outcome or the open-ended questions it sparked. As children revisit panels, they begin to retell the experience to themselves, to one another, and to their parents or classroom visitors. Revisiting helps the experience move forward, keeps the children focused, and deepens their understanding of their experiences. Documentation gives parents and visitors a window into life in the classroom and builds both appreciation for and trust in the school.

environment, helping them to acquire a sense of what the environment is, an awareness of all living things' needs, and some knowledge of how those needs relate to the environment (Gardner 1991). From the children's comments, she added this one to the documentation panel: "How can we get this poop out of the water?" She also added a photo of the fishbowl with its dirty water.

That evening Ms. Putnam matched the concepts she had originally brainstormed with the children's questions (see "Relationship between the Teacher's Ideas and the Children's Interests"). The comparison convinced her to use the children's own questions to begin exploring environmental issues with them. She added two of their most fertile questions to the panel: "How can we clean the water?" and "What will we do with the dirty water?"

Planning for Learning

In educating children about anything, a teacher needs to determine what they already know and find the intersections between her perceptions and their interests. Teachers use this information to decide what to do next (Vecchi 1994). Through analyzing her own brainstorming list and comparing it to the interests children expressed, Ms. Putnam hypothesized that an environmental curriculum in her classroom, sparked by the children's interest in the goldfish, could cover these topics: ecosystem; land, water, and air; food and energy; pollution. The curriculum would emerge as children's investigations and activities led to the evolution of old interests and the development of new ideas. How she prepared the classroom environment and documented the children's experiences would be critical. Ms. Putnam asked herself if she could also:

- Care for an animal in addition to the plants already maintained in the classroom?

- Model environmentally conscious behaviors for the children consistently? For example, could she
  — make sure to turn out lights *whenever* the class left the classroom or sunshine provided adequate light and each time tell the children her actions were taken to save energy?
  — teach the children to conserve by running only a trickle of water then turning it off while soaping hands or brushing teeth?
  — set up a system to segregate leftover food, paper, glass, and plastic, and with the children analyze which leftovers could be reused and how? During meals, Ms. Putnam began to play a game with the children, Compost Collection, in which they discussed what leftovers would make good compost. This sparked the children's curiosity about what to do when the compost container was full, and led to a project to develop a compost pile in a remote corner of the play yard.

- Reach beyond the classroom to engage in environmentally friendly efforts? For example, she
  — toured the school with the children to detect how to save resources
  — asked parents to send to school examples of community environmental activities. One family sent an article about the installation of energy-saving light bulbs in the local public libraries. Ms. Putnam read every item to the whole class, and discussed it in depth with those children who were most interested. Often the children had their own theories, which Ms. Putnam recorded, studied,

and later discussed with them. On subsequent days she had them draw pictures or represent their ideas in other materials, like paper, cardboard, clay, wire, or blocks.
— invited parents to help on field trips. One involved a visit to the city's waste recycling plant, another to a nearby stream to look for effects of pollution.

Using Observations and Conversations to Facilitate Learning

For several days after introducing the goldfish, Ms. Putnam left a tape recorder next to the fishbowl to capture the children's comments. As the children observed the fish, she took photos and added two to the panel. All the children visited the fishbowl at least once a day, most two or three times; five children were regulars, sometimes checking on the fish several times a day and naming it Big Eyes. Children's comments on tape ranged from how fish are born to fish weddings, death, play, and fighting. Most often the children wondered how fish get food, what happens when they poop in the water, and how to clean the water.

After observing and revisiting the panel with the children and while excitement was still high, Ms. Putnam revisited the panel again with the five most interested children and asked, "What else would you like to know about the fish?" Questions poured out. Ms. Putnam then asked another question: "How can we find out?" "These two questions are powerful and universally applicable. The first taps the wealth of experiences even very young children have already accumulated. The second stretches them to make connections from one particular bit of information to their other ideas, which adults cannot intuit" (Lewin-Benham 2006, p. 51).

From this discussion Ms. Putnam realized the children knew these things: the fish should be fed just once daily, it pooped a lot, and its water was already dirty. This bothered them, and they wanted to do something about it.

Ms. Putnam asked the five children, "Can you draw pictures showing how we could clean the bowl?" She added two of the children's drawings to the panel. Two days later, she gathered the five children again, revisited the panel, and asked them to use their drawings to describe to one another how to clean the bowl. Their ideas ranged from fantasy—using a magic vacuum that unrolled from a long tube—to reality—finding ways to clean the bowl without hurting Big Eyes, since cleaning utensils might be rough and cleansers could poison him. Danielle, one of the children, had been to a pet store where she gleaned this information, which she then shared with the others during one of their many small group discussions.

Ms. Putnam suggested that the group discuss which method would be best and then make one drawing to represent it. Several more days passed as the children debated among themselves, sometimes arguing fiercely, often joined by Ms. Putnam. They finally agreed on how to clean the bowl: Catch Big Eyes in a fish net (Danielle had seen this in the pet store also), put him quickly into a pitcher of clean water, empty the old water, carefully scour the bowl, then pour in Big Eyes, clean water and all. The group collaborated on making one drawing of this process, which Ms. Putnam added to the panel.

Big Eyes Dies!

Because the class had not allowed the changing water to stand overnight so the chlorine could evaporate, Big Eyes did not survive the change. Ms. Putnam had not told the children this vital knowledge, something she knew but, in the excitement, had forgotten to share with them. The children were distraught. Ms. Putnam blamed herself. The children saw how sad she was.

"Hey! I know," Joey exclaimed. "Let's go to the pet store and buy a new fish!"

Teacher and children cried—all still sad about Big Eyes, Donnie and Charles in distress at Ms. Putnam's sadness, Danielle and Darrell not to be left out, Ms. Putnam upset at her omission and deeply moved by the children's compassion.

"What are we gonna do with Big Eyes?" asked Joey. Crying ceased as the children began a conversation that became animated. Many ideas later, they toured the yard and found an ideal spot to bury Big Eyes—under the pussy willow, their favorite with its soft, silky-haired blooms. Ms. Putnam added a photo of Big Eyes's grave to the documentation panel. She saw the echoes of this powerful experience in many of the projects that emerged later that year.

Emerging Projects

The experience with Big Eyes sparked a new project on the environment with these themes: What happens when dirty water is poured on the earth? What is earth? What would happen to Big Eyes in the earth? Ms. Putnam documented the earth project on a second panel. A small group went with her to the pet store to buy a new fish in response to Joey's suggestion (the subject of a third panel). The children were full of questions about how stores find fish. This led to a project on ecosystems that support different fish. By year's end the children's evolving interests led to:

When the children learned how dangerous plastic can be to wild animals, they organized a Plastic Patrol and involved their families in a clean-up day.

- Questioning what's in water and how evaporation works.
- Reading the fish food label, which prompted a big project on food sources.
- Carefully watching the ceaseless swimming of the new fish, which led to a project on energy.
- Discussing how pollutants get into air and water.
- Studying the labels on cleansers, which resulted in a search for environmentally friendly cleaning products and replacing commercial cleansers with homemade solutions of baking soda, vinegar, and water, natural products that the children learned would not pollute.

When the children learned how dangerous plastic can be to wild animals, they organized a Plastic Patrol and involved their families in a clean-up day. When they learned that fish poop makes good fertilizer, they went on a hunt for other waste to recycle, and visited their town's recycling center.

Each project involved only a small group, generally different for each project. Ms. Putnam documented every project on its own panel. Usually the entire class toured each panel, led in small groups by the children involved. With one group, Ms. Putnam wrote to parents discussing how to use the classroom's environmentally friendly practices at home. The whole class read the letter; several children added words and drawings, and everyone carried a copy home.

It was possible for Ms. Putnam to teach to a small group for two reasons. First, there were two adults in the classroom. Second, the classroom environment was richly prepared. "In practice this means . . . [the teachers] trust the environment as much as they trust one another, and create a three-member team from two teachers and an environment. Their painstaking organization results in environment-guided activity that is as valuable as teacher-guided activity" (Lewin-Benham 2006, 14–15).

A Year in Review

At the end of the year Ms. Putnam reviewed her teaching and the children's learning. Projects on a wide range of areas covered 10 different panels. She had learned to be more thoughtful about when to add her own knowledge to the children's explorations. This is the essence of emergent curriculum: the learning that results for children and teacher from the teacher's knowledge and skills through collaboration with the children. Because the teacher scaffolds the children's ability, it makes it possible for her knowledge to merge with, expand, or alter their knowledge. What the children learned was evident in their

- favorite books, like *Cactus Hotel,* about a saguaro's life cycle and relationship to other desert plants and animals;
- daily vocabulary, which now included words like *environment, relationship, impact, pollutant, and earth-friendly;*
- drawings, which showed increasingly thoughtful ideas about the environment;
- interest in food content, concern about clean air and water, and knowledge of the plants and animals that lived near the school;
- comments, like Joey's after burying Big Eyes: "You see, we're all connected to everything, fish to insects, insects to earth, earth to goldfish, what we eat to earth. It's all connected."

Conclusion

Ms. Putnam's experience illustrates how to raise preschool children's environmental awareness. Her approach was grounded in the social constructivist theory that we learn through relationships with others who mediate our interactions with things around us. Her approach was influenced by Reggio Emilia school practices, especially belief in children's ability; attentive listening to children's ideas; collaborative small-group projects including the teacher; the use of a well-designed environment as a third teacher; extensive use of various materials as vehicles for children to express and reformulate ideas; and documentation.

Teachers wanting to raise children's environmental awareness can use a fish, a plant, an insect, a book, an environmentally focused local event, or many other things. Wherever they start, teachers should allow plenty of time for conversation and should use the children's own reactions, comments, and questions as the basis for what they do next.

The interconnectedness of everything on our planet dovetails with a teaching approach based on collaboration and a theory of learning based on relationships. In this case the children's interest in the life and death of a goldfish enabled the teacher to arouse their concern for the well-being of the environment and to help the children think and act in ecologically sound ways.

References

Bronfenbrenner, U. 2004. *Making human beings human.* London: Sage.

Edwards, C., L. Gandini, G. Forman, eds. 1998. *The hundred languages of children: The Reggio Emilia approach—Advanced reflections.* 2nd ed. Greenwich, CT: Ablex.

Feuerstein, R., P. Klein, A. Tannenbaum. 1991. *Mediated learning experience (MLE): Theoretical, psychosocial and learning implications.* London: Freund.

Gardner, H. 1991. *The uschooled mind.* New York: Basic Books.

John-Steiner, V., C.P. Panofsky, & L.W. Smith. 1994. *Sociocultural approaches to language and literacy.* New York: Cambridge University Press.

Jones, E., & J. Nimmo. 1994. *Emergent curriculum.* Washington, DC: NAEYC.

Lewin-Benham, A. 2006. *Possible schools: The Reggio approach to urban education.* New York: Teachers College Press.

NAREA (North American Reggio Emilia Alliance). Online: www.reggioalliance.org.

Perkins, D. 1992. *Smart schools.* New York: Free Press.

Reggio Children. Online: http://zerosei.comune.re.it/inter/reggiochildren.htm.

Resnick, L.B., & M.W. Hall. 1998. Learning organizations for sustainable education reform. *Daedalus* 127 (4): 89–118. Online: www.instituteforlearning.org/media/docs/learningorgforsustain.pdf.

Rinaldi, C. 1992. Lecture. Ida College, Newton Centre, Massachusetts, June.

Vecchi, V. 1994. Lecture/Study Seminar. "Experience of the Municipal Infant-Toddler Centers and Preprimary Schools." June. Reggio Emilia, Italy.

ANN LEWIN-BENHAM, AB, was founder/director of the Model Early Learning Center (MELC) and Capital Children's Museum in Washington, D.C. Her recent book, *Possible Schools:* The *Reggio Approach to Urban Education,* tells MELC's story. Ann writes and lectures on early education.

Further resources on environmental education—a bibliography and a listing of curriculum activities—are available through **Beyond the Journal** at www.journal.naeyc.org/btj.

Fostering Prosocial Behavior in Young Children

KATHY PREUSSE

ccording to the National Center for Education Statistics (2001), there are over 21 million children under the age of six in center-based child care programs in the United States. Programs vary in their content, but one of the aspects common to all is the social context in which learning and care occurs. All early childhood teachers have a tremendous responsibility to meet the developmental needs of the whole child, and more than that, to help children develop the prosocial skills necessary to succeed in a group setting, as well as in society.

Social Development in Young Children

From infancy, children are active participates in a complex world. Interactions with parents are the first type of social exchange infants experience. Healthy exchanges create a bond or attachment. Attachment is a sense of connection between two people that forms the foundation for a relationship (Pruitt, 1998). Exchanges such as facial expressions, movements, and verbal interactions help create an attachment or bond. Experts feel that the first year of life is a critical period for bonding. Bonds create a sense of trust that supports an infant's exploration of the world and serves as a base for future development (Raikes, 1996). "Numerous studies have shown that infants with secure attachments to their mothers and fathers are at an advantage for acquiring competencies in language and in cognitive, social, and emotional development" (Raikes, 1996, p. 59). If attachment does not occur, children may have problems later in life and may display asocial behaviors (Wardle, 2003).

Today, with an increasing number of children enrolled in center-based programs, educators and caregivers play an important role in promoting the development of prosocial skills. "The teacher-child relationship is an extension of the primary parent-child relationship, and teachers invest in building supportive relationships with families around their common interest, the child" (Edwards & Raikes, 2002, p. 12). Many programs have been designed based on the principle that attachment is vital to the social development of young children. Some centers have focused on the importance of attachment and relationships by creating small groups or 'families.' In these programs, an early childhood teacher is assigned to a group of children over an extended period of time, sometimes several years, which is

called looping. Primary caregivers provide children predictability, consistency and a secure base, which helps promote the development of trust. It is from this base the child call explore his physical and social environment. According to Howes and others (cited in Raikes, 1996, p. 61) "There are multiple advantages of secure-based behavior for infants: infants explore more, have more productive play, and interact more and more resourcefully with adults in group settings when their attachments to teachers are secure." Furthermore, children with a secure teacher-child relationship tended to have more positive peer relationships (Raikes, 1996).

During the preschool years, children are developing a sense of independence and capacity for cooperation. As they become more verbal, self-aware, and able to think about another person's point of view, they become more able to interact with peers (Berk, 2002). Furthermore, children at this age move from parallel play to more advanced levels such as associative and cooperative play. It is through cooperative play that children experience play in groups in which they must set aside their needs for the good of the group (Wardle, 2003). Thus, they are developing positive social skills.

Early social development is complex and closely intertwined with other areas of development: cognitive, physical, emotional, linguistic, and aesthetic. The National Association for the Education of Young Children (NAEYC; Bredekamp & Copple, 1997) emphasizes the need for socialization and the development of social skills as a vital part of early childhood education. They advocate principles that educators should use as a guide to developmentally appropriate practices. Listed below are five of these principles. As you can see socialization is intertwined and important to each of these principles (as well as the remaining ones not listed).

- Development and learning occur in and are influenced by multiple social and cultural contexts.
- Children are active learners, drawing on direct physical and social experiences as well as culturally transmitted knowledge to construct their own understandings of the world around them.
- Development and learning result from interaction of biological maturation and the environment, which includes both the physical and social worlds that children live in.

- Play is an important vehicle for children's social, emotional, and cognitive development as well as a reflection of their development.
- Children develop and learn best in the context of a community where they are safe and valued, their physical needs are met, and they feel psychologically secure (cited in Bredekamp & Copple, 1997, p. 10).

Prosocial behaviors are crucial to children's well being. Thus, it is our responsibility as early childhood educators to provide opportunities for the development of necessary social skills.

Play

Play is a common form of interaction between and among children. "Children do not construct their own understanding of a concept in isolation but in the course of interaction with others" (Bredekamp and Copple 1997, p. 114). Some of the social skills fostered through play are the ability to work towards a common goal, initiating and/or keeping a conversation going, and cooperating with peers. Attachments are formed with other children of similar interests and can lead to friendships. Friendship can be defined as "a mutual relationship involving companionship, sharing, understanding of thoughts and feelings, and caring for and comforting one another in times of need" (Berk, 2002, p. 377). Many of the social skills children develop at this time are listed in this definition. As social skills become more developed, friendships and interactions can become more complex.

Prosocial Skills

Prosocial behaviors allow a child to interact with adults and children in a successful and appropriate manner (Wardle, 2003). The interaction should be beneficial to one, the other, or both parties involved. An added component is the "individual's ability to perceive the situation and be aware when a particular set of behaviors will result in positive outcomes" (cited in Cartledge & Milburn, 1986, p. 7). According to this, a child needs more than specific skills. A child also needs the ability to navigate specific situations.

Prosocial behaviors can be grouped into three distinct categories: sharing (dividing up or bestowing), helping (acts of kindness, rescuing, removing distress), and cooperation (working together to reach a goal) (Marion, 2003). Other experts include showing sympathy and kindness, helping, giving, sharing, showing positive verbal and physical contact, showing concern, taking the perspective of another person, and cooperating. Kostelnik et al. (1988) placed prosocial behavior in two categories: cooperation and helpfulness. The authors defined cooperation as the act of working together for a common goal. Helpfulness was defined as the act of removing distress from another person.

Developing Prosocial Skills

Many experts have looked at the process of developing prosocial skills. A child must develop cognitive competencies, emotional competencies, and specific skills in order to develop prosocial

behavior (Marion, 2003). For example, in order to share a child must have: 1) The cognitive ability to recognize him/herself as able to make things happen; 2) The emotional capacity to empathize with the other person; and 3) The ability to perform a specific skill.

It is the combination of these three elements that result in the formation of a social skill such as sharing.

Another expert, Vygotsky, viewed socialization as two fold. First, cognition is related to social engagement, and secondly, language is a critical tool for communication within a social context (cited in Berk & Winsler, 1995). Vygotsky emphasized the importance of sociodramatic play. Play is a means by which children interact, but it is also through this social interaction that cognitive development occurs. Researchers have found that preschoolers who spend more time at pretend play are more advanced in intellectual development, have a higher capacity for empathy, and are seen by teachers as more socially competent (Berk & Winsler, 1995).

The development of prosocial skills can be viewed as a three-part process. In the recognition step, a child must be able to determine if someone needs the child must decide whether to help or not to act. Thirdly, a child must and performing an appropriate behavior for that situation (Kostelnik et al., 1988).

Click and Dodge looked at the social problem solving aspect of social development (cited in Berk, 2002). They developed an information-processing model that looked at 1) a child's ability to engage in several information-processing activities at a time, 2) a child's mental state, and 3) peer evaluation and response. They listed the activities a child must do in order to deal with the problem and come up with a solution. They are: "Notice social cues; Interpret social cues; Formulate social goals; Generate possible problem solving strategies; Evaluate probable effectiveness of strategies; Enact response" (cited in Berk, 2002, p. 378).

In addition, the child must have knowledge of social rules, memory of past experiences, and expectations for future experiences. Lastly, peer perspectives and responses to a child's problem solving techniques greatly impact future interactions between the children involved (Berk, 2002).

The Teacher's Role

It is the teacher's role to facilitate and encourage prosocial behaviors, provide activities that foster appropriate skills, provide necessary assistance, and develop a social network that supports children in their efforts. Teachers must provide activities that help children identify various social skills and help them understand why the skill is needed (Johnson et al., 2000).

The National Association for the Education of Young Children (NAEYC) pointed out that "preschoolers are capable of engaging in truly cooperative play with their peers and forming real friendships. However, development of these important social skills is not automatic for children. They need coaching and supervision to learn and maintain appropriate behaviors with others" (cited in Bredekamp & Copple, 1997, p. 116).

How can teachers help children develop the skills and behaviors needed to act in a prosocial manner? According to NAEYC the classroom is a place to learn about human relationships. Children should have the opportunity to:

- Play and work with others
- Make choices and encounter the consequences of those choices
- Figure out how to enter play situations with others
- Negotiate social conflicts with language
- Develop other skills that characterize socially competent human beings (cited in Bredekamp & Copple, 1997, p. 118).

Facilitating Positive Interactions

Teachers can facilitate positive play interactions for children through the use of a variety of strategies. These strategies include: 1) emphasizing cooperation rather than competition, 2) teaching games that emphasize cooperation and conflict resolution, 3) setting up classroom spaces and materials to facilitate cooperative play, 4) using literature to enhance empathy and caring, and 5) encouraging social interactions between children of different abilities whether it is social, emotional, or physical (Honig & Wittmer, 1996). Research has shown children benefit greatly from effective, positive play situations. Klein, Wirth, and Linas (2003) listed several approaches for facilitating quality play situations. These approaches include: 1) Focusing on the process by asking exploratory questions; 2) Building on children's interests and elaborate on their play; 3) Labeling emotions and feelings that children are expressing through their play; 4) Providing materials that encourage and extend exploration and 5) Providing open-ended materials such as blocks or pretend props.

Howes and Stewart (cited in Honig & Wittmer, 1996) found that children who are involved in high-quality care and have supportive parents learn how to recognize and regulate emotional signals when playing with peers.

Helping Children Make Choices

Teachers should help children make choices and deal with the consequences of their decisions. The teacher's role is to plan activities that help children think through a problem. It is also necessary to repeat the learning activity or similar activity several times (Kostelnik et al. 1988). Through this repeated step-by-step process children can learn how to identify the different path choices, apply reasoning to the process, and formulate a decision.

Promoting Entry into Play Groups

Young children frequently need encouragement to enter play-groups, whether it is to enter an ongoing group, initiate a contact with a friend or being approached by others. Children enter playgroups in a variety of ways, some more successfully than others. Preschoolers tend to enter groups in one or a combination of ways: 1) approaching and watching with no verbal or non-verbal attempt to participate, 2) starting the same activity

as another child and blending into the ongoing activity, 3) making social greetings or invitations, 4) offering informational statements or questions, 5) making overt requests to join, or 6) approaching and trying to control group or get attention (Ramsey, 1991).

Preschool playgroups can be fluid, with children entering' and leaving quite frequently. Teachers can respond to these already formed groups to "insure the equal participation of all children, help the group work towards a desired goal, and enrich the activity so that all the children can have a meaningful role" (Ramsey, 1991, p. 120). In some instances teachers may prefer arranging playgroups. This helps reduce children's anxiety and widens their range of contacts. Again, equal and active participation by all members and a common goal are important (Ramsey, 1991).

Helping Negotiate Conflict

Teachers need to help children develop negotiating skills to handle conflict situations. Children must use social problem solving skills to resolve issues in a matter that benefits them and is acceptable to others (Berk, 2002). Marion (2003, p. 56) suggested six steps for teaching conflict resolution:

- Identify and define the conflict.
- Invite children to participate in solving the problem.
- Work together to generate possible solutions.
- Examine each idea for how well it might work.
- Help children with plans to implement the solution.
- Follow up to evaluate how well the solution worked.

Peer mediation is another strategy used by teachers to negotiate conflicts. Peer leaders are seen by other children as being credible and serve as role models (Wardle, 2003). This method is used most effectively in elementary schools because of the skills required to implement the process. The "friendship table, or talk-it-over table;" is suggested for preschoolers. The teacher's role is to remove the children to a neutral site, and facilitate the conflict resolution process (Wardle, 2003, p. 393).

Promoting Self-Control

Teachers should provide as many opportunities for young children to develop other necessary skills needed to achieve social competency. Self-control is one of the skills. Harter and Shaffer (cited in Marion, 2003, p. 56) said, "Self-control is an essential part of how children learn, is important in a child's growth and development, and is fundamental in preserving social and moral order." Self-control or self-discipline refers to the ability to internally regulate one's own behavior rather than depending on others to enforce it (Kostelnik et al., 1988). Children demonstrate self-control when they I) control their impulses, wait, and suspend action, 2) tolerate frustration, 3) postpone immediate gratification, and 4) initiate a plan and carry it out over time (Marion, 2003).

If it is an internal process, how can teachers foster the development of self-control? Kostelnik et al. (1988) suggested four strategies:

- Use direct instruction to let children know what are appropriate behaviors, inappropriate behaviors, and alternative behaviors. For example, restricting certain behaviors ("Five more minutes on the swing.") or re-directing children's behaviors ("Don't bounce that ball inside. Go outdoors instead.").
- Model right from wrong so children can learn by example. Modeling can be nonverbal (returning library books on time) or verbal ("I'm petting the kitten very gently.").
- Introduce logical consequences to influence future behavior ("Wear an apron so paint doesn't get on your shirt.").
- Integrate emotions, development, and experience to help children make an internal map. A child can use this chart to categorize past events, interpret cues, envision various responses, and then respond appropriately ("When you share the chalk with Tommy it makes him happy.").

Self-control evolves over time. Teachers should provide repeated experiences for children to practice self-control and refine their behavior.

Environment and Curriculum

The teacher's role should include preparing the classroom environment for optimal prosocial learning opportunities and providing a comprehensive curriculum that enhances the development of prosocial skills. Opportunities for prosocial skill development should be evident in all classroom areas. To illustrate, here are some examples:

- Placing marble mazes (or other exploratory activities) in the science area that can be played by two or more children. Encourage verbal discussion as well as problem solving.
- Introducing a variety of books that deal with perspective taking, feelings and emotions in the literacy corner.
- Arranging the housekeeping area to include a dollhouse with people of many cultures represented.
- Providing rainbow ribbons in the music area so children can come together in dance to express themselves.
- Placing giant floor puzzles in the manipulative area so that children can work together towards a common goal.
- Playing a parachute game where cooperation is necessary during large motor times.
- Promoting helping skills and acts of kindness by setting up opportunities in the dramatic play area such as a pet hospital.
- Preparing muffins and sharing them as a cooking experience.
- Including open-ended materials in the block area.
- Facilitating play groups for those reluctant to join in.
- Setting up bath time for baby dolls in the sensory table. Model caring and helping behaviors.
- Supplying paint, brushes and a very large piece of paper for the whole class to make a mural in the art area.

- Displaying children's work in the class room at their level.

Teachers must also implement curriculum that emphasizes prosocial themes and concepts. Activities and experiences should focus on the development of selfworth as well as respecting others. One such curriculum is Moonie's Kindness Curriculum which is distributed by Children's Kindness Network (moozie@ childrenskindnessnetworkorg). The curriculum emphasizes respect for self, family, friend, community, animals, and the environment. Activities included promote kindness, caring and sharing (Herr et al., 2004).

Conclusion

Prosocial behavior is essential to the well being of children. Children must learn to act in an appropriate manner, one that is both beneficial to them and to others. With so many children participating in group settings, positive interactions are a necessity. The development of these skills allows children to interact with others in a socially accepted manner.

The development of prosocial skills begins in infancy with the development of healthy attachments to parents and caregiver(s). The early years are the time for children to develop prosocial skills by interacting with other children. Moreover, it is the role of early childhood teachers to facilitate the development of these behaviors in young children. Positive play opportunities, modeling, coaching, optimal room environments, and carefully designed curriculums lay the foundation.

References

Berk, L. (2002). *Infants, children, and adolescents*. Boston, MA: Allyn & Bacon.

Berk, L., & Winsler, A. (1995). *Scaffolding childrens learning: Vygotsky and early childhood education*. Washington, DC: NAEYC.

Bredekamp, S., & Copple, C. (Eds.; 1997). *Developmentally appropriate practice in early childhood programs*. Washington, DC: NAEYC.

Cartledge, G., & Milburn, J. (Eds.; 1986). *Teaching social skills to children*. New York, NY: Pergamon Books, Inc.

Edwards, C., & Raikes, H. (2002). Extending the dance: Relationship-based approaches to infant/toddler care and education. *Young Children*, 57 (4), 10–17.

Herr, J., Lynch, J., Merritt, K., Preusse, K, Wurzer, R. (2004). *Moozie s Kindness Curriculum: Preschool*. Breckenridge, CO: Children's Kindness Network.

Honig, A., & Wittmer, D. (1996). Helping children become more prosocial: Ideas for classrooms, families, and communities. *Young Children*, 51 (2), 62–70.

Johnson, C., Ironsmith, M., Snow, C., & Poteat, G. (2000). Peer acceptance and social adjustment in preschool and kindergarten. *Early Childhood Education Journal*, 27 (4), 207–212.

Klein, T., Wirth, D., & Linas, K. (2003). Play: Children's context for development. *Young Children*, 58 (3), 38–45.

Kostelnik, M., Stein, L., Whiren, A., & Soderman, A. (1988). *Guiding children of social development*. Cincinnati, OH: South-Western Publishing Co.

Marion, M. (2003). *Guidance of young children*. Columbus, OH: Merrill Prentice Hall.

National Center for Education Statistics. (2001). *Table 44. Percentage distribution of preschool children under 6 years old*. Retrieved June 24, 2004, from: www.nces.ed.gov/programs/digest/d01/dt044.asp

Pruitt, D. (Ed.; 1998). *Your child: Emotional, behavioral, and cognitive development from birth through preadolescence*. New York, NY: HarperCollins.

Raikes, H. (1996). A secure base for babies: Applying attachment concepts to the infant care setting. *Young Children*, 51 (5), 59–67.

Ramsey, P. (1991). *Making friends in school: Promoting peer relationships in early childhood*. New York, NY: Teachers College Press.

Wardle, F. (2003). *Introduction to early childhood education: A multidimension al approach to child-centered care and learning*. Boston, MA: Pearson Education, Inc.

KATHY PREUSSE is the Senior Instructional Specialist and the Head Teacher for the Child and Family Study Center at the University of Wisconsin-Stout in Menomonie, WI.

Early Literacy and Very Young Children

This article was adapted from Before the ABCs: Promoting School Readiness in Infants and Toddlers, a publication written by Rebecca Parlakian for ZERO TO THREE's Center for Program Excellence.

REBECCA PARLAKIAN

Early (or emergent) literacy is what children know about reading and writing before they can actually read and write. It encompasses all the experiences—good and bad—that children have had with books, language, and print from birth onward. Because these experiences unfold in the context of relationships, they are linked to and dependent on social–emotional development.

When one imagines an infant or toddler, it is often difficult to conceptualize what early literacy "looks like" for such young children. Schickedanz (1999) has identified several commonly observed early literacy behaviors for infants and toddlers that providers may use to recognize the emergence and progression of very young children's early literacy skill development. These behaviors include:

1. *Handling books* Physically manipulating books (e.g., page turning and chewing).
2. *Looking and recognizing:* Paying attention to and interacting with pictures in books (e.g., laughing at a picture); recognizing and beginning to understand pictures in books (e.g., pointing to pictures of familiar objects).
3. *Comprehending pictures and stories:* Understanding pictures and events in a book (e.g., imitating an action seen in a picture or talking about the events told in a story.
4. *Reading stories:* Verbally interacting with books and demonstrating an increased understanding of print in books (e.g., babbling in imitation of reading or running fingers along printed words).

What does research tell us about early literacy development in the first 3 years of life? The short answer is, not enough. There are several significant gaps in our understanding of the antecedents of early literacy skills, one being the period from birth to 3. Few longitudinal studies follow children into kindergarten or elementary school to confirm the ways and extent to which early interventions, either in the home or caregiving setting, shape later competencies in reading and writing.

The National Early Literacy Panel (NELP), funded by the National Institute for Learning and administered by the National Center for Family Literacy, has been charged with synthesizing the existing research regarding the development of early literacy in children ages birth to 5. The NELP does plan to analyze preschool children separately from kindergarten children. Although the NELP's report is not yet released, researchers Strickland and Shanahan recently shared preliminary findings highlighting the skills and abilities that "have direct links to children's eventual success in early literacy development" (2004). These skills included oral language ability, alphabetic knowledge, and print knowledge.

Oral Language Development and Literacy

Language development provides the foundation for the development of literacy skills. Speaking, reading aloud, and singing all stimulate a child's understanding and use of language. Studies linking oral language to literacy address vocabulary growth and listening comprehension. Oral language development is facilitated (a) when children have many opportunities to use

---

At a Glance

- [F]or infants and toddlers, education and care are "two sides of the same coin."
- Instructional strategies that are most appropriate to the early years include *intentionality* and *scaffolding*.
- Intentionality means thoughtfully providing children with the experiences they need to achieve developmentally appropriate skills in early literacy.
- Scaffolding is the continuum of supportive learning experiences that more competent others (adults or peers) offer to children as they master a new strategy or skill.

language in interactions with adults, and (b) when they listen and respond to stories that are read and told to them (Strickland & Shanahan, 2004). A growing body of research affirms this link between children's early language skills and later reading abilities (Strickland & Shanahan, 2004).

Parents are essential supports of their children's language development. The more time that parents spend talking with their children, the more rapidly their children's vocabulary will grow (Hart & Risley, 1999). Listening to books being read—and having the opportunity to discuss illustrations, characters, and storylines—is also important. The experience of shared reading, whether with parents or other caring partners, is integral to language development. Research in this area finds that the repeated reading and discussion of a story enhances a child's receptive and expressive vocabulary (Senechal, 1997).

> **Being able to communicate and being understood by those around them is a powerful achievement for very young children.**

Language development occurs gradually across the first 3 years of life, and indeed, throughout childhood. Speaking, reading, and writing are reciprocal, interactive skills, each supporting the other's development. For example, toddlers engaged in a pretend-play dramatic scenario (e.g., talking into a plastic banana "phone") possess not only the oral language skills required for this "conversation" but also the ability for symbolic thought, which is integral to understanding that letter symbols can represent sounds and vice versa.

Being able to communicate and being understood by those around them is a powerful achievement for very young children. It is also a critical social–emotional skill originating in the reflexive communication (such as crying, cooing, body and facial movements) that is apparent from birth. Intentional communication emerges as very young children are increasingly able to use gestures and words to convey needs, desires, and ideas. Most important expressive language (such as spoken speech) helps children communicate, to connect with another: to request, protest, greet or take leave of someone, respond to a comment, ask a question, solve a problem, and share their feelings and ideas (Weitzman & Greenberg, 2002). These interactions form the basis of the child's relationships with family members and the outside world.

Alphabetic Knowledge and Literacy

By listening to others and speaking themselves, children develop phonemic awareness—the insight that every spoken word can be conceived as a sequence of phonemes (Snow, Burns, & Griffin, 1998). An example of phonemic awareness is recognizing that *bug, bear,* and *button* all start with "b." Because phonemes are the units of sound that are represented by the letters of an alphabet,

an awareness of phonemes is key to understanding the logic of the alphabetic principle. Learning the letters of the alphabet and recognizing the sounds within words are two skills that form the foundation for later decoding and spelling—which is linked to learning to read. Research has shown that phonemic awareness and alphabetic knowledge (an understanding of the names and shapes of the alphabet) predict whether a child will learn to read during his first 2 years of school (National Reading Panel, 2000).

Print Knowledge and Literacy

Print knowledge is a recognition of the many uses of the printed word and an understanding of how printed language works. The research base here emphasizes the importance of infusing the caregiving environment with print. For example, when children are provided literacy "props" (menus, newspapers, magazines, tablets, writing utensils, etc.), they will incorporate these items into their play (e.g., "reading" a menu and playing restaurant; Neuman & Roskos, 1992). This play offers repeated opportunities for children to practice and expand early literacy skills.

Exposure to environmental print—the print that appears on signs, labels, and products in our everyday environment—also contributes to a child's early literacy skills (Kuby, Goodstadt-Killoran, Aldridge, & Kirkland, 1999). Often, awareness of environmental print emerges organically in a child's life—for example, when a toddler learns to "read" a fast-food sign or recognizes the meaning behind a stop sign. Infant-family professionals can promote children's awareness of and facility with recognizing environmental print by pointing it out, discussing it with children, or integrating it into play activities (e.g., pointing out street signs on walks or noting labeled play spaces).

Social–Emotional Development and Literacy

For babies and toddlers, all learning happens within a relationship. The social–emotional context of a child's most important relationships—parents, family members, and infant–family professionals—directly affects young children's motivation to learn to read and write. In short, for infants and toddlers, the learning of a new skill and the emotional context in which the learning takes place are equally important (National Research Council, 2001).

Social–emotional skills are an integral part of school readiness because they give very young children the skills they need to communicate, cooperate, and cope in new environments. Over the long term, social–emotional skills contribute to a successful first year of school. For example, research has shown that the quality of children's relationships with their kindergarten teachers predicts how well those children adapt and learn, that year *and* the next (Bowman, 2001). In addition, at the end of the kindergarten year, the children who were considered to have made a positive adjustment to school also had the most friends, were able to maintain those friendships over time, and established new friendships across that first year (National Education Goals Panel, 1997). A positive adjustment to kindergarten is an important achievement: Children who are not successful in the early years of school often fall behind from the start (Peth-Pierce, 2000).

Children who are not successful in the early years of school often fall behind from the start.

School readiness means that children enter the classroom able to form relationships with teachers and peers, listen and communicate, cooperate with others, cope with challenges, persist when faced with difficult tasks, and believe in their own competence. The relationship between school readiness and social–emotional development can be summarized in five key points (adapted from Bowman, 2001):

1. Responsive, supportive relationships with parents, caregivers, and other significant adults nurture a child's desire to learn.
2. Learning requires a solid foundation of social–emotional skills.
3. The development of social–emotional skills depends on, and is responsive to, experience.
4. Children acquire new experiences within the context of relationships with the significant adults in their lives; this is why, for infants and toddlers, education and care are "two sides of the same coin."
5. Social–emotional development and academic achievement *are united priorities*. They represent a developmental continuum, a gathering-up of all the skills, abilities, and attributes that children need to succeed in school and, later, in life.

Social–emotional skills help children to adapt and be resilient, to resolve conflict, to make sense of their feelings, and to establish a new network of supportive satisfying relationships to depend on and grow within. Social–emotional skills enable children to concentrate on learning.

Cognitive Development and Literacy

Cognitive development—a crucial part of school readiness—is the natural product of warm and loving families, experienced and well-trained caregivers and enriching environments. Infants and toddlers do not need organized instruction to develop their cognitive skills. Young children's everyday activities and experiences provide ample opportunity for infusing learning into play.

It is possible to introduce cognitive skills such as literacy during the infant and toddler years. Rote learning, flash cards, and one-size-fits-all approaches, however, are developmentally inappropriate for very young children. Drill and practice may reduce children's natural curiosity and enthusiasm for the learning process and so undermine their interest in learning.

Toddlers who feel pushed to read, for example, may become frustrated and fearful, and they may begin to associate those negative feelings with books. Although introducing emergent literacy skills is important, these abilities are unlikely to flourish in very young children when presented out of context as isolated skills (National Association for the Education of Young Children, 1995).

Until the body of research on the early learning skills of the birth-to-3 population becomes more robust, infant–family professionals are challenged to "translate" successful, research-based instructional strategies for older children to meet the needs of infants and toddlers. Instructional strategies that are most appropriate to the early years include *intentionality* and *scaffolding* (Collins, 2004). Rather than use a didactic approach, adults who work with infants and toddlers can creatively integrate these strategies into the day-to-day "teachable moments" that unfold during their natural interactions with very young children.

Intentionality, in this context, means thoughtfully providing children with the support and experiences they need to achieve developmentally appropriate skills in early literacy (and other domains). For example, an intentional provider may offer 14-month-olds the opportunity to pick up raisins and cereal by themselves (which builds fine motor skills critical to writing) and then later offer children crayons to experiment with (which gives them direct experience with writing and drawing). Intentionality is at play here when the provider recognizes the relationship between these experiences, offers these experiences purposefully, and understands the shared developmental goal they both support.

Infants and toddlers learn best when the adults in their lives provide opportunities for exploration and learning in their everyday routines and interactions. The concept of intentionality underscores the role that planning, knowledge, and expertise play in devising and introducing these opportunities. It is the cumulative effect of intentional teaching—the thoughtful repetition of early literacy experiences, the introduction of literacy props into play, modified teacher behavior (e.g., pointing to words on the page), and the creation of language-rich, stimulating environments—that yields the early and important learning that takes place in very young children ages birth to 3.

Scaffolding, a concept introduced by Vygotsky (1962), refers to the continuum of supportive learning experiences that more competent others (adults or other children) offer to children as they master a new strategy or skill (Kemple, Batey, & Hartie, 2004). Children need engaged, responsive adults in their lives who offer them appropriate opportunities to question and problem solve, to hypothesize and take action, to (safely) fail and try again. The richest opportunity for learning—in which children experience a challenge as they pursue a task but do not struggle so intensely as to become frustrated—is called the one of proximal development (Vygotsky, 1962). To help children perform in this zone, teachers must provide scaffolding that incorporates the development of new skills and concepts on the foundation of established ones. This scaffolding requires that teachers know each child in their care—their skills, achievements, and needs—and offer a careful balance of planned, teacher-initiated activities and child-initiated ones, as well. In working with infants and toddlers, a teacher could initiate the practice of reading to children one-on-one each day while placing books at the child's level to enable child-initiated, spontaneous exploration, as well.

The more time that parents spend talking with their children, the more rapidly their children's vocabulary will grow.

In working with older toddlers, skilled teachers can combine a child-initiated interest that arises in the classroom—for example, a passion for castles—and create a series of teacher-initiated early literacy activities that are responsive and flexible. Using the castle example, such activities might include:

- drawing pictures of castles (which helps build fine motor skills for writing);
- reading books about castles; asking older toddlers to dictate stories to the teacher about castles; and
- making a cardboard box castle for the classroom and encouraging children to "act out" storylines using the castle prop (which creates opportunities to expand vocabulary—*moat, knight, king, queen, drawbridge*, etc.).

This "castle" project may last for several days (or weeks), depending on the children's intensity of interest. By remaining observant and responsive to the children's engagement with the topic and activities, teachers can gauge when the children's interest has shifted and when it might be time to introduce a set of early literacy-based activities around a new theme.

Supporting and nurturing early literacy and language skills in infants and toddlers is complex. These skills cannot be developed in isolation but, rather, emerge together with a child's growing competency in all domains—including the social–emotional, motor, and cognitive domains. When providers can recognize and observe each child's current stage of development, they are better positioned to use the strategies above to appropriately extend and build upon a child's existing skills and abilities.

Parents, School Readiness, and Early Literacy

Relationships—especially those between parent and child—play a critical role in ensuring that infants and toddlers are adequately prepared for school. Parents' beliefs about the appropriate ways to express emotion, resolve conflict, persuade, and cooperate with others have a profound influence on toddlers' abilities to get along with peers, follow rules, and cooperate with adults—and ultimately, to be ready for school (Morisset, 1994). In addition, children's positive, satisfying relationships with parents set the tone for equally positive, secure relationships with preschool teachers (DeMulder, Denham, Schmidt, & Mitchell, 2000). This crucial achievement is an important predictor of a successful transition to early education environments (Bowman, 2001).

Parents are the most important people in a child's life. Parents' attitudes toward education, their aspirations for children, the language models and literacy materials they provide, and the activities they encourage all contribute to children's language development. Parental behaviors also influence children's early learning. For example, research shows that the type of at-home language environment is the most powerful influence on children's language growth (Educational Research Service, 1998). Preschool children who live in homes where literacy is supported amass 1,000 to 1,700 hours of informal reading and writing encounters before entering school, whereas children without similar family support may enter school with only about 25 hours of literacy experiences (Adams,1990). Not surprisingly, most children who have difficulties learning to read have been read to one tenth as much as those who are the most successful with acquiring this skill (Adams, 1990).

When infants and very young children receive what they need from their parents, they learn to believe that the world is a good place, that it is safe to explore, and that loving adults will provide comfort, affection, and security. Children who do not receive this loving care expend a great deal of energy trying to ensure that these needs are fulfilled by someone, sometime. How much energy do these children have left for learning and exploration—and, later, for the new concepts and challenges that are a part of going to school?

The Role of Infant–Family Professionals in Supporting Early Literacy

The adults who populate the lives of very young children (including family members and the professionals who support them) make important contributions to children's school readiness. In working with infants and toddlers, teachers and child-care providers are reminded that care and education are not separate activities. They unfold together—one leading to the other, one supporting the other.

Children begin kindergarten with 5 years of accumulated life experiences. Because each set of experiences is unique, children have different perspectives on education, different approaches to relationships with adults and peers, and different levels of competency with social–emotional and academic skills. The ability of direct-service professionals to individualize their approaches to specific children and families is crucial to ensuring that services are meaningful and effective.

Infant–family professionals can support the development of very young children's school readiness skills in several ways.

Responding to children's individual needs and temperaments. Staff members in all infant–family fields can respond to children as individuals, build on their strengths, and support their development. Staff members in infant–family programs must be excellent observers of children. Responsive staff members search for the meaning behind infants' and toddlers' gestures, gurgles, cries, and glances. They wonder why particular behaviors occur, come up with educated guesses to explain why, and interact with children to determine whether their guesses are correct.

Introducing Literacy Concepts to Young Children

Teachers can introduce early literacy concepts to infants and toddlers in a variety of fun, meaningful, and developmentally appropriate ways.

Oral Language

Read to very young children: The most important thing that providers can do to support children's emerging literacy skills is read to them and discuss the stories, at the children's pace and based on their cues.

Talk to children: Children learn language when adults talk to them and with them.

Rhyme and sing: Rhyming activities such as songs and poems promote very young children's knowledge of sounds of speech.

"Narrate" the child's day: Providers can describe what happened that day, which creates opportunities to expand children's vocabulary.

Alphabetic Knowledge

Repeat letter sounds: Providers can point out and say the letters they see in signs or books.

Make a game of repetition: Children love knowing what comes next in a story and anticipating a picture or phrase.

Sing the ABC song and read alphabet books: Both verbal and visual experience with letters help children learn the alphabet.

Play with letters: Arranging and rearranging magnetic letters, alphabet blocks, and puzzles help children with letter recognition and letter sounds.

Use the child's name: Providers can teach children their own names and the sounds that make up their names.

Print Awareness

Make literacy part of playtime: Providers can stock children's play spaces with literacy "props."

Encourage children's own writing: Make paper and writing utensils (markers, crayons, fingerpaint, chalk) available to children. Let infants "write" in applesauce or yogurt.

Point out signs in your neighborhood: When taking walks, providers can look for opportunities to point out stop signs, street signs, and school crossing signs.

Show how adults use writing: Providers can encourage children to watch as they write notes to themselves or colleagues, make a shopping list, or compose the class's weekly update for parents. Providers can also give older toddlers the opportunity to "write" (dictate) notes to one another and family members.

Help children "read" their food: When preparing meals and snacks, providers should read children the words on the food labels, or ask them to "read" the labels to themselves.

Read while you're out and about: Pointing out and reading the signs that say "women" and "men," "exit" and "entrance," and "open" and "closed" are easy ways of sensitizing children to environmental print. Point to the words while reading them aloud to children.

Encouraging children's curiosity and exploration. If caregivers select all the "lessons" that are to be learned or provide an environment that is not stimulating, children will push to do activities that interest them or to create their own stimulation. Often children are told "No," "Stop," or "Bad"—not because these children are not learning, but because they are following their own learning agenda or searching for experiences that interest them. Although setting some limits is important and helps keep children safe, it is equally important to allow children to engage in self-directed learning—that is, to follow their interests and allow them to become immersed in new ideas. This approach supports their development of persistence, motivation, critical thinking, and logical thinking skills.

Introducing early literacy and numeracy concepts in developmentally appropriate ways. A program that serves infants and toddlers can introduce literacy concepts in ways that are fun, meaningful, and developmentally appropriate for very young children (Collins, 2004).

Appreciating the magic of everyday moments'. Children often develop social–emotional skills not in specially planned lessons but in the context of their daily interactions and experiences—such as napping, eating, playing, and diapering (Lerner, Dambra, & Levine, 2000). When staff members use these everyday moments to support and expand children's current repertoire of social–emotional skills, they help prepare young ones to enter the larger world with all of its demands.

To help parents do the same, staff members should emphasize the important learning that takes place in everyday interactions. For example, the give-and-take of parents imitating their babies' babbling teaches children about turn-taking and communication and, from a social–emotional perspective, that they are important, loved, and listened to. Observing this ongoing, daily learning also encourage parents' pride in and enjoyment of their children.

Establishing strong working relationships with families. When interactions between parents and staff members are open and collaborative, parents receive the support they need to learn and grow in their new roles as mothers and fathers. Parents are then better able to support their children's development with affection, responsiveness, and sensitivity. Staff members can provide parents with an outlet in which to explore the questions and challenges associated with child rearing; wonder about their children's behavior, needs, and motivations; and brainstorm about how best to respond.

Recognizing and respecting family culture. By entering a dialogue with parents about how they want their child raised and what family or cultural practices they value, staff members let families know that they are respected partners in the program. If it is difficult to incorporate families' wishes into program practices, a solid foundation of respect and openness makes negotiating these differences easier and more helpful for everyone.

Reducing parents' anxiety about school success. A newborn does not need expensive "developmental" toys or flash cards to become intellectually curious and academically successful. Staff members can help parents understand that the foundation of school readiness is in supportive, nurturing relationships that provide children with a safe "home base" from which they can explore, learn, and grow. This close parent–child bond also helps children develop the key social–emotional competencies that are necessary for a successful transition to school.

Providing anticipatory guidance. When staff members help parents anticipate their children's developmental changes, parents are better prepared to support their children's learning. Armed with accurate information, parents can respond to their children's changing developmental needs in appropriate ways. Parents' ability to meet their children's needs contributes to a greater sense of competency and confidence, which in turn strengthens the family as a whole.

> **Speaking, reading, and writing are reciprocal, interactive skills, each supporting the other's development.**

Supporting inclusive environments. Very young children with special needs may face unique challenges in achieving the skills (social–emotional or otherwise) necessary to enter school. Inclusion is an important intervention because it draws children with disabilities into the mainstream. Ongoing interactions with typically developing children may help support the development of children with disabilities. Inclusion is also important for children whose development is more typical, because diversity helps them to broaden their experiences and learning and to develop empathy.

Conclusion

Developing early literacy skills across the first 3 years of life is a critical ingredient in ensuring that children are school-ready at age 5. By using all domains of development as well as all their senses, children develop the foundational skills necessary for cultivating a lifelong love of literacy. Supported by healthy relationships formed early in life with parents and caregivers, children experience the world as both safe and exhilarating, they view new challenges as exciting, and they believe themselves to be competent learners. In short, infants and toddlers

have a lust for life and learning. When we reject the notion of children as passive "sponges," we are able to truly follow in "the wake of a curious, motivated, social child who is dying to learn" (Lally, 2001).

References

Adams, M. J. (1990). *Beginning to read: Thinking and learning about print*. Cambridge, MA: MIT Press.

Bowman, B. (2001, December). *Eager to learn*. Plenary presentation at the 16th Annual National Training Institute of ZERO TO THREE, San Diego, CA.

Collins, R. (2004, April). *Early steps to language and literacy*. Workshop presented at the meeting of the National Head Start Association, Anaheim, CA.

DeMulder, E. K., Denham, S., Schmidt, M., & Mitchell, J. (2000). Q-Sort assessment of attachment security during the preschool years: Links from home to school *Developmental Psychology, 36*(2), 274–282.

Educational Research Service. (1998). *Reading aloud to children*. ERS Info-File #F1-342. Arlington, VA: Author.

Hart, B., & Risley, T. R. (1999). *The social world of children learning to talk*. Baltimore: Paul H. Brookes.

Kemple, K. M., Batey, J. J., & Hartie, L. C. (2004). Music play: Creating centers for musical play and exploration. *Young Children, 59*(4), 30–37.

Kuby, P., Goodstadt-Killoran, I., Aldridge, J., & Kirkland, L. (1999). A review of the research on environmental print. *Journal of Instructional Psychology, 26*(3), 173–183.

Lally, R. (2001, December). *School readiness*. Plenary presentation at the 6th Annual National Training Institute of ZERO TO THREE, San Diego, CA.

Lerner, C., Dombro, L., & Levine, K. (2000). *The magic of everyday moments'* [series]. Washington, DC: ZERO TO THREE.

Morisset, C. E. (1994, October). *School readiness: Parents and professionals speak on social and emotional needs of young children* [Report No. 26]. Center on Families, Communities, Schools, and Children's Learning. Retrieved January 25, 2002, from http://readyweb.crc.uiuc.edu/library/1994/cfam-sr/cfam-sr.html

National Association for the Education of Young Children. (1995). *NAEYC position statement on school readiness*. Revived January 24, 2002, from www.naeyc.org/resources/position_statements/psredy98.htm

National Education Goals Panel. (1997). *Getting a good start in school*. Retrieved January 23, 2002, from http://www.negp.gov/Reports/good-sta.htm

National Reading Panel. (2000). *Report of the National Reading Panel. Teaching children to read: An evidence-based assessment of the scientific research literature on reading and its implications for reading instruction.*

Writing First!

Putting writing before reading is an effective approach to teaching and learning.

Peter Elbow

The expression "writing and reading" violates the habitual rhythm of our tongues. We usually say "reading and writing," so it sounds as though I'm putting the cart before the horse. But I call *writing* the horse. Nothing can be read unless it was first written.

Consider this scene. First graders in their classroom are writing stories—or rather drawing pictures and writing pieces of their stories underneath each picture. Here's part of one story:

A picture with two human figures.

Text: "Me and Mommy went to Star Market."

An obscure picture of two shapes intersecting.

Text: "I opened the car door and it bumped the car next to us."

A picture of two human figures with lots of bubbles coming out of one of their faces.

Text: "The man shouted at Mommy."

I standardized the text of this story. What the student actually wrote for the first picture was this: "me an mommmy wn to staa maaktt." Besides the spelling problems, the letters vary wildly in size and wander around the picture; there are often no spaces between words (see Calkins, 1983). Nevertheless, every word is there, and the child can read it back to you word for word (as long as you don't wait too long to ask). A teacher or parent who gets to know that child's tricks of spelling can pretty reliably read the writing.

Teachers or parent helpers often compile these pictures and type the text in standard "grown-up" spelling, then bind the pages together with a hard cover to make a book. Students "write" multiple books during the year, which the teacher displays in a prominent spot in the classroom library. Students learn to read by reading their own and their classmates' books. This scene is happening in many kindergarten, 1st grade, and 2nd grade classrooms. I'd call it the most far-reaching change in education—in our very conception of literacy—that has happened in centuries.

First graders are not well positioned for reading: They can read only the words they have learned to read or sound out—a fairly small lexicon. But they are beautifully positioned for writing: They can *write* all the words they can *say*. Even younger children who don't know the alphabet can write if they have seen other people write: They just scribble, scribble, scribble—but with meaning, and they can "read" their writing back to you. All that's needed is to invite them to use invented spelling or kid spelling, whatever letters come easily.

Once this door is opened, teachers find that it helps teach reading. The process of writing helps children comprehend written language and control letters and texts, an understanding that they need for reading. Children no longer think of books as something impersonal—like arithmetic workbooks—written by a corporate, faceless "they." They realize that books are the products of people like themselves trying to communicate with other people like themselves.

Donald Graves and several others deserve enormous credit for this discovery: Very young children can write *before* they can read, can write *more* than they can read, and can write *more easily* than they can read—because they can write anything they can say (Calkins, 1983; Graves, 1983; Harste, Woodward, & Burke, 1984; Sowers, 1982). Why did it take us so long to discover this root, brute fact? Plenty of children through the ages must have scribbled meaningful writing before they could read or spell. Plenty of grown-ups must have noticed. But somehow no one *really* noticed; or else they noticed and called it aberrant or wrong.

Input or Output?

We could blame our blindness on the phrase "reading and writing," but that phrase—and the sequence it implies—merely encapsulates a deep cultural construction embedded in everyday language. The word *literacy* literally means power over letters—that is, over both writing and reading. But used casually (and in government policy and legislation), literacy tends to mean *reading*, not writing. The words *academic, professor,* and even *teacher* tend to connote a reader and critic more than a writer, so deeply has the dominance of reading infected our ways of thinking.

The word *learning* also tends to connote reading and input—not writing and output. Our very conception of learning favors reading over writing because the concepts of learning and reading draw on the same root metaphor. *Learning is input:* taking things in, putting things inside us. People think of listening and reading—not talking and writing—as the core activities in school. (An old tradition has not fully disappeared: Talking is the crime and writing the punishment.) If we stop to think about it, we will realize that students learn from output—talking and writing. But we don't naturally think of learning as talking and writing. Notice, for example, how many teachers consider assessment or testing as measuring input rather than output. Tests tend to ask, in effect, "How well have you learned others' ideas?"

When I ask about a more writing-friendly model of assessment, educators suggest questions like this: "How well can students build new thoughts out of what they have studied?" That's a good model—yet notice how it's still a covert test of input. We need to stretch our cultural habits to realize that we could also have tests that ask, "What new ideas can the student come up with?" Such a model may seem to be an inadequate test of learning, yet it would in fact measure learning and reflect skills that students need for school, work, and life.

In most school and college courses, reading is more central than writing. There is usually only one writing course: some kind of "freshman writing workshop." A sprinkling of creative writing or other advanced writing courses is available to comparatively few students. Departments other than English and journalism typically have no writing courses at all.

Of course, writing is assigned in many courses across many disciplines, although some students in large universities manage to avoid writing for their entire college career. But when writing is assigned, it traditionally serves reading: The student summarizes, interprets, explains, integrates, or makes comparisons among readings.

The Unexamined Dominance of Reading

Our sense of reading as the horse and of writing as the cart derives from a metaphor of learning that students are vessels to Fill with knowledge. But if we put the real horse forward and emphasize writing, we make use of a better metaphor: *Learning is the making of meaning.* This helps explain much that is otherwise paradoxical. For example, the more we write and talk, the more we have to write and say. The greater the number of words that come out of us, the greater the number of words we find left inside. And when students feel empty—"I have nothing to say, nothing on my mind"—the cause is not insufficient input but insufficient output. Talking and writing put words and thoughts *into* students' heads. These facts are not contradictory when we understand that learning consists of making new connections, and thus new meanings.

When we stop privileging reading over writing and put the real horse—writing—in front, we stop privileging passivity over activity. I grant the usefulness of the currently fashionable formulations: that reading is "really writing" (actively creating meaning), and writing is "really reading" (passively finding what culture and history have inscribed in our heads). These

formulations carry genuine and useful truth, but in the end, writing promotes more psychological and physical engagement than reading.

Reading tends to imply, "Sit still and pay attention," whereas writing tends to imply, "Get in there and *do* something."

For example, reading tends to imply, "Sit still and pay attention," whereas writing tends to imply, "Get in there and *do* something." Reading means that the teacher and the author chose the words; writing means that the student chose the words. Reading asks, "What did *they* have to say?", whereas writing asks, "What do *you* have to say?" Reading is consumption; writing is production. Putting reading first encourages passivity by locating agency and authority away from the student, keeping it in the teacher or the institution. It locks schools into sending students a pervasive message: Don't speak until spoken to, and don't write your own ideas until you prove you can correctly reproduce the ideas of others. When we make writing as important as reading, however, we help students break out of their characteristically passive stance in school and learning.

We also shouldn't overlook the importance of the physical dimension. Students are more awake and involved after they write than after they read. The next time a class discussion turns listless, stop and have everyone read a helpful piece of text. But notice how much more energized students become if—in the same situation—you ask them to write for a few minutes. The physical dimension can even enliven reading. Reading out loud—especially if the student uses gestures—has a positive influence on cognition.

Reading's dominance is linked to a cultural fear: "We must put reading before writing—input before output—or else we'll invite romantic solipsism and rampant individualism. Students will disappear into cocoons of isolation." This fear rests on a model of individual development that most readers of this journal will recognize as misguided—a kind of parody of Freud and Piaget: "Children start out as egocentric little monads dominated by the desire to stay separate and egocentric. They cannot become 'decentered' or social without a terrible struggle." It's as though we fear that our students are each in their own little bathrooms, and we must beat on the door and say, "What are you *doing* in there? Why have you been in there so long with the door locked? Come out and have some wholesome fun with us!"

A different model of development that derives from thinkers like George Herbert Meade, Mikhail Bakhtin, and Lev Vygotsky now seems more acceptable: Our children *start out* social and intertwined. Their little selves are not hermetically sealed atoms; instead, they are deeply enmeshed in the important figures in their lives. We don't have to struggle to make children connect with others—they already are naturally connected. We don't have to bang on the bathroom door to make them listen to, collaborate with, and feel part of the people and cultural forces around them. They may not want to listen to *us*, but that doesn't make them private and solipsistic. (It's usually the more private and solipsistic kids who listen best to us teachers.)

Separateness and autonomy are not qualities that children start out with but rather qualities they gradually achieve—a process marked by struggle and setbacks throughout adolescence and young adulthood. It can be a slow and difficult process for individuals to achieve that sense of self that enables them to think and act in ways that their community may disapprove of. Writing, in this instance, is a particularly powerful tool for helping adolescents listen, reflect, converse with themselves, and tackle both cultural messages and peer pressures.

Write Movies of the Reader's Mind

We saw how writing helps 1st graders learn the difficult process of reading. Writing can help students at the college level as well, by providing them with a metacognitive understanding of the nature of the reading process. Most students have been taught by writing teachers to draft, get feedback, and revise (even if many of them skip this sequence when they can). Most students can see how writing is a process of slowly constructed meaning, often socially negotiated through feedback. They have learned that clarity is not what we start with but what we work toward. Fewer students are prey to the once-common myth that good writers sit down and immediately produce excellent writing out of some magical genius place in their heads.

> **People think of listening and reading—not talking and writing—as the core activities in school.**

But reading is much quicker and more hidden than writing. Students are therefore more prey to the myth that reading is a process in which experts look at texts and immediately see perfectly formed meanings hidden there—meanings that ordinary folk can't see. Students have a harder time understanding that reading is just like writing: a process of cognitive (and social) construction in which *everyone* builds up meanings from cues in the text, using as building blocks the word meanings already inside readers' heads. Just as in writing, clarity is not what we start with in reading but what we work toward.

We can use writing to help students comprehend this concept. When they understand it, they read better. What helps clarify the process is capturing elusive "rough drafts of reading"—what I call "movies of the reader's mind." I present a text in fragments. After each fragment, I have students quickly write down everything that's going on in their minds: their reactions, their

interpretations. For example, after being given the title and the first several sentences of a text, a student might write, "It seems to be about *X*. Some kind of analysis or story or argument. I have a hunch that I'm going to like this piece." After reading the next couple of paragraphs, the student might write, "Oh, now I see it's doing something different from what I thought. It's making me think of *X* and *Y*, and it's reminding me of *Z* from my past experience [my past reading]." I try for three to five interruptions of this kind, regardless of the length of the piece. I also have students record changes in their reactions and interpretations after they read the piece a second time. The reflective writing after the first fragment might take only two minutes—but the writings get longer with subsequent fragments. This process flushes out the misreadings and wrong takes that are inevitable even with expert readers. It often helps for the teacher to be the guinea pig for the class and record movies of his or her mind with a text encountered for the first time (see Curtis, 2001).

The Horse *and* the Cart

I'm *not* arguing that reading is less important than writing. Nor am I saying, "Let's put writing first because students already read well." Many students are remarkably *bad* at reading. But weakness in reading often stems from neglect of writing. Students will put more care and attention into reading when they have had more of a chance to write what's on their minds and when they have been given more opportunities to assume the role of writer. This is not an either/or argument, and the writing/reading connection is not a zero-sum game.

References

Calkins, L. M. (1983). *Lessons from a child on the teaching and learning of writing.* Portsmouth, NH: Heinemann.

Curtis, M. (2001). *The original text-wrestling book.* Dubuque, IA: Kendall/Hunt.

Graves, D. (1983). *Writing: Teachers and children at work.* Portsmouth, NH: Heinemann.

Harste, J., Woodward, V., & Burke, C. (1984). *Language stories and learning lessons.* Portsmouth, NH: Heinemann.

Sowers, S. (1982). Reflect, expand, select: Three responses in the writing conference. In T. Newkirk & N. Atwell (Eds.), *Understanding writing: Ways of observing, learning, and teaching.* Chelmsford, MA: Northeast Regional Exchange.

PETER ELBOW is Emeritus Professor of English at the University of Massachusetts in Amherst, Massachusetts. He is the author of *Writing Without Teachers* (Oxford University Press, 1973), Embracing Contraries (Oxford University Press, 1986), Writing with Power (Oxford University Press, 1998), and Everyone Can Write (Oxford University Press, 2000). He is coauthor with Patricia Belanoff of the textbook *Being a Writer* (McGraw-Hill, 2003).

The Sweet Work of Reading

**Kindergartners explore reading comprehension using
a surprisingly complex array of strategies.**

ANDIE CUNNINGHAM AND RUTH SHAGOURY

ndie, a kindergarten teacher, sits before her class of
5- and 6-year-olds and holds up the book *Owl Moon*
(Yolen, 1987) for the students to see.

"Open up the part of your brains that's brilliant," Andie tells
them. "We're learning a new strategy today. You're going to use
your brains to make a picture of the book. Ready?"

Andie directs her students' attention toward the fresh piece
of butcher paper on the easel. She points out the sticky notes and
pens. "It's time to read *Owl Moon*," she says. "As I read, pay
attention to the place in your brain that makes a picture of the
part of the book that's most important to you."

She starts to read, and the class enters the hushed night of
owl-calling. Faces turn to the book; from time to time, the students use their "owl voices" to hoot with the owls in the story.

When she finishes, Andie asks the students to decide on the
one picture in their heads that's most important to them. "When
you're ready," she says, "get your pen and paper and draw your
one picture. Be specific and detailed."

Slowly and intentionally, Megan picks up a sticky note and
pen and walks to a table to draw her picture. Austin looks up at
the ceiling, smiles, picks up his pen, and settles down to work.
Lacey scrunches up her face, squeezing her eyes shut. "I'm still
thinkin'," she says. "I gotta choose 'cuz I got five in my head."

This kindergarten is a workshop of readers and thinkers who
take seriously the work of making meaning from books. Andie
has set the tone for their comprehension work through deliberate instructions and by providing her students with the tools
they need. Students are writing about their reading. They use
fine-line black pens to make meaningful marks on large sticky
notes that serve as placeholders for their thinking.

This lesson is not reproduced from a published reading program, nor is it a yearly unit trotted out for every new group of
kindergartners. This particular book choice was in response to
Carrie's interest in becoming an expert in trees and Kenya's
desire to learn more about big birds and where they live.

Building on Interests

As a kindergarten teacher-researcher and a university researcher,
we have been investigating what is possible for young children

as they acquire literacy skills. Educators concerned with
kindergarten curriculum are all asking the same questions:
What reading comprehension skills do today's kindergartners
truly require? What skills do they need to become avid learners
in school and in the world, active and compassionate citizens,
and their best selves?

Building on their interests helps students make authentic connections.

Contemporary researchers (Harvey & Goudvis, 2000; Keene
& Zimmermann, 1997; Miller, 2002) have shown how readers can explore comprehension using a range of strategies (see
"Reading Comprehension Strategies"). The students in Andie's
class are teaching us that kindergartners can use these important comprehension strategies to bring their home knowledge
into school. Some students realize for the first time that their
understanding of a book is important. As they make text-to-self
connections in books that the teacher reads to them, students
learn the importance of schema—what they bring to a text in
terms of their background knowledge and life experiences.
As they tap into their knowledge of the world and make connections, they are more prepared to go on to other important
reading comprehension skills, such as text-to-text connections,
inferences, questioning, and synthesis. For example, when we
read *Too Many Tamales* (Soto, 1993), with its central theme of
losing an important object, the students made bridges from the
book to each of their schemas. Daniel remembered misplacing
a screw for a toy truck headlight; Ryan relived the memory of
losing a ring in a swimming pool; Bao Jun detailed her loss of
a cat in China.

Student interests create our reading curriculum. Nathaniel's
interest in pumpkins led to our decision to read *Pumpkin Circle*
(Levens, 1999). We read *Miss Twiggly's Treehouse* (Fox, 1966)
to focus on Bianca's interest in studying friendships. Building
on their interests helps students make their own authentic connections, the foundation of our work together. The lesson on

Reading Comprehension Strategies

- *Making connections*—between texts, the world, and students' lives (sometimes called text-to-text, text-to-world, and text-to-self connections). Readers bring their background knowledge and experiences of life to a text.
- *Creating mental images.* These "mind pictures" help readers enter the text visually in their mind's eye.
- *Asking questions.* Readers who use this strategy actively ask questions of the text as they read.
- *Determining importance.* This strategy describes a reader's conscious and ongoing determination of what is important in a text.
- *Inferring.* When readers infer, they create new meaning on the basis of their life experiences and clues from the book.
- *Synthesizing.* Although this strategy is sometimes considered a retell, synthesizing is a way of spiraling deeper into the book. Readers might explore the text through the perspective of different characters to come to new understandings about the character's life and world.

making mental pictures from *Owl Moon* is not isolated from the rest of the students' lives. They paint what they know, write and tell stories, and read books that link their background knowledge to this new academic world.

A Community of Learners

Andie's classroom is in a K–3 school in Portland, Oregon, that has the highest number of families living in poverty in the district. Of its 540 students, more than 85 percent receive free or reduced-price breakfasts and lunches. There are six half-day kindergarten classes, each with 20–25 students. Students speak at least 13 languages other than English; the school employs two full-time, in-house translators for Spanish and Russian families.

Many languages swirl through the classroom. During daily calendar work, for example, we usually count in Russian, Spanish, and English, thanks to the help of parents who are teaching us to count in their home languages. Sharing our home languages, experiences, knowledge, and questions is an important element of becoming a community. Comprehension and community go hand in hand as the students learn to work together and do the hard work that goes along with making meaning out of difficult texts.

Bringing each student's schema to the classroom discussion is challenging. It requires thoughtful planning on the part of the teacher and ample time for learners to grapple with meaning so they can contribute their ideas to the community.

Mind Pictures

This morning, the students wrestle with important "mind pictures" that they have in their heads as a result of listening to *Owl Moon*. Lacey shows her completed picture to Ruth, a university researcher. "This is a big tree where the man was calling out," she says.

Benjamin shows his drawing to Andie. "This is the guy who is telling her to be quiet," he says, pointing to the two figures on the sticky note. Benjamin shows her the arrow between the two figures, indicating from which direction the voice is coming. He points to two large orbs hovering over the people. "This is the owl's eyes," he says. As the students finish drawing on their sticky notes, they carry them to Andie, who records their words on the notes and sticks them on the butcher paper.

Together we look at and read the individual writing and drawing on the sticky notes, noticing first the differences. For example, Carrie has drawn a picture of an owl landing on a branch, whereas Ivan focused on one of the characters, the Grandpa. Andie reinforces the idea that although everyone is bringing a different schema to the story, they have all drawn owls, trees, and people. The chart has stimulated rich new discussions of the story. With contributions from each class member secured, conversations have a grounded place in which to flourish.

Digging Deep

Readers who care about making sense of the books they read don't give up on stories when meaning eludes them. They come back and struggle with the text until they make sense of it. There is an excitement to uncovering layers of meaning when we spiral back to difficult texts. Few kindergartners are taught how to experience this kind of "hard fun" when they read. But when we give them a chance to play with it, they rise to the challenge.

When Andie finishes reading *Almost to Freedom* (Nelson, 2003), Austin's first words are, "There were a lot of words in there!" This book is challenging. Besides having "lots of words," it tells the painful story of a young girl fleeing slavery on the Underground Railroad.

"Yeah," Nathaniel piggybacks, "like a hundred million words. I want to keep it in the room and read it the next day and the day after that and the day after that."

Nathaniel understands that the more we revisit those tough reads with millions of words, the better our chances of discovering their riches. Throughout the year, we explore such provocative books as *The Three Questions* (Muth, 2002), a retelling of a philosophical tale by Leo Tolstoy; *The Cats of Krasinsky Square* (Hesse, 2004), set in Poland during World War II; *Where Is Grandpa?* (Barron & Soentpiet, 2001), a story of one family dealing with death and loss; and *Visiting Day* (Woodson, 2002), in which a little girl tells of looking forward to her weekly visits to her dad in prison.

Kindergartners are capable of far more sophisticated reading strategies than educators often suspect. As they write, draw, paint, and move their bodies to the stories, they dig deep to make sense. Students might use clay to portray their mental images, dramatize what is important to them in a book, or paint watercolors of their inferences. With these strategies, they have a firm foundation for building reading success.

Synthesizing Meaning

Synthesizing is one of the most complex strategies that readers use to spiral into deeper layers of meaning. Readers "hold their thinking" as they progress through a book. In other words, they keep track of how their thinking is evolving, using their schemas to make inferences. They come to view the book and the world through new lenses.

This week, we dig into synthesizing with the clever picture book *No Such Thing* (Koller, 1997), in which a human child and a monster child are repeatedly assured by their mommies that the other doesn't exist—that there is "no such thing." It's a perfect book for seeing the world through another's eyes and gaining insights about perceptions other than one's own.

Early in the week, the students hold their thinking by writing and making drawings on sticky notes of what they remember from the book. When they finish, they place their notes on Andie's anchor chart. Later in the week, on the third reading of the book, Andie tells her students to use a new lens as they read the book:

> Decide who you are going to think like. The boy? His mom? The monster? Or the monster's mom? You'll be bringing your schema and using it to think like that person.

At the end of the reading, Carrie and Megan crawl under one of the tables and pretend they're lying in bed. Some boys head to the coat rack where they peer back over their shoulders. Around us, we see children pretending to be the little monster and the little boy. Bianca behaves as though she were the mother, looking in the door at her little boy.

After a few moments, the chime ringer rings the bell and the students return to the circle area. Andie tells the students that they can act out their characters for the class and that everyone will try to guess who they are.

Austin volunteers to start. He lies on the floor in the middle of the circle. It turns out he is being the monster screaming "AAAAHHHHH!" When it's his turn, José also lies in the middle of the floor, but he shakes his head no to all the guesses. He explains, "I was the boy at the end of the book when he was under the bed."

"Did that actually happen in the book?" Andie asks.

"No," José tells us. "They were just *gonna* switch when the book ends."

"José made a great inference!" Andie exclaims. "He used clues to figure out what was going to happen next—even after the book ends. Sweet work!"

As kindergartners write, draw, paint, and move their bodies to the stories, they dig deep to make sense.

The students take turns acting out different roles. Shy Bianca walks slowly to the center of the circle and hugs her arms tight around herself, rocking from side to side. We guess that she's the monster or the boy being scared.

"No," she says. "I'm huggin' the boy. I'm the mom huggin' the boy."

Bianca lived the book through the mom's eyes, sharing two different parts of the book as she moved: the mother looking at the boy through the doorway and the mother hugging her son. She spiraled deeper as she synthesized meaning.

Too many educators think that there's "no such thing" as kindergartners making sophisticated inferences that help them synthesize what they read. These students show what is possible.

A Nourishing Environment

Kindergartners face enormous challenges. Most of the students in Andie's class have little or no alphabet knowledge when they enter the classroom in the fall. English is a second or third language for many of the families in this impoverished working-class community. Instead of viewing kindergarten as a garden of children, we prefer the metaphor of a tide pool:

> Kindergartens, like tide pools, are a meeting place of two systems. The land and the sea meet at tide pools, and organisms in tide pools must adapt to adjust to the drastic changes in environment that come with the changing of the tides each day. (Barnhart & Leon, 1994, p. 7)

This image helps remind us of the way in which children must adjust to the differing environments of home and school at the cultural meeting place that is kindergarten. Kindergartners need specific learning tools. They need honor and respect to thrive. They need similar souls nearby, without the threat of predators. They need a climate that invites and supports their learning, and they need plenty of time to link literacy with their lives in the challenging world of school (Cunningham & Shagoury, 2005).

Building bridges between the books in the classroom and what students have learned in their first five years takes work. A publisher-designed curriculum might not connect to these children's lives at all. By incorporating students' interests into the curriculum, we can create a community in which we learn together. Within that community, students can learn the kind of reading comprehension skills that will help them become readers who turn to books for meaning, understanding, reflection, and pleasure.

References

Barnhart, D., & Leon, V. (1994). *Tidepools: The bright world of the rocky shoreline.* Upper Saddle River, NJ: Pearson Educational.

Cunningham, A., & Shagoury, R. (2005). *Starting with comprehension: Reading strategies for the youngest learners.* Portland, ME: Stenhouse Publishers.

Harvey, S., & Goudvis, A. (2000). *Strategies that work: Teaching comprehension to enhance understanding.* Portland, ME: Stenhouse Publishers.

Keene, E., & Zimmermann, S. (1997). *Mosaic of thought: Teaching comprehension in a reader's workshop.* Portsmouth, NH: Heinemann.

Miller, D. (2002). *Reading with meaning: Teaching comprehension in the primary grades.* Portland, ME: Stenhouse Publishers.

ANDIE CUNNINGHAM teaches kindergarten at Harold Oliver Primary School in Portland, Oregon; rupali@easystreet.com.

RUTH SHAGOURY is Mary Stuart Rogers Professor of Education at the Graduate School of Education and Counseling, Lewis & Clark College, 0615 S. W. Palatine Hill Rd., Portland, OR 97219; shagoury@lclark.edu.

The Overdominance of Computers

Our students need inner resources and real-life experiences to balance their high-tech lives.

Lowell W. Monke

The debate churns on over the effectiveness of computers as learning tools. Although there is a growing disillusionment with the promise of computers to revolutionize education, their position in schools is protected by the fear that without them students will not be prepared for the demands of a high-tech 21st century. This fallback argument ultimately trumps every criticism of educational computing, but it is rarely examined closely.

Lets start by accepting the premise of the argument: Schools need to prepare young people for a high-tech society. Does it automatically follow that children of all ages should use high-tech tools? Most people assume that it does, and that's the end of the argument. But we don't prepare children for an automobile-dependent society by finding ways for 10-year-olds to drive cars, or prepare people to use alcohol responsibly by teaching them how to drink when they are 6. My point is that preparation does not necessarily warrant early participation. Indeed, preparing young people quite often involves strengthening their inner resources—like self-discipline, moral judgment, and empathy—before giving them the opportunity to participate.

Great Power and Poor Preparation

The more powerful the tools—and computers are powerful—the more life experience and inner strength students must have to handle that power wisely. On the day my Advanced Computer Technology classroom got wired to the Internet, it struck me that I was about to give my high school students great power to harm a lot of people, and all at a safe distance. They could inflict emotional pain with a few keystrokes and never have to witness the tears shed. They could destroy hours of work accomplished by others who were not their enemies—just poorly protected network users whose files provided convenient bull's-eyes for youth flexing newfound technical muscles.

I also realized that it would take years to instill the ethical discipline needed to say *no* to flexing that technical power. Young people entering my course needed more firsthand experiences guided by adults. They needed more chances to directly connect their own actions with the consequences of those actions, and to reflect on the outcomes, before they started using tools that could trigger serious consequences on the other side of the world.

Students need more than just moral preparation. They also need authentic experiences. As more students grow up spending much of their time in environments dominated by computers, TV, and video games, their diminished experience with real, concrete things prevents them from developing a rich understanding of what they study on computers. The computer is a purely symbolic environment; users are always working with abstract representations of things, never with the things themselves. In a few months my students could learn to build complex relational databases and slick multimedia presentations. But unless they also had a deep knowledge of the physical world and community relationships, they would be unable to infuse depth and meaning into the information they were depicting and discussing.

Do Computers help Achievement?

Educational technology researchers, who tend to suffer from a severe inability to see the forest for the trees, typically ignore the impact that saturating society with computers and other screen environments is having on children. University of Munich economists Thomas Fuchs and Ludger Woessmann recently examined data from a study of 174,000 15-year-olds in 31 nations who took the Programme for International Student Assessment tests. They found, after controlling for other possible influences, that the more access students had to computers in school and at home, the *lower* their overall test scores were (2004). The authors suggest that rather than inherently motivating young people or helping them learn, computers more likely distract them from their studies. But there may be other problems behind this phenomenon that point to inherent contradictions in the use of educational technology.

For example, although we know that computer programs can help small children learn to read, we also know that face-to-face interaction is one of the most important ingredients in reading readiness (Dodici, Draper, & Peterson, 2003). As a result of increased time spent with computers, video games, and TV the current generation of elementary students will experience an estimated 30 percent fewer face-to-face encounters than the previous generation (Hammel, 1999). Thus, teachers may be employing the very devices for remediating reading problems that helped cause the problems in the first place.

Nearly everything children do today involves technologies that distance them from direct contact with the living world.

The issue is not just balancing computer time with other activities in schools. Both inside and outside school, children's lives are dominated by technology. Nearly everything a child does today—from chatting with friends to listening to music to playing games—tends to involve the use of technologies that distance children from direct contact with the living world. If the task of schools is to produce men and women who live responsible, fulfilling lives—not just human cogs for the high-tech machinery of commerce—then we should not be intensifying children's high-tech existence but compensating for it. Indeed, as advanced technology increasingly draws us toward a mechanical way of thinking and acting, it becomes crucial that schools help students develop their distinctly human capacities. What we need from schools is not balance in using high technology, but an effort to balance children's machine-dominated lives.

To prepare children to challenge the cold logic of the spreadsheet-generated bottom line, we need to teach them to value what that spreadsheet cannot factor in: commitment, loyalty, and tradition. To prepare them to find meaning in the abstract text and images encountered through screens, we need to first engage them in physical realities that screen images can only symbolize. To fit students to live in an environment filled with human-made products, we need to first help them know and respect what cannot be manufactured: the natural, the living, the wild. To prepare students to live well-grounded lives in a world of constant technological change, we need to concentrate their early education on things that endure.

The Cost of Failing to Compensate

Anyone who has spent time in schools knows that what is keeping today's youth from succeeding academically has nothing to do with a lack of technical skills or access to computers. Rather, it is the lack of qualities like hope, compassion, trust, respect, a sense of belonging, moral judgment, stability, community support, parental care, and teacher competence and enthusiasm that keeps so many students imprisoned in ignorance.

Ironically, what students will most need to meet the serious demands of the 21st century is the wisdom that grows out of these inner human capacities and that is developed by community involvement. If the 20th century taught us anything at all,

it should have been that technology can be a very mixed blessing. Children entering elementary schools today will eventually have to wrestle with the mess that their elders have left them because of our own lack of wisdom about technology's downside: global warming, increasingly lethal weapons, nuclear waste, overdependence on automobiles, overuse of pesticides and antibiotics, and the general despoiling of our planet. They will also have to take on ethical conundrums posed by advanced technology, such as what to do about cloning, which decisions are off-limits to artificial intelligence devices, and whether or not parents should be allowed to "enhance" the genetic makeup of their offspring (only the wealthy need apply).

Those decisions should not be left to technicians in labs, CEOs in boardrooms, or politicians in debt to those who stand to profit from the technology. Our children should be at the decision tables as adults, and we want them to be able to stand apart from high technology and soberly judge its benefits and detriments to the entire human race.

How can young people develop the wisdom to judge high technology if they are told from the moment they enter school, implicitly if not explicitly, that they need high-tech tools to learn, to communicate, to think? Having been indoctrinated early with the message that their capacity to deal with the world depends not on their own internal resources but on their use of powerful external machines, how can students even imagine a world in which human beings impose limits on technological development or use?

Where to Go From Here

Keep to Essentials in the Early Years

So how, specifically, should educators make decisions and policies about the appro priateness of digital technologies for students of different ages?

One approach to tackling this dilemma comes from the Alliance for Childhood. During the last eight years, the Alliance (whose board of directors I serve on) has engaged educators, children's health professionals, researchers, and technology experts in developing guidelines for structuring a healthy learning environment for children, and has developed a list of essential conditions. Educators should ask themselves to what extent heavy use of computers and the Internet provides children in the lower grades with these essential school experiences:

- Close, lining relationships with responsible adults.
- Outdoor activity, nature exploration, gardening, and other encounters with nature.
- Time for unstructured play as part of the core curriculum.
- Music, drama, puppetry, dance, painting, and the other arts, both as separate classes and as a catalyst to bring other academic subjects to life.
- Hands-on lessons, handicrafts, and other physically engaging activities that provide effective first lessons for young children in the sciences, mathematics, and technology.

- Conversation with important adults, as well as poetry, storytelling, and hearing books read aloud.

This vision places a high priority on a child's direct encounters with the world and with other living beings, but it does not reject technology. On the contrary, tools are an important part of the vision. But at the elementary level, the tools should be simple, putting less distance between the student and the world and calling forth the students own internal resources.

Schools must also be patient with children's development. It would strike anyone as silly to give the smallest student in a 2nd grade class a scooter so that the child could get around the track as fast as the other kids his or her age. But our society shows decreasing willingness to wait for the natural emergence of students' varying mental and emotional capacities. We label students quickly and display an almost pathological eagerness to apply external technical fixes (including medications) to students who often simply aren't ready for the abstract, academic, and sedentary environment of today's early elementary classrooms. Our tendency to turn to external tools to help children cope with demands that are out of line with their tactile and physically energetic nature reflects the impact that decades of placing faith in technical solutions has had on how we treat children.

Study Technology in Depth After Elementary School

After children have had years to engage in direct, firsthand experiences, and as their abstract thinking capacities emerge more fully, it makes sense to gradually introduce computers and other complex, symbolic environments. Computer hardware and software should also become the focus of classroom investigation. A student in a technological society surrounded by black boxes whose fundamental principles he or she does not understand is as functionally illiterate as a student in a world filled with books that he or she can't read. The only thing worse would be to make technology "invisible," preventing children from even being aware of their ignorance.

By high school, digital technologies should take a prominent place in students' studies, both as tools of learning and as tools to learn about. During the last two years of high school, teachers should spend considerable time outfitting students with the high-tech skills they will need when they graduate. This "just-in-time" approach to teaching technical skills is far more efficient—instructionally and financially—than continually retraining younger students in technical skills soon to be obsolete. In addition, students at all education levels should consciously examine technology's role in human affairs.

Techno-Byte

Percentage of U.S. students who used computers in school in 2003:

- 97 percent of high school students.
- 95 percent of middle school students.
- 91 percent of students in grades 1–5.
- 80 percent of kindergarten students.
- 67 percent of nursery school students.

—National Center for Education Statistics, 2005

I am not suggesting that we indiscriminately throw computers out of classrooms. But I do believe it's time to rethink the past decision to indiscriminately throw them in. The result of that rethinking would be, I hope, some much-needed technological modesty, both in school and eventually in society in general. By compensating for the dominance of technology in students' everyday lives, schools might help restore the balance we need to create a more humane society

The irony of postmodern education is that preparing children for a high-tech future requires us to focus our attention more than ever before on the task of understanding what it means to be human, to be alive, to be part of both social and biological communities—a quest for which technology is increasingly becoming not the solution but the problem.

References

Dodici, B. J., Draper, D. C., & Peterson, C. A. (2003). Early parent-child interactions and early literacy development. *Topics in Early Childhood Special Education, 23*(3), 124–136.

Fuchs, T., & Woessmann, L. (2004, November). *Computers and student learning: Bivariate and multivariate evidence on the availability and use of computers at home and at school.* CESifo Working Paper Series (#1321). Available: www.cesifo.de/~DocCIDL/1321.pdf

Hammel, S. (1999, Nov. 29). Generation of loners? Living their lives online. *US. News and World Report*, p. 79.

Author's note: The Alliance for Childhood has produced two publications to help parents and educators guide children toward a healthier relationship with technology: *Fool's Gold: A Critical Look at Computers in Childhood*, and *Tech Tonic: Towards a New Literacy of Technology* (both available online at www.allianceforchildhood.org).

LOWELL W. MONKE is Assistant Professor at Wittenberg University in Springfield, Ohio; 937-342-8648; lmonke@wittenberg.edu.

Meeting the Challenge of Math & Science

Barbara Sprung

Two 4-year-olds are in the block area. There are only two double-unit blocks on the shelf and the children know they need four to make a rectangular base for their structure. (Another child has used many blocks in a special building and has requested that it be left up until her dad can see it at pick-up time). As they observe the remaining blocks in the cubby, one child says, "I have an idea." He takes the two remaining doubles and four single blocks from the shelf. He places two single blocks alongside a double and sees that they are of equal length. Both children are excited to see that the two single-unit blocks can be used in place of one double-unit block, and they can build their rectangle after all.

These children have made a math discovery that uses the skills of observation, problem-solving, creative-thinking, geometry, and fractions!

On another day, Amy and Eric are working at each side of the double easel. The paint colors of the day are blue, yellow, and white, and there is a can of plain water for cleaning the brushes. The classroom rule is not to mix paint colors in the cans. Eric is busy painting a sun on the top of his paper. Next, he plans to make a blue sky around the sun. As Eric leans around the easel to see what Amy is painting, his blue brush hits the yellow sun. Eric is surprised to see that his "sun" has turned green and he shows Amy, who begins to chant, "Eric made a green sun, Eric made a green sun." Eric says, "Look Mrs. Sumner, look what happened to my painting."

Eric and Amy have had a science experience. They have discovered that two colors can combine to make a third color. They have experienced firsthand that yellow and blue make green.

Seizing Teachable Moments

These two anecdotes tell a story: Math and science are everywhere in your classroom! The challenge is to take these wonderful "teachable moments" that happen all the time and intentionally incorporate them into the curriculum. As early childhood teachers, we need to learn to seize these teaching and learning opportunities, and to let children know that you value their discoveries and ideas by sharing them with other children and adults in the classroom. When I was teaching kindergarten, Yigal, an Israeli boy in my class, brought in a retractable measuring tape, which was obviously a treasure for him. We used it at various times during the morning to measure areas of the classroom that he designated, and we wrote a story for the class library, entitled "Yigal's Measuring Story." Yigal's interest in math was validated, all the children became interested, and Yigal gained some much-needed recognition and stature among his classmates.

Sometimes the lessons might be for an individual child or a small group, and other times the moment may turn into a lesson or book that can benefit the entire class!

Math and Science Around the Room

In addition to acting on children's discoveries, there are many ways you can promote math and science skill development in your learning centers. As children engage in the activities, you'll discover that math and science activities enhance all those other skill areas we work so hard to develop in early childhood classrooms, including literacy and language, social/emotional, physical, small- and large-motor, eye-hand coordination, and observation. Let's start by taking a look at how you can integrate math learning into your classroom centers.

Block Area Math

The unit blocks that are standard equipment in most early childhood classrooms are a multi-disciplinary curriculum in themselves. Think about the potential of this area for developing math awareness and skills. Through blocks, children gain experience with geometry, shape recognition, fractions, and counting, as well as spatial relations, creative thinking, problem-solving, and decision-making, which are essential higher-order skills. They are also fun—and enjoyment is an important component of learning.

For a change of pace, try conducting a math lesson right in the block area with small groups of children at a time. Here's what you can do:

- Ask children to sit in a semicircle.
- Place one block of each size in a row on the floor and name all the different block types with children: unit, half unit, double, quad, and wedge.

- Together, describe the shapes of the blocks, for example: rectangle, square, and triangle.
- Pose a challenge or brain teaser: "Can someone tell us one interesting thing he or she notices about the blocks?" If no one volunteers, give children a clue by placing the half-unit on the unit block. Children may notice that:
  - Two half-units equal (are the same as) one unit.
  - Two units equal one double.
  - Four units equal one quad.
- After you have thoroughly explored all the possibilities for combining the blocks on the floor, ask: "Can someone find other blocks in the cubby to match up?" If needed, give an example by putting two half-circles together to make a whole circle.
- Place the semicircle block in front of the children and ask, "Does anyone see something about this block and the way we are sitting?" Help children observe that they are sitting in a semicircle—the same shape as the block only much larger. This comparison will provide children with an early experience in scale, a concept they will learn more about in the upper elementary grades.
- As a final step, create an experience chart to document the lesson.
- Repeat the math lesson with other small groups until everyone has had a chance to participate.

During a math lesson in the block area, children are gaining many other important skills. They are building literacy skills by listening, talking about their discoveries, and using math vocabulary and word recognition, for instance: "This block is a rectangle;" "This one's a triangle;" "This one is half as big as that one;" "This one is twice as big;" "Look, Mrs. Sumner put two halves together and made a whole circle;" "This is fun."

As children engage in block-building they learn to organize their play, share materials, negotiate with others, and cooperate with their building partners. So, this one area of the classroom offers opportunities for planned lessons, experiential learning, math and science skill-building, and a host of other interdisciplinary skills.

Dramatic-Play Area

As the year progresses, the dramatic-play area might be turned into a food store or a restaurant for a week. Either scenario will provide children with math experiences, including the use and value of money for buying and selling; pricing items for sale and creating price lists or menus; and counting items to buy and sell. Children can use play money of different denominations or make their own money from construction paper. As they engage in this play, children will gain math vocabulary and additional practice in higher-order thinking skills—organizing, decision-making, problem-solving—and the essential early childhood skill of cooperative play. Here's how to begin:

- Call a class meeting to talk about the idea of creating a store or restaurant.
- Let the children decide between the two ideas.

Quick-and-Easy Learning Center Ideas

These few activities are just the tip of the iceberg: You will be able to discover many other ways to highlight the math and science opportunities that abound in your classroom. Here are some other quick ideas:

- Experiment with the concepts of wet and dry using clay.
- Cut sponges into shapes for sponge painting.
- Have children sort and count Legos and other stacking toys by size and color.
- Use the water table for "sink or float" experiments. Provide a variety of objects and have a supply of pencils and picture charts nearby so children can record which items sank and which items floated.
- In the spring, blow bubbles outdoors using a variety of found materials as bubble makers—plastic strawberry containers a plastic cup with a hole in the bottom, or pipe cleaners. To make a strong bubble solution; mix a gallon of distilled water with liquid dishwashing detergent and two ounces of glycerin (available in the hand lotion section of drug-stores). Let children experiment with various bubble makers, wind direction, and their breath to make discoveries.

- Take a neighborhood field trip to a store or restaurant. If the choice is a restaurant, ask for a menu to take back to school. If the choice is a store, select one that doesn't sell too many items (a bodega or deli).

After the Field Trip:

- Hold a planning meeting to assign jobs.
- Make the play money.
- Set up the restaurant or shop (use play food or pictures of items cut from magazines or drawn by the children).
- Keep the restaurant or shop up for at least one week, or as long as interest lasts. Ask children to help to take the store or restaurant apart.

While the restaurant or store is active, observe and keep notes on children's discussions. You will learn about their ideas concerning the use of money and how the "real world" works. After the activity is complete:

- Call a class meeting to talk with children about the activity.
- Ask children to talk about how it felt to be a customer or a worker.
- Print children's comments on sheets of chart paper.
- Talk about observations that you made, especially about children's use of numbers and money, and about how well they cooperated.
- Relate the activity to how real stores and restaurants work.

Home-School Connection

In today's early childhood programs, there is a growing emphasis on skill-building. Families can become willing partners in providing developmentally appropriate math and science experiences at home. Here are ways to partner with families:

- Through your regular school communication channels—family letters, newsletters, online messages—share information about the math and science activities you are doing in the classroom.
- If family members work in a job related to math and science, ask them to come for a visit to talk about their work.
- Send home directions for making Oobleck, or other cooking activities, so that families can try them out with children.
- Encourage parents to take children on "Shape Hunting Walks." These can be easily done on the way to the supermarket or playground.
- Suggest that letting children help with chores—such as sorting laundry, pairing socks, putting groceries into sets, and sorting silverware—is a great way to reinforce math skills.
- If possible, arrange a school and family trip to a local children's science or discovery museum.
- Encourage families to visit their local science resources—children's museums, aquariums, parks, science museums, and botanical gardens.
- Give parents some ideas for "bathtub science"— providing measuring cups, funnels, and tubes as bathtub toys. They can also provide a variety of sink and float objects—a small rock, a plastic spoon, and other small and large plastic objects.
- Invite family members into the classroom to participate in activities where extra adults would be helpful.

Outdoor Area

Learning about shapes is a standard part of the early childhood curriculum but, too often, we begin and end with children being able to recognize and name the shapes—the square, rectangle, triangle, and circle. Think about taking the study of shapes outside the classroom and into the hallways, the gym, on a walk around the school, and, most fun of all, into the playground or park. Try a playground scavenger hunt to find shapes. To get ready:

- Make a large chart with a set of shapes you have cut from construction paper glued down the left margin.
- Gather enough pieces of stiff cardboard and small clips to make a "clipboard" for each pair of children. Tie a string around a pencil and attach it to the clip.
- Place sets of shape cutouts, drawing paper, and glue sticks on each of the work tables.

The Playground Activity:

- At class meeting time, tell children about going on a "Shapes Scavenger Hunt."
- Divide the class into pairs and ask each pair to sit at a table.
- Ask each pair to glue a row of shapes onto a piece of paper down the left side. (Be sure your sample chart is set up in a place where all the children can see it.)
- Attach the shape charts to the cardboard clipboard.
- Explain that every time someone sees a shape on the playground they should put a mark next to that shape with the pencil.

As children hunt for shapes, you may need to clue them in to shapes in different places around the playground, for instance: the frame of the slide might have triangles; the fence might have squares or diamond shapes; and the climbing equipment could be a stack of rectangles. If needed, ask some questions:

- "Does the door to the yard have a shape we know?"
- "How about the steps, are they made of shapes we know?"
- "Has anyone looked at the fence yet?"

Back in the Classroom:

- Ask children to sit at their tables with their clipboards.
- Ask them to count the number of marks they made next to each shape, and write the number on their charts.
- Circulate around the tables to help children count and write the numbers.
- Add up the cumulative numbers for each shape.
- At meeting time (it could be the next day), bring out the large shape chart you made and demonstrate how you tallied up all the shapes children found. For example, next to each construction-paper shape, draw a smaller shape representing each one found by the children. Then, count out loud: "Ricky and Sam found four rectangles. Jake and Jamala found three rectangles. Daniela and Karim also found three, and Kari and Irene found five. All together we found 15."
- Continue tallying for each shape on the chart.

Science is Everywhere!

Important science concepts are continuously being investigated all around the classroom. In the block area, for example, children are learning by trial and error that a wide base creates a stronger building (balance); that if the building is too asymmetrical (symmetry), or if it is too high and narrow, it will fall down; and that they must be aware of themselves and others or they might bump into their own or someone else's building (spatial relations). As children are working on their buildings, you can introduce these terms. They will love the sound of these new "grown-up" words, and will begin to use them as they work together!

Block Area Science

Try a small-group "What will happen if…?" lesson in the block area:

- Invite children to sit in a semicircle.
- Ask them a "What will happen if…?" question. For example: "I've been wondering, what will happen if I try to build a tall building with this one unit block on the bottom?"
- Invite children to respond with their ideas and then say, "Let's experiment and see what happens." As you build together, you may want to pause and say, "Should we build it higher? What do you think will happen?"
- Depending on the result of the experiment (most likely the building will collapse), ask children why they think it happened. What was the problem? If the building does collapse, explain that many times scientists have to repeat an experiment, but they learn from their mistakes.
- Ask children if anyone has another "What will happen if…?" question and continue to experiment.

From time to time, try "What will happen if…?" questions in the block area with other small groups of children. The experimentation will reinforce what they are already learning through trial and error during block play.

Cook Up Some Learning!

If you cook with children, you already are doing math and science in a very "real-world" context. Following recipe charts and measuring ingredients are math activities, and as they stir, beat, and bake children are engaging in chemistry. They also are experiencing the properties of solids and liquids as they watch the batter, which is a liquid, become a solid cookie, cake, or bread.

When doing these cooking activities, let children know that cooking is a form of science, and build science words into the activity. For example, a class story about a cooking experience might say something like:

"Today, we made pancakes for lunch. We measured and mixed water and milk—which are liquids—with eggs and flour. After we stirred everything together, the mixture was like a thick liquid. When the ingredients were cooked, our pancakes turned into solids."

Art Area

Eric and Amy's discovery in the opening anecdote can be turned into a wonderful color-mixing activity. Of course, color-mixing often happens by chance as children paint or use markers, but it can so easily be turned into an intentional science experience. To prepare:

- Cover the tables with newsprint.
- Put several pieces of drawing paper on each table (one for each child in the group, plus extras).
- On one table, place small containers of red, yellow, and white paints; on another table, put containers of blue,

yellow, and white; on a third table, red, blue, and white (repeat the process for each additional table).

- Put a small piece of sponge near each container. Have extra pieces on hand.
- Explain to children that in this activity they will work like scientists, experimenting with mixing different colors of paint.
- Assign children to tables and demonstrate how to dip a sponge lightly into the paint and make a print on the paper.
- Let all the children try the sponge painting, using a different sponge for each color.
- After a bit, if children haven't already done so, ask them to put one color over the other and see what happens.
- Circulate around the tables as children are working and help them notice the color changes.
- Ask some questions to spur their observations, such as, "Did anyone put white paint over the other colors? Please tell us what happened."

After about 15 minutes of experimentation, ask children at each table to talk about their discoveries. Begin by asking one child to name the colors of paint that she worked with, and then ask each child to report on one discovery. There will be repetition as the children report, but that is a way to reaffirm for everyone that blue and yellow create green, red and yellow create orange, red and blue create purple, and white makes the colors lighter. As a finale, you may want to ask: What do you think will happen if we combine all the colors together?

- Let children make guesses (they may know from experience at the easel), and then try it!
- Document the experiment on an experience chart that records each child's contribution.
- Revisit the scientific process with children around this activity.

Oodles of Oobleck

Many teachers regularly make play dough for, or with, children. This simple mixture of flour, water, and salt provides much fun, experimentation, and imaginative play. Oobleck is a wonderful variation of play dough, and provides engaging experiences with solids and liquids, since it has the properties of both. The added value of Oobleck is that it is an excellent medium for introducing the scientific process. And, because it reverts quickly to a smooth powder (once the water dries up), it appeals to children who are reluctant to touch "yucky" substances.

Oobleck consists of two parts cornstarch to one part water, with a few drops of food coloring added (optional). The water should be added to the cornstarch slowly and stirred with a popsicle stick. (You may need to add a drop or two of extra water or a sprinkle of extra cornstarch to get the right consistency.) For the whole class, two cups of cornstarch and one cup of water (to which food coloring has been added) will be enough. It's best to make it in an aluminum cake pan or a plastic deli container.

The Oobleck is ready when it resists a hard smack, but a finger gently pushing against it goes right in. Once the Oobleck is made, you can:

- Gather a small group of children around the table in the art area, which has been covered with newsprint or a plastic cloth and say, "Today, we're going to do a science experiment with something new."
- Mix the Oobleck in front of the children or have a batch ready in advance.
- Give each child a small lump of Oobleck for experimentation.
- Let them make it into a ball and watch it melt through their fingers like a liquid (remind children that it's both a liquid and a solid).
- While children are playing, ask: "Does anyone want to guess what this stuff is?" "What do you observe about Oobleck?" "Can you make it into a ball?" "Then what happens?"
- Suggest putting one finger into the Oobleck. Ask what children notice when they do that.
- Try putting a penny or other small object into the Oobleck. What happens? (The object sinks out of sight.)
- When children have finished experimenting, print their discoveries on the chart paper.
- Let children know that they have been working like scientists using a special process. Make a scientific-process chart for the classroom that includes the following:
  - First we *Wondered*—What is this gooey stuff?
  - Then we *Predicted*—Guessed it might be flour or goo
  - Then we *Tried it*—Experimented
  - Then we *Found Out*—We used our senses
  - Then we *Talked About It*—Documented our discoveries

As a follow-up activity, children can make their own Oobleck. You will need a deli container for each child, popsicle sticks for stirring, scoops, small pitchers of water with the food coloring added (two to three drops is all you need). The formula is the same, two parts cornstarch to one part water, with adjustments as needed.

Library Links

At story time, read *Bartholomew and the Oobleck* by Dr. Seuss. The book is quite long, so you can plan to read it in parts.

As a follow-up to the color-mixing activity, read *Little Blue and Little Yellow* by Leo Lionni. It's a wonderful story about color-mixing and other important things!

As an early childhood teacher, you're familiar with creating a curriculum that excites young children and stimulates learning. You already do many activities that are inherently about math and science. However, it's important to label these activities as math and science experiences—for yourself and for the children in your classroom. Affirm children's discoveries as math or science, and, whenever possible, turn their discoveries into lessons for everyone. It is so important to create an attitude in children that says, "Math and science, I like them—and I can do them!" ECT

BARBARA SPRUNG has over 40 years of experience in early childhood education. Currently, she is co-director of the Educational Equity Center at AED (Academy for Educational Development).

Beyond Community Helpers

The Project Approach in the Early Childhood Social Studies Curriculum

My fellow teachers and I would sit down and plan out the year, starting with the theme "All About Me," moving on to "My Family," and eventually arriving at "Community Helpers," yet I sometimes asked myself, "What exactly are we learning here, and why?"

TED L. MAPLE

Traditionally, early childhood educators address the gaping hole in their planning books under the "social studies" header by teaching a smattering of thematic units. When I began teaching my kindergarten and 1st-grade classes, my approach was no exception. My fellow teachers and I would sit down and plan out the year, starting with the theme "All About Me," moving on to "My Family," and eventually arriving at "Community Helpers." Although the progression of these topics seemed to follow what I understood to be logical child development theory, I was concerned that the children and I were not making as much sense out of what we were discussing as we could have. The songs, books, poems, games, centers, and art activities I planned to accompany these units were fun, and certainly not harmful; yet I sometimes asked myself, "What exactly are we learning here, and why?"

My whole style of teaching changed when I began to study the project approach. According to Lilian Katz (1994),

A project is an in-depth investigation of a topic worth learning more about. The investigation is usually undertaken by a small group of children within a class, sometimes by a whole class, and occasionally by an individual child. The key feature of a project is that it is a research effort deliberately focused on finding answers to questions about a topic posed either by the children, the teacher, or the teachers working with the children. The goal of a project is to learn more about the topic rather than to seek right answers to questions posed by the teacher.

After listening to Katz speak at a local professional meeting, reading *Engaging Children's Minds* by Lilian Katz and Sylvia Chard (2000), and seeing a project in action at a local elementary school, I gradually stopped being a teacher who relied heavily on pre-planned thematic units of study. I began to value children's interests and questions above what came next in the thematic teaching resource book on the shelf in our staff lounge.

My transformation in teaching style did not happen overnight, nor did I become a "projects purist"—using one way to teach everything when working with young children. But I soon found the difference between merely covering material laid out months in advance, and what Katz called "uncovering" rich, meaningful, and interesting topics with children's ideas as the driving force (personal communication, August 6, 2001).

Social Studies and the Project Approach

Most early childhood educators now know the importance of planning experiences for social studies, or any other content area, that are integrated, meaningful, and of high interest (Seefeldt, 2001). Many teaching methods use these criteria, but the project approach goes further. A project is unique because it does not simply introduce subject matter that integrates content area, it also provides a meaningful context for that subject and draws interest by connecting with children's background experiences. A project does all these things while providing an opportunity to attend to curriculum goals and standards, as well as addressing desirable dispositions (e.g., making sense of an experience, showing persistence in seeking solutions to problems, grasping the consequences of actions) as goals for learning (Helm & Katz, 2000).

The goal of social studies is to "promote civic competence"; for young children, this begins with finding their own voice (National Council for the Social Studies [NCSS], 2002). According to a position statement from NCSS called *Social*

Studies for Early Childhood and Elementary School Children Preparing for the 21st Century (1988), "Children can also develop, within the context of social studies, positive attitudes toward knowledge and learning and develop a spirit of inquiry that will enhance their understanding of their world so that they will become rational, humane, participating, effective members of a democratic society." Children need opportunities to function as part of a community of learners if they are to gain the skills and dispositions that lead to civic competence, and grow into contributing members of society.

Katz and Chard (2000) point to "community ethos" as an important benefit of the project approach. They write: "Community ethos is created when all of the children are expected and encouraged to contribute to the life of the whole group, even though they may do so in different ways" (p. 9). In order to grow into positive, contributing members of a democratic society, children must learn to work together, appreciate and respect differences in others, and play a role in the common good.

Wood and Judikis (2002) identify "six essential elements" of a community: 1) common purpose or interest among the group, 2) assumption of mutual responsibility, 3) acknowledgment of interconnectedness, 4) mutual respect for individual differences, 5) mutual commitment to the well-being of each other, and 6) commitment by the members to the integrity or well-being of the group. While the phrase "classroom community" and "community of learners" are common slogans among teachers and teacher educators, do we really understand the concept of "community"? It may be beneficial for us to keep Wood and Judikis's definition in mind when striving to build community in our classrooms. Children best learn to work in a group, respect others, and work toward a common goal by experiencing these traits—and ultimately civic competence—as part of real events, much like those made available through the project approach.

Explorers' Express: A Post Office Project

My first teaching assignment was in a kindergarten/1st-grade multiage classroom at a suburban elementary school. By most standards, this was a fairly innovative school that embraced mixed-age grouping and followed a year-round calendar. The teaching staff was very dedicated to integrated thematic instruction. I knew this was not quite the same as the project approach, but it was fairly compatible with what I thought I could do. I also found that the school's philosophy and system for curriculum planning was, while somewhat shortsighted, flexible enough for me to embed project work in my own classroom.

According to the thematic instruction model, we (the teachers) were to devise a yearlong theme, and choose sub-themes or "components" within that theme to serve as guides for all our curriculum planning. Since our school calendar was divided into three trimesters, each had its own component. The primary (kindergarten and 1st-grade) team's sub-theme for the winter of 2000 was the ever-popular theme of "Community Helpers." Most early childhood teachers have used this concept in their classroom at some point in their teaching careers, to fill the social studies section of their lesson plan. This type of study often would involve a survey of all the different jobs or occupations people have in a local community. This is a fine idea, but often ends up being a very shallow endeavor in which a smattering of careers, from police officer to truck driver, are only superficially examined.

Our trimester began just this way. Children had an opportunity to share what their mothers and fathers did for a living. We had guest speakers, books, poems, songs, learning center activities, and all the necessary parts of a thematic study one could easily find in a teacher-store book. As we were making our way through the different community helpers, we came to the postal worker. I remembered the mail project I learned about three years ago when watching Lilian Katz speak and suddenly became excited. Here was a way out of the "community helpers" doldrums.

Projects begin in many different ways. Some of the best projects happen spontaneously; a teacher carefully observes children at work and play, and chooses a topic based on their questions and interests. Other times, teachers may plan a project based on curriculum goals and what they know to be an appropriate area of study. This project began the second way. I chose the topic based on what I thought would provide many opportunities for firsthand experiences and that would connect to something within most of the children's existing experiences. I decided it would be a much better use of our time if we were to look at one occupation or career in-depth, as opposed to lightly covering all the "community helpers" we could think of throughout the trimester. We had to study something the children were somewhat familiar with, which left out jobs like sailors (we lived in Indiana), soldiers, politicians, and the like. The postal worker was perfect. Also, this being my first full-fledged project, it helped to know that it had been done before by the preschool children Katz mentioned.

Getting Started

How was I to begin? I already had some books about postal workers that I had gathered for the community helpers theme. Beginning a project with a book seemed too familiar, however. I wanted to try another technique to grab the children's interests. It need not be glamorous, but should be interesting and familiar. On the first day of the project, we sat down for the morning meeting and I pulled out a box of envelopes I had "borrowed" from the school supply closet. I took one of the envelopes out and we talked about it.

Immediately, the children began talking about the mail and, more important, talking about their own mailboxes, mail carriers, and times when they had received or sent mail. Some of the children, as many children would in a similar circumstance, began playing with the envelope I had passed around and started taking it apart. I recognized that through their actions the children had asked their first questions: What is an envelope and how is it made? Questions are the main ingredient to any good project, and they are what distinguish project work from other types of instruction. I became very excited to see it actually working!

I then invited the children to explore the envelopes. They proceeded to take them apart and examine the rounded corners and the edges covered with dried glue. I gave the children a piece of plain white paper and challenged them to make their own envelopes. I wanted to see if they could discover the answer to their own questions. I was not sure how well their homemade envelopes would hold a letter, but I think this project got off to a good start and set the tone for a child-centered, question-driven investigation.

Delving Deeper

Our discussions about the mail continued as we read some informational books about postal workers and the post office. The children continued to share stories about times when they mailed a letter with their parents, or when they actually went to the post office. A class field trip to the local post office seemed the next logical step when the children began to ask questions pertaining to how the mail system works, such as, "Where do the letters go when we put them in the mailbox?" I called the post office and set up a class trip, which would turn out to be one of the highlights of our post office project.

We prepared for the trip by reviewing some guidelines concerning safety around the machinery they might see, and compiling some questions for the postal workers. The post office manager, Mrs. Smith, was our tour guide, and the children really did an exceptional job of listening carefully to her instructions as they were shown around the lobby and "behind the scenes" at the post office. They saw the postal materials that the clerks sold at the front desk. They were able to see a customer make a purchase, and watched the clerks weigh the package and make the transaction.

Next, we entered the back room of the post office. The children gasped as they looked around the huge area, and all the things that were going on. The first area Mrs. Smith showed the children was the mail-sorting machine. She explained that the envelopes were sorted by ZIP code, and asked the technician to show the children how it worked. The children were fascinated by it all—the machine, the computers, and especially when the sorter broke down and had to be serviced right before our eyes. I took several pictures to ensure that we had it well-documented. A parent who came along for the trip videotaped the event so we could revisit what we had experienced.

Mrs. Smith introduced us to several mail carriers who were getting ready to go out on their routes. She showed the children many of the different machines that they used to help them sort and deliver the mail more efficiently, different tools the mail carriers used (such as carts, bins, and bags), and the post office boxes. The trip culminated with a walk outside to look at the inside of a mail truck, and we had a conversation with a mail carrier getting ready to go on his route. Although the tour was mostly a passive one, which I would later learn how to avoid, I believed the group gained much from the experience.

Bringing It Together

When we returned to school, the children sat down to write in their individual journals and draw pictures of the experience. The next day, I asked our school secretary to call down to our classroom when the school's mail carrier arrived to deliver the day's mail. When she did, we dropped everything and went down to see and talk with her. This was a nice way to connect our previous trip to real life. We saw a carrier in action, and she became the expert who would be able to answer any questions that were remaining from the day before.

During choice time, the children began to show what they were learning about mail and the post office in different ways. Allie drew a picture on the dry erase board of the sorting machine from the post office trip. Another group of children built mail trucks with Legos. As they pursued these activities, the children demonstrated what part of the mail process interested them the most. After much discussion, we decided as a class to make our own post office right there in the classroom. The planning began. First, we would need a name. The children came up with several ideas, but finally voted for "Explorers' Express" (the "Explorer" is the school mascot). In order to plan for the creation of Explorers' Express, the group reflected on what they had learned from the visit to the real post office.

We talked about how the postal workers all had different jobs and had to work together in order to complete the big task of delivering the U.S. mail. We also would have to work together in order to make our mail system work. After reviewing what we had learned so far from our reading, the expert's insight, and the field trip, we broke the mail process down into four basic tasks: delivering and picking up mail, sorting mail, producing stamps and envelopes, and selling stamps and envelopes. Each child chose an operation that most interested him or her. Four interest groups were formed to produce stamps and envelopes, sell the items, deliver and pick up mail, and sort the mail for delivery.

As the stamp and envelope group produced stamps (some were mass-produced, and others were "special edition" stamps made individually), the mail clerks set up a makeshift post office using our puppet stand. Some of the children wrote messages on the front, describing the price of stamps, hours of operations, etc. One child brought in a toy cash register, and soon they were ready for customers. Meanwhile the mail carriers devised mail bags made of paper and staples (which they later would find ineffective for large packages) and sat down with me to divide the school into "mail routes." There were 30 classrooms in the school, so each of the six mail carriers had five classrooms on a route. Each carrier chose a color, and we painted the mailboxes on his or her route that color to help remind them which classrooms were theirs. The color code system also helped the sorting group.

When the mail came in (either picked up by the mail carriers or brought in by "customers"), the members of the sorting group put a dot on the back of the envelope with a marker. The marker color matched the color of the mailbox to which it would be delivered. The sorting group knew what color to put on the envelope because the sender had to put the classroom number in the address area on the front of the envelope. We had devised a chart to help the sorters do their job. For example, if the envelope said, "John Doe, Rm. 16" on the front, the sorters would look for the number 16 on the chart and mark the letter with the appropriate color. They then would put the letter in the corresponding mail carrier's bin to be delivered that afternoon.

Every part of this project was planned and carried out by the children and teacher together. On most occasions, a problem was posed by the teacher to the children, and then discussed—or vice versa. On no occasion was an action taken unilaterally. Some of the children took on extraordinary roles in the Explorers' Express. David, a child advanced beyond most in reading, writing, and math, became our unofficial "Postmaster General." He helped children count money, write signage, tell time, etc. He kept us in line and on time. Another child, Jason, became so engaged in the mail project, his mother joked with me that it was bordering on obsession. He had his mother buy him a planner, and he "scheduled meetings" with various members from various groups in the Explorers' Express. He would go home at night and devise new plans for the next day, write countless letters to friends, and make new stamp designs.

The mail carriers soon became school-wide celebrities. Older children waved at them as they went down the hall. Every classroom in the school participated in the project. Children were lined up outside of our room every morning from 9 a.m. to 9:30 a.m. The post office opened and closed on time every morning, without fail. Kindergartners who had never learned how to tell time before this project were learning now because they had a purpose. In three weeks, we processed over 1,000 pieces of mail. After those three weeks, we closed the Explorers' Express mail service and celebrated our accomplishments. We made a scrapbook together that documented the experience, which each child took home. The book told the story of an unforgettable classroom project that lasted for a total of nine weeks.

The Impact of the Project Approach on Children

What is the point of spending nine weeks talking about mail? In an atmosphere of rigorous standards and academic accountability, this question is sure to be asked. The real reason I spent so much time focused on one seemingly insignificant topic is simple. The primary purpose was not to teach children about the mail system, but rather how to be empirical, strive for accuracy, and work cooperatively. It was not really terribly important to me that the children in my classroom learn about the different parts of a post office. I did want them to learn, however, how to carefully observe people, places, things, and events. My goal was for the children to become active participants in a group that had a common goal and supported each other in their search for knowledge and truth. I hoped for them to become citizens of our classroom and school community. Those are the dispositions that in-depth projects help to foster and strengthen in children, and they are crucial.

When these goals are kept in mind, a project can be a transformational experience for children and teachers. A child's background, developmental level, behavior problems, or other traits and features that typically separate the haves from the have-nots are diminished by project work because the children are allowed to pursue their own interests and be challenged at their own levels. Children often transcend their problems or differences, and come to life in the joyous exploration of a topic that has meaning and is of interest to them.

My students have been transformed by projects in many ways—both individually and as a whole. Billy, a child with behavior and emotional problems, could not sit still for more than two minutes of circle time or last for five minutes on the playground without creating a disturbance. When I brought in a collection of bike parts for the children to explore during a project on bicycles, Billy took leave of his typically destructive and distracting behavior for the day. I watched him become engrossed in figuring out how the bike parts fit together and how they work, and I observed him testing his theories for 45 minutes. For a child who has difficulty sticking with one task for more than five minutes, this was a wonderful thing to behold.

The personality of Calbert, a socially awkward kindergartner who struggled academically, also emerged during the workings of a project. He was a member of the sorting group for the post office project, whose job it was to sort the incoming mail for the mail carriers to deliver around the school. The sorting group needed a location to sort the mail and, for whatever reason, chose the loft in our classroom as the "sorting room." One day Calbert had a great idea. He decided that since the loft was up high, and the mail needed to come back down, they should have a mail chute to send the mail down to the carriers' boxes for delivery. The group loved the idea, and they got busy working together to bring Calbert's idea to fruition. They first tried to slide the envelopes and packages down the steps, but had the difficulties one might expect. They used trial and error to test several different methods, and finally were able to use long cardboard pieces to create a tunnel that would guide the mail pieces down between the wall and the steps. This was all accomplished with Calbert leading the way; from that moment on he had a new sense of pride and confidence.

Another unique attribute of projects is the opportunity they provide for service learning. Projects that offer these experiences, according to NCSS's position statement on service learning, provide: 1) relevant opportunities to connect civic life with practical community problem solving; 2) an increased awareness of children's immediate surroundings and its unmet needs (as well as opportunities to learn strategies to meet those needs); and 3) enhancement of "democratic values and attitudes" (NCSS Citizenship Select Subcommittee, 2000). The Explorers' Express gave the children all these experiences, and our classroom community grew together because of it.

Conclusion

According to NCSS, the "primary goal of public education is to prepare students to be engaged and effective citizens." To reach that goal, the NCSS position statement titled Creating Effective Citizens explains that students should participate in activities that "expand civic knowledge, develop participation skills, and support the belief that, in a democracy, the actions of each person make a difference … as they work to solve real problems" (NCSS Task Force on Revitalizing Citizenship Education, 2002).

When given the opportunity to become an active, participating member of a community of learners, a child learns to be an effective citizen. We need not lecture young children about the historical roots of our democratic republic, or go through the silly, artificial motions of participating in a mock election, in order to teach them about citizenship and democracy. What we must do is provide opportunities for children to be part of an endeavor that celebrates our ideals through cooperative group efforts, in which they strive to better themselves by developing the disposition to find things out and respect each other's individual differences and talents. That is where democracy begins for our children.

References

Helm, J. H., & Katz, L. (2000). *Young investigators: The project approach in the early years.* New York: Teachers College Press.

Katz, L. G. (1994). *The project approach.* Champaign, IL: Children's Research Center. (ERIC Document Reproduction Service No. EDO-PS-94-6)

Katz, L. G., & Chard, S. C. (2000). *Engaging children's minds: The project approach* (2nd ed.). Stamford, CT: Ablex Publishing

National Council for the Social Studies Citizenship Select Subcommittee. (2000). *Service learning: An essential component of citizenship education.* Retrieved September 3, 2004, from http://socialstudies.org.

National Council for the Social Studies Task Force on Early Childhood/Elementary Social Studies. (1988). *Social studies for early childhood and elementary school children preparing for the 21st century.* Retrieved October 28, 2003, from http://socialstudies.org.

National Council for the Social Studies Task Force on Revitalizing Citizenship Education. (2002). *Creating effective citizens.* Retrieved October 28, 2003, from http://socialstudies.org.

Seefeldt, C. (2001). *Social studies for the preschool/primary child* (6th ed.). Upper Saddle River, NJ: Merrill Prentice Hall.

Wood, G. S., & Judikis, J. C. (2002). *Conversations on community theory.* West Lafayette, IN: Purdue University Press.

TED L. MAPLE is Director, Success by Six, Indianapolis, Indiana, and former Director, St. Mary's Child Center, Indianapolis, Indiana.

Physical Fitness and the Early Childhood Curriculum

RAE PICA

You can hardly open the newspaper these days without reading headlines about the children's obesity crisis in the United States. The problem of overweight and obese children is growing at a faster rate than the problem of adult obesity, and the primary culprit is physical inactivity. Children today lead much more sedentary lifestyles than their predecessors, and society places less and less value on movement and recreation, as evidenced by reductions in physical education programs and recess in schools across the country.

Obese Children Bound for Lifelong Health Problems, Experts Warn

Children's Fitness: Whose Responsibility?

Should the physical fitness of young children be the concern of early childhood professionals? Or is it a matter for the family, and the family alone, to worry about? Consider that 40 percent of five- to eight-year-olds show at least one heart disease risk factor (Berenson 1980; Ross et al. 1987; Bar-Or et al. 1998). Heart disease is the leading killer of adults in the United States, accounting for more than half of all deaths every year (U.S. DHHS 1990). With risk factors appearing in children as young as five, cardiovascular disease may become an even greater threat in future generations. Furthermore, the Centers for Disease Control (CDC 2005) reports that from 1979 to 2000, annual hospital costs for obesity-related conditions in children ages 6 to 17 rose from $34 million to $127 million.

As early childhood professionals we have a duty to educate the whole (thinking, feeling, *moving*) child.

Given these alarming facts, the state of children's fitness is clearly the responsibility of all who are involved with children. As early childhood professionals we have a duty to educate the whole (thinking, feeling, *moving*) child. Moreover, teachers of preschoolers can be more realistic than parents in their assessment of children's physical activity levels (Noland et al. 1990), and preschool teachers' prompting of children has a positive influence on those levels (McKenzie et al. 1997).

Also significant, inactive preschool children were almost four times more likely than their active peers to gain body fatness as they enter first grade (Moore et al. 1995). And body fatness established in childhood tends to carry over into adulthood (Bar-Or et al. 1998). So too does physical inactivity (Moore et al. 1995).

Thus, childhood fitness is an issue upon which early childhood professionals can have a significant impact. By ensuring that children stay active while in our care, we can help combat obesity and promote healthy lifestyles from the beginning.

Playing tag, marching, riding a tricycle, dancing to moderate- to fast-paced music, and jumping rope are other forms of moderate- to vigorous-intensity exercise for children.

Definitions of Physical Fitness

It's important to understand what physical fitness is and how it applies to children (as opposed to adults). The National Association for Sport and Physical Education (NASPE) describes physical fitness as

> a condition where the body is in a state of well-being and readily able to meet the physical challenges of everyday life. Most experts believe physical fitness is the result of practicing a physically active lifestyle. For young children, appropriate movement tasks and experiences can enhance overall body strength, bone density, and developmental functioning of the cardiovascular system. (NASPE 2002, 18)

Physical fitness comprises two components: health-related fitness and skill-related fitness. The latter includes balance, agility, coordination, power, speed, and reaction time. However, it is the former that is relevant to our discussion about young children. Health-related fitness incorporates cardiovascular endurance, muscular strength, muscular endurance, flexibility, and body composition.

Cardiovascular Endurance

Cardiovascular endurance is the ability of the heart and lungs to supply oxygen and nutrients to the muscles. Someone with great cardiovascular endurance has a strong heart—a heart that is larger and pumps more blood per beat than the heart of an individual who is not fit. Good cardiovascular endurance results when an individual exercises regularly. Typically, aerobic exercise improves cardiovascular fitness; but for children, we think of aerobics in a different way than we do for adults.

Young children, particularly before the age of six, are not ready for long, uninterrupted periods of strenuous activity. Expecting them to perform organized exercises for 30 continuous minutes, as an adult does, is not only unrealistic but also could be physically damaging. At the very least it can instill an intense dislike of physical activity.

Developmentally appropriate aerobic activities for children include moderate to vigorous play and movement. Moderately intense physical activity, like walking, increases the heart rate and breathing somewhat; vigorously intense movement, like pretending to be an Olympic sprinter, takes a lot more effort and results in a noticeable increase in breathing. Playing tag, marching, riding a tricycle, dancing to moderate- to fast-paced music, and jumping rope are other forms of moderate- to vigorous-intensity exercise for children.

Muscular Strength

Strong muscles are necessary not only for performing certain actions, like throwing a ball for distance, hanging and swinging, climbing, and carrying heavy books or groceries, but they also prevent injury and help us maintain proper posture. As an added bonus, increasing muscle strength increases strength in tendons, ligaments, and bones.

Strength training—also known as resistance or weight training—is the best way to build muscular strength. For adults, strength training usually means working with weights and equipment. For children, such a regimen is not appropriate. It is never a good idea to modify an adult strength-training program for use by children. Adults' bodies are fully developed; children's are still growing. Adults have long attention spans and the motivation to endure the monotony of repetitive exercises; children do not. Adults can follow specific instructions for proper form and understand the risks in handling strength-training equipment; children cannot. For these reasons the best strength training for children uses children's own weight in physical activities they typically enjoy, like jumping, playing tug-of-war, and pumping their legs to go higher on a swing.

The best strength training for children uses children's own weight in physical activities they typically enjoy, like jumping, playing tug-of-war, and pumping their legs to go higher on a swing.

Muscular Endurance

Muscular endurance, which is related to stamina, is the muscles' ability to continue contracting over an extended period of time. Children's muscular endurance is important because "a child who has good muscular endurance will enjoy and have greater success in his/her daily work activities, in play, and in sporting and athletic competitions" (Landy & Burridge 1997, 8).

Muscular endurance is tied to muscular strength, so many activities and exercises benefit both. However, muscular endurance also depends on skill level. A skilled individual can perform movements efficiently, meaning she can sustain movement for longer periods of time. This ability comes with practice and perseverance. A child, having less practice than an adult in most skills, tends to use maximum force and contract more muscles than needed to perform a movement. Therefore, he cannot sustain the movement as long as a skilled mover.

Flexibility

This fitness factor involves the range of motion around joints. People with good flexibility can bend and stretch without effort or pain, and they can take part in physical activities without fear of muscle strain, sprain, or spasm.

Most young children are flexible, and girls tend to be more flexible than boys. Boys who are inactive start to lose their flexibility at around age 10; inactive girls, at 12. However, if children are physically active, they will continue to be flexible.

Adults should encourage children to work specifically on their flexibility, using gentle, static stretches that take a muscle just beyond its usual length (without pain) and holding a stretch for at least 10 seconds. Activities such as stretching to pretend to climb a ladder, reach for something on a high shelf, shoot a basketball through a hoop, or tie shoes, pick flowers, or pet a cat—as well as hanging and swinging from monkey bars—help increase flexibility. Two cautions regarding stretching; first, children should work their own limbs through their range of motion because an adult can easily stretch a child's muscles and joints too far. Second, children should be warned against ballistic stretching—bouncing while stretching. Ballistic stretching can cause small tears in the muscle fibers, and it is not as effective as static stretching.

Body Composition

The final component of health-related fitness is the body's makeup in terms of fat, muscle, tissue, and bone, or the percentage of lean body tissue to fat.

Due to the burgeoning childhood obesity crisis, a lot of attention is focused on body weight. Weight alone, however, is not a good indicator of fitness. For example, some children are simply large-boned and thus heavier than other children. Also, muscle weighs more than fat, so two children may have the same weight but very different body composition, one having muscle and very little fat and the other having too much fat.

Physical activity, and particularly aerobic and muscle-strengthening activities, is the key to combating body fat.

Physical Activity Recommendations

The position of the National Association for Sport and Physical Education is that "all children birth to age five should engage in daily physical activity that promotes health-related fitness and movement skills" (2002, 2). Their guidelines for physical activities for young children state that young children should not be sedentary for more than 60 minutes at a time, except when sleeping (NASPE 2002). NASPE recommends that toddlers accumulate daily at least 30 minutes of structured physical activity and at least 60 minutes (and up to several hours) of unstructured physical activity. Preschoolers should engage in the same amount of unstructured

Movement Suggestions

Here are some suggestions for encouraging children's active movement.

Arrange the environment to allow for movement. Is there room indoors for you and the children to dance or play Follow the Leader, to set up an obstacle course, or to twirl hoops around various body parts? Does the outdoor environment have open areas for running, jumping, rolling, and other active play and games? Is there equipment for safe climbing, hanging, and swinging?

Buy equipment and props with movement in mind. Choose items like parachutes, plastic hoops, jump ropes, juggling scarves, ribbon sticks, and balls in a variety of shapes, sizes, and textures. Purchase enough so all children have access. Invest in tricycles, scooters, and climbing equipment.

Demonstrate enthusiasm for physical activity. Children learn by watching the important adults in their lives. If you spend the majority of your time in sedentary activities, that is what the children will want to do. But if you spend time playing actively with them, the children will have a wonderful role model.

If rainy or very cold weather forces the children to stay indoors, break out the juggling scarves. Do the children need to take a break or burn some energy? Take them for a walk. With all the excitement you can muster, set off to see and hear everything you can in the block around the school or center.

Too often activities such as running laps or doing pushups are meted out as punishment, linking negative associations with physical activity in children's minds. But a teacher's playful, enthusiastic attitude toward physical activity helps children form positive associations with movement.

Help children understand why movement is important. Recognizing why physical activity is necessary promotes a positive attitude toward fitness that endures beyond childhood. All it takes is a well-placed word or two. For example, as children stretch: "It's important to stretch after exercising so your muscles don't get all bunched up." Or to stimulate children's natural curiosity: "Wow! Chasing bubbles really got my heart pumping. It's healthy to do that sometimes. Is your heart going faster too?"

Children should understand why you offer activities like chasing bubbles, dancing, and pretending to jump like rabbits and kangaroos. And they should have a voice in deciding which physical activity they take part in. Would they rather play Statues or Cooperative Musical Chairs? Choice is a necessary ingredient in fostering intrinsic motivation, and intrinsic motivation goes a long way toward ensuring lifelong fitness.

---

activity but accumulate at least 60 minutes daily of structured physical activity.

Physical activity, and particularly aerobic and muscle-strengthening activities, is the key to combating body fat.

The key word is *accumulate*. No longer are we told that to attain benefits, we must perform 30 minutes of uninterrupted aerobic activity. Rather, new recommendations from such groups as the Centers for Disease Control, the National Institutes of Health, NASPE, and the American Heart Association recommend 10- to 15-minute "bouts" of at least moderate-intensity physical activity, adding up to 30 minutes, on most or all days of the week.

This is good news for children, who are not equipped physically, emotionally, or cognitively to participate in strenuous, nonstop, 30-minute exercise sessions. Children are naturally intermittent movers, so the concept of physical activity in bouts is ideal for them.

When children jump like rabbits and kangaroos, they develop muscular strength and endurance and, depending on how continuously they jump, cardiovascular endurance.

Fitting Fitness into the Curriculum

Given the increasing emphasis on accountability and academics, physical activity is in danger of falling by the wayside in the early childhood curriculum. Indeed, more and more early childhood professionals say they have trouble fitting movement into the program because they're too busy preparing children for academics.

Developmentally appropriate practice dictates that we educate the whole child. Furthermore, academics and physical activity are *not* mutually exclusive. A number of researchers (Martens 1982; Hannaford 1995; Sallis et al. 1999) have found that regular physical activity contributes to improved school performance. For example, in one study, 500 Canadian students spent an extra hour a day in physical education class and performed better on tests than children who were less active (Hannaford 1995). A neurophysiologist, Hannaford states that because movement activates the neural wiring throughout the body, the whole body, and not just the brain, is an instrument of learning.

Here are some suggestions for fitting physical activity into the schedule.

Use Movement Across the Curriculum

Young children are experiential learners, and the more senses they use in the learning process, the more they retain (Fauth 1990). Brain research has shown us that the mind and body are *not* separate entities—that the functions of the body contribute to the functions of the mind (Jensen 2000). Moreover, Gardner's recognition of the bodily/kinesthetic intelligence (1993) supports the use of the body and body parts as a way of learning and knowing.

Active Start—Physical Activity Guidelines for Children Birth to Five Years

National Association for Sport and Physical Education (NASPE)

The guidelines presented below support NASPE's position that all children birth to age five should engage in daily physical activity that promotes health-related fitness and movement skills.

Infants (Birth to 12 Months)

1. Infants should interact with parents and/or caregivers in daily physical activities that are dedicated to promoting the exploration of their environment.
2. Infants should be placed in safe settings that facilitate physical activity and do not restrict movement for prolonged periods of time.
3. Infants' physical activity should promote the development of movement skills.
4. Infants should have an environment that meets or exceeds recommended safety standards for performing large muscle activities.
5. Individuals responsible for the well-being of infants should be aware of the importance of physical activity and facilitate the child's movement skills.

Toddlers (12 to 36 Months)

1. Toddlers should accumulate at least 30 minutes daily of structured physical activity.
2. Toddlers should engage in at least 60 minutes and up to several hours per day of daily, unstructured physical activity and should not be sedentary for more than 60 minutes at a time except when sleeping.
3. Toddlers should develop movement skills that are building blocks for more complex movement tasks.

4. Toddlers should have indoor and outdoor areas that meet or exceed recommended safety standards for performing large muscle activities.
5. Individuals responsible for the well-being of toddlers should be aware of the importance of physical activity and facilitate the child's movement skills.

Preschoolers (3 to 5 Years)

1. Preschoolers should accumulate at least 60 minutes daily of structured physical activity.
2. Preschoolers should engage in at least 60 minutes and up to several hours per day of daily, unstructured physical activity and should not be sedentary for more than 60 minutes at a time except when sleeping.
3. Preschoolers should develop competence in movement skills that are building blocks for more complex movement tasks.
4. Preschoolers should have indoor and outdoor areas that meet or exceed recommended safety standards for performing large muscle activities.
5. Individuals responsible for the well-being of preschoolers should be aware of the importance of physical activity and facilitate the child's movement skills.

Excerpted with permission, from the National Association for Sport and Physical Education (NASPE), an association of the American Alliance for Health, Physical Education, Recreation and Dance, *Active Start: A Statement of Physical Activity Guidelines for Children Birth to Five Years* (Reston, VA: NASPE, 2002), 5–11.

When children have opportunities to get into high, low, wide, and narrow shapes, they increase their flexibility (one of the five fitness factors). They also learn about mathematics and art because these are quantitative ideas (math), and shape is both an art and a mathematics concept. If they practice these shapes with partners, the concept of cooperation, a social studies skill, is added. When children jump like rabbits and kangaroos, they develop muscular strength and endurance and, depending on how continuously they jump, cardiovascular endurance. They explore the concepts of light/heavy, big/small, up/down, and high/low. These are also quantitative math concepts, but physically experiencing them enhances word comprehension, which contributes to emergent literacy.

Regardless of the content area or concept being explored, there is a way for children to experience it physically. Doing so benefits children because they learn best by doing and it promotes physical fitness.

A brain break can be any kind of physical activity that gets the blood flowing and provides a change of pace.

Take "Brain Breaks"

Research (Jarrett et al. 1998) shows that individuals—but particularly children, due to their stage of brain development—accomplish more when their efforts are distributed over time rather than concentrated. In other words, we all need the occasional break! If the break lasts at least 5 to 10 minutes and consists of moderate- to vigorous-intensity movement, it qualifies as a fitness bout.

A brain break can be any kind of physical activity that gets the blood flowing (and glucose and oxygen to the brain) and provides a change of pace. However, if you want to focus particularly on cognitive benefits, cross-lateral movements are an excellent choice, because they require the two hemispheres of the brain to communicate across the corpus callosum (the matter connecting the two hemispheres) (Hannaford 1995).

Cross-lateral movement is anything that requires the left arm and right leg, or vice versa, to move simultaneously. Walking, marching, creeping, and crawling all fit this category. You can also lead an activity that requires children to cross the midline of the body—the vertical line that runs from the top of the head to the feet and divides the body into left and right sides. For example, lead the children in reaching one arm at a time across the body, or in alternatively touching right elbow to a lifted left knee and the reverse (Dennison & Dennison 1989).

Use Transitions to Promote Fitness

Children move from one activity to another during transitions, so they may as well move in ways that are both functional and fun. Promote flexibility by challenging children to move in a tall, straight shape or a crooked shape; by tiptoeing; or on three body parts. Enhance children's muscular strength, muscular endurance, and cardiovascular endurance by challenging them to hop, skip, or jog lightly.

Teach Movement Skills!

Most people believe children automatically acquire motor skills as their bodies develop—that it is a natural, "magical" process that occurs along with maturation. The truth is that maturation influences only part of the process, allowing a child to execute most movement skills at an immature level. A child whose skill stays at the same level will lack confidence in her movement abilities and is unlikely to take part in physical activities beyond childhood. The end result is an individual who is not physically fit.

Just as other skills are taught in early childhood, so too must movement skills have a place in the curriculum. Carson (2001) tells us that engaging in unplanned, self-selected physical activities—or even a movement learning center—is not enough for young children to gain movement skills. She points out that families and teachers "would not advocate learning to read or communicate by having their children enter a 'gross cognitive area' where children could engage in self-selected 'reading play' with a variety of books" (p. 9).

Conclusion

The notion of leaving cognitive or social/emotional development to chance is ludicrous. Yet we feel no similar sense of absurdity at the idea of leaving physical development to chance—that all we need to do is let children play and they will be prepared for all the physical challenges life brings their way.

Yes, the pressure to focus on academics is fierce and, unfortunately, mounting. But as early childhood professionals who understand how young children really learn, and who keep in mind the whole child, we must withstand the pressure and do what will best prepare the children for the future—cognitively, affectively, *and* physically. Society may place less and less value on movement, but we do not have to. By helping children to be more physically active, early childhood professionals can help combat the obesity crisis and promote lifelong physical fitness.

References

Bar-Or, O., J. Foreyt, C. Bouchard, K.D. Brownell, W.H. Dietz, E. Ravussin, A.D. Salbe, S. Schwenger, S. St. Jore, & B. Torun. 1998. Physical activity, genetic, and nutritional considerations in childhood weight management. *Medicine and Science in Sports and Exercise* 30 (1): 2–10.

Berenson, G.S., ed. 1980. *Cardiovascular risk factors in children: The early natural history of atherosclerosis and essential hypertension.* New York: Oxford University Press.

Carson, L.M. 2001. The "I am learning" curriculum: Developing a movement awareness in young children. *Teaching Elementary Physical Education* 12 (5): 9–13.

Centers for Disease Control. 2005. Preventing obesity and chronic diseases through good nutrition and physical activity. Online: www.cdc.gov/nccdphp/publications/factsheets/Prevention/obesity.htm.

Dennison, P.E., & G.E. Dennison. 1989. *Brain gym.* Ventura, CA: Edu-Kinesthetics.

Fauth, B. 1990. Linking the visual arts with drama, movement, and dance for the young child. In *Moving and learning for the young child*, ed. W.J. Stinson, 159–87. Reston, VA: AAHPERD.

Gardner, H. 1993. *Frames of mind: The theory of multiple intelligences.* New York: Basic Books.

Hannaford, C. 1995. *Smart moves: Why learning is not all in your head.* Arlington, VA: Great Ocean.

Institute for Aerobic Fitness. 1987. *Get fit.* Dallas: Author.

Jarrett, O.S., D.M. Maxwell, C. Dickerson, P. Hoge, G. Davies, & A. Yetley. 1998. Impact of recess on classroom behavior: Group effects and individual differences. *Journal of Physical Education, Recreation, and Dance* 53 (3): 55–58.

Jensen, E. 2000. *Brain-based learning: The new science of teaching and training.* San Diego: The Brain Store.

Landy, J., & K. Burridge. 1997. *Fifty simple things you can do to raise a child who is physically fit.* New York: Macmillan.

Martens, F.L. 1982. Daily physical education—A boon to Canadian elementary schools. *Journal of Physical Education, Recreation, and Dance* 53 (3): 55–58.

McKenzie, T.L., J.F. Sallis, J.P. Elder, C.C. Berry, P.L. Hoy, P.R. Nader, M.M. Zive, & S.C. Broyles. 1997. Physical activity levels and prompts in young children at recess: A two-year study of a biethnic sample. *Research Quarterly for Exercise and Sport* 68 (3): 195–202.

Moore, L.L., U.D.T. Nguyen, K.J. Rothman, L.A. Cupples, & R.C. Ellison. 1995. Preschool physical activity level and change in body fatness in young children. *American Journal of Epidemiology* 142 (9): 982–88.

NASPE (National Association for Sport and Physical Education). 2002. *Active start: A statement of physical activity guidelines for children birth to five years.* Reston, VA: Author.

Noland, M., F. Danner, & K. Dewalt. 1990. The measurement of physical activity in young children. *Research Quarterly for Exercise and Sport* 61 (2): 146–53.

Ross, J.G., R.R. Pate, T.G. Lohman, & G.M. Christenson. 1987. Changes in body composition of children. *Journal of Physical Education, Recreation, and Dance* 58 (9): 74–77.

U.S. Department of Health and Human Services. 1990. Health, United States, 1989 and Prevention Profile. DHHS pub. No. (PHS) 90-1232. Washington, DC: U.S. Government Printing Office.

RAE PICA is a movement consultant and author based in Center Barnstead, New Hampshire. She speaks throughout North America and has shared her expertise with such groups as the *Sesame Street* Research Department, Gymboree, and the Head Start Bureau.

Promoting Creativity for Life Using Open-Ended Materials

WALTER F. DREW AND BAJI RANKIN

reative art is so many things! It is flower drawings and wire flower sculptures in clay pots created by kindergartners after visiting a flower show. It is a spontaneous leap for joy that shows up in a series of tempera paintings, pencil drawings of tadpoles turning into frogs, 3-D skyscrapers built from cardboard boxes or wooden blocks. It can be the movement and dance our bodies portray, the rhythmic sound of pie-pan cymbals and paper towel tube trumpets played by four-year-olds in their marching parade, the construction of spaceships and birthday cakes.

What is most important in the creative arts is that teachers, families, and children draw upon their inner resources, making possible direct and clear expression. The goal of engaging in the creative arts is to communicate, think, and feel. The goal is to express thought and feeling through movement, and to express visual perception and representation through the process of play and creative art making. These forms of creative expression are important ways that children and adults express themselves, learn, and grow (Vygotsky [1930–35] 1978a, 1978b; Klugman & Smilansky 1990; Jones & Reynolds 1992; Reynolds & Jones 1997; McNiff 1998; Chalufour, Drew, & Waite-Stupiansky 2004; Zigler, Singer, & Bishop-Josef 2004).

This article is based on field research, observations, and interviews about the use of creative, open-ended materials in early childhood classrooms and how their use affects the teaching/learning process. We identify seven key principles for using open-ended materials in early childhood classrooms, and we wrap educators' stories, experiences, and ideas around these principles. Included are specific suggestions for practice.

Principle 1
Children's Spontaneous, Creative Self-expression Increases their Sense of Competence and Well-being Now and into Adulthood.

At the heart of creative art making is a playful attitude, a willingness to suspend everyday rules of cause and effect. Play is a state of mind that brings into being unexpected, unlearned forms freely expressed, generating associations, representing a unique sense of order and harmony, and producing a sense of well-being.

Play and art making engender an act of courage equivalent in some ways to an act of faith, a belief in possibilities. Such an act requires and builds resilience, immediacy, presence, and the ability to focus and act with intention even while the outcome may remain unknown. Acting in the face of uncertainty and ambiguity is possible because pursuing the goal is worthwhile. These actions produce a greater sense of competence in children, who then grow up to be more capable adults (Klugman & Smilansky 1990; Reynolds & Jones 1997; McNiff 1998; Zigler, Singer, & Bishop-Josef 2004).

Children and adults who are skilled at play and art making have more "power, influence, and capacity to create meaningful lives for themselves" (Jones 1999). Those skilled at play have more ability to realize alternative possibilities and assign meaning to experiences; those less skilled in finding order when faced with ambiguity get stuck in defending things the way they are (Jones 1999).

In Reggio Emilia, Italy, the municipal schools for young children emphasize accepting uncertainty as a regular part of education and creativity. Loris Malaguzzi, founder of the Reggio schools, points out that creativity

> Seems to emerge from multiple experiences, coupled with a well-supported development of personal resources, including a sense of freedom to venture beyond the known. (1998, 68)

Many children become adults who feel inept, untalented, frustrated, and in other ways unsuited to making art and expressing themselves with the full power of their innate creative potential. This is unfortunate when we know that high-quality early childhood experiences can promote children's development and learning (Schweinhart, Barnes, & Weikart 1993).

The Association for Childhood Education International (ACEI) has enriched and expanded the definition of creativity. Its 2003 position statement on creative thought clarifies that "we need to do more than prepare children to become cogs in the machinery of commerce":

> The international community needs resourceful, imaginative, inventive, and ethical problem solvers who will make a significant contribution, not only to the Information Age

in which we currently live, but beyond to ages that we can barely envision. (Jalongo 2003, 218)

Eleanor Duckworth, author of *The Having of Wonderful Ideas* (1996), questions what kinds of people we as a society want to have growing up around us. She examines the connection between what happens to children when they are young and the adults they become. While some may want people who do not ask questions but rather follow commands without thinking, Duckworth emphasizes that many others want people who are confident in what they do, who do not just follow what they are told, who see potential and possibility, and who view things from different perspectives. The way to have adults who think and act on their own is to provide them with opportunities to act in these ways when they are young. Given situations with interesting activities and materials, children will come up with their own ideas. The more they grow, the more ideas they'll come up with, and the more sense they'll have of their own way of doing things (E. Duckworth, pers. comm.).

Principle 2
Children Extend and Deepen their Understandings through Multiple, Hands-on Experiences with Diverse Materials.

This principle, familiar to many early childhood educators, is confirmed and supported by brain research that documents the importance of the early years, when the brain is rapidly developing (Jensen 1998; Eliot 2000). Rich, stimulating experiences provided in a safe, responsive environment create the best conditions for optimal brain development. the years from birth to five present us with a window of opportunity to help children develop the complex wiring of the brain. After that time, a pruning process begins, leaving the child with a brain foundation that is uniquely his or hers for life. The key to intelligence is the recognition and creation of patterns and relationships in the early years (Gardner 1983; Jensen 2000; Shonkoff & Phillips 2000; Zigler, Singer, & Bishop-Josef 2004).

Rich, stimulating experiences provided in a safe, responsive environment create the best conditions for optimal brain development.

The importance of active, hands-on experiences comes through in the stories that follow, related by several early childhood educators.

At the Wolfson Campus Child Development Center in Miami, program director Patricia Clark DeLaRosa describes how four-year-old preschool children develop some early understandings of biology and nature watching tadpoles turn into frogs. The fact that this change happens right before their eyes is key to their learning. The children make simple pencil drawings of the characteristics and changes they observe.

One day during outdoor play, the teachers in another class see that children are picking flowers from the shaded area and burying them. This leads to a discussion with the children about how to prepare a garden in which to grow flowers and vegetables. Children and teachers work together to clear weeds and plant seeds. They care for the garden and watch for signs of growth. Over time they observe the plants sprouting, leaves opening, and colorful flowers blooming. The direct, hands-on experience inspires the children to look carefully and to draw and paint what they see.

Another group of children in the same class takes walks around downtown Miami. The children then talk about what they saw, build models, look at books, and explore their new understandings in the block play area.

DeLaRosa describes a classroom that includes a number of children who display challenging behaviors. Some of the architectural drawings the children produce during a project on architecture amaze her. They demonstrate that with a concrete project in which children are deeply interested, and with teachers who guide them and prompt them with stimulating materials and related books, children's accomplishments can far exceed expectations. Because the children have direct and compelling experiences and multiple ways to express their thoughts, curiosity, and questions, the teachers are able to help them focus and produce, expressing their thoughts and feelings in a positive way.

When an architect supplies actual building plans of a house, the children become even more active. They make room drawings and maps of the house, all the while conversing and building vocabulary. They roll up the plans in paper tubes and carry them around like architects. Because the children are deeply involved in the project, DeLaRosa reports, they experience significant growth in critical thinking and creative problem solving. With questions like "How can we build it so it stands up?" and "Where's the foundation?" they show a growing understanding of the structure of buildings and a deep engagement in the learning process.

Claire Gonzales, a teacher of four- and five-year-olds in Albuquerque, points out how open-ended materials allow children choices and independence, both crucial in stimulating genuine creativity. Children make things without preconceived ideas. When teachers support authentic expression, there is no one right or wrong way—there is space to create.

Gonzales describes a child who is fascinated by a stingray he sees on a visit to an aquarium. He is inspired to make a detailed, representational drawing of the stingray that goes beyond anything he has done before. Gonzales relates how he was able to use his memory and cognition to revisit the aquarium because the stingray made such a deep impression on him. The child recalled the connection he made with the stingray and represented the creature's details—the eyes, the stinger, the gills.

Key to this kind of work by children is the teacher's respect for both the child and the materials and the availability of open-ended materials like clay, paint, and tools for drawing and writing. Materials can be reusable resources—quality, unwanted, manufacturing business by-products, otherwise destined for the landfill, which can serve as much-needed, open-ended resources:

cloth remnants, foam, wire, leather, rubber and wood (See "A Word about Reusable Resources.") Open-ended materials are particularly effective because they have no predetermined use (Drew, Ohlsen, & Pichierri 2000)

Margie Cooper, in Atlanta, Georgia, works with Project Infinity, a group of educators inspired by the schools of Reggio Emilia. She speaks of the values of seeing art making not as a separate area of the curriculum but rather as an extension of thinking and communication. Art making can be especially valuable for young children whose verbal skills are not well developed because the diverse materials offer a variety of ways to communicate. We can learn a lot from children who show a natural affinity for materials, gravitating to them without fear or intimidation. Cooper notes that adults often approach materials, familiar or unfamiliar, with apprehension. Learning from children's openness to materials is important so as not to teach children the fears or discomforts we as adults may have.

Principle 3
Children's Play with Peers Supports Learning and a Growing Sense of Competence.

Duckworth underscores the importance of this principle, emphasizing that by working and playing together in groups, children learn to appreciate not only their own ideas and ways of ding things, but also each other's. a child can learn that others have interesting methods and ideas that are worth paying attention to and that can contribute to his or her interests as well.

In a kindergarten classroom in Worcester, Massachusetts, five- and six-year-old children study flowers together before a visit to a flower show. The children see and discuss with each other pictures of flowers painted by Vincent Van Gogh, Claude Monet, and Georgia O'Keeffe. They use some of these pictures as inspiration for their own sketches and paintings. They explore flowers with different colors, paints, paper, brushes, and print making.

To give the field trip a focus, the teacher, Sue Zack, organizes a scavenger hunt. At the flower show, the children work in small groups, searching for wolves, sunflowers, tulips, a large fountain, waterfalls, goats, a yellow arrangement of flowers, and a Monet painting.

By working and playing together in groups, children learn to appreciate not only their own ideas and ways of doing things, but also each other's.

At school the children make flower creations using recycled materials. At first, they have difficulty making their top-heavy flowers stand up. Then one child discovers that he can use the recycled wire available on the table to hold the flower upright. Others encountering the problem use their classmate's solution.

When children discover how difficult it is to make flowers from clay, one child suggests, "We can use the clay to make a vase and put flowers in it instead." So the project turns into making clay pots. Zack describes the children as being so involved that they seem unaware of her presence nearby. They are engrossed in their flower pots, expressing their thoughts to each other while working and using adjectives such as *smooth, bigger, huge, longer, taller, bumpy, dusty, sticky,* and *cold.* All the children are proud of their work, eager to show and share with one another. "Did you make yours yet?" "Where did you put yours?" "What flowers do you have on yours?" "I have a dandelion and tulips." "My flowers go right from a side to the bottom."

Here are children excited to be working in small groups and deeply connected to a sense of themselves. They do not look for external motivation or recognition. Rather, they express something direct and clear from within themselves as individuals. This is a wonderful example of endogenous expression, where children draw on their inner resources and express themselves from within.

Learning in a social setting is extended when children use diverse materials and symbol systems such as drawing, building, talking, making, or writing. the interaction among these various symbol systems—that is, different languages children use to express themselves—promotes and extends thinking in individuals and within the group.

Promoting interaction among these expressive languages fosters children's development and learning. And the languages encompass a variety of subjects, which leads to the next principle.

Principle 4
Children Can Learn Literacy, Science, and Mathematics Joyfully through Active Play with Diverse, Open-ended Materials.

When children play with open-ended materials, Duckworth says, they explore the look and feel of the materials. They develop a sense of aesthetics by investigating what is beautiful and pleasing about the material. The wide variety of forms of different kinds of materials, along with suggestions of things to do and to look at, flows over into artistic and scientific creation. These experiences naturally lead to conversations among children that they can write or draw about or make into books or other literacy or science experiences. Play helps children develop a meaningful understanding of subject matter (Kamii 1982; Christie 1991; Stupiansky 1992; Althouse 1994; Owocki 1999; Jensen 2001; VanHoorn et al. 2002).

The more children use open-ended materials, the more they make them aesthetically pleasing by fiddling, sorting, and ordering, and the more they see the potential in the materials and in themselves. "Knowing your materials is the absolute basis for both science and art. You have to use your hands and your eyes and your whole body to make judgments and see potential," states Duckworth.

Cathy Weisman Topal, coauthor with Lella Gandini of *Beautiful Stuff* (1999), points out that children develop power when they build individual relationships with materials. When children have the chance to notice, collect, and sort materials, and when teachers respond to their ideas, the children become artists, designers, and engineers. When children are simply given materials to use without the chance to explore and understand them, the materials do not become part of their world. Weisman Topal relates,

> When a child says, "Oh, I need some of that red netting from onions," he demonstrates that he has experience, knowledge, and a relationship with the material, a connection. It is not somebody else's discovery; it is the child's. Whenever a child makes the discovery, it's exciting, it's fun. The child is the researcher and the inventor; this builds confidence. (Weisman Topal, pers. comm.)

Children's explorations come with stories. Histories, associations, and questions. From the questions come the next activities, investigations, and discoveries. A natural consequence is descriptive language; children naturally want to talk about—and maybe draw about—their discoveries. "Not many things can top an exciting discovery!" says Weisman Topal. Organizing and dealing with materials is a whole-learning adventure. Working in these modes, the child produces and learns mathematical patterns and rhythms, building and combining shapes and creating new forms.

When children have the chance to notice, collect, and sort materials, and when teachers respond to their ideas, the children become artists, designers, and engineers.

Teachers can promote language, literature, mathematics, and science through creative exploration. Margie Cooper points out that skill-based learning and standardized testing by themselves do not measure three qualities highly valued in our society—courage, tenacity, and a strong will. Yet these three characteristics may have more to do with success in life than the number of skills a person may have mastered.

Principle 5
Children Learn Best in Open-ended Explorations when Teachers Help Them Make Connections.

Working to strengthen a child's mind and neural network and helping the child develop an awareness of patterns and relationships are the teacher's job. Constructive, self-active, sensory play and art making help both children and adults make connections between the patterns and relationships they create and previous knowledge and experience. The brain, a pattern-seeking tool, constructs, organizes, and synthesizes new knowledge.

Teachers integrate playful, creative art making with more formal learning opportunities such as discussion, reading, writing, and storytelling. They ask questions and listen to the children so that the more formal learning activities are connected closely to the children's ideas and thinking. Teachers provide concrete experiences first: investigating, manipulating, constructing and reconstructing, painting, movement, and the drama of self-activity. Then the reflection and extension involving literacy, science, and mathematics that follow are meaningful. Zack in Massachusetts gives us a good example of this when she organizes a scavenger hunt at the flower show, encouraging children to make connections between their interests and activities at the show.

Principle 6
Teachers are Nourished by Observing Children's Joy and Learning.

A central tenet in the schools of Reggio Emilia is the idea that teachers are nourished by children's joy and intelligence. DeLaRosa clearly demonstrates this tenet as she describes teachers working with children on the architectural plans:

> Watching the teachers guide, interact, and work with the children makes me feel extremely excited—joyful just to see the gleam in their eyes. You know the children are thinking, you see them creating and producing and playing with purpose. I am proud to see teachers taking learning to higher levels, not sitting back festering about this problem or that. They could hang on to the fact that they have a hard time with some of the children . . . but they don't. They look at the positive and move on. (Pers. comm.)

Teachers and children learn together in a reciprocal process. The exciting work of the children inspires the teachers to go forward. Children are looking for more, and the teachers think, "What else can I do to bring learning to the next level?" "How can we entice them to go further?" "What new materials can I introduce?" and "I can see how to do this!" At times the teachers set up and move ahead of the children, and at times the children move ahead of the teachers. When teachers see what children can accomplish, they gain a greater appreciation for them and for the creative arts and materials.

In addition, the work that children do, while inspired by experiences teachers and parents provide, is at the same time an inspiration to all adults who notice. Sue Zack notes,

> The flower unit forced me to make the time to listen, reflect, and write down observations of the children. It felt good! It is what I need and what the class needs in order to be a group that communicates, experiences life, creates, learns, and cares about each other. (Pers. comm.)

Principle 7
Ongoing Self-reflection among Teachers in Community is Needed to Support these Practices.

It is vital for teachers to work and plan together to promote children's creativity and thinking. By meeting together regularly over a few years, teachers connected with Project Infinity in Atlanta have developed the trust to have honest conversations with each other regarding observations of children and classroom experience—not an easy task. They are doing research and constructing knowledge together about how children build relationships (M. Cooper, pers. comm.). Just as children learn and grow in community, so do their teachers (Fosnot 1989).

Conclusion

Play and the creative arts in early childhood programs are essential ways children communicate, think, feel, and express themselves. Art making, fiddling around with bits of wood and fabric or pieces of plastic and leather, reveals the gentle spirit creating simple forms and arrangements, touching the hands, hearts, and minds of young children—and adults.

Children will succeed when they have access to a wide variety of art-making materials such as reusable resources, and when they are surrounded by adults who see and believe in the creative competence of all children and are committed to their success in expressing themselves. As we trust the process, as we encourage and observe the emerging self-initiative and choice making of the children, we come to more fully understand the intimate connection between the spirit of play and the art-making process.

Word about Reusable Resources

Many of the materials used in art-making and play experiences can be discards donated by local businesses. Fabric, yarn, foam, plastic moldings, gold and silver Mylar, paper products, wood, wire, and a world of other reusable materials provides early childhood teachers and families with hands-on resources for creative learning.

Most businesses generate an abundance of unwanted by-products, overruns, rejects, obsolete parts, and discontinued items and pay costly fees to dispose of them. Throughout the nation, manufacturers dispose of their discarded materials in landfills and incinerators.

Through the establishment of a local Reusable Resource Center, high-quality, unwanted materials serve much-needed resources for creative play, the arts, mathematics, science, and other creative problem-solving activities for early childhood education.

In this way businesses become a powerful force to improve early childhood education while reducing disposal costs, improving their bottom line, helping their community, and communicating a strong message that they are in business not just to make a profit but also to make a difference.

(For information on Reusable Resource Centers near you or for training and technical assistance in developing a reuse program in your community contact Reusable Resource Association, P.O. Box 511001, Melbourne Beach, FL 32951, or visit www.reusableresources.org.)

Given these optimum circumstances, children surprise and delight us—they create structures and thoughts no one has seen or heard before. We adults develop a greater appreciation for the children and for the power of creative art making and materials, thus providing a strong motivation for adults to continue teaching and children to continue learning in this way.

In this era of performance standards and skill-based/outcome-based education, it is more important than ever for educators and families to articulate the values and support the creativity of play and exploration as ways to meet the standards—and to go beyond them.

References

Althouse, R. 1994. *Investigating mathematics with young children.* New York: Teachers College Press.

Chalufour, I., W. Drew, & S. Waite-Stupiansky, 2004. Learning to play again. In *Spotlight on young children and play*, ed. D. Koralek, 50–58. Washington, DC: NAEYC.

Christie, J.F., ed. 1991. *Play and early literacy development.* Albany: State University of New York Press.

Drew, K., M. Ohlsen, & M. Pichierri. 2000. *How to create a reusable resource center: A guidebook for champions.* Melbourne, FL: Institute for Self Active Education.

Duckworth, E. 1996. *The having of wonderful ideas and other essays on teaching and learning.* 2nd ed. New York: Teachers College Press.

Eliot, L. 2000. *What's going on in there? How the brain and mind develop in the first five years of life.* New York: Bantam.

Fosnot, C.T. 1989. *Enquiring teachers, enquiring learners: A constructivist approach for teaching.* New York: Teachers College Press.

Gardner, H. 1983. *Frames of mind: The theory of multiple intelligences.* New York: Basic Books.

Jalongo, M.J. 2003. The child's right to creative thought and expression. *Childhood Education* 79: 218–28.

Jensen, E. 1998. *Teaching with the brain in mind.* Alexandria, VA: Association for Supervision and Curriculum Development.

Jensen, E. 2000. *Brain-based learning.* San Diego, CA: Brain Store.

Jensen, E. 2001. *Arts with the brain in mind.* Alexandria, VA: Association for Supervision and Curriculum Development.

Jones, E. 1999. The importance of play. Presentation for "The Play Experience: Constructing Knowledge and a Community of Commitment," symposium at the NAEYC Annual Conference, New Orleans.

Jones, E., & G. Reynolds. 1992. *The play's the thing: Teachers' roles in children's play.* New York: Teachers College Press.

Kamii, C. 1982. *Number in preschool and kindergarten: Educational implications of Piaget's theory.* Washington, DC: NAEYC.

Klugman, E., & S. Smilansky, eds. 1990. *Children's play and learning: Perspectives and policy implications.* New York: Teachers College Press.

Malaguzzi, L. 1998. History, ideas, and basic philosophy: Interview with Lella Gandini. In *The hundred languages of children: The Reggio Emilia approach—Advanced reflections*, 2nd ed., eds. C. Edwards, L. Gandini, & G. Forman, 49–97. Greenwich, CT: Ablex.

McNiff, S. 1998. *Trust the process: An artist's guide to letting go.* Boston, MA: Shambhala.

Owocki, G. 1999. *Literacy through play.* Portsmouth, NH: Heinemann. Available from NAEYC.

Reynolds, G., & E. Jones. 1997. Master players: Learning from children at play. New York: Teachers College Press.

Schweinhart, L.J., H.V. Barnes, & D.P. Weikart. 1993. *Significant benefits: The High/Scope Perry Preschool Study through age 27.* Monographs of the High/Scope Educational Research Foundation, no. 10. Ypsilanti, MI: High/Scope Press.

Shonkoff, J.P., & D.A. Phillips, eds. 2000. *From neurons to neighborhoods: The Science of early childhood development.* Report of the National Research Council, Washington, DC: National Academies Press.

Stupiansky, S.W. 1992. *Math: Learning through play.* New York: Scholastic.

VanHoorn, J., P. Nourot, B. Scales, & K. Alward. 2002. *Play at the center of the curriculum.* 3rd ed. Upper Saddle River, NJ: Merrill/Prentice Hall.

Vygotsky, L. [1930–35] 1978a. The role of play in development. in *Mind in society: The development of higher psychological processes*, eds. M. Cole, V. John-Steiner, S. Scribner, & E. Souberman, 92–104. Cambridge, MA: Harvard University Press.

Vygotsky, L. [1930–35] 1978b. The prehistory of written language. In *Mind in society: The development of higher psychological processes*, eds. M. Cole, V. John-Steiner, S. Scribner, & E. Souberman, 105–20. Cambridge, MA: Harvard University Press.

Weisman Topal, C., & L. Gandini. 1999. *Beautiful stuff: Learning with found materials.* New York: Sterling.

Zigler, E., D.G. Singer, & S.J. Bishop-Josef, eds. 2004. *Children's play: The roots of reading.* Washington, DC: Zero to Three Press.

WALTER F. DREW, EdD, is a nationally known early childhood consultant whose inspiring workshops feature hands-on creative play with open-ended reusable resources. As founder of the Reusable Resource Association and the Institute for Self Active Education, he has pioneered the development of Reusable Resource Centers as community-building initiatives to provide creative materials for early childhood programs. He is an early childhood adjunct faculty member at Brevard Community College in Melbourne, Florida, and creator of Dr. Drew's Discovery Blocks.

BAJI RANKIN, EdD, is executive director of NMAEYC, lead agency for T.E.A.C.H. Early Childhood New Mexico. Baji studies the Reggio Emilia approach and is committed to building early childhood programs with well-educated and -compensated teachers who find renewal through promoting children's creativity.

Index

Index

Test Your Knowledge Form

We encourage you to photocopy and use this page as a tool to assess how the articles in *Annual Editions* expand on the information in your textbook. By reflecting on the articles you will gain enhanced text information. You can also access this useful form on a product's book support Web site at *http://www.mhcls.com/online/*.

NAME:

DATE:

TITLE AND NUMBER OF ARTICLE:

BRIEFLY STATE THE MAIN IDEA OF THIS ARTICLE:

LIST THREE IMPORTANT FACTS THAT THE AUTHOR USES TO SUPPORT THE MAIN IDEA:

WHAT INFORMATION OR IDEAS DISCUSSED IN THIS ARTICLE ARE ALSO DISCUSSED IN YOUR TEXTBOOK OR OTHER READINGS THAT YOU HAVE DONE? LIST THE TEXTBOOK CHAPTERS AND PAGE NUMBERS:

LIST ANY EXAMPLES OF BIAS OR FAULTY REASONING THAT YOU FOUND IN THE ARTICLE:

LIST ANY NEW TERMS/CONCEPTS THAT WERE DISCUSSED IN THE ARTICLE, AND WRITE A SHORT DEFINITION:

We Want Your Advice

ANNUAL EDITIONS revisions depend on two major opinion sources: one is our Advisory Board, listed in the front of this volume, which works with us in scanning the thousands of articles published in the public press each year; the other is you—the person actually using the book. Please help us and the users of the next edition by completing the prepaid article rating form on this page and returning it to us. Thank you for your help!

ANNUAL EDITIONS: Early Childhood Education 07/08

ARTICLE RATING FORM

Here is an opportunity for you to have direct input into the next revision of this volume.
We would like you to rate each of the articles listed below, using the following scale:

1. **Excellent: should definitely be retained**
2. **Above average: should probably be retained**
3. **Below average: should probably be deleted**
4. **Poor: should definitely be deleted**

Your ratings will play a vital part in the next revision.
Please mail this prepaid form to us as soon as possible.
Thanks for your help!

RATING	ARTICLE	RATING	ARTICLE
_____	1. Children at Risk	_____	22. One District's Study on the Propriety of Transition-Grade Classrooms
_____	2. Preschool Pays	_____	23. Successful Transition to Kindergarten: The Role of Teachers & Parents
_____	3. The High/Scope Perry Preschool Study and the Man Who Began It	_____	24. Second Time Around
_____	4. Class and the Classroom	_____	25. Making the Case for Play Policy: Research-Based Reasons to Support Play-Based Environments
_____	5. The Preschool Promise		
_____	6. Kindergarten Learning Gap	_____	26. Essential Contributions from Playgrounds
_____	7. The New First Grade: Too Much Too Soon?	_____	27. From Policing to Participation: Overturning the Rules and Creating Amiable Classrooms
_____	8. Taking a Stand: Strategies for Activism		
_____	9. Creative Play: Building Connections with Children Who Are Learning English	_____	28. Heading Off Disruptive Behavior
		_____	29. Building Positive Teacher-Child Relationships
_____	10. Children of Teen Parents: Challenges and Hope	_____	30. Unprotected in the Classroom
_____	11. Supporting Grandparents Who Raise Grandchildren	_____	31. The Plan: Building on Children's Interests
		_____	32. One Teacher, 20 Preschoolers, and a Goldfish
_____	12. The Dynamics of Families Who Are Homeless: Implications for Early Childhood Educators	_____	33. Fostering Prosocial Behavior in Young Children
_____	13. The Uniqueness of Infancy Demands a Responsive Approach to Care	_____	34. Early Literacy and Very Young Children
		_____	35. Writing First!
_____	14. Reading Your Baby's Mind	_____	36. The Sweet Work of Reading
_____	15. The Trouble With Boys	_____	37. The Overdominance of Computers
_____	16. What Does It Mean to Educate the Whole Child?	_____	38. Meeting the Challenge of Math & Science
_____	17. What Can We Do to Prevent Childhood Obesity?	_____	39. Beyond Community Helpers: The Project Approach in the Early Childhood Social Studies Curriculum
_____	18. Back to Basics		
_____	19. Stop the Insanity! It Takes a Team to Leave No Child Behind	_____	40. Physical Fitness and the Early Childhood Curriculum
_____	20. Uniquely Preschool	_____	41. Promoting Creativity for Life Using Open-Ended Materials
_____	21. Rethinking Early Childhood Practices		

BUSINESS REPLY MAIL
FIRST CLASS MAIL PERMIT NO. 551 DUBUQUE IA

POSTAGE WILL BE PAID BY ADDRESSEE

McGraw-Hill Contemporary Learning Series
2460 KERPER BLVD
DUBUQUE, IA 52001-9902

NO POSTAGE
NECESSARY
IF MAILED
IN THE
UNITED STATES

ABOUT YOU

Name

Date

Are you a teacher? ☐ A student? ☐
Your school's name

Department

Address　　　　　City　　　　State　　　　Zip

School telephone #

YOUR COMMENTS ARE IMPORTANT TO US!

Please fill in the following information:
For which course did you use this book?

Did you use a text with this ANNUAL EDITION? ☐ yes ☐ no
What was the title of the text?

What are your general reactions to the Annual Editions concept?

Have you read any pertinent articles recently that you think should be included in the next edition? Explain.

Are there any articles that you feel should be replaced in the next edition? Why?

Are there any World Wide Web sites that you feel should be included in the next edition? Please annotate.

May we contact you for editorial input? ☐ yes ☐ no
May we quote your comments? ☐ yes ☐ no